CREATING A PROGRESSIVE COMMONWEALTH

MAKING THE MODERN SOUTH
David Goldfield, Series Editor

CREATING A PROGRESSIVE COMMONWEALTH

Women Activists, Feminism, and the Politics of Social Change in Virginia, 1970s–2000s

MEGAN TAYLOR SHOCKLEY

LOUISIANA STATE UNIVERSITY PRESS
BATON ROUGE

Published by Louisiana State University Press
Copyright © 2018 by Louisiana State University Press
All rights reserved
Manufactured in the United States of America
First printing

DESIGNER: Michelle A. Neustrom
TYPEFACE: Cassia
PRINTER AND BINDER: Sheridan Books, Inc.

LIBRARY OF CONGRESS CATALOGING-IN-PUBLICATION DATA

Names: Shockley, Megan Taylor, author.
Title: Creating a progressive commonwealth : women activists, feminism, and the politics of social change in Virginia, 1970s–2000s / Megan Taylor Shockley.
Other titles: Making the modern South.
Description: Baton Rouge : Louisiana State University Press, [2018] | Series: Making the modern South | Includes bibliographical references and index.
Identifiers: LCCN 2018018057| ISBN 9780807169360 (cloth : alk. paper) | ISBN 978-0-8071-7031-1 (pdf) | ISBN 978-0-8071-7032-8 (epub)
Subjects: LCSH: Feminists—Virginia—History. | Feminism—Virginia—History. | Women's rights—Virginia—History.
Classification: LCC HQ1438.V8 S56 2018 | DDC 305.4209755—dc23
LC record available at https://lccn.loc.gov/2018018057

The paper in this book meets the guidelines for permanence and durability of the Committee on Production Guidelines for Book Longevity of the Council on Library Resources. ∞

CONTENTS

Acknowledgments vii

A Brief Feminist Timeline of Virginia in the 1970s xi

Introduction 1

1 Origins 10

2 The Battle for the ERA 49

3 Abortion Rights and Reproductive Justice 96

4 Ending Violence against Women 134

Conclusion: Assessing Progress and Evaluating the Path Forward 175

Notes 195

Bibliography 245

Index 259

ACKNOWLEDGMENTS

This is the book I needed to write, although I did not know it when I embarked on the study. The project grew out of the collaborative effort Cindy Kierner, Jennifer Loux, and I undertook for the Library of Virginia to look at Virginia history through a gendered lens. It was then that I understood just how much of my work and my career as a professional historian has been made possible by the feminist activists who fought to change the commonwealth in the late twentieth century. A few pages dedicated to these women in the larger work did not do them justice, and so I determined to write a book about them and the issues for which they fought. While they did not succeed on every level, and they were not without their own prejudices and shortcomings, feminist activists made Virginia a better place, and helped to move the South forward on women's issues.

This book is truly a collaborative effort. I could not have written it without the assistance of many feminists, both activists and academics. First, I must thank the women who took time out of their busy lives to meet with me, share their inspirational stories about how they lived and how they worked to better the lives of Virginia women. These self-defined feminists, all listed by name in the Works Cited section and quoted extensively throughout the book, represent, to me, the heroes of Virginia. They spent countless hours, used their own money and raised more from others, and sacrificed work and sometimes family time to fight for women's rights in the commonwealth. It is to them that I dedicate this book. I am so grateful not just for the time I was privileged to spend with them, but also for the work they did to make Virginia women's lives immeasurably better. Their stories are archived as transcripts and digital recordings at Virginia Commonwealth University (VCU) in the Virginia Feminist Oral History Project. They graciously allowed open access so other scholars can make use of their stories.

I have been fortunate to have worked with fantastic archivists and public historians throughout the commonwealth. Though it's hard to believe, I have been working at VCU's Special Collections on various projects for over twenty years. Through all of that time and to this day I count on Ray Bonis. From making sure collections were processed in time for my use, to pointing out and allowing me access to unprocessed records or records currently being reprocessed, he has been unfailing in his support of my work. I am lucky to be able to work with Ray; Wesley Chenault, director of VCU Special Collections; and Yuki Hibben, assistant director, as well as Laura Muskavitch, archivist, who have been collaborators in the feminist oral history project. Thanks, too, to Cindy Jackson, comic arts specialist, for always being ready to assist and answer questions! I have also been privileged to work at the Library of Virginia for two decades with some wonderful people. They have patiently listened to all of my stories, pointed me in some important directions, and made collections available to me. I value so much the time I have spent with Sandra Treadway, Mari Julienne, Gregg Kimball, Brent Tarter, Mary Dean Carter, and all the editors and archivists I've been associated with through my work at the LVA. A special thank you goes to Jessica Tyree, who worked tirelessly to process the voluminous National Organization of Women–Virginia Chapter records for me. Mona Farrow at Old Dominion University came in early and stayed late just so I could have more access to records, and both she and Mel Frizzell made my research in the Tidewater much easier. Christine Cheng at George Mason's Special Collections and Marc Brodsky at Virginia Tech's Special Collections, as well as the archivists at the College of William and Mary, also went out of their way to assist me in securing access to materials in a timely and efficient fashion, working around my oral history schedule. If you have not gathered as much, there is a wealth of manuscript sources on Virginia women's activism, and my book can only address a few of the critical issues I researched for many years. It is my hope that other scholars will avail themselves of these sources and continue to work on this vital history.

I received material support from many sources to assist in the production of this book as well. From professional development grants for travel, to a University Research Completion Grant that paid for transcriptions and other related costs, Clemson University provided considerable financial backing for my work. I received a Guy Kinman Fellowship from the Virginia Museum of History and Culture that enabled me to work in their collection of LGBT-related publications and records. The Clemson MA students including

John Gause, Clelly Johnson, Patrick Kent, Connie Wallace, and Brett Zeggil volunteered their transcription services, for which I am grateful. My team of transcribers also included Bea Burton, Elaine Bowen Fowler, and Matt Gottlieb, whose work made this book possible. In addition, Dana Friedman McGuire, Kevin McGuire, and their family, as well as Shu Wang and Todd Holland and their family, in Montgomery County, hosted me while I conducted interviews in the New River Valley and parts west.

As with all collaborative efforts, this work benefited from the support of many. I have always profited from the many panels and conversations with other researchers in post-1945 feminism including Nancy Baker, Sandra Treadway, and LaShonda Mims. Janet Allured has been a constant friend and colleague, offering guidance, support, and a deeply thoughtful reading of my first draft. Her comments have made this work immeasurably better. Marjorie Spruill also read a draft and provided tremendous assistance in helping me contextualize the movement within larger social forces. David Goldfield read the manuscript and offered excellent suggestions for revision. I also want to thank those who read the final copy of the manuscript and often helped to clarify details, including Lee Perkins, Emily McCoy, Kate McCord, Beth Marschak, Suzanne Keller, Lisa Beckman, Betsy Brinson, Denise Lee, Pat Winton, Sandra Brandt, Mary Dean Carter, Bonnie Atwood, Mary Wazlak, Karen Raschke, Georgia Fuller, Mary Coulling, Elizabeth Smith, Stephanie Tyree, and Terrie Pendleton. I am grateful for all of the readers' support and advice; the book is immeasurably better because they took the time to provide feedback. My Clemson colleagues and friends have lived with this book as long as I have—Stephanie Barczewski, Criss Smith, Linda Li-Bleuel, Rachel Chico Moore, Caroline Dunn Clark, Lee Wilson, Brenda Burk, and Vernon Burton in particular have helped me keep my focus on the work and my perspective on the present as the 2016 election and its subsequent headlines drew my attention and ire. Cindy Kierner has shared hotel rooms and her Fairfax home with me, and we have spent countless hours talking about our work, kids, and Jersey roots. Her pointed assessments of my work have made me a better writer through the years. I must give a special thank you to Matt Gottlieb, who has helped track down articles, kept me in the loop in terms of recent Virginia developments, and Simone Roberts, whose incredibly helpful readings of early first-chapter drafts enabled me to develop a narrative path and whose Facebook posts keep me in the loop in terms of feminist activism in the Old Dominion. I am also grateful to LSU Press, particularly editors Rand Dotson and Neal Novak, and copyeditor Stan Ivester, for their support throughout the writing and revision process.

In addition, this work would not have been possible without the support of family. My family has helped to watch my son Scott while I write and research. Elaine Bowen Fowler and her husband, Jeff, are family to me. Elaine has been my best friend since we were music majors at the University of Richmond, and I have shared life with her as I crashed on her floor doing research for my dissertation, graduated to a small guest-room in Ashland while conducting research for the third book, and then on to the Fowler Funhaus as I completed research for this book. Elaine has been my constant cheerleader, advocate, and partner in all sorts of schemes, and this work is better due to her unflagging support—and transcription skills! Whether pushing me to finish my five hundred hours of yoga training or whatever academic work I'm trying to complete, Elaine can get me through any crisis. Jeff Shockley and my son Scott have modeled what it is to be feminists. For twenty years Jeff has supported my career, moving to follow me, and has most recently taken on the role of non-commuting partner in our relationship, running Scott to his myriad activities and providing support so that I can continue to teach in Clemson. I cannot thank him enough for enduring my eight-hour weekly commute and nights away, research trips, and other absences associated with academic careers. He is a talented professor in his own right, and he is a great academic and a dad. Scott is only ten, but he probably knows more about social injustice than most kids his age, having been on the receiving end of many discussions about contemporary issues related to this book and more. He has watched me research and write this book from beginning to end, and he has been patient through the process. I hope that he will continue the struggle for social justice as he grows up. Thanks, guys, for being awesome feminist activists.

Writing this book has been painful, uplifting, and exciting. Given that the election gave us a president who has openly used language of sexual predation, has acknowledged disrespecting and even assaulting women, and that Hillary Clinton's loss in the election to him despite her historic popular-vote margin, we clearly have a long way to go until we have achieved full gender equality in this country. But the women in this book, named and unnamed, furthered the cause in innumerable ways. To them, and to all feminists who have put personal and professional lives on hold to fight for women's rights, I am grateful.

A BRIEF FEMINIST TIMELINE OF VIRGINIA IN THE 1970s

1973   ERA first introduced in the General Assembly.
1974   Creation of Virginia ERA Central.
1974   Establishment of VOKAL (Virginia Organization to Keep Abortion Legal).
1974   Foundation of Virginia ERA Ratification Council.
1975   First major ERA rally to coincide with the hundred-mile march from Alexandria.
1975   COSAR (Virginia Committee on Sexual Assault Reform) organized by local anti-rape organizations.
1975   Introduction of changes to the criminal code regarding rape (defining different degrees of assault).
1976   General Assembly passes law to compensate victims or localities paying for rape kits.
1977   ERA "Facts for Action" Speakout, Teach-In, and March.
1977   ERA Caravan begins, and Jim Thomson is defeated.
1978   LERN Rally (Labor for ERA Now).
1978   Eastern District Court upholds an injunction filed by the ACLU against antiabortion trespassers in Fairfax.
1979   Planned Parenthood determined to prioritize lobbying against consent-based abortion laws.
1979   Richmond's YWCA opens its first shelter.
1979   Virginians Against Domestic Violence formed as coalition of grassroots activists/organizations.
1980   Virginians Organized for Community Expression (VOICE) organized as pro-choice group.

1980 Virginians Allied Against Sexual Assault organized.
1981 SB 158, which instituted a form of rape shield law and dropped the demand for proof of resistance for rape passed.
1982 ERA fails to be introduced for the last time before expiration in the House, is not ratified in Senate.
1983 Virginia General Assembly passes a law allowing for victim impact statements.
1989 Douglas Wilder (pro-choice) elected as governor.
1990 Five antiabortion bills defeated.
1991 Katie Koestner takes her story of sexual assault at William and Mary national.
1994 Waiting-period and parental-consent laws passed.
2002 Marital rape law passed.

CREATING A PROGRESSIVE COMMONWEALTH

INTRODUCTION

[T]hat particular group of women that were working so hard and so intensely from 1970 to 1985, as Marianne Fowler put it the other day, we really borrowed from our futures. Some of us borrowed from our health, some of us borrowed from our career, I certainly borrowed from my career to do it. So there is a price to be paid, there's a sacrifice to be made. But if you look at the wider picture... the experiences I've had, the people I've met.... You know, it's been great.
—GEORGIA FULLER, former chair, NOW Task Force on Religion; former Virginia NOW state coordinator; PhD in anthropology

When a group of Virginia Commonwealth University (VCU) students stood outside the administration building of the Virginia General Assembly on a cold day in January 2015 to demand that the Equal Rights Amendment be put on the docket of the House Privileges and Elections Committee, they probably had little idea that they were just the most recent activists in an effort that began in the early 1970s. In fact, Virginia feminism has a long and significant history, from the first women claiming rights in the early 1600s.[1] Virginia feminists in the late twentieth century built on this long history of women's activism. They demanded progress for women's rights, including passage of the Equal Rights Amendment, maintenance of abortion rights upheld by the Supreme Court in *Roe v. Wade,* and a change in laws and social attitudes on issues of violence against women. As they battled recalcitrant legislators, they enjoyed some short-term success, but also helped Virginia to become a more liberal commonwealth, one that today is represented at the state and federal levels by a slate of progressive politicians. Virginia feminists took a two-pronged approach to change; politically, they engaged with an often-hostile General Assembly to change the laws for the betterment of the commonwealth's women. In addition, they worked at the grassroots level to reshape their communities by educating the public and creating or safeguarding institutions that protect and empower women, like reproductive-health clinics and domestic-violence shelters. Feminist political activism and grassroots campaigns to build or safeguard feminist institutions like reproductive-health clinics and women's shelters had a positive impact on women in Virginia.

This book has several goals. It is one of a growing number of studies that seek to correct the historiographical record that tends to locate feminist activism in metropolitan areas outside the South. It situates Virginia in its rightful place as an important site of feminist activity, especially as one of a few crucial swing states in the battle to ratify the Equal Rights Amendment and as a state that has seen feminist protest against recent conservative legislation. It reveals the diversity of Virginia's activist women, who represented many organizations scattered throughout the whole of the commonwealth. The histories of the movement, told by the participants themselves, address the issues outlined above and give us much better insight into the motivations and memories of feminist activists. In addition, they provide a resource for scholars and community members to draw on when trying to better understand the women's movement in Virginia.

Feminist Scholarship

In the late twentieth century, feminists battled to open up to women myriad economic, educational, and social opportunities that were nonexistent prior to the 1970s. Historians Ruth Rosen, Sara Evans, Alice Echols, and others have argued that, despite 1980s setbacks like the failure to achieve ERA ratification, along with abortion-rights rollbacks, glass ceilings, and persistent workplace discrimination, activists' efforts to claim more political, social, and economic rights were met with great success by the end of the twentieth century. However, these historians focus primarily on the work of national and local leaders working in the Northeast, upper Midwest, and West. Indeed, historians have often dismissed the importance of women's social movements in the South because of the region's more traditional and patriarchal society, as well as its reluctance to enforce federal civil rights mandates, its fear of federal insertion into matters considered local, and its poor record on ERA ratification.[2]

Recently, scholars have begun to explore grassroots feminist activism to better understand local activists' impact on the nation as a whole, a trend that encompasses more studies of southern feminism. They have found that these women were critical at the state and local level in bringing feminist issues to the forefront in their communities, introducing many people to key feminist concepts, even when they did not necessarily self-identify as feminists. These studies have also explored feminist activity before the 1960s and 1970s, the period which is often identified as the second wave of the American women's movement. These studies are instructive, and together tell a much more detailed story of feminism. From several comparative city studies that include a southern locale, to studies of feminism in key southern cities, scholars are beginning to uncover the work of southern feminists. Articles about the ERA and the emergence of anti-violence activities, as well as lesbian activism, illustrate that more historians are engaging with this complex region, associated with southern belles more than feminist activists. In her book on Louisiana feminists, Janet Allured celebrates this growing body of literature that is bringing southern feminism to light.[3] Together, these studies contribute to a growing body of literature on feminism in the southern states.

To dismiss southern women's feminist activism, and in particular, feminist activities in Virginia, is to miss the larger story of women's importance to structural shifts in society. For example, from the 1970s on, Virginia National Organization for Women members from across the state lobbied legislatures to pass the ERA, keep reproductive rights safe, and pass more stringent rape and domestic-violence laws; filed lawsuits against corporations and demonstrated for equal economic opportunities; and helped to establish domestic-violence shelters and women's centers throughout the state. One of the most notable aspects of Virginia NOW was its geographic reach. From Alexandria to Appalachian Alleghany County, Norfolk to rural Rockbridge County, women worked together to advance the goals of economic, political, and social equality. The persistence of activist efforts in rural areas challenges the dominant historiographical narrative that locates the majority of feminist activism in urban centers.

Feminism and Conservatism in Virginia

Competing social forces have always buffeted the commonwealth. The "cradle of democracy," home of many leading revolutionaries and the Bill of Rights, Virginia also embraced slavery, the Confederate cause, and Jim Crow laws, as did the rest of the South. Virginia often presented itself differently, however. From commonwealth hero Thomas Jefferson agonizing over the institution of slavery—but never actually manumitting his slave population, to being a late addition to the Confederate cause but producing Robert E. Lee as commander of the Confederate forces, serving as the Confederate capital, and becoming one of the centers of the "Old South" apologist Lost Cause ideology after the Civil War, Virginia is somewhat schizophrenic.[4]

Virginia still struggles with the legacies of one-party rule, massive resistance to civil rights, and strong forces of both progressivism and conservatism within its own borders. Virginia's history is one of iron-fisted rule by a small cadre of privileged white men. When feminists began engaging with the legislature in the 1970s over the ERA and reproductive rights, they faced senators and delegates who were used to having total dominance, thanks in large part to Harry Byrd and his three-decade rule over Virginia politics.

Some of these legislators had built the massive resistance movement against desegregation when they met in a special 1956 General Assembly session. In this session, they passed laws that included closing any school that integrated and stopping NAACP lawsuits that had been effective in targeting school-district policies. Eventually the General Assembly created a pupil-placement board that forced all black students desiring entry to white schools to apply through a centralized state board. Massive resistance in Virginia culminated in a U.S. District Court ruling against the effort in 1959, although Prince Edward County shut down its schools rather than comply. There, African American students went without a publicly provided education while white students attended a private academy that received financial support from the county until a court decision reopened the schools in 1964. Though some white women supported the efforts of the legislature, both black and white women were instrumental in trying to fight school closures in Virginia.[5] Virginia legislators spoke of economic progress as they maintained state-supported eugenics programs and traditional gendered hierarchies. Virginia sometimes appears more progressive than Deep South states, but it is by no means as forward-thinking as many northeastern states, for example. This caused the commonwealth to align with either national or southern trends at different points in the feminist movement of the late twentieth century. Virginia's racist policies often escaped national notice because much of the work of segregation was done administratively and legislatively, rather than at the hands of violent police action as in the deeper South.[6]

Women faced their own kind of massive resistance in the commonwealth, and for centuries they had fought for the full rights of citizenship. In the twentieth century, white women demanded access to equal education. Rather than open up the University of Virginia to women, the legislature created a coordinate college system that established Radford, Mary Washington, and James Madison universities. The legislature and board of trustees successfully kept full-time residential female students out of the University of Virginia until 1970, just three years before activists began fighting to ratify the ERA. It would not be until the twenty-first century, after a hard-fought court battle, that women could matriculate at the Virginia Military Institute. African American and white women fought for voting rights, equal access to education, and welfare benefits during the Depression, and employment during World War II. African American women emerged as leaders in the civil rights movement in Virginia after Reconstruction, and white allies assisted in civil rights efforts in the twentieth century. When feminist activists battled the General Assembly and worked in their communities to further change, they built on a long tradition of women's activism in the commonwealth.[7]

As Virginia's feminists forged ahead in the late twentieth century, a competing force emerged from the commonwealth, one that would become a national movement that threatened the progress of feminists. Thomas Road Baptist Church in Lynchburg became a hotbed of conservatism after concerted efforts by its leader, Jerry Falwell, to roll back progress made by women activists and the LGBT community in the 1970s. Falwell had emerged as a preacher reacting against the civil rights unrest in Lynchburg, speaking against civil rights and maintaining a segregated church until at least 1971. He then turned his ire to feminism and progressivism, attacking abortion, ERA, LGBT rights, and pornography, and ultimately founding the Moral Majority as a way to mobilize evangelicals to vote. Falwell and his conservative allies are responsible for founding Liberty University in 1971, and at his height he had an audience of between six and thirty million.[8]

On the other side of the state in Virginia Beach, Pat Robertson used his Christian Broadcasting Network, founded in 1961, to promote evangelical Christianity. Like Falwell, Robertson founded a university, Regent, in 1977 to promote conservative values. As his network became more popular in the 1980s, Robertson's star rose and he eventually eclipsed Falwell. Robertson's anti-LGBT, anti–sex education, anti-feminist, and antiabortion values drew voters, and he founded the Christian Coalition in 1989 after his failed 1988 run for president. By 1984, the Christian Coalition had about one million members and a budget of twelve million dollars.[9]

But at the same time, the commonwealth itself was changing, and not just in metropolitan Northern Virginia. In the early twenty-first century, Virginia progressives gained ground as more Democratic governors, lieutenant governors, attorneys general, and a slate of U.S. senators were elected statewide. Progressives in the Northern, Central, Tidewater, Southside, and Western regions all contributed to these victories. Virginia was also the named the test case for same-sex marriage, and women are continuing the fight for more political representation through Emerge Virginia, an organization dedicated to helping women secure elected offices at all levels of the commonwealth. Still, in a state where the General Assembly presented a transvaginal ultrasound antiabortion bill in 2012 that narrowly missed becoming law, feminists acknowledge that there is much work to be done.

Feminism and Oral History

The arguments made in this book rely on two main sources: manuscript collections and oral histories. The manuscript collections are housed in repositories across the state and tell the story of how groups like the Federation of Business and Professional Women's Clubs (BPW), the American Association of University Women (AAUW), the League of Women Voters (LWV), the Southern Women's Rights Project of the ACLU (SWRP), the National Organization for Women (NOW), and others worked to advance change. The material from organizational records and personal papers are enhanced by the stories told by women who were active in promoting feminist issues or culture in Virginia. Oral histories can tell how women felt about the changes they tried to make, how they defined success and failure, and how they developed their ideologies. The way in which they remembered their work reflects how they viewed change.

Doing oral history is a feminist project unto itself, one that countless scholars have advocated as a way to allow women to tell their own stories. Recognizing that the women I interviewed were crafting their own narratives, I attempted to let them speak for themselves as much as possible, particularly when discussing the origins of their activist or feminist ideals and what they view as the results of their work. I tried to ask a combination of questions that Alicia Rouveral explains in an article as "life review" and "oral history" questions.[10] I wanted to understand how women came to support feminist causes, so I asked them to talk about their lives and the influences in them. But I also asked questions about feminist movements in Virginia, the challenges they faced, the support they received, and the differences feminism made (or didn't make) on public policy and in the greater culture. I then relied on the transcribed interviews to write the book, weaving them into the story with other documents.

In the text, you will hear stories that reflect both diversity and commonalities in women's experiences. However, I also recognize that I am a part of the story, as I am retelling the histories they shared with me. As a feminist, I focused interviews on the work that they did and allowed them to both interpret and assess their own activities. In so doing, I tried to understand the complexity of how activists defined achievement in the face of what often appeared to be loss, as well as the ways in which they saw themselves and society change.[11] The oral histories reflect a geographic diversity—I traveled through the state meeting with women, and I attempted to secure representation from diverse groups of feminists. They were active in many organizations that promoted feminist issues, either as volunteers or professionals, or their work contributed to building feminist culture or communities. Some of their efforts could not be detailed in the book due to page-length constraints, but they were deeply engaged with feminist issues and became active in promoting these in the last quarter of the twentieth century.

The story is incomplete, however. Time constraints and the vagaries of personal lives necessitated that I only collect two dozen interviews, and the women with whom I met were ones I discovered in archival sources and who could be found and responded to my contact, or by referral, so it is a limited group. Chapter 1 will introduce readers to these women and explain further the limitations of the interview process, as well as why most of the women I interviewed were white and college-educated, as were the majority of self-identified feminists. You will hear their voices throughout this book, as they remember and analyze their own values and actions as well as the women's movement as a whole. The women interviewed had the opportunity to weigh in on their own experience after I concluded writing the book. I have on occasion edited their phrasing, often with their input after they reviewed the work, but I have changed none of the meaning or impact of their statements. The original transcripts can be found in the Virginia Feminist Oral History Project at Virginia Commonwealth University.

The story is also incomplete because the women I interviewed tended to be college-educated, and most were white professionals. Class, race, and other divisions were present in the Virginia feminist movement, as they were in the national movement, and I will examine these issues at greater length. Moreover, the archival sources I reviewed tended to privilege the story of middle-class professionals, as well as white women.

This book focuses on how Virginia's women fought for feminist change by looking at three major initiatives of the feminist movement in the late twentieth century: passage of the ERA; protection of abortion rights accorded by *Roe v. Wade*; and the securing of more legal and social rights for survivors of domestic and sexual violence. I chose these issues because they precipitated some of the largest conflagrations between women activists and legislators in the General Assembly where women's rights were concerned, and because all three are unresolved and continually addressed by feminists today. As a result, this study is necessarily incomplete, as it does not address educational or employment equity, or LGBT rights, as those changes came mainly through federal court decisions and not from Virginia legislation, despite activists' best efforts. There are other key aspects of the feminist battle I have left unexplored in this effort, like the creation of a feminist culture through the efforts of community builders, but I hope that other scholars will help to fill in the rest of the story of feminism in Virginia, and in the larger southern region as a whole.

Feminist Issues: Time Frame

The book is structured topically, rather than chronologically, with chapters addressing ERA ratification, the struggle to maintain abortion access, and the battle to end sexual and domestic violence against women. Because feminists have engaged in addressing myriad overlapping issues, a topical approach enables the reader to see just who and what organizations focused time and attention on particular issues. A topical approach highlights the major actors who fought for women's rights by taking on different issues, but it does obscure the fact that this change was all occurring simultaneously.

Chapter 1 explores the background and motivations of the Virginia feminists interviewed for this book as well as the political climate of Virginia on the eve of the feminist movement. Chapter 2 examines the battle for the ERA, which was the single issue that united the most feminist activists and sparked calls for changes in other areas of society. Chapter 3 addresses the battle to maintain safe and legal abortion in Virginia. Chapter 4 focuses on how feminists changed laws pertaining to and cultural values related to domestic and sexual violence. In the conclusion, feminists themselves reflect on the changes they wrought, from what worked to what they left undone, as well as what they would like to see activists do today.

The story of Virginia feminist activism explains how women fought an intransigent legislature and brought women's issues to the forefront of a conservative society, how activists remember their victories even in the face of so many legislative defeats, and how they conceptualize change as they look back over fifty years of the state's history. Given the conservative climate of Virginia when feminist activism began to emerge in the 1960s, it is stunning to see what has happened in the commonwealth.

Even if southern feminists lost some policy and legislative battles, the "paradigm shifted" because of the work they did.[12] Virginia feminists were able to push the commonwealth further than other southern states. Virginia has moved from a solidly reliable Republican state to a battleground state, one that can be counted on recently to secure Democratic electoral victories at the national level. While some of this can be attributed to in-migration in the twenty-first century, historic bastions of conservatism like Henrico and Chesterfield counties have elected Democratic representatives to the General Assembly in 2017. The sociopolitical climate of Virginia has also shifted dramatically, suggesting that the work of Virginia women activists to educate the public about women's issues and urge the General Assembly to pass legislation benefiting women made an important impact on the commonwealth.

1
ORIGINS

So in Western Culture, it's very binary, good and evil, men and women.... And I think for me, feminism was more holistic.... So it wasn't just about legal rights by any means. It was really a whole different way of looking at things... in my mind there was no such thing as something that wasn't a "woman's issue."
—BETH MARSCHAK, founding member, Richmond Lesbian-Feminists; former chair, Third District National Women's Political Caucus–Virginia

In the second half of the twentieth century, the Old Dominion was changing as activists fought to destabilize racial and gender oppression. What forces would shape the commonwealth's future remained to be seen at mid-century. As the General Assembly's massive resistance to civil rights gave way to grudging acceptance of at least institutional desegregation, if not actual social equality, feminists began to engage with the legislature and educate the public on women's equality.

Women who promoted feminism in the commonwealth came to the movement in many ways. Many factors shaped their ideology and motivated their activism—from their families, to their experiences with social justice, religion, and civil rights growing up, to their battles for equality in the workplace, and their encounters with feminist literature which was burgeoning in the 1960s and 1970s. These women shared the common belief that their efforts mattered to Virginians.

Whether native Virginians or transplants, these women encountered a commonwealth buffeted by change. Virginia became more industrialized, urbanized, and populous in the 1940s.[1] As World War II brought in new industries, it also ushered in a new round of civil rights activism that would intensify as African Americans continued to claim equality. As they looked to reshape their society, however, women activists faced a power structure that continued to be dominated by white male leaders, many of them hostile to change, and by traditional culture. Virginia feminists faced challenges, particularly from those who benefited from male privilege in politics, the workforce, and society. Virginia's recent tradition of massive resistance to desegregation, as well as its long-standing history of power brokers controlling the General Assembly, created particular challenges for Virginia feminists.

A Privileged Patriarchy: The General Assembly

The Virginia General Assembly promoted the interests of the white men who had dominated the political and economic system of the commonwealth since its founding. At the turn of the twentieth century, both African Americans and non-elite whites found themselves unable to gain from gaining power. In fact, new voter qualifications enumerated in the new state constitution of 1902 created an electorate smaller than that of the colonial period. Accruing poll taxes, for example, hurt the already economically disadvantaged.

The Virginia legislature naturalized racialized privilege and power and survived fairly intact through the late twentieth century. With politico Harry Byrd controlling the system of government from the 1920s through the 1960s, Virginia's legislature continued as a reactionary and exclusive terrain. When Byrd politicians were in charge at the assembly, not only did Virginia stand in the way of civil rights reform, but it also became a place where citizens' individual concerns were not taken seriously. The legacy of his political machine dominated after Byrd's death, as the politicians who had been part of that camp remained in office. Many of the very same legislators opposed the ERA and other reforms that would have benefited women. While other legislatures, like Louisiana, Illinois, Oklahoma, and North Carolina, were also conservative bastions of white male privilege, the implications of Virginia's long-standing Byrd machine lasted long into the twentieth century.[2]

Women seeking to change Virginia's long-standing system of male privilege, seen in its inheritance, divorce, domestic-violence, and other laws, faced serious challenges in confronting not only hostile legislators' ideologies but their actions. For example, in 1979 Delegate Clinton Miller of Woodstock found himself under attack when he told a racist and sexist joke at an all-male civic-club meeting. He importuned men to "go home and claim their equal rights by insisting on cooking, cleaning, and sewing as well as laying claim to 'Tupperware parties, soap operas, and afternoon tea with the boys.'" Men should be expected to earn more because of their level of education, he said. He also launched pointed criticisms at Congress for providing an extension to pass the ERA.[3]

Feminists and their male allies in the commonwealth did not allow this kind of disrespect to go unchallenged. Backlash against Miller was swift. Juanita Sanders, chair of the Harrisonburg Democratic Committee, for one, said in a press release that his "blatant attack on all women is unwarranted and filled with false and demeaning statements." She called his comments about women and African Americans "condescending" and "insulting" and threatened that the voters would remember in the fall election. Miller seemed surprised by the backlash. He defended himself by saying he had given the talk in Staunton before to a mixed audience and it had gone over well. According to a one newspaper report, he claimed that "it would be racist if he as a white man could not tell the same jokes as a black comedian." And using a common method anti-feminists used to deflect women's critiques of poor behavior, he called his detractors "uptight and sensitive."[4]

Miller's jokes and comments were symptomatic of a much larger problem at the General Assembly, revealed in a 1980 *Washington Post* story about male legislators that showed just how much of a bastion of chauvinism Virginia's legislature remained. Reporters Karlyn Baker and Pat Bauer interviewed over 24 women who worked at the capitol, from legislative assistant to lobbyist, and all 9 (out of 140) female legislators. From Common Cause lobbyist Barbara Pratt recalling when Delegate Thomas Moss kissed her on the cheek in an elevator and later made a sexually charged comment about an elevator to her while she was in a meeting monitoring a bill, to Delegate Elise Heinz recounting when Delegate Don McGlothlin of Buchanan invited her to "sit on his lap" and warned her "that kind of attitude wasn't the way women accomplish things in Richmond" when she rebuffed him. The *Post* article depicted the General Assembly as a group of men whose privilege had run amok, well beyond the realm of common decency. Reporters termed the situation for women workers "low-level sexual harassment."[5]

Women interviewed for the article noted that the harassment they encountered was personal and political. The male legislators' attitudes toward them personally appeared to be reflected in their views on legislation affecting women. Reporters noted that six of the nine women legislators were willing to go on the record to explain the problem. They found that the women believed "attitudes held by certain of their male colleagues make work difficult or at times affect legislation." And although the women interviewed were ready to say that not all men were problematic, writers of the report concluded that "there is a heavy sexual undercurrent in their dealings with the male-dominated political and bureaucratic establishment here."[6] As a freshman delegate and the only woman on the powerful Courts of Justice Committee in 1978, Mary Sue Terry remembered Democratic Delegate Richard Crandall (Roanoke) grabbing at her skirt as she was giving a prayer before a committee dinner. Clive DuVal's legislative aide Joann Spevacek explained when she went to speak with a Delegate about a bill, "all the time I was talking he was looking my body up and down.... I went into the meeting feeling like a legislative aide and I came out feeling like a whore." Some female lobbyists said that there was one "senior legislator" who said their bills might get more favorable treatment if they met him in his hotel room later in the evening. Although these could well have been rumors, a lobbyist recounted one woman who took him up on his offer and whose "bills got treated more favorably."[7]

The harassment of women in the General Assembly mirrored the problematic legislative climate for Virginia women. Reporters noted Virginia's property and divorce codes were among the worst in the nation, and any proposed changes to sexual-assault, property-rights, or divorce laws "makes the predominantly conservative and middle-aged male lawmakers nervous." Many women said they stayed silent for fear of reprisals. Some also said the General Assembly's climate was worse than that of Congress or northeastern private-sector businesses in which they had worked.[8]

Some of the *Post*'s descriptions must have astonished Virginia readers. Delegate Mary Sue Terry said that, when the wrong legislators get together, "they're like a fifth grade boy." Heinz claimed that several delegates physically assaulted her, and Jean Marshall Clarke, who was at this point the former NOW state coordinator, told reporters that it was fine meeting legislators one-on-one in their home offices, "But boy, you get them in Richmond and it's like one big fraternity party or locker room." Heinz described men who "snicker, giggle, and poke fun at [legislation affecting women] like a bunch of adolescents." Delegate Mary Marshall said they also refused to take women's issues seriously, instead passing bills favorable to women by in favor of "serious business." And one male delegate said, "If you go off the record, you'd probably get every single male here to tell you they [women] are less effective and if they were being honest with themselves they'd say it's because they're women." He said, "It's an unfortunate thing because so many of the women have so much to offer." He refused to go on the record because he feared political reprisal.⁹

When confronted by these charges, male delegates reacted in ways that suggested just how chauvinistic the legislature really was. According to reporters, the men they spoke with "shrug[ged] off such incidents as jokes or even expressions of affection." Delegate Moss reiterated Miller's claims that women were "too sensitive" and opined, "I guess we're going to have to walk around like zombies." Delegate McGlothlin denied remembering anything about the incident with Heinz, but claimed that he probably didn't do it because he only did that with people he knew well. He suggested he may do that to her if she returned the next year.¹⁰

Many lawmakers were, in the words of *Post* reporter Pat Bauer, "indignant" at the charges. Republican Delegate Warren Barry read the original article in a joking fashion on the record, saying "This isn't reporting the news.... This is creating the news out of half-truths, innuendo, and the wishful thinking of some paranoid individuals." According to Bauer, "Barry drew loud laughter from the delegates when he read portions" of the article, and described Moss and Heinz as "sex objects." He also stated, "Anybody who knows Tom Moss knows that if Tom Moss wanted to put the moves on a woman it wouldn't be to kiss her on the cheek, that's for sure," and Democratic Delegate James Almand said the entire incident was "much ado about nothing," according to Bauer. In a voice vote, the delegates did agree to allow Speaker A. L. Philpott to investigate any allegations brought to him, however.¹¹

Such allegations may well have not concerned Speaker Philpott, given his own indiscretions. In 1984, Philpott was roasted in an event sponsored by the "Circus Saints and Sinners" club, an all-male charitable business organization. In this year, only men who worked at the General Assembly in some capacity were invited. The women present were strippers in pasties. Former chairperson H. H. Howren objected to no women being invited but said to the press: "All they [the dancers] do is come in and take off a veil or something.... I guess they could not be accused of exploiting sex. They just come in and flip their bulbs at the guys." Democratic Delegate Vivian Watts of Fairfax said, "I can't think of anything to say that I wanted to be quoted on." Four hundred men turned out for the event, and the reporter suggested women delegates were loath to openly criticize the gathering, as Philpott made committee assignments.

Women from local NOW chapters picketed the event. The organizer, lawyer James Baber, told the reporter the protestors were "an awfully ugly bunch" and claimed that women "should stay at home, raise children, clean the house and take care of their husbands." Richmond NOW president Lynn Bradford remembered that incident: "we weren't protesting the strippers per se, we were protesting the idea that this... is an acceptable form of entertainment for our legislators. And I will never forget... [after her statement and Baber's insult]... the news anchor, the expression on his face was just killing. I mean it was like, did he say that?" The article covering the event said delegates outside were "chuckling at nearby pickets and the media coverage of the event." Still, some tried to stay away from the "entertainment." Philpott said he was staying out of the room with the strippers, asking "You think I'm some kind of nut, with all your cameras out there?"[12]

The protests fell on deaf ears. The Saints and Sinners held a similar event for Democratic Delegate Norman Sisisky of Virginia Beach, and six hundred people showed up. This time, according to activist Judy Goldberg, because women's groups were not notified in advance, they were not there to picket. But she still protested on behalf of women in the commonwealth, especially because the organizer of this event was said to have remarked, "I think that some of these liberation movements go a little too far."[13]

Harassment continued well past the 1980s. Karen Raschke loved being a lobbyist, first for Virginia Power, where she could deliver the money, and then for Planned Parenthood, where she could deliver the votes. She recalled, though, that women lobbyists spent an inordinate amount of their time discussing which legislators would proposition in what kinds of ways, who might be sleeping with whom, and the standard pickup lines of legislators in the 1990s. She remembered being put in compromising positions from which she had to cleverly extricate herself, and she was even the target of some rumors that she had slept with a legislator when she had only taken him out to dinner. Bonnie Atwood also recalled stories of harassment told by other professional lobbyists, although she did not experience any problems herself.

Although legislators may have learned not to make harassment public for fear of reporters' exposés, the feminist movement could not prevent individuals from continuing to demean women working at the capitol. Women had to manage these individuals as best they could. Raschke noted that she helped form a women's lobbyist group that provided camaraderie and support to each other, partly in response to the fact that they still faced these conditions.[14]

* * *

Civil Rights and the Commonwealth

In the 1940s African Americans across the country and in the commonwealth fought for entry in choice wartime jobs held generally for whites; filed lawsuits against segregated schools; and desegregated public restaurants, transportation, and other facilities. They fought for change that challenged long-standing Jim Crow traditions in Virginia. Their efforts opened the path for feminists, as they provided a model of successful protest and change.

Virginia did not witness the large-scale physical violence leveled at civil rights activists as did states in the lower South (with the significant exception of a particularly brutal police takedown of peaceful demonstrators in Danville, Virginia), but white leaders' program of "massive resistance"—legislative and judicial programs designed to withstand federal demands for change for segregation—managed to hold back change in a way that did not capture as much national attention. In this way, Virginia could appear more progressive, but maintain the same levels of segregation that the Deep South did, as it escaped national notoriety.[15]

Without a national spotlight on it, Virginia's legislature successfully delayed integration. For example, it created onerous programs that required African American students to "apply" to white schools, dragging their feet on federal court orders, and supporting local closures of schools. These programs worked for some time. Even though Supreme Court decisions had ordered desegregation in 1954 and again in 1959, Suzanne Keller still lived through it in 1970, when an entirely black high school was integrated with her high school that had been populated by middle-class whites and a few African Americans.[16]

But federal action effected significant change. First, a federal order forced Prince Edward County's schools to reopen in 1959, effectively ending massive resistance in Virginia. Then, the Supreme Court determined miscegenation laws unconstitutional in the landmark 1968 decision in *Loving v. Virginia*. These cases threw a national spotlight on Virginia, and revealed that perhaps the commonwealth was not quite as different from the rest of the South as people might have believed.[17] It was civil rights activists who first launched large-scale assaults against the privileged patriarchy of Virginia, and who opened the way for feminists to claim equality for all women.

* * *

Feminists Come of Age

Virginia feminists came from a variety of backgrounds. As they told their stories, each wove a narrative to explain her feminist identity and activist inclinations. Perhaps because they are well-versed in the concept of personalizing the political, the women interviewed for this project clearly articulated their own experiences and were adept at self-analysis. Their memories point to a few commonalities of experience—namely that, good or bad, families, communities, and schools influenced them tremendously early in life, introducing them to ways to be strong and independent women. As young adults, experiences in college and/or in the workforce made them aware of gender discrimination.

Feminists hailed from diverse geographic regions. Some grew up in rural Virginia, others in Richmond, the Tidewater, and still others in the suburban Northeast. Often they learned as girls that social injustices ran deep, and that they were often the victims of gender, class, and racial constraints. Many realized early on, as Mary Ann Bergeron said, "I knew I was not going to be content [with] what was expected of women in the world. I knew that."[18] Later Bergeron would serve as president of her local NOW chapter and co-coordinator of Virginia NOW.

Many women active in promoting feminism were native Virginians. Only one of those interviewed grew up in what is generally considered the most progressive area of the commonwealth, Northern Virginia. Instead, they came from rural Urbanna, Iron Gate (far Western Virginia), Draper and Washington County (far Southwest Virginia), Norfolk (Tidewater), and Richmond.

Other women who would join Virginia's feminist movement were born outside of the state. Mary Ann Bergeron and Karen Raschke hailed from New Jersey, Georgia Fuller and Kristi Van Audenhove from Maryland, and Lee Perkins from Massachusetts, for example. For them, either their own careers or those of their husbands brought them to the commonwealth. Bergeron's husband took a job in Richmond. Terrie Pendleton, born in a suburb of Philadelphia, returned to Richmond for a job after her stint in the army. Van Audenhove ultimately became the director of the Virginia Sexual and Domestic Violence Action Alliance (VSDVAA) after holding similar positions in Maryland and in the commonwealth. Raschke had attended the University of North Carolina and then Wake Forest Law School, then worked in Charlottesville before landing in Richmond.

Early Education

Many women interviewed, including those in rural areas, saw their primary and secondary schools as formative. Boots Woodyard grew up on a farm in Washington County, Virginia. When she was just in high school, because of a World War II teacher shortage, she and one other female student were pulled out of their classes. She says this terrible experience prompted her to remain childless. Also, instead of going to a teacher's college, she took business courses, became a bookkeeper, and ultimately served as the head accountant of the United Mine Workers union and president of the Federation of Virginia Business and Professional Women. Another rural feminist from Draper, Virginia, Holly Farris, remembers the poverty of so many students in her school, which made her very aware of power and class systems. Her first social justice action was as an elementary student, when she wrote to the school board protesting the extremely dangerous fire hazard caused by the oiling of the old wood floors in the schoolhouse. As the daughter of a relatively privileged family, she often felt out of place in her rural school setting, and she looked to get out of town—although she settled back into her family home as an adult.

It was not only rural women who remembered school as a place where they experienced gender inequality. Beth Marschak, who moved to Richmond as a child, was a founder of the Richmond Lesbian-Feminists. Marschak's parents were supportive of her, although they refused to purchase a softball glove for her as it went beyond their accepted gender norms. Marschak remembers her parents backing her up when she ended up in the principal's office for throwing rocks at the boys in retaliation for their throwing rocks at the girls. Her parents supported her refusal to take home economics in school. Marschak was a motivated student. She took two languages and two sciences in one year, despite the fact that her female guidance counselor wondered why, as Marschak "would just be getting married and raising children anyway." But a teacher helped her get into the Latin course she desired. She also remembered how angry she was that she could not participate in a car model competition for GM as it was closed to girls: to this day she has not owned a GM vehicle. And as the first in her immediate family to go to college, she faced challenges that at the time she did not know how to handle—including her rejection from the University of Virginia because of her gender. In retrospect, she said she would have been willing to challenge UVA's rejection in court had she known that was an option. She was interested in law and nuclear chemistry at that time, so she refused to attend the teacher-focused colleges suggested by the University of Virginia. Instead, she went to Westhampton College, the women's coordinate college associated with the University of Richmond.[19]

Richmond native Mary Dean Carter, another Richmond Lesbian-Feminists founder, remembered challenges from her early years also related directly to the struggles of her divorced mother. She recalled, "I grew up in the fifties and early sixties. It was very much a southern culture and southern ladies, and very much of that decorum that you had to follow as a woman." But her mother, whom she described as "traditional as far as a lot of things" was also an "independent thinker." Carter also pointed out that "divorce was really a no-no. People were still biased in their attitudes towards children from divorced families, and parents who were divorced." Watching her mother struggle affected Carter's understanding of how women were disadvantaged. Carter attended Westhampton College because she did not want to be a teacher, and it afforded her more opportunities than her other potential choices.[20]

Some feminists received an education further afield, which had an impact on their worldviews. Mary Coulling, a women's historian active in fighting for ERA and other issues as a member of the League of Women Voters in Lexington, spent many years as the child of missionaries in China, and Muriel Elizabeth Smith moved to India with her missionary family. Smith remembered moving to India in 1946, and witnessing Indian independence as a formative experience in her life. She recalled how two women from the village proudly displayed the marks on their hands to show that they had voted. As she said, "here were women who had grown up in a British colony, who had no rights, all of a sudden had arrived at the polling place, and had voted.... Even as a teenager I caught the excitement at that time. And that excitement has continued to be much of the excitement that has led me into feminist work."[21]

Family

For many, family members provided feminist role models. Mary Coulling explained that her grandparents had also been missionaries in China, and her mother trained to be a nurse. As she noted, "both my mother and my grandmother, who were missionaries, were early feminists." She made clear that for a woman to leave rural Due West, South Carolina, after the Civil War was unusual enough: to travel to China herself was something quite special. Coulling's mother was a role model; she chose an education at Bryn Mawr College over a debut in Baltimore, although she admitted that her grandfather made her mother eventually "come out" anyway. However, she, too, chose the missionary life after meeting her future husband, who was the son of missionaries from China.[22]

The work of women family members inspired many feminists. Some, like Coulling and Holly Farris, talked about the strength of their grandmothers. In Farris's case, one was a major buyer of hospital supplies, lived in hotels, and was a less-than-domestic career woman, while the other was a "typical country grandmother" who could handle farm chores and taking care of children with ease, as Sarah Payne's daughters remembered about their own grandmother. Bonnie Atwood recalled the time her mother left home to take a job in Washington, D.C., during World War II. She became incensed when she had left her luggage at Union Station in search of a hotel and was continually turned away because desk managers thought she was a prostitute. She finally secured lodging by angrily showing her offer letter. Like Marschak's mother, she continued to work outside the home through Atwood's childhood, and Atwood remembered the difficulties she had finding childcare in Northern Virginia. Although, like Carter, Virginia Beach resident Mary (Denyes) Wazlak remembers her medical professional family as "conservative," Wazlak's mother was a nurse who worked outside the home. Her parents showed her a documentary about illegal abortion when she was just eleven, an event that had a strong impact on her life. Terrie Pendleton described growing up with her mother, grandmother, and aunt in a "matriarchal" household outside of Philadelphia. Her grandmother, the first black registered nurse in the county, was a community leader and supported Pendleton through some difficult times in high school. Pendleton credited her strength to the support she found living with three strong women and many siblings and cousins.

Sometimes men were the strongest positive influence recalled by feminists. Kate McCord remembered her father as a role model. A history professor at William and Mary, he served on the town council and was extremely involved in "bridging town and gown," and working through community organizations to improve the local quality of life. He and her mother allowed her to join antinuclear demonstrations on campus in the 1980s. Another native Virginian, Sandra Brandt, chair of the Virginia Women's Political Caucus (VWPC) and member of the Democratic National Committee, remembered growing up in Norfolk with her stay-at-home mother and her father, who was foreman of the local transportation union. She attended meetings and political events with her father: "It was lots of fun." She continued to be interested in politics and still works with unions today.

In other cases women's negative family experiences encouraged the development of their feminist values. Kristi Van Audenhove grew up with an abusive father and experienced other violence, but she had no way to understand domestic violence at the time. She remembered that she was lucky to have nonfamilial role models who enabled her to succeed, even when home was not a safe haven. She noted, however, that she knew nothing different at the time, so when she did grow to understand the violence, it had a strong effect on her. Eventually Van Audenhove attended the all-female Hood College, and it was there she took an internship at a domestic-violence shelter where she began to analyze her own experience.

Emily McCoy also had a family member—a husband—who was influential in getting her involved in feminist activities. She worked as a computer programmer at IBM and became active in NOW because her husband attended a church that was a "hotbed of feminism" and told her a feminist professor from Mary Washington College said she should subscribe to *Ms.* magazine and get involved in the movement. McCoy did and got on a NOW mailing list. She worked with an ERA canvass first and ultimately ended up using her computer-programming skills for phone banking, and she never left. She has served as legislative cochair and state coordinator, as well as in a host of other roles. She is still active in NOW today.

Others explained that they challenged conservative family traditions. Georgia Fuller remembered her father telling her younger sisters, "'don't be smart like Georgia; she'll never get married. Don't be athletic like Georgia; she'll never get married . . . don't be . . . assertive like Georgia, she'll never get married.' So my whole idea was, 'who the hell wants to get married?'" Fuller found support outside of her family, in the Jewish community. She said that, unlike her own family, the parents of her Jewish friends expected their daughters to go to college, so she found affirmation for the first time in her life when she spent time with her friends and their families.

Feminist artist Lisa Beckman remembers her native Virginian mother and Navy father, who had wholeheartedly adopted what he saw as traditional Virginian values—manners and gentility—when they moved to Chesapeake in her early teens. She already understood what they wanted from her: "for me to grow up and marry a sailor . . . and if I had to I could be a secretary for a while . . . and then I would just have a houseful of children." She chose a different life, and ultimately when her family rejected her for refusing to follow that path, she found a strong feminist community that supported her and her choices. She remembered the painful experience: "My parents were horrified." And as she noted, "For me to become the independent person I'd like to think I am, even then, was to alienate my family.... It was really sad. Because that was never the intention." Even Sandra Brandt, whose father took her to political events and union meetings, remembered her father expecting her to just get married. She attended Old Dominion University, worked through school, and paid for it herself just to show him how serious she was about a career.

Influences from Civil Rights and Social Justice Movements

Many white women who grew up to be feminist leaders were very sensitive to the social injustices faced by African Americans in Virginia, and for some, it had an impact on their ideology. As with many other feminists across the country, these women came to the movement because they were influenced by the civil rights movement. As Elizabeth Smith explained, "I would say that civil rights ... was always the core that provides the energy for [my work]." Although she attributed that to her early experience in India, she even ran for city council in Richmond in the 1980s because she saw simple economic justice, prison, and welfare issues as part of her Christian outlook and intrinsically intertwined with civil rights issues. She did it because of her "desire to be some sort of a bridge between the two communities, the black community and the white community."

Other white women explained early experiences with racism that affected them. Mary Coulling remembered being upset when she saw college-educated African Americans forced to take janitorial jobs at Virginia Military Institute. Coulling, who had attended Agnes Scott College, said, "They were getting below minimum wage. It was appalling." She did not believe that, as a "lowly, lowly secretary," she could do anything about it but "treat them as human beings." Melanie Payne-White, who became the first director of Alleghany County's first women's shelter, remembered how the civil rights movement affected her: "I just couldn't believe humans could do something like that to another person." She even took psychology courses at George Mason University to better understand what was happening. Suzanne Keller recalled moving with her military family from a more egalitarian army base in Germany to Petersburg in 1966 as a culture shock: "it was very parochial, very racist ... very classist."

But the challenges these white women activists faced were minor in comparison to the ordeals experienced by the African American feminists I interviewed. Two of them grew up in a segregated Virginia, and their experiences shaped their lives in important ways. Bessida White remembered growing up in the rural Tidewater town of Urbanna, with a population of around six hundred. She graduated from high school in 1965, and although some black students had begun to attend the white high school in her junior year, she did not. She explained that her mother, a school teacher, needed her job, and that her father could not afford to alienate white customers. She remembered that a local bus driver was fired for sending her daughter to the formerly all-white school, and had to endure burning crosses on her lawn in retaliation.

White did what she could, however, which included attempting to desegregate the lunch counter at Marshall's Drug when she was just fifteen. She had her own protocol: "I always got a chicken salad sandwich and a limeade. ... And they would put my sandwich in waxed paper ... and my limeade in a cup ... and I would proceed to undo it and eat it. The person next to me of course got theirs in a glass and a plate, so we went through that for a couple of years, I guess." She also said that, because white and black societies were so segregated, she didn't have an idea of everything that went on in the white school or white parts of the county except, when she went to pick up her schoolbooks from the central bookstore one year, she noticed what was not taught at her school, "like calculus, and Latin...."

Like many other black women who came to define themselves as feminists, White began her career as a civil rights activist.[23] She received tremendous support from her local black community, and she attended college as her grandmother and mother had done before her. At Virginia State, she participated in many civil rights demonstrations and joined SNCC and the Black Panthers. She recalled, "In fact it's so funny, my daughter said ... 'why do we always have to protest? Why can't we just be like normal folks do?'"

It was this sense of activism that eventually led her to the women's movement, as a leader in the VWPC and founder of the Richmond chapter of the National Black Feminist Organization, especially as she began to experience racism within the civil rights movement. She remembered: "So you know, we didn't progress. And I think too, that the other piece that I left out, that was my really realizing what was going on, was what was ... how very sexist folks like Stokely Carmichael were...." But as many other African American women who got involved with the movement concluded, she recognized that, while all African Americans understood well the problems caused by racism, not all "got" sexism.[24]

Denise Lee had a different experience in Chesapeake, Virginia. She recalled: "I remember when I was in the eighth grade how systematically some of our black kids were taken... but no white kids were made to come to [our school]." After that, the all-black high schools were shut down, but the white high schools were kept open. After returning to Chesapeake from New York City in eleventh grade when her Navy father was relocated, she recognized what she had lost with the new high school—the history, the tradition, and the sense of community. An honor student whose Navy dad and working mom instilled in her and her sisters the critical importance of an education, she was stunned when she was called to the principal's office after she challenged busing and what had happened to the black high school. She noted, she thought it "interesting" that someone could think she "could possibly start a riot," as being an activist was not what she set out to do. She did ask to continue a black history program that had been started by African American students at the school, but concluded that "Maybe the fact that I called the school racist, that I thought it was systematic racism that got rid of [the segregated African American high schools]" that made the principal take notice of her.

Lee did not think of herself as an activist at this time. Unlike White, she was not involved in student protests in the 1970s at Norfolk State University, which she attended while living at home. Instead, she focused on her education. Still, she admitted that she "was not afraid to speak my mind...." Although she did not participate in demonstrations or protests, Lee had no trouble sharing her strong political opinions, a trait that would later serve her well when she became state coordinator of Virginia NOW.

Although as a student not yet claiming an activist identity, Lee was well aware of the challenges she faced as a professional African American woman in a predominantly white workforce. Lee advanced quickly through the ranks as a talented analyst with Caterpillar Corporation and later Honeywell. As one of the few African Americans in Peoria, Illinois, and facing racism and sexism on the job in the 1980s, Lee had to handle many detractors and racist challenges over the years. She saved Honeywell money right away by poring over the financial records to find cost savers, and even created a leadership tool, but it wasn't enough. She remembered that being the only woman and African American at the company did not mean she would get accolades—in fact, she had to work much harder to be respected even half as much as everyone else.

Even being an analyst did not make her immune from discrimination. One night when she was at a business conference, a friendly game of poker in which she was the only woman—and the only African American—quickly devolved. After she got confused about the rules, a white man with whom she worked called her the "n-word" and, as she remembered, "the whole room just got so silent... I just got up and left." She said that, even though he apologized at the office, nobody knew how to respond, and "It was a disaster." She said, "it just reiterated that no matter what you do, that's what they see you as. That's what they see you as. No matter what I had accomplished, no matter what I had done, no matter how sociable we all were. When... I'm not doing what you think I should do, that's what you resorted to calling me." She remembered, "It was a more important lesson for me. And it was a clear lesson. It was a hurtful one, but nevertheless. That's what I tell everybody, you can do whatever you do, but recognize who you are."

The South did not have a monopoly on racism at the time, and school segregation affected Terrie Pendleton as well. Terrie Pendleton grew up in a suburb of Philadelphia, but her community, Ardmore, was very heavily African American, and she was somewhat insulated, and isolated, from what was happening outside of her community. She described it as "apart from, but also integral to," a larger surrounding white community. She, too, experienced segregation until sixth grade because of residential patterns, when she was bused outside of her community. Like so many other African American children, Pendleton had to leave her own school and friends to attend a school outside her district—it was never the white children who seemed to get bused to the historically African American schools. About her experience, she explained, "what I remember about that was the change of feeling about leaving a school in your own community and going to a school outside... with people that you don't know. And that was really traumatic, I think, for a lot of us." All three African American women interviewed for the project saw from an early age and continued to witness that their position as African American women made them vulnerable to assaults on many levels. For all three, this vulnerability would inform their feminist positions.

Some white feminist leaders gained experience as demonstrators and workers for the civil rights movement. Beth Marschak joined the Woody Guthrie Community Center in Richmond while she attended Westhampton College (University of Richmond) as an undergraduate. She participated in many Southern Christian Leadership Conference–led demonstrations, in Petersburg and outside of the state. She remembered getting arrested in several different demonstrations but was jailed only once, in 1972, when demonstrating in North Carolina for the tribal rights of the Tuscarora nation. Muriel Elizabeth Smith recalled taking a YWCA-sponsored bus from Oberlin College in Ohio to participate in a civil rights march for equal housing in Washington, D.C.

Betsy Brinson also came to the movement after being an activist in other organizations. Moving to Virginia from North Carolina and eventually becoming the head of the ACLU Southern Women's Rights Project (SWRP), she participated in several demonstrations in Greensboro while she was a student at the North Carolina Women's College (now the University of North Carolina at Greensboro). She remembered being picked up by the police for demonstrating in front of a segregated movie theater, and being warned by the dean of students that if she participated again she would be expelled. When asked about the source of her determination to fight for civil rights, Brinson said, "... I'd been reading what was going on in the country, certainly, and my mother was originally from New England and, you know, we talked about these things at home.... What was right... what was fair."

Georgia Fuller, who would later be director of NOW's National Religious Task Force as well as Virginia state NOW coordinator, also became involved in feminism through her work with civil rights and social justice. She recalled that, when she worked for a social gospel–based group in Brooklyn, she hadn't realized how segregated her Maryland neighborhood was. She thought her religiously diverse neighborhood was integrated, "but I... hadn't realized how little I knew until I went up there and I started looking differently at the whole idea of injustice...." Through this work she supported civil rights, and as she noted, "There was a natural transition for women of that era to the feminist movement when we suddenly see, in our white consciousness, that African Americans should not be called boys, but we were still willing to let people call us girls, you know?"

It was Fuller who most described her activism through a lens of religion and social justice, which developed through her civil rights efforts. She explained that, as an anthropologist, not only could she see that to sustain the movement would require a "viable subculture" but also that successful movements were tied to religion. As she explained: "I was also very aware that every movement that had ever succeeded in America had a very prominent religious component, like the whole social gospel ministry with the labor movement [as well as civil rights and anti-war movements]." Because of this understanding and interest, Fuller focused her efforts on "bringing [religion] into the feminist movement" as well as working for equality in religious denominations and affirming feminist spirituality in different artistic venues.

Influences from the Antiwar Movement

Other women came to their activism like thousands of others across the country, as they participated in campus protests during the 1960s and 1970s. Many feminists of the late twentieth century found their voices with the anti–Vietnam War protests, as well as the protests many students had against what they viewed as repressive college administrators or policies.[25] Bonnie Atwood went to George Mason College (now George Mason University) as a commuter student, then left to tour with the Ice Capades for a year. Upon returning to college in 1967 she remembered the charged atmosphere: "I noticed a difference in the students and the professors. Something was happening. And I think by the end of that calendar year I recognized it as just boiling anger over the Vietnam War." She became angry, too, and participated in many antiwar protests. Atwood remembered that, when she was arrested and her name made the paper, her family "were embarrassed at first." But she continued to protest, and she explained her parents' change of heart: "We managed somehow after years and years of discussion to get them to separate [criminal behavior from civil disobedience]." Her father accepted this, and her mother became "a real champion" for Atwood in everything she undertook.

Beth Marschak's first official protest was against the Kent State killings. She cut classes and headed to the capitol building in Richmond. She was reluctant to join in at first, fearing arrest might hurt her prospects for a good job, but she decided to march anyway. Although she did not get arrested that day, she continued to do "much more risky" things in the future because she had decided that she could live with the consequences. Other Westhampton students like Mary Dean Carter attended antiwar protests, and Marschak remembered her participation as a vehicle through which she met other like-minded progressives. Melanie Payne-White did get arrested during an antiwar protest, and recalled that her father was none too happy about it.

Some women's antiwar experiences became family affairs. For Suzanne Keller, the war hit close to home, as her father was stationed in Vietnam for a tour. She remembered her sister being against the war, but "For me, my father going to war was much more of a personal separation...." When she went to

Virginia Tech she participated in protests, and her sister produced an underground paper in Petersburg. Holly Farris recalled going on buses to Raleigh to protest the war as a student at the University of North Carolina. Her father, who was a World War II combat veteran, was a pacifist, as was her mother, and both of them were happy, in her words, "to package me off to become an activist." They supported her and her views in front of her extended family, which was much more conservative. Bergeron did not recall actively protesting because, "Well, this was slightly before the flower children, just slightly before, but we did care about nuclear weapons. We did care about peace. We did care about Vietnam[.]" Her husband at the time ended up deploying there.

Many activists across the country said they became feminists when supposedly liberal men failed to treat them as equals in the movement. They saw the disconnect between men's stated progressivism and their chauvinism. For these women, discussion of and action against the war led them to more progressive arenas in which they could further their own activist identities. It also gave some women experience in public demonstrating. Bonnie Atwood remembered a distinct connection between the antiwar movement and feminism when she attended her first feminist meeting in Washington, D.C., after reading about it in an underground newspaper: "We talked about the men in the antiwar movement being disrespectful of the women in the antiwar movement and how we were tired of being pushed around." She had not experienced that disrespect personally, "But I could see what they were talking about, because in all the groups, there was a lot of expectation that the women were responsible for the meals, and the men were going to make all the decisions, it was that whole dynamics. And we were starting to articulate it. That's what was like a sheet of ice that broke."[26]

Workplace Inequality

Like many employed women across the country, a good number of women interviewed for this project faced the challenges of chauvinism by taking personal action and engaging in the feminist movement, once they recognized that there was an outlet for them to do so. Women had always faced discrimination in securing employment, and getting equal pay, benefits, and promotions. Throughout the twentieth century, women used what was available to them to do battle with discriminatory employers and their practices, from demanding action from their unions, to collectively lobbying for anti-discrimination laws through groups like the Federation of Business and Professional Women, to using federal government agencies like the National Labor Relations Board, the Fair Employment Practices Committee, and the Equal Employment Opportunities Committee to seek redress. While not all of the women who worked to advance the goals of equality in the workplace would call themselves feminists, many did embrace the feminist movement of the late twentieth century after having their own run-ins with discrimination.[27]

Some Virginia women recognized their unequal treatment in the workforce, which launched some into feminist actions. Hailing from a family whose roots in far Western Virginia were deep, Sarah Payne became a nurse and served in World War II but became incensed when she learned that women made far less than men. She and her daughter, Stephanie Tyree, fought for the ERA, began a NOW chapter in the rural Allegheny Highlands, and helped to start the first domestic-violence shelter in the area. As Tyree noted, her husband watched her move gradually toward feminism as she saw more inequality: "I was so infuriated that women didn't have equal rights, and the more you get into it, you'd find that not only did you not have equal rights, but that you didn't have diddly squat, and they were bound and determined in Richmond and in Washington to keep it that way."

Other women transitioned into feminism over time but identified an occupational experience as a defining moment. Another lifelong Virginian, Lynn Bradford, remarked on her conservative upbringing—she was a devotee of William F. Buckley in high school and belonged to the "ultraconservative" group Young Americans for Freedom because the Young Republicans were too moderate. But over time she changed. She heard a campaign speech by Flora Crater, lieutenant governor candidate in 1973, when she was at William and Mary that "just made a lot of sense." She recalled, though, "I don't remember a specific incident or issue that radicalized me ... issues of fairness were important to me, and it gradually dawned on me that there were a lot of things that were not fair in the world." Bradford recalled touring a factory in 1973 while still in college. As she said, "they wanted to go to the South, they had wanted to hire women, because they could pay them half," according to the manager who spoke with them. She remembered, "and what gets me to this day, is that man was proud of that."

Sometimes specific workplace experiences affected feminists. Mary Ann Bergeron got involved with NOW while working as a consultant in the 1970s. She was doing sexual-harassment prevention training for companies "who were becoming aware that they had wonderful women in their workforce, but these women had no formal or informal training in how to move forward" and recognized that women faced problems that had held them back. Lee Perkins remembered that, when she lived in Washington, D.C., a friend told her to look in the men's section of the newspaper "because that's where the good jobs were" but not thinking much about it until she involved herself in the women's movement. She recalled an incident in 1965, when she worked as a researcher at the Smithsonian, a male intern from Northeastern University physically attacked the African American secretary. Perkins recalled: "I mean, [he] tore her blouse, and I knew that my time was limited there when I called the police. And they wanted to settle it in house, and I said, 'you can't have guys attacking women.' And they said, 'well, she's not really a woman.' And I said, 'She's over twenty-one.' And they said. 'She's black, they're used to that.' So the inherent racism was I think more overt than the sexism." She left shortly thereafter for a better job at the Library of Congress, but she understood that taking a stand hurt her chances of working on an oceangoing research vessel, which she had wanted to do.

When Beth Marschak took a job as a grocery clerk during college, she recognized that it was the women who had the dead-end, low-paying jobs, while men became managers. This influenced her feminism by "caus[ing] me to be much more open to a class analysis of things...." Terrie Pendleton faced a challenge more grave—as a lesbian in the military during the 1970s, she, her partner, and their lesbian friends faced "witch hunts." She and her friends lived in fear of being discovered, until she finally decided she did not want to be career military and the stress wasn't worth it. She left the army and moved back to Germany, living as a civilian with her military partner.

Others saw problems in attempting to get into the workforce. According to Karen Raschke, in college she generally focused on boys and sports. But at Wake Forest Law School in 1982, she went to the dean and said she would refuse her degree if the school didn't take down a sign advertising for a "male partner." She remembered: "I don't know how much I now, looking back... really knew what I was willing to give up...." Mary Dean Carter recalled a similar situation when she went on the job market: "When I first started job hunting I was faced with a lot of discrimination... the first thing they want to know, well when you go in to apply they give you a typing test." She finally confronted an employment agent about this, which got results with a better job. She had, however, found a position on her own by this point.

Towards the Development of Feminist Philosophies/Identities

Some feminists encountered what conscious-raising groups of the 1970s would call a "click" moment, which they often remembered vividly. Some were drawn to the movement by feminist literature. Lisa Beckman remembered as a teen being introduced to *Ms.* magazine by her friend whose mother was more progressive than her own parents. She described the excitement of learning more about feminism: "We would run out and keep watching at the local pharmacy ... and look for [*Ms.*] on the stands, and we had one of our other best friends ... who was a pharmacy delivery boy in high school, and he'd give us the heads up [when it was delivered]." She used her lunch money to buy the magazine. "When I would read it, I would cry ... " she remembered. She talked with her friend about women's issues, forming what amounted to an informal consciousness-raising group among like-minded women. Feminist literature also grabbed Suzanne Keller's attention. She remembered the Virginia Commonwealth University Bookstore stocking *Off Our Backs,* a radical feminist newspaper from the D.C. area. She credits discovering that newspaper and her attendance at a conference on women and prison for having propelled her to be a more active feminist. As she said, "yeah I thank God for whoever was ordering that *Off Our Backs*, you know." In 1975 it introduced her to feminist theory that would continue to be important to her as she worked on the feminist bookstore collective in Richmond and was active in the Richmond Lesbian-Feminists. Mary Dean Carter remembers a similar experience at a Westhampton class in female psychology. After reading an assigned book, "It was an instant click. It was like one of those aha moments inside. Oh my God, wow! This is really like, 'Oh wow, I'm a feminist, wow.'"

Others recounted personal experiences from college that affected their philosophies about the necessity of working for change. Kate McCord remembered that she learned about building consensus through the Oberlin co-op experience. This would be particularly useful to her in her position as communications coordinator of VSDVAA. She explained: "and so that was a value that I think I carry through to the rest of my work ... because that's how you change hearts and minds." Mary Wazlak recalled working for a suicide-prevention program and dealing with a particularly terrible situation where a young woman was pregnant. Wazlak remembered the dilemma the woman was in, exacerbated by the fact that the woman was Catholic and had been sexually assaulted: "They have names for date rape now. They didn't have that term then ... we had all agonized with her.... We kept thinking, what is the alternative?" This would stay with Wazlak and helped to inform her strong opinions on reproductive choice.

Others tested activist strategies or found kindred spirits in college. Carter remembered attending a demonstration against the restrictive curfews faced by Westhampton women—curfews that applied only to female students, and not the men on Richmond College's campus. As she noted, while nothing happened at the time, she thinks it may have changed the following year. Marschak was actually called into the dean's office for wearing slacks—which she promptly informed the administrator was against no rule—and Carter recalls that the year she attended was the first year in which women didn't "have to" wear skirts. Bonnie Atwood and Lisa Beckman found feminist friends in college who affirmed their ideologies and their choices, which was the experience of many other feminists in the 1970s.

The Limits of Sisterhood: Feminist Schisms

It is no surprise that most of the women interviewed for this project were white, college-educated, and middle-class. This was true of feminists across the country—and it speaks to a larger issue many historians have articulated, notably, the preponderance of these women in the formal mainstream feminist movement.[28] The lack of women of color and of working-class women in the movement was a problem noted at the time and has been continually addressed by scholars. Every woman I interviewed had a post-secondary degree, and many had degrees beyond the BA. And while the feminists with whom I spoke represented great geographic diversity, I spoke with only three African American women out of the total two dozen.

This homogeneity among the women who told me their stories is acknowledged by the women themselves. Although Sarah Payne and Stephanie Tyree explained that the NOW chapter they founded in their mountain town had both black and white members, many Virginia women pointed out that, while members of organizations attempted to be inclusive, they were not successful. They often related their own efforts to reach beyond traditional membership, to little avail.

African American feminists saw it happening at the time. Bessida White recalled: "Well, oftentimes I was the only black woman.... There were times when there were one or two others ... but ... if you look at the old stuff from the political caucus, women's center, you know, the Richmond women's festival groups, you aren't going to see many." She said there were some women from outside of professional classes, explaining "I guess there was some diversity, but you know,... probably not a lot of poor women... but there were certainly people from across the state who had different backgrounds." Denise Lee became active in her local NOW chapter over the 1989 *Webster* decision that restricted abortion access. At the first meeting, she noted she was the only African American woman there out of about eight to ten people. After working with her local chapter and serving as state legislative cochair, Lee eventually became state coordinator.

Terrie Pendleton, founder of Lesbian Womyn of Color, had an explanation for the dearth of black women in white-dominated organizations. She opined, "black women... don't think about feminism in the same way as white women do... it's not a construct of political activism for them, it's a way of being for them. It has always been that, in our minds that we are some way or another, feminist." Citing the fact that black women have always acted in ways to empower themselves and others which we would define as feminist, "Feminism has always been a part of the African American language. Although we maybe never said it's feminism." But she said some African American women rejected the term "because they considered it to be a white ideology. And they're not going to buy into that." Referencing the famous question attributed to Sojourner Truth, "Ain't I a Woman," Pendleton said that feminism must be "flexible enough to encompass black feminism under its umbrella" and accept her experiences as a valid and legitimate expression of the "woman's experience."

It was not only African American women who noticed the preponderance of white women in the Virginia movement. Mary Ann Bergeron remembered she did not experience the problem in the North, whereas in Virginia, "We had to work hard to get African American women into NOW....That had not been an issue in any other place we lived...." Tyree noted that her rural NOW chapter was "a really diverse group," but when they would go to the conferences, they would see "more middle-aged white women."

NOW and VWPC were not the only groups that had a disproportionate number of white middle-class women. Photos and newsletters from the Virginia BPW, League of Women Voters, and American Association of University Women reflected a fairly homogenous membership. There were some notable exceptions. Ruth Harvey Charity served as state ERA coordinator for AAUW, and Rosalind Exum was the president of Virginia AAUW and chair of the

Virginia ERA Ratification Council for a time. Together with Denise Lee and Bessida White, who served as state Virginia Women's Political Caucus (VWPC) coordinator at one point, they appeared to constitute African American women's leadership in predominantly white women's groups in the late twentieth century.

It wasn't that white women did not want African American women to join these organizations. Zelda Nordlinger noted that Ruth Harvey Charity failed to receive a notice about a state VWPC meeting and urged the coordinator to send her a note explaining the oversight as unintentional. She told the coordinator, "It cannot be stressed too much that the Caucus *must* gain the support of Negro women if we are to be effective."[29] In the 1970s, Del Dobbins, minority affairs chair of Northern Virginia NOW, wrote articles in the newsletter to try to educate members about African American women's issues. By the 1980s, NOW was focusing on a "Minority Outreach Committee" to try to reach out to African American women, and the AAUW in Norfolk reported that it was having difficulty securing women of color as members.[30]

Concern over diversity of membership continued through the end of the century. In 1990, President Marian Patey stated in Arlington NOW's annual report: "The diversity of participation in the chapter is sadly lacking. I have found, as the current president, an undercurrent of apathy when broaching the subject of addressing the needs of 'women of color' in our locale. We need help!" And feminists in the western commonwealth were having little luck recruiting African American women, too. Montgomery County NOW's Susan Anderson reported that, although the chapter tried to recruit women of lower income through sliding scale dues, all meetings were open to the public and widely advertised, and they represented diverse sexual orientations and religions and had several men. "We are, however, composed of predominately white, middle-income members."[31]

Virginia NOW was concerned enough about the lack of diversity that in 2004 they dedicated their state conference to the theme "Building Bridges for Tomorrow: Cultural and Racial Diversity & Feminism." One of the stated goals of the conference was "To improve alliances between NOW, traditionally viewed as a white women's organization, and other diverse social justice organizations." Speakers included the director of the National Coalition for Asian Pacific American Community Development; Nancy Redd, first African American Miss Virginia, who received a BA in women's studies and graduated from Harvard; Lori Montenegro, National Telemundo anchor; and Viola Baskerville, African American Virginia Delegate.[32]

Why was it so hard to recruit African American women into NOW, LWV, AAUW, and other progressive women's organizations that had been populated primarily by white women? Across the country, this was a problem acknowledged by some white feminists and many activist women of color. African American women in the Combahee River Collective, members of the National Black Feminist Organization, and Asian American and Latina feminists were pointing out problems. They challenged myopic class- and race-based assumptions of many middle-class white women and insisted on acknowledging the interconnection between racism and sexism. They demanded that white feminists recognize the problems poor women of all racial-ethnic backgrounds faced.[33]

Many scholars argue that women of color stood at the vanguard of feminist thought because they were the first to identify multiple interlocking oppressions that affected women, but still they did not have a central role in what became defined as the "feminist movement." They were not becoming activists in reaction to white feminists or black men in the civil rights and black power movements, but instead had historically been activists on their own and their communities' behalves.[34] Often, as sociology professor Deborah K. King wrote in 1988, African American women's experience within the larger feminist movement was one of "invisibility and marginality."[35] Although African American women well understood racism and sexism as "interactive oppressions that circumscribe our lives," and were active in working for social justice through many institutions, she claimed "Feminism has excluded and devalued black women, our experiences, and our interpretations of our own realities at the conceptual and ideological level."[36] Feminism's failure to grasp the complexity of black women's experience affected African American's view of and participation in the movement, King explained.[37]

In Virginia, African American women tried to explain the chasm between black and white women. In her series on racism and feminism published in 1975, Del Dobbins explained why more women of color didn't join NOW—"Prevalent in NOW is an assumption that the organization can be all things to all feminists. The problem with that is, it ignores the reality of racism." She also said that many African American women felt "subtle pressure" to "be 'women' first and third world second." She questioned how anyone could separate the two. While she noted that "feminist dialogue" was prevalent in NOW, "exposure to the life experiences of minority feminists" was not. She chided her fellow NOW members: "We cannot afford to sit on a remote hill dictating the 'right way' if we have not experienced the reality, the pain, and the suffering of racial oppression. We cannot and should not make guesses, we have to hear it like it is from those who know."[38] Dobbins's series of articles written during her tenure as Minority Task Force chair of Virginia NOW reflect a desire to educate white NOW members on the problems faced by women of color. Illustrating an important point of contemporary black feminist theory, she demanded that white women recognize their own bias.

Bessida White founded a National Black Feminist Organization (NBFO) chapter in Richmond which held several seminars on black feminism. The NBFO took on issues of racism and sexism in the mid-1970s to publicize the ways in which African American women had to negotiate inequality. The chapter planned a seminar in 1975 called "Double Jeopardy: To Be Black and Female" at Virginia Union University. Topics to be discussed related to black professionals, incarcerated black women, women in the media, healthcare, and the ERA and its intended effect on poor and minority women. Savannah Williams, Afro-American studies instructor at Virginia Commonwealth University and Virginia Union University; Georgia Randall, leader of work in prisons; Bunny Strachan, reporter; Marie Montroy, former nurse at the Medical College of Virginia (MCV); and Phyllis Boanes, assistant professor of history at Virginia State, were on the panel. Later that year at a seminar held at Virginia Union University, black men came together at an NBFO-sponsored panel to describe black feminism. A reporter wrote that the sixty people who showed up heard Freddy Ray, graduate student at Virginia Commonwealth University, say that he thought black liberation and women's liberation were a "direct contradiction of terms"; although he claimed to be sympathetic to black feminists, he also was reported to have said: "I see black feminism as a countermovement to stop black liberation" because the women's movement did not concern itself with racism. He was supported "vocally" by at least one woman there, who said, "We as black people have a habit of waiting for white people to come up with statistics."[39] In this way, these two audience members articulated the alienation many African Americans felt from white feminists.

But the other five speakers supported the need for black feminism. Napoleon Peoples, Virginia Commonwealth University counselor, said "If black sisters feel the need for liberation, black men must stand by them. They need liberation too. Sisters, unity is the key issue no matter what the goal." Philip Bladen, White's husband, said that he "doesn't think there has been a conscious effort" to privilege the issue of black women in the mainstream feminist movement, but that he was a feminist and believed that traditional gender norms hurt everyone. The reporter then wrote that "Ms. White took the floor to say it bothered her to separate feminism and that she had only recently started to think in terms of black feminism. 'I have never heard a feminist say her or his goal was not the liberation of total humankind.'"[40]

White faced some resistance from African Americans in the Richmond community. In 1985, in an article assessing the effect of ERA lobbying and feminism on the state, White noted that she received pushback for studying feminist theory in college: "I was described as a woman who left her husband for women's lib." She pointed out that this fact was untrue, because except for in 1968 when he was in Vietnam, they'd been together. White said that many African American women's reaction to her claims of feminism was "Maybe for those white women, but not for you, sister." However, she said black women did indeed support women's rights, even if they weren't "in the forefront of the feminist movement."[41]

While Dobbins and White were promoting what black feminism meant to them, other African American women questioned the need for alliances with white women at all. In 1982, African American activist Pat Blackwell gave a talk to the Northern Virginia NOW chapter (NOVA NOW). The member of the Fairfax County NAACP and chair of the Human Relations Advisory Committee made quite an impact. According to Carole Marcoux, author of the newsletter article, Blackwell "gave voice to the perceptions that many black women have about feminists, in order to make visible the wall of myths, misunderstanding, and silence that obscures common concerns and experience." Marcoux explained that Blackwell asked why she had just recently been invited to NOW. She wondered if the ERA's failure was causing the chapter to look for other "causes." Marcoux claimed Blackwell queried: "Why, if we were truly seeking equal rights, did we continue to 'sleep with our white master?' Why did the women's movement steal the tactics of the black civil rights movement?" Marcoux noted pushback from some white women there, but chapter members asked Blackwell to return—with African American friends—to continue talking.[42]

When the ACLU's Richmond-based SWRP sent two African American women to an ERA conference in Louisiana, one originally from Washington, D.C., reported experiencing extreme hostility from African American women. In an article for an ACLU women's rights report, Sheila Iverson told Liz Wheaton of the Richmond central office that "[the community members] thought I was trying to convince them to support an issue which might somehow work against them. Because of this, because I was working on ERA, I was isolated from the black community. Just because you are the same race, it doesn't mean that you can automatically relate or that you will be welcomed into the community." Like Dobbins, she described the problem of intersectionality: "We're always being asked, 'Are you a woman first or a black first?' It's like being split in two. But I'm always a woman, always black. I can't change either, and I don't want to."[43]

Ultimately, Iverson believed that the conference fostered good conversation but that African American women would just continue to work for their local communities, as they saw problems there that were more important than sexism. In an earlier draft of the article, Iverson made a statement that did not make it to the final edition, claiming black women were skeptical—"And there is still a distrust of the women's movement, with a lack of senstivity [sic] or even outright racism on the part of white feminists."[44] The hostility Iverson encountered suggests that racial tension in this situation impeded the ACLU's ability to work on the ERA in Louisiana. The SWRP was attempting to reach out and build bridges, but perhaps the historic oppressive racial hierarchies of the South were too much to overcome here, perhaps especially when the field workers sent in were outsiders.[45]

In Richmond, the annual conference of the National Association of Black Women Attorneys held a workshop titled "The Involvement of Black Women in Feminism and Other Progressive Movements" that articulated national debates in the black community on a local level. Bessida White discussed intersectionality of race and gender with Demeter Frazier of Massachusetts. She believed that racism and sexism were "both important" and should be addressed simultaneously, but Edythe Rogers of Richmond disagreed and said that racism was much more problematic for African American women. A news report explained Frazier claimed that she had seen some feminist movements fail and that "Working with racist white women does not help the cause of black feminist [sic] either because the issues, particularly those affecting poor women, are not addressed...." Rogers, who was one of the conference organizers, had "serious problems with the term feminism" as "its [sic] like falling into a trap defined by someone else." Echoing the sentiments of many in the civil rights struggle, "She said those involved in the black feminist movement should nto [sic] dilute the strength of the struggle by lashing out at black men. 'They too are victims of the same system.'..." The reporter claimed that "Ms. White, a Richmond Lawyer who acted as moderator for the discussion, opened a can of worms, so to speak, when she said that 'sexism runs rampant' in black institutions, especially in the male black church, which is male-dominated." This sparked a major debate, but ultimately, Frazier and White maintained that racism and sexism were inseparable problems for African American women.[46]

It wasn't just national organizations with large membership bases where African American women felt excluded, either. In Richmond, Terrie Pendleton started the Lesbian Womyn of Color after feeling that she was not fully embraced by the entire Richmond Lesbian-Feminist community. Although she said that there were women like Beth Marschak, Suzanne Keller, and Mary Dean Carter who were very welcoming, she recalled that others did not make her or other women of color feel at home. She believed one of the biggest problems in the wider lesbian community stemmed from racism she believed the owner exhibited at the local lesbian bar, Babe's. She remembered that, even in the 1980s and early 1990s, "every African American lesbian knew that when you came in there, you were not going to be really welcomed, and you were damn invisible... you just didn't, you just weren't seen... you weren't a person. You weren't there. Can you believe that?.... It was... as divisive as any community in Richmond. It was no different. Isn't that a damn disgrace."

If African American women went to Babe's with white friends, they often found themselves isolated from other black women who might have been in the bar at the time, as they were associated only with the white women with whom they had come. "So the cycle of the craziness of prejudice and distortion and racial tension was just in a circle, you know." She believed that this stemmed from African American women's fear that they would not be accepted: "You are brainwashed into this construct" of heterosexuality and race, and "you understand who the dominant culture is and you do everything to try to be accepted into it." As surprised as she may have been to discover racism at a lesbian bar, this was often the case in other lesbian-friendly bars across the country.[47] For her and her friends, Lesbian Womyn of Color became a safe place to gather.

Were white Virginia feminists trying to be exclusionary? Perhaps in the case of Babe's owner, yes. In many other situations, it appeared that they very much wanted to be inclusive, but they did not reach out to African American women or their organizations on a regular basis in order to build bridges over the chasm that centuries of racial oppression had wrought. LWV chapters in Northern Virginia, for example, focused a tremendous amount of energy and effort on studying and advocating for affordable housing and environmental protection, issues that crossed class and race lines. LWV chapter newsletters discussing better schools and voter registration also reflected the concerns of a broader community. Bergeron believed many African American women lacked the time and resources to participate in NOW activities, but NOW tried hard to reach out. NOW chapter reports bemoaning their own homogenous membership, their focus on diversity, and their attempts to understand African American women's positions, many feminists showed an interest in inclusivity.

In retrospect, some white feminists acknowledged that they may not have tried hard enough to reach out to African American women. Beth Marschak pointed out the problem in organizations like NOW and other groups she termed "liberal" rather than "progressive" in Richmond: they had "more discomfort about differences. So this group which was more predominantly white middle-class women [NOW]... might be stay at home [mothers]." And, while they constantly discussed the need for more inclusivity, Marschack suggested that they did not address what was "important to black women" so could never ameliorate the problem.

This was not just a problem intrinsic to the organizations in which Marschak held membership. Former LWV Richmond president (Muriel) Elizabeth Smith said that her group had a problem with diversity, and often chafed at her more radical suggestions. As she explained, "The League has never been terribly... comfortable with the perspective that I bring." Describing herself as "a little bit too far to the left" and "too quick to point out the racism that's apparent to me, but not necessarily to them," she said, "it takes something to tolerate [me] on the boards, you know."

The ACLU was also concerned about being representative of all people, and so its staff was aware of the race divide in the feminist movement. Betsy Brinson, executive director of the SWRP, wrote:

> Overall, southern feminist activists gave little attention to the inclusion of black women in the women's movement. It was not a malicious oversight; there was so much else to do to ratify the ERA, to encourage political and legal reform, to make pro-choice abortion a reality. We gratefully

accepted when our black sister feminists offered help but we did little to reach out to black women; we assumed that the extension of legal rights for women included *all* women. And our energy was limited. Like most of our foremothers, we did what we could.

But for many white women feminism is not the sum of social reform. Prison reform, school desegregation, voter law, abolition of capital punishment contribute significantly to the quest to eliminate both racism and sexism. No person can be free until we are all free.[48]

African American women were present and active in supporting feminist causes in Virginia, but not in numbers representing the overall population of the commonwealth. Instead, they joined other women when they saw issues that mattered to them and their communities and joined with white feminists to support issues like the ERA, reproductive rights, and domestic and sexual violence. Patricia Hill Collins calls this "flexible solidarity," an idea she introduced at a 2016 talk at Clemson University. Black women were in flexible solidarity with groups and individuals on all causes addressed in this work, either as members of their own community groups or as representatives of white-dominated women's organizations, but feminists never achieved diversity in the movement.[49]

Lesbian Feminism in the Commonwealth

Although self-described feminists involved in many organizations tended to be white and college-educated, not all were straight. As in another bastion of conservatism, Louisiana, lesbian feminists were extremely active and vocal in supporting women's causes.[50] Early on in the national women's movement, this created some tensions, as feminists feared being defined as "man-hating lesbians." This tension manifested itself most notoriously when in 1969 Betty Friedan, one of the founders of NOW, called the "threat" of lesbians to feminism a "lavender menace," a distraction from what she saw as key feminist goals. In response, lesbian feminists organized as a "Lavender Menace" group, fighting for recognition of themselves as legitimate participants in the movement and for the importance of LGBT issues.[51]

As conversations about lesbian inclusion happened nationally, Virginia feminists were struggling with these issues in the commonwealth. Virginia was a historically conservative state. Its legal system was designed to take children of lesbian and gay parents away in the case of a divorce, and there existed no civil rights for same-sex couples or members of the LGBT community. In the last quarter of the twentieth century, Virginia was not necessarily a safe place to come out.[52]

Some feminist organizations in Virginia were not openly welcoming of lesbians. Mary Dean Carter remembered that "there was one point in time where NOW was worried that lesbians would make them look bad, or hurt the cause or something to that effect." Although there "were a fair number of lesbians who were coming to the meetings," Carter said there was an "undertone" of concern in the Richmond chapter. She explained that, while it wasn't overt and not everyone felt that way, "They wanted to pass the ERA and they felt like lesbians might hurt the cause, but it was never really said." Carter was active with NOW for about two years but then moved on because "As I started to come out and recognize and embrace my lesbianism I felt more drawn to the work in the Richmond Lesbian-Feminist Organization." Holly Farris got involved with NOW because of a flyer or handout she had seen at an LGBT meeting and other information she had seen as a graduate student at UVA, but she remembered Charlottesville NOW "was very, very, very strongly heterosexual" to the point of being "squeamish about lesbians" in the mid-1980s. She felt that NOW's sole focus was on reproductive rights at that time, and members did not concern themselves with LGBT issues then. However, Farris was later elected state coordinator, so clearly not all NOW members in Virginia felt this way.

Even the YWCA appeared concerned about being defined as pro-lesbian, some recalled. Former board member Bessida White said that the YWCA asked the Richmond Women's Center to find alternate quarters in the 1970s after the center published a newsletter containing a lesbian-oriented poem and drawing. She defined the incident as a mixed blessing; the publicity put the Women's Center on the front pages of the paper and brought in some contributions. And Marschak admitted "The women's center was eventually evicted from the Y for promoting lesbianism. Which we were doing I guess." But the eviction caused the center to lose its footing and it "eventually faded out." Betsy Brinson also remembered that the YWCA asked the book cooperative run by the Lesbian-Feminists to leave because it "needed space." That may well have been the case, but some tension over lesbian activism may well have made Brinson say, "I always questioned whether or not that was the issue."

There was also some trouble in the VWPC. Bessida White remembered that, although there were lesbian members, "for political reasons" the group did not want to focus on lesbian issues. As a result, national organizers had to come down from Washington, D.C., to speak with the group. White recalled the organizers asking the local activists to imagine themselves in the Deep South and to replace lesbian with black, which showed that "there's a problem." When she was a VWPC local chair, Marschak remembered being told by a friend that a state leader thought membership was dropping because Marschak was a lesbian. As she pointed out, membership in feminist organizations was dropping after ERA failed to pass in 1982, so it was not outside of the norm.

But concern over overtly supporting pro-lesbian issues continued long after NOW and other organizations had embraced lesbian rights, in some cases. In 1986, Alison Bradner, assistant state coordinator of NOW, explained that, although she was a lesbian, she had "put [lesbian rights issues] on a back burner" because of the difficulty of gaining traction in Virginia.[53] In 1997, Christy Burns, Richmond NOW chapter president, wrote in her annual report: "On Gay & Lesbian issues, particularly, there seems to be a *potential* rift. Older members don't necessarily wish to appear as radical. I tend to favor doing more work on G/L issues and hope to bridge any resistance. We are having a program on it in May."[54]

Although NOW in particular ultimately created a task force for lesbian and gay issues, and many other feminists did step forward to defend the rights of all women, it took longer for some feminists to "get on board," as it were, to see issues of sexuality as human rights. As Betsy Brinson suggested: "It was still hard for a lot of women to be inclusive of lesbian feminists . . . and their agendas. And even though there were some similarities, . . . you had more traditional women's groups who had trouble with some of that." This issue would continue to come up in the late twentieth century, but by the new millennium women's rights activists fully embraced the fight for equality for all women, regardless of sexuality, on multiple fronts. This change reflected the societal trend of acceptance of full equality for the Lesbian/Gay/Bisexual/Transgendered/Queer (LGBTQ) community.

As a result of mixed reactions to their presence, lesbian feminists also joined the movement in "flexible solidarity" with straight women. From the beginning of the anti-violence movement, lesbians were a force. They were active in creating a same-sex-partner anti-violence program with Virginians Against Domestic Violence, for example, and they continue to be a presence in the VSDVAA as trained professionals today. Lesbians also formed their own supportive communities, like the Richmond Lesbian-Feminists, to share in social activities, educational events, and often to partner with other feminist organizations on the ERA, abortion, and anti-violence efforts.[55] As they moved into the last decade of the twentieth and the early twenty-first century, NOW activists and other feminists began to promote LGBTQ rights as part of a feminist agenda, but fear of being branded as lesbians during the ERA battle did limit the extent of some feminists' progressive ideology.

Domesticating Feminism for a Southern Audience

Reluctance to embrace lesbian rights in the second quarter of the twentieth century perhaps came from women's reaction against negative media stereotypes about feminists. In the early days of the feminist movement, Virginians worked to counter these images often promoted by the national media, and as southerners living in a much more conservative environment with clearly prescribed traditional gender norms, their work was cut out for them. Feminists seeking to work more with mainstream organizations and to lobby legislators and citizens who might be on the fence for change sometimes downplayed their own progressiveness. Men with traditional views still held the reins of power. Thus, women often portrayed themselves as concerned mothers and wives in order to make feminism appear less threatening.

Then, as now, more radical feminist actions got the press, which sometimes obscured all of the daily lobbying, canvassing, letter-writing, and interpersonal communication done by other feminists. When Americans in the late 1960s and early 1970s looked at images in the media, they often saw "zap actions"—short, audacious demonstrations meant to be ironic, gain publicity, and make points about women's status in society. For example, feminists crowned a sheep in a demonstration outside the 1968 Miss America pageant, to challenge strict cultural standards of beauty which they believed hurt women. The Women's International Terrorist Conspiracy from Hell (WITCH) held demonstrations in which feminists dressed up like witches and "cast hexes" on Wall Street, and protested institutions that had failed to hire women or perpetuated patriarchal social structures. They passed out flyers at a New York City bridal fair calling the exhibitors "whoremongers," actions meant to be thoughtful but also humorous. Bonnie Atwood remembered going to D.C., dressing up in witch outfits, and "it was always something... having to do with putting hexes on government powers or something like that. It was Guerilla Theater so it was fun.... I mean, it was part art, and part politics."[56]

But not everyone was laughing. And to be fair, not all radical feminists probably thought through the implications of what they believed was political satire. Atwood said that she and her friends did not necessarily think about the ramifications of their activities. When someone asked what the purpose of a radical zap action was and another replied it was to embarrass conservatives, Atwood remembered someone questioning: "'why would you want to embarrass them?' which I thought was really a brilliant question. And I ask it today when I see certain demonstrations. Is your purpose to embarrass someone? Because that's not a lofty...goal." When more mainstream "liberal" feminists, who sought to effect change through existing sociopolitical structures, focused on their status as wives and mothers, they were countering the actions of many radical feminists, who believed that the structures themselves were broken and only consciousness-raising to create dramatic philosophical change would bring women equality.[57]

This was especially true in the South. Because of conservative societal norms, feminists often focused on presenting very traditional gender norms.[58] Many Virginia feminists adopted a conciliatory demeanor while demanding change, especially as they cultivated media in the commonwealth. For example, Richmond NOW cofounder Holt Carlton held strong feminist opinions which she voiced freely, but in 1973, *Richmond Mercury* reporter Mike Braun described her as a fifty-eight-year-old "native Richmonder" and former mayor's granddaughter who spoke "quietly, almost gently," to him in her "attractive northside home." And Carlton was willing to play along with those images—she told Braun that she was "no ballbuster." While she acknowledged to him that she had been angry and that other feminists continued to be angry, "Now that I can speak without being emotional about [feminist issues], I find there are more and more people willing to listen."[59]

Sympathetic reporters often described women activists as "passive feminists." When Madeline Havelick of the *Potomac News* described a group that gathered in Prince William County to start a NOW chapter, she said, "they looked as though they might have been attending a cooking demonstration." She noted: "Some of the attendees expressed concern for the radical image that NOW has perpetuated." The coordinator of the meeting, Mrs. Kathy Sobrio, told Havelick that most NOW members were not radical. Havelick described them as "married women, mothers who are serious, and businesslike." Sobrio acknowledged the place of what Havelick called "the radical element." In another article, reporter Joan Mowrer said Sobrio spent several hours explaining to her that NOW "is not made up of a bunch of kooks, bent on burning bras, castrating their husbands, and leaving dishes for cockroaches to clean." She described Sobrio as a stay-at-home mother by choice raising two daughters. Mowrer interviewed another local NOW leader, Janet Barr, wife of a former fire marshal, who joined because she realized that after staying home with two girls for ten years she had a lot of time available. Taking a course on women's issues at a community college got her interested in the movement.[60]

Nowhere was the collusion of reporters and feminists in "domesticating" feminism more clear than in the coverage of Zelda Nordlinger. Nordlinger led a delegation of women to "de-sexgregate" Richmond Thalhimer's lunchroom in the 1960s, helped to found the Richmond Women's Liberation group that would become the first local NOW chapter, filed lawsuits against companies for discriminatory hiring practices—and won. This was a woman who took her daughters to karate class in the 1970s to teach them to be strong. In a feature on feminism, Richmond reporter Emma Livingstone featured a picture of Nordlinger in a dress with her two children and quoted her as saying, "in any kind of social movement there has always been a radical element.... Here in Richmond we have more conservative views. In history there must be all kinds of influences used to achieve a goal."[61]

A report in the *Chesterfield News-Journal* described resident feminist Zelda Nordlinger as "no wild-eyed radical or sour-faced screwball. She's a very sincere woman who happens to feel very strongly and ardently about equality for women in all facets of living, and doesn't mind stating her views whenever the subject comes up[.]" Noting Nordlinger's long-standing feud with the conservative editor of the *Richmond Times-Dispatch,* the reporter explained, "her forthright views on women's lib and equal rights for women come across without histrionics or any Bella Abzugness.... She leaves outrageous remarks to nationally prominent women's libbers like Betty Friedan and Gloria Steinem, but she admits she's not above baiting her audience—particularly male—in order to evoke gasps and raised eyebrows, and loves it when it works...." Nordlinger herself said to Michael Braun of the *Richmond Mercury*: "People have the concept that women's liberationists are a group of non-human radicals. This is a very bad image.... We do not see ourselves as being a threat to anyone." She compared NOW to the NAACP in its moderation.[62]

This cannot be dismissed as an aberration of the early 1970s, either. In 1986, NOW Assistant State Coordinator Alison Bradner of Norfolk told Mike D'Orso of the *Virginian-Pilot*: "A massive demonstration does get attention.... It gets you a two-minute spot on the TV news, but it doesn't really educate anyone on the issues. You're going to get your point across better... if you sound rational and logical and don't come across as a screaming lunatic."[63]

But there were legitimately angry feminists out there, and even as they tried to promote less "radical" images of feminism for the average Virginian, women's rights activists accepted the importance of those women. Georgia Fuller remembered that, during consciousness-raising sessions, women would often get furious as they came to grips with what they realized had been deep-seated and long-standing discrimination they faced in their lives, and that those who facilitated consciousness-raising groups would have to work to help them through their emotions so that they could move beyond the anger to action. And as Richmond NOW cofounder Holt Carlton told reporter Mike Braun, "But even the militants can be useful. We wouldn't get anything done if it weren't for them. The so-called 'women's libber' hurts; she screams because she can no longer hold back her pain. We need to understand her." Bessida White explained to reporter Douglas Durden, "I tell people I have a right to be angry.... The feminist movement has to make people realize we insist upon being human, which means we can be angry."[64] Anger is a powerful emotion and can move people to act; to ignore or downplay the legitimate anger women felt in service to making people more comfortable with feminism may have been a bit disingenuous.

As much as some feminists acknowledged that women had a right to be angry, many feared any actions that others could deem "radical." As reporters positioned them against prevailing negative stereotypes, they reinforced the concept that more radical feminists were threatening and, possibly, too much for Virginia to handle. This would cause some women to leave the movement, or not get involved as deeply as they could. Bessida White, for example, claimed she never joined NOW because it was "too milquetoast." Bonnie Atwood chose to align with more radical feminists in D.C. rather than the NOW chapters in Northern Virginia. And Georgia Fuller moved to other projects when NOW began to focus more on lobbying than on the direct actions she favored.

Sometimes, different concepts of how Virginia feminists should present themselves divided women. This division was manifested over organizational strategies around women's issues. Others might say that, no matter how Virginia feminists acted, they faced an uphill battle with a General Assembly filled with legislators whose responsiveness to women and women's issues ranged from uncommitted to open hostility.

It was this commonwealth, and in front of this legislature, that women fought for their rights to equality and safety. When demanding ratification of the Equal Rights Amendment, working to maintain access to legal abortion, and fighting for legal and cultural changes in the response to sexual and domestic violence, women faced a commonwealth steeped in white patriarchal tradition, and a society that was slowly changing as a result of the civil rights movement. Considering how opposed Virginia legislators appeared toward progress in the first seventy years of the twentieth century, it is a wonder that feminists made the gains they did. When Virginia women engaged in activism, their backgrounds, stories, and influences guided their choices.

2
THE BATTLE FOR THE ERA

[W]e wanted equality of rights.... And all of the fears about wanting equality of rights that were thrown in our face were military service, unisex bathrooms, etc. Well what do we have now? We do not have the ERA, but we have military service and we have unisex bathrooms.
—MURIEL ELIZABETH SMITH, former Virginia ERA Ratification Council chair and Richmond League of Women Voters president

No other feminist issue in the commonwealth drew together as many diverse groups working for a single goal as the battle for ratification of the Equal Rights Amendment, which began in 1972 and ended with defeat in 1982. ERA ratification brought together a broad coalition in Virginia, from labor unions to the League of Women Voters. Like activists in other southern states like Louisiana, Texas, and North Carolina, Virginia club women, unions, and feminist organizations joined as sometimes unlikely allies to try to get the ERA passed.[1] Although it ended with defeat, the battle to ratify the ERA ultimately helped to define the major feminist issues of the late twentieth century.

The ERA had been part of the feminist agenda since shortly after the passage of the Nineteenth Amendment. While not all suffragists supported the amendment in the 1920s, members of the National Women's Party and others believed the ERA was a necessary step in codifying equality in the Constitution. As feminists realized Title VII of the 1964 Civil Rights Act was not advancing gender equality at the desired pace, activists renewed their efforts to support passage of the ERA. Many stepped forward to support the amendment, including Republicans and Democrats, and finally, the labor movement got on board. Women launched a massive lobbying effort in Congress in the early 1970s, led in part by Virginian Flora Crater, who gained some notoriety by running as an independent candidate for lieutenant governor in order to promote women's issues. Her widely circulated newsletter, *The Woman Activist*, updated feminists on lobbying efforts in Congress, and she and her compatriots, "Crater's Raiders," helped convince Congress to pass the ERA in 1972.[2]

The ERA read simply, "Equality of rights under the law shall not be denied or abridged by the United States or by any State on account of sex," giving Congress the power to enforce this through legislation. Opponents argued that the ERA would institute a draft for women, enable easier access to abortions, institute "homosexual marriage," "make" housewives work, infringe on states' rights, and force the integration of men's and women's bathrooms. Scholars argue that the real fears of anti-ERA activists were the eroding of what they perceived to be traditional family values. Many women anti-ERA activists believed that they gained special societal status as housewives and mothers, and they fought an emotional battle to stop the ERA. More often than not, conservative religious values informed anti-ERA activists as well. Led by Phyllis Schlafly, STOP-ERA chapters and other anti-ERA groups grew quickly throughout the country in reaction to the ERA's passage, working to either stop state legislatures from ratifying or getting it rescinded where it had been ratified.[3]

By the time of its defeat, thirty-five of the required thirty-eight states had ratified the amendment. Of the southern states, only Texas, Tennessee, Kentucky, and West Virginia had ratified, and by the end of the battle Tennessee and Kentucky had rescinded ratification (as did Idaho).[4] The South stood in the way of ERA ratification, just as it had with the woman suffrage amendment. Yet throughout the national struggle, Virginia activists believed that, despite the deep conservatism of their legislators, they had a chance. Often citing both Virginia's deep roots as the "cradle of democracy" during the early national period, even as they recognized the patriarchal General Assembly that thwarted progressive efforts on many fronts, Virginia's feminists positioned themselves as part of a national and regional struggle for equality.

The battle for the ERA in Virginia is significant because it introduced many women to lobbying and it prompted thousands of women to involve themselves in organized activist efforts. Although the ERA ultimately did not get ratified in Virginia, it kept women's issues at the forefront of General Assembly sessions. As a result, women made gains as the General Assembly passed other laws to benefit them, progress which also occurred in other states.[5] Looking at Virginia enables us to see how grassroots activists navigated the byzantine committees of the General Assembly, as well as how they dealt with recalcitrant legislators. As in other states, grassroots activism brought ERA issues to the public and garnered widespread support, but legislative intransigence caused the ERA's ultimate demise.[6] Scholars and politicians debated what kinds of change the ERA could effect, but most agreed that its symbolic meaning—that of altering traditional gender norms—had the most impact on legislators. In the South, legislators' concern over maintain traditional gender roles joined with their historic distrust of federal incursion, making pro-ERA advocates fight an uphill battle.[7]

Building Support in the Commonwealth

Virginia activists began to lay the groundwork for promoting ERA ratification as it moved through Congress by claiming that the amendment would bring significant change to women. It received overwhelming approval by Congress, with a vote of eighty-four to eight in the Senate after being approved by a large margin in the House. Both of Virginia's senators and all of Virginia's representatives voted for the amendment in Congress.[8]

Virginia women perceived real inequities they thought the ERA could address. In 1972, Audrey Capone, Annandale newspaper editor, wondered why "any woman, particularly one who is engaged in business or a profession could object to this legislation." Noting that Virginia's laws still referred to women as chattel, she rejected the premise that only a "radical" or a "card-carrying liberationist" would support the ERA. Her analysis explained that it would give equal pay, Social Security benefits, and property rights and encapsulated the basic premises of most proponents.[9] In 1972, however, it seemed that the Virginia Women's Political Caucus (VWPC), which later also became known as the National Women's Political Caucus-Virginia, had the strongest early statewide push for ratification. The VWPC had organized to get women elected to all levels of office and was prepared to lead support for the ERA in Virginia. In just two years of existence the VWPC had grown to one thousand members. In the first year the ERA was up for ratification, the VWPC led a letter-writing campaign, petition drives, and lobbying efforts and compiled an ERA fact kit for each legislator.[10]

There had been a few other efforts to promote the ERA in 1972, but not at the level necessary to mount opposition against what they would face on the anti-ERA side. Mary Holt Carlton, graduate of the University of Richmond's Westhampton College, prominent clubwoman, social-services consultant,

NOW member, and self-described "dyed in the wool Virginian," weighed in on the pro-ERA side in an attempt to convince fellow Virginia Federation of Women's Clubs (VFWC) members. She noted the long-standing patriarchal tradition of the South that included gendered stereotypes and pointed out that passing the ERA would acknowledge that change had already happened, despite stereotypes.[11] While the VFWC broke with its national organization and refused to support the ERA, League of Women Voters (LWV) members were also early supporters. As former LWV Richmond president Muriel Smith remembered, Richmond leaguers were fairly conservative, overwhelmingly white, and ranging in age from thirty to their sixties. They supported the ERA reluctantly at first, but were convinced by the position of the national organization, which had endorsed ERA in 1972. The Richmond league emerged as one of the leaders in the battle for ratification.[12]

In February 1973, the amendment went before a joint House-Senate Privileges and Elections Committee. The committees determined whether legislation would go to the floor for a vote. The House committee was particularly notorious for keeping legislation off of the floor, and eight of the fifteen members had been on the committee since 1965. Its powerful chair, Jim Thomson, Democrat from Alexandria, was a brother-in-law of Harry Byrd Jr. and had been in the General Assembly since 1956. He was a powerful opponent of the ERA.

Between eight hundred and one thousand women appeared at the joint session of the House/Senate Privileges and Elections Committees in 1973, including Phyllis Schlafly, who testified against it. Women debated the meanings of equality and the ramifications of the bill, including issues related to homemakers, women in the military, and employment. Schlafly brought up the issue that would most concern traditional legislators: that somehow the ERA would change definitions of womanhood.[13]

Pro-ERA activists did not win. The Senate Privileges and Elections Committee took no action on the amendment and the House Privileges and Elections Committee voted to "pass by indefinitely" (kill) the ERA for the year. Legislators created a task force to study the ramifications of ERA, and hearings were eventually set for September to allow for Virginians to weigh in on the amendment.[14] Although ERA proponents focused on women being recognized as legal citizens, Schlafly's reported testimony, "There are a few women who want to be treated like a man, but most women don't," and elderly former suffragist Adele Clark's testimony against the ERA may have helped to sway lawmakers' decisions.[15]

Across the country, ERA activists were simply unprepared for the level of antagonism they encountered in legislative hearings.[16] To proponents, their arguments seemed reasoned and self-evident justifications for the ERA, so they were caught off-guard by the vociferous opposition. Organized in January 1973, Virginia's STOP-ERA (Stop Taking Our Privileges) took off quickly under the leadership of Alyse O'Neill, who had been chosen by Schlafly, and Eva Scott, Republican from rural Amelia County, emerged as a House anti-ERA leader.[17] Mormons in Virginia would later join these nascent forces and used their church structure to spread anti-ERA information and mobilize members to join in STOP-ERA demonstrations and to lobby the General Assembly.[18]

Pro-ERA activists were surprised by the efforts of the antis.[19] Virginia NOW sent a letter to its members stating that the opposition was "'well-organized, well-funded, and experienced.'"[20] In Virginia, as in neighboring North Carolina and other unratified states across the country, activists found themselves unprepared for the "vindictiveness" and "scare tactics" of the anti-ERA women.[21] Delegate Dorothy McDiarmid, sponsor of the amendment in the House, blamed Schlafly for the "'fanning of fears'" in the commonwealth.[22] No matter the reason, it was clear that ERA activists were unprepared for the February hearings to turn out that way.

While there had been some pro-ERA efforts before the hearing, it was clearly not enough. League ERA coordinator Buffie Scott blamed the fact that they started "too late" to mount an "extensive public educational campaign" against the "scare tactics" of the antis. In addition, she explained that, because the antis were able to turn the ERA into an "emotional, controversial issue," the General Assembly did not want to deal with the ERA at that time.[23] The Fairfax Area LWV said ERA ratification should have been "almost automatic" in 1973 but for the anti-ERA women who "came into the state and frightened the living daylights out of a great many women who promptly organized public demonstrations and wrote to their legislators and frightened the living daylights out of them, albeit it was a different fear." The chapter called the claims of the anti-ERA activists "false or exaggerated."[24]

In response to the shock of 1973, activists got serious. The fifteen-hundred-member Virginia chapter of the National Council of Jewish Women, the 111-group-strong Congress of Women's Organizations, Church Women United, and the League of Women Voters, among others, determined to secure the ERA's ratification. Virginia NOW announced ratification its top priority and named Arlington lawyer Elise Heinz its legislative coordinator. The state organization also launched a research project seeking to actively support and oppose candidates based on their opinion of the ERA and began to organize more earnestly.[25]

The September ERA task-force was almost a "replay" of the original joint session meeting. Once again Phyllis Schlafly flew to Virginia to testify against the ERA, and Adele Clark also took the stand. On the pro-ERA side, Natalie Cooper of the LWV argued the ERA would provide "massive legal, moral, and symbolic impact" and, while she did acknowledge Virginia's own amendment, she said all citizens of the United States deserved rights, too. She denounced women having to go to court to win equality, and claimed the ERA was a "matter of simple justice."[26] Flora Crater referenced the Supreme Court's 1973 decision in *Archer v. Johnson,* which essentially nullified Virginia's antidiscrimination amendment and necessitated the ERA. Farmville native and lawyer Nina Horton Avery testified, and Vera Henderson of Virginia Beach's NOW chapter argued the ERA would help end employment discrimination. Although their testimony was compelling, the chair of the ERA Task Force, Harold Wren of T. C. Williams Law School at the University of Richmond said that there would not be much real effect on the laws of Virginia. And although turnout for this Task Force hearing was lighter than the February turnout, one newspaper reported that anti-ERA speakers outnumbered advocates six to one, as speakers were scheduled by how many letters each side sent to legislators.[27]

That fall, a group of activists originally from Northern Virginia formed Virginia ERA Central. The organization's goals were to lobby the legislature, act as a clearinghouse for information to share with other pro-ERA groups, and help coordinate all pro-ERA activities. Virginia ERA Central recruited members from NOW, ACLU, AAUW, BPW, Common Cause, and VWPC.[28] The LWV appointed Lela Spitz of Salem and Natalie Cooper of Lynchburg as state ERA coordinator and co-coordinator, respectively, perhaps in an attempt to reach out to western areas of the state. Although they determined it would be best for their members to work through LWV and not Virginia ERA Central, so as not to confuse legislators or repeat actions, LWV pledged to work with the new organization to effect change.[29] The Tidewater Coalition for the ERA also formed during this period, with seventeen local member organizations, including the local AAUW chapter.[30]

Although Virginia's early supporters' arguments focused on both real and ideological reasons why the U.S. Constitution needed the ERA, just as ERA activists did throughout the country,[31] proponents in Virginia had to address one particularly problematic issue. As pro-ERA activists had acknowledged in their testimony, Virginia's legislature had added a state constitutional amendment in 1971 that banned discrimination based on sex and race. This made the commonwealth one of only three states at the time of ratification which had already theoretically banned gender discrimination.[32] Virginia ERA activists had to explain why Virginia needed "extra" federal protections.

But Virginia did not have a strong record on women's rights. Nancy Joyner, research assistant to the University of Virginia's Institute of Government, observed, "Historically Virginia's record on equal rights has been short of laudable." She noted that, even with the state constitutional amendment, the Supreme Court determined in 1973's *Archer v. Johnson* that women with children under the age of sixteen could be exempted from jury duty, something that ERA proponents like Flora Crater used as evidence of gender imbalance.[33] Still, a spokesperson for Virginia Wives and Mothers for the ERA used Virginia's constitution to defend the passage of the ERA, explaining "We are fortunate to be Virginians, whose state constitution already prohibits discrimination on the basis of sex. The same safeguards should be provided to all women, and men too, throughout our Republic."[34]

Throughout the ratification decade, Virginia's ERA proponents pointed out the inequalities in property and divorce laws that could be remedied by the amendment. They would write much about this issue, as several laws in Virginia were outdated compared with those in the rest of the country. Virginia ERA Ratification Council (VERARC) published a pamphlet that circulated widely in this decade. Titled "Women of Virginia: Rights You Are Denied," it asked: "Do you realize that the privileges and pleasures you enjoy in your marriage are available mainly through the good graces of your husband?" The pamphlet explained that, because Virginia was a "separate property" state, each spouse controlled the property he or she purchased or received, which would include property purchased by a sole wage-earner in the household. Moreover, at the time of the ERA's introduction to the state legislature, as VERARC noted, Virginia still had dower and curtesy laws, meaning a widow would receive only one-third of the property and children two-thirds should a husband die without a will. VERARC explained that, although a widow could challenge a will in which she was disinherited, she could not claim property gifted to her or even funds in a bank account in the event of a divorce. A divorced wife in Virginia at the time was not entitled to half of the property, and the pamphlet stressed that Virginia was one of three states in which marital property was divided solely upon the discretion of the divorce court. The pamphlet concluded that "many of these Virginia laws adversely affect the rights of women... and are contrary to the requirement of equal treatment under the Equal Rights Amendment." It warned women: "Don't deceive yourself—this is YOUR problem."[35]

ERA proponents also cited systemic gender discrimination in the workforce. As they did nationwide, activists in Virginia gave examples of how discrimination affected women and might be eradicated through the amendment. Often they touted the ERA's potential for promoting wage equality. Prominent Richmond attorney Sylvia Clute argued in 1975 that women faced difficulty in getting their cases handled by the Equal Employment Opportunity Commission. She recounted her experience in a job interview with the dean of T. C. Williams School of Law, who also ended up sitting on the Virginia ERA Task Force. She claimed that, when she told him she had three children, he said a woman with that many children couldn't teach in law school, "as though this was a self-evident truth that any reasonable person would have known." She also noted that a law school dean asked her friend if her husband had "allowed her to go" to school.[36]

The Virginia League of Women Voters strongly supported the ERA on the basis of equal opportunity, too. Leaders explained to members, "Sex discrimination knows no bounds." They argued that all discrimination was "destructive" and that the only way to address this problem was by securing ratification of the ERA.[37]

"Respectable" Feminists

Southern patriarchy was strong, and southern standards of decorum expected restrained behavior from "ladies." Proponents often found themselves on the defensive. Like their counterparts nationwide, pro-ERA activists fought against prevailing negative stereotypes established publicly by the anti-ERA movement early on in the Virginia fight. Schlafly damaged their position by attacking them as women who "wanted to be men," which set the tone for the battle which would rage for decades. Although anti-ERA proponents used these stereotypes in the few states left to ratify the ERA, the historic conservatism of the South may have made women's refutations of stereotypes more urgent and critical. That the South had only three of the thirty states which had ratified the amendment by 1973 suggests that the conservative and patriarchal South, historically rife with racialized gender hierarchies, loomed large in ERA activists' regional battle. This problem would have an effect on the national ratification process.[38]

As early as the February hearings in 1973, Virginia Wives and Mothers for the ERA co-chair Cynthia Popinko rose in defense of the respectability of activists. She told a reporter: "We have become seriously disturbed with the way these well-financed, right wing pseudo-organizations speak for us, and there are great numbers of us." The article also featured a statement from her co-chair from Western Virginia, Mrs. Garrison Ellis, who made sure to note, "We are the same sort of women who make up the General Federation of Women's Clubs, League of Women Voters, Church Women United, and many other widely respected organizations that support the ERA."[39] During the later September hearings, those sentiments remained the same. Nina Horton Avery reflected many attitudes when she told a reporter that she didn't support newer women's liberation groups: "I don't think they're helping us. They have hurt us. A large segment of the public thinks we are all the same." Avery's roots in Virginia were deep: a Farmville native who became a lawyer in Richmond, she was past president of the Federation of Business and Professional Women's Clubs (BPW), American Association of University Women (AAUW), and National Women's Party.[40]

Virginia ERA Central urged its members and friends to avoid playing into negative stereotypes. It established ground rules for activists, warning them to "be on their best behavior." A legislative bulletin article titled "Mind Your Manners" explained that proponents needed to fight for the ERA "with good taste and good manners." It claimed McDiarmid and Elise Heinz had to join a few activists in mollifying a few co-patrons "who had been publicly abused and vilified by an overly enthusiastic pro-ERA constituent."[41]

ERA Central warned that the antis were especially attacking NOW, claiming the organization was behind most pro-ERA activism, and that NOW's "real interests are pro-lesbian legislation and destruction of the family." The article made sure readers understood the false nature of these accusations: "let it be known that NOW members are pretty much like other ERA supporters—happy wives, loving mothers, active in a variety of organizations, particularly concerned with difficulties encountered more by women than by men." It also clarified that NOW cared deeply about many issues, including "the persecution of homosexuals," but that its priority was passing the ERA, and that it had "no legislative program" regarding LGBT equality. It urged readers: "Don't let them convince anybody that all ERA supporters fit the Bella Abzug–Gloria Steinem–Betty Friedan mold. We're responsible citizens of Virginia, not New York radical feminists. We're anxious to admit women to full participation in today's society, not to destroy it."[42] ERA Central's concern over behavior and platforms reflected more moderate activists' concerns about entrenched stereotypes of feminists hurting them as they battled the conservative, mostly male, legislature and ERA opponents.

The fact that pro-ERA activists self-defined as the REAL Virginians showed just how worried feminists were about the movement being misunderstood. When Virginia ERA Central explained its members were homegrown, it reiterated an important point made by many Virginia women's organizations—the outsiders who came to Virginia to oppose the ERA were the radicals. Mrs. Neustadt, president of the Virginia League of Women Voters, noted in a letter to legislators that the national anti-ERA movement marked the commonwealth as a "target area" and local opposition was established by "well-financed, right-wing extremists" who circulated "materials which originated out-of-state[.]"[43] Many pro-ERA charged the antis, or "stoppies," as many Virginia women called them, with being outsiders, while claiming pro-ERA women came from established, respectable, and fairly staid and traditional organizations with Virginia roots.[44] The charge of anti-ERA activists being outsiders was a bit disingenuous; the women who led STOP-ERA efforts in Virginia were certainly commonwealth residents, as were many others who lobbied against the ERA. While it may be true that the national Mormon church funded the Virginia Citizens Coalition, a name chosen to obscure its Mormon and outsider roots, and Schlafly certainly controlled STOP-ERA, which was especially powerful in many unratified states across the country, including in Virginia,[45] pro-ERA Virginians also got support from "outside" forces as they forged ahead in battle.

Some ERA activists raised the specter of lesbianism and radical "women's libbers" in their arguments. Neustadt warned legislators not to fall for the stereotype of all proponents being women's liberationists. And describing herself to a journalist as "a conservative type person in clothing, language, and behavior[,]" Elise Heinz of ERA Central stated emphatically to a reporter, "we are not bra-burning screaming lesbian harpies. We are just our own natural selves, trying to let legislators know that many women in Virginia are in favor of ERA."[46]

Although both groups were in defensive mode, their responses may well have helped to feed into negative stereotypes of feminists and certainly did not help the cause of LGBT equality, even as they tried to embrace any and all women willing to fight for the ERA. Downplaying the radical nature of some activists' feminist ideologies while privileging the positions of leaders as wives and mothers reified negative stereotypes held by conservative Virginians and would eventually cause tension between activists. These tensions would later emerge as divisions in the movement.

The 1974 Session, the "Secret Memo" and Its Ramifications

By the legislative session of 1974, pro-ERA groups were well organized and hopeful. Pro-ERA activists continued to lobby the legislature for the 1974 session. The LWV announced the ERA could be its top priority, and freshman delegate Evelyn Hailey of Norfolk told a reporter, "If you ask me what I consider to be the most important issue in the minds of the women who have contacted me thus far, I'd say it is passage of the Equal Rights Amendment."[47] Virginia ERA Central established a headquarters at Richmond's Raleigh Hotel, funded entirely by donations. While it had enough to establish this space, it asked for more to cover lobbying expenses. It assured supporters, "The ERA Central will be alive and present in Richmond as long as necessary." Over 200 ERA supporters from groups including NAACP, NOW, BPW, VWPC, the State Commission on the Status of Women, and Virginia ERA Central feted 120 legislators at a breakfast sponsored by the Congress of Women's Organizations. As longtime Richmond activist Zelda Nordlinger explained, "We will be lobbying E.R.A. with Ham & eggs." Turnout was larger than Virginia ERA Central expected.[48] Moreover, the National Federation of Business and Professional Women had given $250,000 to fund pro-ERA work in the state.[49]

The ERA Task Force Report, which had been commissioned by the legislature to determine how the ERA would affect Virginia, came out in February 1974. Written by five legal scholars, it concluded the ERA would have little effect on existing Virginia laws, something legal experts across the country had already been suggesting. However, the few changes that would occur, according to the experts, were positive. The Virginia Military Institute could not continue as a single-sex institution; rape laws would have to protect male victims; prison facilities would need to be equalized; and in terms of labor, the ERA would help enforce the Equal Pay and Civil Rights acts. The one female task-force member, Carroll Kem Shackelford, suggested family-law courts would have to recognize husbands and wives as equal partners. Both sides saw this report as helpful to their position, and one committee member said it was designed just to help inform the legislators, not to convince them one way or another.[50]

The activists were ready to face the men of the House Privileges and Elections Committee the second time around. Virginia ERA Central sent out a notice instructing supporters to get to the committee meeting early. At least six hundred people attended the hearing, and according to the LWV ERA state coordinator, Lela Spitz, pro-ERA activists outnumbered antis three to one. She described the path taken by the pro-ERA forces, a "Parade of Proponents," in which seventy-five representatives of organizations spoke for thirty seconds each to illustrate the widespread support for the ERA in the commonwealth. Speakers included men and several nuns. Spitz remarked that the first two anti-ERA speakers were not even present and that, although Schlafly appeared again, "several of her points had already been refuted."[51]

At this point ERA activists learned the strength of the obstacles they faced in the General Assembly. First, the House Privileges and Elections Committee dismissed the hearing participants. Then, Jim Thomson circulated a thirteen-page "secret memo," which he said came from Attorney General Andrew Miller. The memo stated that the ERA would require Virginia to institute coed dorms and bathrooms. Thomson did not allow enough time for delegates to study the memo; instead, he made committee members immediately return documents after reading. Not only did this memo contradict the findings of the task force, which said those facilities were covered under a citizen's constitutional right to privacy, but it also represented a violation of procedural rules. Thomson presented what amounted to testimony in a non-hearing setting, when only a vote would be allowed. In addition, according to Lela Spitz, he refused to allow committee members to verify the origins of the memo, study it, or refute it. The bill to ratify went down to a twelve-to-eight defeat in the committee.[52]

Reaction to the committee's actions was quick. Delegate Dorothy McDiarmid said on the floor of the House she had never seen, and hoped to never see again, an incident of this nature. Flora Crater wrote in the Virginia edition of her national newsletter, *The Woman Activist,* a reference to Virginia's specific role in building the early U.S. democracy: "How denigrating it is to see the sons of the Founding Fathers use their legislative skill to subvert the democratic process while considering the rights of women." Arthur Giesen, a pro-ERA Republican delegate from Stanton, stated: "Regardless of the merits of the ERA, actions such as were used by the attorney general and Chairman

Thomson are a clear usurpation of power." Spitz queried: "Why was the memo prepared at all? Why was it prepared so late? Why was it given only to the most vocal ERA opponent?" She also questioned why it was specifically kept from McDiarmid, the ERA's chief sponsor. Reactions came so swift and strong that Andrew Miller had to say the memo had no legal position in Virginia, and he blamed one of his assistants for writing it. Delegate Carrington Williams said that, although the memo did not change votes, the committee should resolve to only have "full, open and public discussion" in the future.[53]

The committee's actions galvanized ERA proponents. Supporters gave Thomson a child's potty seat filled with a floral arrangement and a note reading, "To Watergate on the James [River]—Miller & Thomson, Plumbers, Inc," referencing the nefarious Watergate break-in to the Democratic Party Headquarters orchestrated by Nixon and his allies. This delegation of supporters included LWV women, NOW women, members of the VWPC, and representatives of the Democratic State Central Committee and Charlottesville City Council. Thomson was unmoved, and, going on the offensive, said it reflected "the caliber of people [for the ERA] and the methods and conduct they had stooped to."[54]

The actions of the committee angered pro-ERA activists and made them more determined to change the political system.[55] The VWPC submitted a public letter criticizing the actions of the committee, and the over four hundred signatures affixed to the document attest to how far ERA support in Virginia had moved in just one year. The letter's signatories included residents from as far west as Tazewell County and Abingdon, as far into the Southside as Farmville, and everywhere in between, from Northern Virginia, to the Tidewater, to the Shenandoah and New River valleys in the West. Republicans and Democrats signed, as did a member of the NAACP and National Association of Colored Women's Clubs, Common Cause, and the ACLU, among others. The document shows that ERA supporters spanned the breadth of the commonwealth and held diverse political positions as well as organizational memberships.[56]

The actions of the House Privileges and Elections Committee appeared to help pro-ERA forces gain traction. In 1974 a group of women founded the Virginia ERA Ratification Council, comprised of pro-ERA organizations, including BPW, LWV, NOW, and Common Cause. The group elected Flora Crater as its first leader. The organization determined to serve as a clearinghouse of information so that member organizations could coordinate actions.[57] Other groups sprang to action, including the African American women's organization Women for Political Action, founded in Norfolk several years earlier by civil rights activist and club woman Vivian Carter Mason. Tidewater NOW invited Mason to speak on African American women following a pro-ERA slide show it presented at a meeting at the local YWCA.[58]

Virginia NOW published the *ERA Supporter's Handbook* in 1974, a thick booklet designed to help supporters speak more authoritatively on the issues. NOW Virginia sold these handbooks for just one dollar. The League of Women Voters recommended it to its members as a useful resource and as a way to collaborate with NOW. It gave information "(a) so you can explain the current state of the law which makes ERA necessary, and (b) so you can jump down the 'Stoppies's' [sic] throats when they misrepresent what the courts did in 'Phyllis's favorites.'" The manual provided a bio of Schlafly, too: "She is a politically ambitious person who can and does use any issue... to frighten and confuse a Generally uninformed electorate...."[59]

The manual also advised on how to debate the ERA, including avoiding other issues like divorce laws and abortion. It encouraged activists to stop any "coupling of issues" that could "cause a negative reaction regarding the ERA." This focus suggested the ongoing concern with image, especially when the manual listed antis like the KKK and the John Birch Society against which supporters could position themselves.[60]

Many women chose to make the ERA a single-issue campaign to avoid controversy. Even as they fought, Heinz reminded them to watch their attitude: a newspaper report said she warned lobbyists not to confuse the ERA with abortion or go "selling women's lib."[61] LWV explained to members that Lela Spitz believed "total cooperation with every group for positive action is essential."[62] But total cooperation did not necessarily mean working with other women who promoted issues that would "distract" from the ERA, or who appeared too "radical," something that would continue to haunt the activists until it came to a head later.

No matter how women approached the legislators, the ERA was doomed in the 1975 session.[63] The House killed the bill in committee and the Senate voted it from the floor back to the committee. Yet when Richmond NOW president Mary Parsiani assessed the loss, she wrote, "All of us who have put in so many, many hours should take heart...." She explained activists "did a good job of lobbying and putting pressure on representatives—even if they are not sensitive to constituent pressure." Parsiani urged the women to get over their "bitterness and the feeling of helplessness" because, as she said, "We, as feminists, cannot dwell on our defeats."[64]

Escalating the Battle

Parsiani's words could not have been more prophetic in a climate like Virginia's, where committee power dominated the General Assembly and legislators seemed content to let a small group keep the amendment from seeing a full recorded vote. The failure of the General Assembly to respond to lobbying made many proponents take a new direction—which was going to demand more involvement and money from activists. In fact, Lulu Meese went to a Chicago hotel to meet with several political consultants, including Joe Rothstein and Jill Buckley, who in 1982 was called "one of the few successful women in the industry" by the *Washington Post*.[65] Lulu Meese reported on the meeting to the VERARC board. She came away understanding that, if Virginia activists wanted the ERA to succeed, they needed to raise more money and work harder. Meese told the state board that, according to this group, the ERA had a better chance to succeed in Virginia than in other states that were "targeted" by national groups, and that Virginia *had* to pass the ERA in order for the amendment to be ratified.[66]

Even before this meeting, local activists moved toward engaging more directly in the ERA battle. In 1975, its first year of existence, Charlottesville NOW held a fundraiser to support the ERA while Richmond NOW, Virginia Nurses' Association, and other groups raised money for VERARC. Virginia AAUW's legislative chair Ellen Griffee pointed out that only Mississippi and Virginia had failed to vote on the amendment in either legislative chamber. Asking "Has our 'cradle of democracy' been rocking so long that Virginia is asleep and neglecting her responsibility[,]" Griffee called on AAUW members to give money directly or through the AAUW to VERARC and to participate in any direct actions planned. The VWPC raised money too, saying it would "contribute as much as we possibly can to the coalition's fundraising effort," especially to help establish an office and support head lobbyist Elise Heinz in her battle.[67]

Activists also looked to change the makeup of the 1976 General Assembly. Fundraisers helped to support more direct electoral action, as pro-ERA activists determined ousting hostile legislators was one of the few solutions available to them. As Anne Lunde, BPW legislative chair, said, "It is the opinion of the Legislative Committee that if we are to achieve ratification of the Equal Rights Amendment, we must have some new members in the General Assembly in 1976. So... BE SURE TO VOTE YOUR CONVICTIONS this November."[68] The VWPC decided to give financial support to three pro-ERA candidates from

Lexington, Hillsville, and Radford, all typically conservative areas of the commonwealth, and local caucuses gave contributions to a candidate in Hinton and one in Northern Virginia. VERARC used financial support to conduct a telephone poll with all candidates. Led by Susan Blair and Marianne Fowler, the poll secured answers from 67 percent of the candidates, so voters could understand exactly whom they supported. In a press release before the election, the VWPC released overall results: the majority of legislators favored the ERA, so McDiarmid called upon them to support its release from committees.[69]

In fact, the VWPC said activists had no choice. To its members, the VWPC stated simply, "Unless we have some assurance that ERA will not die a fourth time in committee, we have no alternative to trying to deprive the committee of its murderous opposition; a cat may have nine lives, but the ERA only has only seven." And "Virginians for ERA" and Common Cause were putting pressure on the House to vote to discharge the bill from committee by surveying delegates on the issue. This, the VWPC argued, would at least show who the ERA's enemies were, as it did when the Senate had to vote publicly on returning the ERA to committee. Pressure was so strong in the 1975 Senate elections that the VWPC noted a few senators who had voted to return the ERA to the committee were "running scared in their election campaigns now."[70]

This language signaled a new attitude in the pro-ERA camp. Activists' change in strategy was so apparent that the LWV became a bit concerned with the tactics. At a meeting, leaders recognized "There was evidence of strong feeling to defeat candidates who voted against the ERA, despite stated policy of non-partisanship."[71] Because LWV did not pull out of VERARC, however, it must ultimately have deemed the questionnaires nonpartisan enough. VWPC did not concern itself with appearing partisan—its goal was to get more pro-ERA legislators elected to office.

And it worked. The VWPC noted with optimism that pro-ERA forces ousted five anti-ERA senators and encouraged two more to retire, so only fourteen anti-ERA senators were returning to the General Assembly. Referencing an idea unpopular with activists, a proposed state referendum on the ERA, State Coordinator Martha Boyle said, "To those diehards who say they want a referendum on the Amendment we say, 'you just had one.'" She also spoke about the determination of pro-ERA fighters: "Members of our organization and many other ERA proponents in Virginia are tired to the bone of hassling over this issue. But our commitment is more firm than ever and we're not going to give up and slink away."[72]

Demonstrations

This attitude was also present in the willingness of pro-ERA activists to engage in more direct actions in support of the ERA. Coalition members of VERARC determined to organize silent protests during lunchtime every day the General Assembly was in session. Richmond VERARC, AAUW, LWV, BPW, and VWPC all signed on to organize participants one day a week. In addition, NOW began planning for a massive rally on the opening day of the General Assembly in 1975. NOW leaders recognized that for many this was a step too far, explaining: "There has been a lot of opposition to proposals of public rallies and mass gatherings in the past by those actively involved in the ERA struggle. NOW leaders throughout the state, however, feel that it is time to move beyond the 'soft sell' approach. It has not worked so far." Acknowledging the importance of other kinds of ERA work, leaders stressed that it was time to do something "dramatic."[73] According to NOW's Junior Bridges, who was spearheading the planning, the theme of the rally would be "Personhood, Apple Pie, and the American Way." They argued, "Anti-ERA groups have loudly charged that we are anti-American, anti-motherhood, and child-haters. But what is more American than democracy?" Leaders also pointed out the ERA proponents fought for displaced homemakers' rights, day care, and "economic security for the women who choose homemaking as a career[.]"[74]

As NOW members correctly surmised, not everyone was on board with the plan. Member organizations of VERARC had what leaders called a "long and complicated" discussion about VERARC's role in the rally. At a meeting attended by a myriad of representatives from organizations, members determined that the organizations themselves must plan and promote all activities, not VERARC, which would serve only as a coordinator and information clearinghouse. BPW, AAUW, and LVW leaders contacted members by phone to urge them to support the rally, but the LWV-Fairfax area chapter acknowledged some members' reluctance to do so. One leader urged leaguers, "Even though you may not feel that a rally is the best way to demonstrate support, please consider what a small turnout will do to the chances of ratification."[75]

The rally kicked off with participants walking one hundred miles from Alexandria, Jim Thomson's district, to the capital. Designed to coincide with the two-hundredth anniversary of the signing of the Declaration of Independence, as organizer Junior Bridge stated, "The 1976 Bicentennial celebration is a poignant reminder that women are still second-class citizens in the United

States." Thirteen women and one man (the director of Common Cause) participated. Marchers ranged in age from eighteen to sixty-nine and included students, professionals, homemakers, and Kathryn Brooks, a grandmother well known for her LWV and NOW activities. While some were from out of state, the newspaper made sure to comment that Bridge had been a resident of the commonwealth "for 29 of her 31 years." Walkers reported receiving only positive comments along the way (with the exception of two incidents), including offers of coffee and cheers. One recalled talking to a man who said he wished his deceased wife would have had the ERA to protect her rights, and another walker remembered a man saying women had been doing things for men for years and it was time for men to reciprocate. Arriving in Richmond, marchers were joined by local supporters.[76]

The rally itself was a tremendous success, with an estimated one thousand in attendance.[77] Held at Monroe Park, just on the perimeter of Virginia Commonwealth University Campus and a short walk from the Virginia capitol building, it saw supporters from across the commonwealth, from Roanoke and Wytheville to the Tidewater.[78] NOW's national president Karen DeCrow spoke. She reiterated what activists already believed about the centrality of Virginia in the ERA battle: "I'm told the South looks to Virginia like the country looks to Maine [for ratification].... If the South looks to Virginia, the state must ratify the Amendment. The whole country is looking to Virginia. Do your thing...." Elise Heinz, now the coordinator of Virginia ERA Central, talked about the historical impact of women in Virginia, and reminded activists that Virginia had only officially adopted half of all constitutional amendments. She asked, "But are we really like Mississippi? Must we continue to deny our proud early history of national leadership, of intense concern for the rights of individuals?" By calling on Virginia's historic leadership in establishing religious freedom and the Bill of Rights, she placed women in the narrative of the country's founding, reminding Virginia legislators of the commonwealth's important place in history. She also explained: "Make no mistake, *we* are the Virginia women who make a difference politically ... until ERA is ratified, we lack the cornerstone upon which our future progress must rest."[79]

After the rally, a large cohort of marchers walked to the capitol. Their numbers were so numerous—over six hundred, by one reporter's estimates—that they stretched down ten city blocks. Onlookers' reactions ranged from amusement, to "chagrin," to quiet acceptance. Some joined in. But marchers met with resistance at the capitol. Initially told that thirty people could enter the grounds, they were all blocked because someone had called a bomb threat to capitol police. When police told a marcher that it would be a very long wait to get inside, she retorted, "We've been waiting 200 years." Activists faced other challenges as well—not only did Representative Thomson refuse to meet with the delegation that had walked from his district, but the activists were also barred from putting apple pies on each legislator's desk as they had planned. As the marchers finally disbanded at 1:00 p.m., chanting, "we'll be back," one woman said, "You can't say we weren't orderly[.]"[80] After all of this training to walk and organization to make it possible, the failure of the walkers to even secure an audience with Thomson suggested to some that even more militant tactics would be necessary.

The rally was accompanied by increased lobbying efforts on the part of ERA proponents. In addition to the silent vigils organized by the five sponsoring groups from VERARC, LWV Fairfax urged its members to write as many letters as possible to show antis how much support there was, even if their legislators were pro-ERA, as many in the area were. Montgomery County Leaguers followed suit, demanding that legislators release the amendment to a floor vote. The league also gave one thousand dollars to support its own lobbyist, Pat Jensen, who remained in Richmond for the duration of ERA discussions. The AAUW sent seven members to lobby every Tuesday until action on the ERA happened, and Elise Heinz was in the office five days a week, with Martha Boyle of VWPC in on Fridays. They met with unregistered lobbyists from many organizations, including Richmond NOW (under the direction of Louise Wright) who were members of VERARC. These lobbyists learned on the job, moving through the General Assembly with more experienced politicos. While all of this activity did increase the intensity of pro-ERA sentiment, again, not everyone was on board. VERARC noted that on lobbying days not every organization sent enough people to truly make a difference.[81] Silent vigils would continue throughout the campaign until after ERA ratification failed.

So activists stepped up their game—but to what end? First, VERARC unsuccessfully lobbied to get the Democratic Caucus to change the rules so that all amendments would go to the floor. Then the anticipated assistance in the Senate Privileges and Elections Committee did not come through, because only one of the six pro-ERA senators ended up on the committee. When the Privileges and Elections Committee did meet on the amendment, one anti-ERA senator who was notorious for missing the General Assembly chartered a plane to attend the vote. The amendment failed to pass through committee on a vote of eight to seven, and Senator DuVal's motion to discharge the amendment automatically failed as well. Even some pro-ERA senators feared challenging the sacrosanct General Assembly committee system. In the House, McDiarmid attempted to a motion to turn the House into a "Committee of the Whole" to consider the amendment, but this failed as well. By early February, the ERA was dead for another year. And this is exactly how legislators wanted it—they could continue to refuse any formal position on the ERA if they did not have to vote on it during a session.[82]

Once again, actions by the committee held back the potential for change. And once again, activists reacted strongly and prepared to continue the fight. As the Charlottesville NOW newsletter contributor wrote, "Betrayal after betrayal in the Virginia legislature has led to the shelving of E.R.A. for still another year.... So be ready for next January. The only way to win is to fight." In the postmortem meetings, Flora Crater admitted, "ERA is not top priority with any legislator and certainly not with the leadership." She suggested more lobbying and better coordination within the council. AAUW continued its support by determining at its 1976 convention that it would get information out to all members to secure their active participation, and it would financially support VERARC and ERA Central. By the time of the convention it had donated over one thousand dollars to support the lobbying office and to facilitate communication through a phone tree and correspondence.[83]

Counting on Virginia

Once again grassroots activists took center stage after the legislative session of 1976 as they drummed up support for the ERA. Shirley Chisholm spoke to an audience at a public lecture in Portsmouth and demanded the ERA be passed in the commonwealth. She told her audience no one should be discriminated against, and that, as her audience knew, "the struggle... is far from over." NOW Virginia also took the national stage as it planned a month of protest outside the White House in the summer months. Modeling their protest after those of the suffragists at the beginning of the century, the Alexandria chapter called on participants to bring banners similar to those their foremothers had used in their struggle, and NOW members across the commonwealth took part.[84] The ACLU published pamphlets targeting African American women and at some point also began printing Spanish-language pamphlets as well.[85]

As the 1977 General Assembly session approached, Judy Harris, Virginia

NOW state coordinator, announced NOW's plan for grassroots support. NOW members would not only write letters to the editor, speak to myriad women's groups, and participate in news-media programs, but they would also collect signatures on petitions on election day, just two months before the General Assembly would begin meeting, and use the information to create a database from which to draw supporters. In conjunction with these efforts, NOW determined to hire a lobbyist for the duration of the next session. Harris told NOW members, "Please don't despair. I know all of this seems like a big order, but we can do it; we must, if we are to ratify ERA." In Richmond, LWV members reported working directly with VERARC: "Those Leaguers involved are too numerous to mention. All of us have helped with distribution of supportive literature and organizing neighborhood coffees to educate the Richmond area about equality of rights under the law for men and women." And while national ERA strategists turned their sights to North Carolina, Nevada, and Indiana, LWV ERA coordinator Pat Jensen told leaguers, "Obviously no one is counting on Virgninia [sic]." But still, she called on every local league to personally visit their legislators, "to let them know you are there—and so is ERA."[86]

As ERA ratification stalled across the country and the deadline for ratification approached—indeed, in 1975 New Jersey and New York legislators had defeated attempts to add ERAs to their state constitutions and rescission efforts were underway in many states—in 1977 activists looked to the same exact General Assembly as they had previous year. Pat Jensen admitted, "While the picture in Virginia isn't as bright as elsewhere," she was confident that "The degree of commitment to ratification [was] expanding."[87]

In January 1977, Richmond proponents organized a teach-in at Virginia Commonwealth University and a West End Lutheran Church for ERA Week, titled "The ERA: Facts for Action," and an "open air speakout" in Monroe Park featuring Gloria Steinem, held in January while the General Assembly was in session. Bessida White, founder of the National Black Feminist Organization (NBFO) chapter in Richmond, convened the teach-in and gave the plenary talk on "Women and the ERA." Sessions addressed issues like the ERA and the military, the ERA and men, the ERA and African Americans, and the ERA and the law. The sessions closed with a wine-and-cheese fund-raiser at the home of Muriel Elizabeth Smith, LWV Richmond president and VERARC coordinator.[88]

This program had a broad range of support, including NOW chapters, VERARC, local and state VWPC chapters, Virginia Education Association

(VEA), Richmond BPW, Alpha Kappa Alpha, Virginia Nurses' Association, National Black Feminist Organization, YWCA, LWV Richmond, Common Cause, AAUW, Socialist Workers' Party, Richmond Lesbian- Feminists, and Virginia National Chapter of Social Workers. This list reflects the broadest coalition to undertake a major initiative in the name of the ERA, and it would be the last time these groups would work together so closely.[89] Toba Singer, one of the organizers and a member of the Socialist Workers' Party, noted that the Richmond-based speakout drew 650 people, raised one thousand dollars, and brought African Americans, labor, and students to the movement, in addition to garnering great press.[90]

Despite their best efforts, the House of Delegates refused to hear the amendment yet again in 1977. The Senate finally voted on it for the first time, and it won twenty to eighteen, but without the supermajority of twenty-one that the Senate had determined was necessary to pass the ERA. One of the key no votes came from someone proponents thought was in their camp, A. Joseph Canada. His switch was a surprise, and it appeared that perhaps he was trying to get support from conservatives in his upcoming campaign for lieutenant governor.[91]

Dissension in the Ranks

Perhaps it was fallout from the vote, or perhaps it had been a long time coming, but discord over the way the ERA Week activities were planned came out in accusations of discrimination lodged against some main organizers. According to Toba Singer, co-organizer Jean Hellmuth from Richmond's ERA Ratification Council and Richmond NOW's organizer Louise Wright grew hesitant over the plans. In an article penned for *The Militant* magazine, Singer claimed that these organizers refused to support the speak-out tactics, saying, "the ERA had to be won 'quietly.'" She said that these two were also concerned that "a public outpouring of support would anger legislators."[92]

Singer believed that Hellmuth and Wright tried to stop Steinem from speaking. The two also tried to exclude the Socialist Workers' Party as a co-sponsor as they were afraid that "feminists in the coalition were trying to impose a 'feminist image' on the ERA and the movement supporting it." They to stop the speakout, partly because the YWCA, VWPC, and others supported it. Singer said Beth Marschak, speaking as chair of the local VWPC district (who was also the organizing force behind Richmond Lesbian-Feminists) moved in a meeting that no one be excluded from supporting the activities because all who supported the ERA should be embraced. This would include the Socialist Workers' Party and the Richmond Lesbian-Feminists, whose names were absent from a reading of the list of endorsers. Singer also claimed that Betsy Brinson, director of the Southern Women's Rights Project of the ACLU, explained that exclusion would violate the Socialist Worker's Party's First Amendment rights.[93]

While we cannot know if the women Singer accused refuted her accusations, others supported Singer's denouncement of the exclusionary behavior and criticized the local organizers who worked with her, especially after the Richmond ERA Ratification Council dealt with the situation by banning all political parties from membership. Richmond NOW member and original Richmond ERA Council member Juanita White protested the personal politics at play: "I found myself confused by deliberations which seemed to center more around who should be excluded than who should participate, who should be silenced than who would speak out." She complained about the group's original insistence on white leadership in the organization phase. She also noted that the group had been reluctant to support the presence of lesbians in the 1976 demonstration. White decried the move to prevent Gloria Steinem from speaking in 1977, and "the earlier abortive effort to unseat the Socialist Workers' Party and your most valuable worker on the very eve of your great triumph." She concluded "an almost paranoid fear of offending the 'Right People'" was stifling ratification efforts. She also said that, while she would work with the Virginia Education Association and NOW to fight for ratification, she could not work with the Ratification Council. Zelda Nordlinger also protested the decision of the council, calling it "reprehensible and counter-productive" that a "small clique" could degenerate into "red-baiting." In a note she sent to the national *E.R.A. Monitor* she said, "Here in Richmond we are particularly concerned (obsessed?) with image." She considered it a situation worth investigating.[94]

The "obsession" with image can be linked back with many activists' concern to separate the ERA from any other issue. Although neither Marschak nor Brinson mentioned their role in the dustup over the ERA speakout, Mary Wazlak and Marschak recalled points of division during the ERA campaign. Wazlak distinctly recalled that, while she wanted to take part in ERA lobbying, her role in the Virginia Organization to Keep Abortion Legal (VOKAL) made open support impossible. She remembered when she would be at the capital representing VOKAL, and her friends would be there fighting for the ERA: "The ERA group had to do their Equal Rights Amendment stuff, and they didn't want people who hated us for the abortion issue to see us with them on that side of the street, so there were many nights that I walked alone in Richmond from the General Assembly session waving to my colleagues on the other side of the street...."[95] Beth Marschak remembered when the Richmond Lesbian-Feminists walked in the demonstration with a banner, "The ratification council as a group was very uncomfortable with that, just as ... they were not comfortable with socialist groups marching." She recalled: "They did not really want us to be there and to be visible."[96] In both of these cases, liberal feminists likely feared their carefully honed and safely moderate image they had cultivated with the media was being overshadowed by abortion and lesbian rights, two more controversial issues being addressed by feminists at the time.

This concern over image would continue to become more problematic as the ERA ratification battle raged on, especially with regard to lesbian rights. Because many anti-feminists conflated feminism with lesbianism, which at the time many viewed as a deviant sexual orientation, some ERA activists worked hard to disassociate themselves from any semblance of LGBT activism. In July 1977, Pat Watt, Fairfax Area LWV president, wrote about the concern some of her members had with articles they read in the *Washington Post* and *New York Times* about LWV United States directors' meeting with the National Gay Task Force: "Please understand that we fully agree that this may well be a legitimate league concern under our HR [Human Rights] position, but we plead for a low profile in this particular instance." She claimed, "Our members must fight continually to separate the ERA from the issues of gay rights and abortion with which opponents attempt to saddle it." Calling the issues an "albatross," she asked for the LWV to wait until the ERA was ratified before reaching out to LGBT organizations.[97]

Marschak and Brinson, always focused on inclusivity in the ERA and wider feminist movement, also specifically remembered the problems lesbian activists faced. In her position as co-organizer of the Richmond Lesbian-Feminists and chair of the Third District of Virginia Women's Political Caucus, Beth Marschak recalled: "it wasn't like [other ERA activists] had a united front" against lesbians, but they feared targeting. She said "for a lot of them ... the most important thing in the world was the ERA and anything else that could endanger that in any way shape or form just, you know, wasn't going to be happening." But she remembered it not just being about "heterosexism" but also directed at "reproductive health" and anything "issue wise or individual wise that wasn't one hundred percent ERA." Betsy Brinson articulated the problem when she explained: "I think [the tension] was just there.... It was still hard for a lot of women to be inclusive of lesbian feminists and their agendas. And even though there were some similarities, there were... more traditional women's groups who had trouble with some of that."[98]

Dissension continued, possibly because of the tensions many felt after such hard defeats in the legislature. Louise Wright became the Richmond ERA Ratification Council chair, even though several had opposed her position on the ERA activities of 1977. After ERA's defeat and the division over ERA Week planning was exposed, dissension in the ranks of VERARC emerged as well, which came to a head in May of 1977. Some, including the leader of the Virginia chapter of ERAmerica, a national pro-ERA organization established in 1976 to support state efforts, believed the coordinator was not as effective as she could be. The coordinator, Muriel Elizabeth Smith, did not think LWV members had worked hard enough to promote ERA during the legislative session, and thought the Virginia Education Association was not making ERA a priority.[99] Smith remained the chair of VERARC, but this episode suggests the way in which the hard work done by all began to cause strain in the organizations involved in ratification efforts.

Pro-ERA Developments in 1977

Nineteen seventy-seven was a special year, for several reasons, both nationally and in the commonwealth. It was the year designated for the National Women's Conference in Houston, Texas. Congress had set aside federal money to fund a major women's conference in Houston in honor of 1975's International Women's Year, to which delegates from all states would vote on resolutions prioritizing women's needs in America.[100] In Virginia, pro-ERA activists focused on sending delegates who would strongly advocate for the need for the amendment. In the commonwealth itself, an even bigger drama unfolded—every single seat in the House of Delegates was up for reelection. If the ERA was ever to be dislodged from the House Privileges and Elections Committee, this was the time to do it. In addition, the entire slate of state leaders—governor, lieutenant governor, attorney general—were up for election as well.

Politically, proponents geared for battle, their goal to change the makeup of the House. VERARC leaders determined the time had come to be more aggressive in the fight for the ERA. They created a political action committee, Virginia ERA-PAC (VERA-PAC) free from the ties binding the organization to its nonpartisan status, to provide financial and material support to pro-ERA candidates. In a letter to potential donors, VERA-PAC administrators said, "Virginia has become a pivotal state in the national struggle for ratification."[101]

Proponents truly believed Virginia was key to breaking the southern deadlock, where only Tennessee, Texas, and Kentucky languished as the sole pro-ERA states. Their vision was to use political pressure to frighten other legislators into ratifying the ERA. As the letter stated in no uncertain terms, "'If it can happen in Virginia, it can happen here' will become the disconcerting reality haunting all southern politicians." Leaders believed they needed to show politicians that the "safe" vote was the pro vote.[102]

Naming long-time activist Marianne Fowler and noted Richmond psychologist and professional ERA lobbyist Norma Murdoch-Kitt as the coordinators of the PAC, VERA-PAC targeted districts across the state, including in Northern Virginia, along the I-81 corridor in the West, and other places throughout the state with vulnerable legislators. It quickly raised over eighty-seven hundred dollars and continued to raise funds throughout the year. At the same time, Virginia NOW focused on elections as the method of ERA ratification. The groups joined forces, and to support VERA-PAC and drum up grassroots activism, NOW organized an ERA caravan, which would be staffed by NOW officers Jean Marshall Clarke, Carol Pudliner-Sweeney, Patricia Winton, and VERA-PAC coordinator Marianne Fowler. The idea, borrowed from the Indiana NOW chapter, was to get out the vote in areas not often reached by other means. NOW activists credited Indiana's caravan with electing six out of nine pro-ERA candidates and securing a victory there. The key was high visibility. Modeled after suffragist campaigns, the coordinators would come to town, show the suffrage documentary *How We Won the Vote*, narrated by feminist actress Jean Stapleton of *All in the Family* fame, organize information sessions, and secure pledges of money and support. The caravan kicked off in Charlottesville, NOW state coordinator Clarke's home base, in April. It would remain in operation through the early 1980s.[103]

Not to be outdone, the League of Women Voters of Virginia participated in a national LWVUS effort to raise over $1 million to go to unratified states. LWVUS did not target Virginia, despite LWV-Fairfax area president Vivian Watt's plea to LWV-Virginia board president Lulu Meese that "Virginia should be very carefully considered as one of the target states." As the leaders argued,

"Virginia has served as a leader of the South in other issues[,]" and its proximity to the national headquarters would make coordination easy. Still, Virginia's LWV chapters pledged almost $20,000 to the national cause, to which the LWVUS had designated over $200,000 of its operating budget, and other state chapters had pledged almost $826,000.[104] At the same time, across the commonwealth, LWV members gave talks to groups, organized voter drives, got petitions signed, and set up information booths to promote the ERA.[105]

Many other supporters worked to support PAC activities to give a final push to the ERA before its expiration in 1979. From Ashland, where "Hanoverians for ERA" placed weekly Q&A ads in the paper, people mobilized, to Bedford, where Common Cause, LWV, VEA, AAUW, and BPW members worked to raise support and visited their strongly anti-ERA incumbent legislator. Activists in the rural northern-neck area participated in a rally organized by Common Cause's lobbyist Kay Peaslee to support the ERA's passage and the pro-ERA challenger to the incumbent. From Martinsville Common Cause supporters making pro-ERA public service announcements, meeting with Delegates, and doing interviews in local media outlets, to Montgomery NOW members working the phones and raising money with VERA-PAC members, to supporters in South Boston and Halifax promoting the ERA with literature drives, pro-ERA Virginians showed their strength. Even in remote Campbell County, the one known active supporter of the ERA, Pat Brehl, spent an entire day at the local grocery store handing out literature.[106] In Harrisonburg, two hundred people marched the streets in support of the ERA. Many Virginians also participated in the National Walkathon for Equal Rights in August. Designed as a national action to honor radical suffragist and National Woman's Party founder Alice Paul on her birthday and to bring awareness to the ERA, the demonstration involved members of various organizations marching in groups to support the amendment's passage. Across the country, and throughout Virginia, NOW members sponsored walkathons to raise money for the ERA.[107]

During the summer of 1977, Virginia activists also made their presence known on the national stage by electing an entirely pro-ERA slate to the International Women's Year conference in Houston. Each state was to hold a conference open to all women, and at the conference all present would vote on a slate of delegates and resolutions to go before the entire conference in Houston. Twelve hundred women from around the commonwealth attended the conference, held in June at the University of Richmond. Workshops on equal opportunity in work and education, lesbian rights, family and divorce issues, the ERA, women and violence, women and the law, and others were open to all participants. The ERA proponents went to the conference knowing that antis dominated the Missouri conference and elected an entire slate of anti-ERA delegates. They determined that would not happen in Virginia.[108]

Not only did the proponents get their entirely pro-ERA slate elected, but they also secured a resolution endorsing an economic boycott of anti-ERA states, a resolution upholding state abortion laws, and resolutions prohibiting discrimination on all matters, including sexual orientation, along with the support of sex-education programs in schools, the revision of rape laws, and stronger domestic violence programs, minority history education in schools, and equal opportunity for women in sports. Jean Marshall Clarke noted following the conference, "The 31 resolutions passed were OUR kind of resolutions. ... NOW is not so far out! It's great but [sic] the rest of the women are catching up with us and joining us!"[109]

Labor Gets Involved

Perhaps increased activity on behalf of the ERA finally drew labor interests into the movement in Virginia, echoing the efforts in Louisiana, where the AFL-CIO provided a tremendous amount of support.[110] No matter the reason, the entry of unions into a leadership position signaled a turning point. It also signified a shift in labor-union attitudes in the campaign. Earlier in the twentieth century, unions refused to support the ERA because they were concerned it would eradicate protective legislation for women. By the 1970s, labor leaders were convinced supporting the ERA was critical to advancing worker rights.[111]

Labor support mattered in Virginia. Pro-ERA activity had been dominated by middle-class women in established organizations. But labor represented working-class interests and brought the weight of mass membership to Virginia's ERA struggle. Vera Harrison, Viola Crooks, Lizzie Corbin, and Helen Tyson, all members of the women's committee of the Amalgamated Meat Cutters and Allied Workers of North America AFL-CIO Local 593 were largely responsible for this. At their 1977 meeting, feminist members convinced their colleagues to pass a resolution to hold a pro-ERA conference that year. The resolution provided the reasons for ERA support: "Forty percent of all workers in the United States are women. The wage gap between their earnings and the earnings of men continues to widen. Disproportionate numbers of women are being laid off. Women continue to be excluded from many higher paid jobs.

Women generally are victims of economic, political, social, and legal discrimination." Addie Wyatt was the keynote speaker at the conference, sponsored by LERN—Labor for Equal Rights Now. Wyatt had gained fame by being the first woman elected to the International Executive Board of the Meatcutters Union. She was nominated by Carter to be a national delegate at IWY. She and her husband, a minister, had a long history with fighting for labor, African American, and women's rights. Two hundred people came to the conference, which featured panel discussions on the ERA with Southern Women's Rights Project (ACLU) director Betsy Brinson and VEA's Mary Hatwood, VERARC, International Ladies' Garment Workers' Union, and NOW members. The upshot of this conference was a mass rally planned for the General Assembly session in January, fully sponsored by LERN, and voted on unanimously by conference attendees.[112]

Electoral Victories

Although ERA supporters across the state worked to elect proponents, arguably the most intense effort centered on Jim Thomson's district. Thomson was a twenty-year veteran of the General Assembly. In his district three men were running for two seats, and Northern Virginia activists hit Thomson hard. When the Alexandria chapter of the BPW held a dinner for Thomson, the only questions anyone asked were about the ERA, making it clear that this would be an issue for him. Activists spent their time and money to defeat Thomson. Nine thousand letters went out to every known pro-ERA voter in the district. VERA-PAC's "Virginians for the ERA" sent letters to Alexandria voters, noting that Thomson "has actively opposed the ERA for five years and will continue to do so." VERARC members made calls to every registered voter, and three hundred volunteers canvassed the area. NOW members went out with signs to rally in front of his office one weekend. And three thousand ERA supporters attended a town hall meeting where Lily Tomlin said she came all the way from California, according to a *Washington Post* reporter, "to help defeat the strongest anti-ERA candidate in Virginia and probably in the whole country."[113]

The goal of this political work was to create a new political climate in the House of Delegates and with the top leadership of the commonwealth. Was the time and energy spent by activists worth it? In a post-election dissection, Common Cause called the effect "mixed." Many strong ERA supporters returned, and proponents picked up ten new supporters. Elise Heinz won a floater seat in Northern Virginia, although her opponents were also pro-ERA. Pro-ERA Lieutenant Governor Chuck Robb won in a landslide over A. Joseph Canada, the vote-switching senator, as did pro-ERA attorney general candidate J. Marshall Coleman. And in perhaps the most stunning upset of all, Thomson lost his seat to the other two candidates. This defeat sparked celebration among ERA activists everywhere. Jean Marshall Clarke told one reporter, "If we can do it to Jim Thomson, the most powerful legislator in the state, we can do it to anyone. And we won't stop with Thomson." Thomson had been slated to chair the powerful Appropriations Committee in the next General Assembly, so his defeat stunned many of his legislative colleagues. Thomson conceded ERA activists made an impact, telling a Roanoke reporter, "the ladies are entitled to their share of the cadaver...." As ERAmerica's spokesperson Kathleen Currie said, this was the first time ERA activists could successfully "translate popular support into political clout."[114]

When the election dust settled, ERA activists could claim some victory. Common Cause estimated that the House now had forty-seven supporters, thirty-eight opposed, and fifteen undecideds. More important, however, may have been the impact on the ground. As Common Cause's newsletter noted, "Whatever the effect the efforts of the ERA 'contacts' had on the election of the ERA supporters, they made a significant and gallant effort to publicize the issue and to persuade voters to support ERA candidates."[115]

Although ERA supporters did not get everything they wanted out of the election, their efforts had an impact on the commonwealth. Immediately after the election, pro-ERA sentiment in Virginia was running high. ERAmerica commissioned a Virginia survey to determine attitudes in the commonwealth. Results confirmed this simple fact: Virginians were in favor of the ERA. This survey noted that, statewide, 59 percent supported the ERA, 28 percent opposed, and 13 percent were undecided. African Americans overwhelmingly supported the ERA at 69 percent, and more Democrats (64 percent) than Republicans (58 percent) supported the ERA. In no income level or job strata did the ERA fall below 53 percent support, although 80 percent of manual and semiskilled laborers were supporters.[116] Organizations had worked toward a common goal, and it seemed like it might be within reach. NOW and VERA-PAC were united in fighting for the ERA; "after some initial trepidations" about the effect of supporting two separate lobbying efforts, LERN was planning a major rally; and the commonwealth appeared united in its support for the ERA. Additionally, NOW membership had grown by over 100 members per month in each of the last five months of the year, with 147 in November alone. The ERA was not just politicizing women; it was also drawing them into the movement.[117]

Racing against the Clock

In 1978, ERA proponents had to fight for a congressional extension while national organizations determined which states to target and local grassroots activists stepped up their efforts to ratify. Nationally, several major organizations instituted a boycott of non-ERA states. While traditional organizations like the BPW, AAUW, UAW, and AAUW as well as NOW supported the boycott, the newcomer VERA-PAC and other sympathetic groups also got on board. An article in *E.R.A. Time* explained the sanctions were projected to cost nonratified states eighty-five million dollars in three years, and that the National Association of Social Workers, seventy-seven thousand strong, had already canceled a Virginia meeting. Pat Winton said, "We are advised to go back to writing softspoken letters from home or to wearing demure dresses when visiting a legislator to thank him for so kindly seeing us. If we had some glimmer of hope after all those years of plodding away, many of us might have been willing to continue that path. But hope eluded us, and we had nothing to lose."[118]

LERN's march and rally that had been planned at the annual meeting just months before amped up demonstrations in Virginia as well. Endorsed by NOW, Common Cause, Black Women's Awareness, local Virginia ERA organizations, VERARC and its member organizations, which included AAUW, American Camping Association, Federally Employed Women, NAACP, NBFO, and Church Women United, the march drew over thirty-two hundred demonstrators on a Sunday afternoon in January. Marchers were geographically and regionally diverse. In addition to the many trade-union members from all over Virginia supporting the march, AAUW representatives hailed from Northern Virginia and the Shenandoah Valley. Busloads came from Wise County, Staunton, Waynesboro, and other rural areas. Church of the Brethren women hailed from Harrisonburg and Broadway, and Mormons for the ERA also marched. Ardelle Lett, the United Methodist Church women's coordinator, brought women from Newport News, Hampton, and Williamsburg; and the Tidewater YWCA sent three busloads. Good Shepherd Catholics for the ERA, composed of over two hundred families, also marched. Fourteen speakers included Kathleen Nolan, president of the Screen Actors Guild and the only woman international union president; Eleanor Smeal, president of NOW; and William Lucy, president of the Black Trade Unionists and international secretary-treasurer of the American Federation of State, County, and Municipal Employees.[119]

ERA activists continued to work traditional lobbying channels as well. Pat Jensen told leaguers to write to all the legislators and visit their own in Richmond. She said, "Make them realize that equality is coming. Let them know how committed we are. Make them understand that women by the hundreds and thousands believe in the ERA."[120] Activists did just what was asked. From Montgomery County to Richmond to Hampton Roads, ERA supporters lobbied, bought newspaper ads, and ran information sessions.[121] These activities, designed to coincide with the General Assembly session, reflected an intensity of action that legislators could not ignore.

In fact, legislators took up one issue that suggested how much ERA proponents had rattled them. Apparently, General Assembly leaders were in a "fuss" over the state seal, which had been displayed prominently on the ERA Caravan. Depicting an allegorical Virginia in a toga with her foot on the chest of a soldier with the words "Sic Semper Tyrranus"—thus ever to tyrants—the flap began when a NOW member (or members) altered the image to depict Virginia with her foot on a business-suited man with crowns bearing the initials of Thomson and Canada. This led to a "flurry of activity" in the General Assembly about the appropriateness of the seal, as Virginia has one breast bared. Then apparently a discussion took place over whether Virginia needed to be fully covered. Pat Winton queried in VERA-PAC's *E.R.A. Time*, "Is the General Assembly so intent on keeping women in a subservient role that even the state symbol must suffer redesign?"[122] While Emily McCoy recalls the drama as hearsay, she did remember the story that legislators realized all state capital police cars would have to be repainted, so the discussion went nowhere.[123] However, the fact that legislators saw fit to discuss this issue at all reflects how much ERA proponents rattled them.

Proponents would soon learn the extent of their efforts. Delegate McDiarmid introduced the amendment two days after the LERN rally, on the day of a large anti-ERA rally, and, according to some activists, against their suggestion. Although McDiarmid had always seemed to work closely with supporters in the past, this year Jean Marshall Clarke alleged that she could get only five minutes to talk with the delegate before McDiarmid introduced ERA ratification in 1978. Clarke charged that McDiarmid saw some as "radicals who should be home writing letters."[124] Many activists were becoming more radical, perhaps because they had seen previous efforts go nowhere, and perhaps they were ready to take this new strategic direction. In so doing, however, they threatened the image of feminist activism that more mainstream "liberal" feminists had so hoped to cultivate with the media and the legislators of Virginia, so it is not surprising that McDiarmid and others might have been concerned about a more confrontational position.

The amendment, as in years past, went to the House Privileges and Elections Committee which, despite the new faces in the General Assembly, was still weighted with anti votes.[125] Lulu Meese wrote to her representatives to tell her version of the events. The day of the hearing, proponents got to the capitol building ten minutes before it opened. A state policeman barred the activists from entering the building, despite the "extreme cold," although everyone else wanting entry got in. Officer Holloway, she said, would periodically "step outside to issue another unkind order[,]" although the crowds were cooperative. Finally, activists were allowed in just in time for the meeting to begin. Those testifying for the ERA included a lay leader from the Southern Baptist Convention, a representative of the Virginia Council of Churches, the ACLU, Women's Equity Action League, the VWPC, the LWV, AFL-CIO, NOW, and LERN. Muriel Smith, still chair of VERARC, reiterated the message related by many: "We are not an insignificant minority, nor a radical, irresponsible alliance of irrational revolutionaries. We are LOYAL citizens, CONSERVATIVE Virginians, PRAYERFUL church and synagogue members, THOUGHTFUL men and women. We are MAINSTREAM Americans." Proponents once again tried to convince the Privileges and Elections Committee to release it to the floor, while opponents, according to journalist Deborah Woodward, "dodged issues and used emotional labels such as 'communist,' 'neuter,' and 'black widow spider.'" Pat Winton argued the "star" of the hearings was former attorney general Andrew Miller, now a U.S. Senate candidate, whose administration had produced the notorious 1974 memo. Using testimony prepared by Clarke, he refuted the memo point by point. One of the most powerful members of the committee, A. L. Philpott, who had been a supporter of Miller, turned his back on Miller during the testimony.[126]

The committee scheduled the vote for the next day. Pat Winton remembered that "Capitol police were everywhere—in corners, in aisles, in doorways." Betsy Brinson told a national women's publication, "The security that day was the strongest I've ever seen."[127] What happened next was business as usual for the Privileges and Elections Committee—legislators voted against the floor vote. The response was not traditional. While facts are a bit murky, eyewitness testimony suggests that a group of women sang a chorus of Helen Reddy's iconic "I Am Woman." Others began chanting "The Dirty Dozen" and "Remember Thomson." Shortly thereafter, Marianne Fowler, who, according to reports, had been giving an interview, was physically picked up by police and hauled out of the building and off capitol grounds, with proponents following her. Then, Jean Marshall Clarke attempted to reenter the area and was promptly arrested. When she asserted her right to be there, police dragged her across the ground to their police car. She was shoved into the car, and when Fowler attempted to come over to help her, she, too, was arrested. Both were charged with trespass and disorderly conduct, and one officer charged Fowler with assault, claiming she had spit on him. Clarke was later also charged with assault when she allegedly hit an officer with the back of her knee.[128]

The fallout was immediate. The ACLU took up representation of Fowler and Clarke, as Betsy Brinson noted that they were arrested over exercising their First Amendment rights to speak, associate, and organize peacefully. VERARC established an ERA Legal Defense Fund to help cover expenses, which quickly reached over one thousand dollars. Many believed that politicians targeted the two. As Pat Winton said later, Fowler was largely credited for the plan to oust Thomson, so she was well known to legislators. The Democratic Party had already punished her by expelling her from her position as treasurer of the local Democratic Committee. Witnessing the event, Eleanor Smeal admitted to a journalist, "It's not a coincidence that the two people who were arrested were the leaders of the ERA movement in Virginia.... The police action was extraordinary and I believe, extreme." While some delegates supported their right to militant action, others tried to deflect attention by saying that the majority of proponents were more mainstream like Common Cause, and other nonpartisan groups.[129]

Others were not so supportive. Elise Heinz made a statement: "There has been much conversation (in the capitol) that those ERA girls are getting too pushy, too aggressive." A few blamed the tactics on proponent legislators' failure to try to move for a discharge to the floor. McDiarmid said that such a move was no longer feasible, and she suggested that the incident may have been a setup when she that she "felt the lobbyists may have precipitated the disruption after the committee vote." And pro-ERA Delegate Hobson told a reporter, "I don't approve of what went on after the vote. The singing and chanting tactic was not a good idea."[130] Rosalind Exum, then serving as chair of VERARC, reported to her executive committee after attending the ERAmerica conference that "backlash toward ERA supporters' image from capitol incident's media treatment" was discussed as a "less than successful" outcome—as was the "lack of minority outreach" also discussed in the failures category.[131]

Others lay the blame squarely on the shoulders of the Privileges and Elections Committee. Lulu Meese, hardly a radical by anyone's standards, told Virginia Leaguers that she was "reluctant to easily place the blame on any one or two people because so many things have happened during this session that I wonder if any one action is more offensive than any other." She challenged LWV members: "You be the judge of who has committed the greatest offense: (a) The two women who had worked, supported, educated, and then silently watched as twelve men, with no concern as to the legislative process or the fairness of their actions," killed the ERA in committee, or anti-ERA supporters who were demonstrating as well—possibly without even a permit. Dorothy Spinks, legislative chair of the BPW, wrote to a delegate, "We are deeply distressed that twelve men saw fit to deny action on an Amendment to the United States Constitution...." She claimed it reflected their "lack of responsiveness to business and professional women of Virginia who believe sincerely that the Equal Rights Amendment is their only assurance of equal legal rights and responsibilities." An editorial in the *Norfolk Journal and Guide* pointed out that it was the House Privileges and Elections Committee that held up integration during Virginia's notorious massive resistance movement and that there was "nothing wrong" with women fighting for an equal legal basis in the country. Some delegates said blaming the activists was nothing more than "another smokescreen," according to one article, and Delegate Raymond Vickry said "Sentiment in the House is much greater for ERA.... It is not the function of the committee to keep an issue from being voted on year after year. It is contrary to a parliamentary system...."[132]

Fowler and Clarke drew a firestorm with their actions, drawing lines between supporters and defining for activists what everyone personally believed was an appropriate demonstration of anger with the General Assembly. After almost a year, a conviction, and an appeal, charges were dismissed on the grounds that the capitol police had no right to keep them off the property. Betsy Brinson summed up the importance of the event in a press release announcing the final dismissal of charges: "The opposition tactics to make ERA activists look bad have failed. The arrests had served to stimulate pro-ERA supporters around the state." She said that the case was one of the most important the ACLU had handled, and that it had ultimately brought "widespread publicity" to the ERA in Virginia. Clarke herself said, "If our arrest did anything to help the extension of time and the passage of the ERA, it was worth it."[133]

Those who believed the women did more harm than good seemed to be in the minority. While some may have disagreed with their tactics, most were willing to place blame squarely on the men of the General Assembly. For six years the assembly had stalled. Virginia and Mississippi remained the only two states in the union that had not yet brought the amendment for a full House floor vote. The commonwealth was one of the many states below the Mason-Dixon Line that were holding back the change desired by a majority of citizens. As Deborah Woodward concluded: "If the ERA fails to be ratified, a look at a U.S. map will explain why... it will be the firm rejection of the South that kills it."[134]

Final Attempts

From 1979 to 1982, activists continued their efforts. Among the many activities scheduled, Montgomery County Area NOW's chapter held a pig roast to raise ERA funds, and NOVA NOW sold items at a flea market, raising eighteen hundred dollars for ERA ratification efforts. Richmond NOW continued its "Run for Equality" to raise funds, and Kathryn Brooks celebrated her seventy-fifth birthday with participation in another swimathon in Northern Virginia, while Charlottesville ERA walkers raised forty-five hundred dollars for ratification by getting pledges for their ten-mile walk, which was part of a national NOW Walkathon effort. Supporters ran ads in papers with signatures of support, and the AAUW, BPW, Housewives for ERA (HERA), NOW, VWPC, and other groups secured over nineteen thousand signatures in the north and west in order to prove to legislators widespread support and to supply information for the phone banks. BPW, LWV, and AAUW newsletters continued to exhort members to write letters and visit their legislators.[135]

But all was not the same in Virginia, or nationally. Although by 1978, sentiment for the ERA in the South had increased from 43 to 50 percent, and a national survey reported 57 percent of those polled favored ratification while only 40 percent did not, ratifications had stalled out.[136] Moreover, proponents were fighting rescission movements, and a new, conservative force was on the rise—one that would work through the Republican Party to facilitate a shift in politics, which included dropping support of the ERA plank from the national platform and, ultimately, in securing Ronald Reagan's election in 1980. Virginia was at the heart of much of this movement, as Jerry Falwell, pastor of Thomas Road Baptist Church in Lynchburg, Virginia, helped found the Moral Majority with Paul Weyrich. On the opposite end of the state in the Tidewater, the *700 Club* on cable television began attracting a larger viewership as it promoted a conservative social and political agenda under the tutelage of Pat Robertson. Faced with the rise of national and state conservative social forces, ERA proponents became more militant. As SWRP director Betsy Brinson said, "it is time to consider... prayer vigils, sit-ins, demonstrations, hunger strikes and other nonviolent tactics to show the seriousness of our commitment and to allow for more militant expression."[137] Many supporters ramped up their demonstrations as they worked even harder to elect pro-ERA politicians. Because of their proximity to the nation's capital, many Virginia women also took part in national ERA actions.

One such action was the summer 1978 D.C. march to support extending the deadline of ERA ratification. This march, in which 100,000 participated, kicked off six weeks of vigils at the White House. Two hundred activists from Charlottesville, Albemarle, and Waynesboro took buses to the march, and the ACLU chapters brought banners and held a wine-and-cheese reception after the march. While others attended and supported the watch, like the AAUW and NOW, there were noticeable absences. Muriel Elizabeth Smith wrote to the vice-president of the National League of Women Voters that its failure to support the march threatened the movement. She claimed, "Failure of the League to maintain a firm position in support of ERA makes it opportune for splinter groups to rise in prominence.... When responsible national leaders fail to lead coherently and cogently, the women's movement is threatened by dissolution into radicalism." But even if the national LWV stayed away from the march, Virginia Leaguers participated in the vigil and found it "a rewarding experience."[138]

Labor continued to be an important part of planned actions and education, which was critical for bringing more diversity to the Virginia movement. In the summer of 1979, labor planned a mass meeting to educate and rally workers. According to United Food and Commercial Workers' representative Jerry Gordon, Virginia was a "key state" in the battle for ratification. African

American Newport News shipyard computer programmer Cynthia Boyd said, "Women must unite! . . . The United Steelworkers of Local 8888 will not stand idly by and have its female members separated by built-in wage controls of the past." Connie Weiss of the United Mine Workers from Castlewood also noted, "Being a union member means that we stand together as people and workers for one idea, that being fair treatment for all regardless of sex, religion, race, or ethnic background." Suzanne Kelly of the VEA said politicians made it clear that what mattered more was not who was elected, but how much pressure the legislator faced.[139] Six hundred workers attended the LERN conference in Richmond; over 350 of whom were Virginians, according to one news report. The attendees resolved to disseminate a "labor for ERA" pamphlet, train union speakers to participate in forums, and build grassroots support through educational programming.[140] Labor forces pulled together to promote a massive rally in Richmond in 1980. According to newspaper reports, between seventy-five hundred and eight thousand supported the rally. Endorsed by NOW, the Council of Labor Union Women, VERARC, and the Council of Black Trade Unionists, the rally was publicized widely and signified the largest pro-ERA action Virginia would see.[141]

Many women demonstrated before the ERA expired, adding their voices with other proponents across the country. Sixty women picketed Jerry Falwell's church in Lynchburg, including about fifteen students, and women from Lynchburg, Roanoke, Richmond, Arlington, and Alexandria, led by Phyllis Stevens, psychology professor at Sweet Briar College. And on June 30, 1981, ERA activists kicked off a weekly prayer vigil at the capitol, called "A Pillar of Fire." Many Virginia women attended the national prayer vigil at the capitol every Wednesday in the summer, including NOW members from Charlottesville, Rockingham County, and Harrisonburg. Two hundred rallies were held nationwide in conjunction with the national vigil, and Charlottesville held one.[142]

This rally was not the only high-profile demonstration in which Virginia pro-ERA activists participated. In fact, as it became increasingly clear to some that lobbying would never be enough, a cadre of women, calling themselves "A Group of Women," decided to engage in public acts of civil disobedience, with the intention of being jailed, to bring attention to the ERA. Composed of mothers, housewives, teachers, lawyers, and ordained religious women, ranging in age from their thirties to their fifties, many embraced feminism later in life. Using the suffragists of the early twentieth century, and in particular Alice Paul, as their model, these women demonstrated in Washington, D.C. In

August of 1980, the women chained themselves to the door of the Republican National Committee headquarters to protest the removal of the ERA from its national platform. The RNC declined to press charges. In 1981, the founder of Mormons for ERA and Virginia resident Sonia Johnson, Georgia Fuller, and nineteen others were arrested for chaining themselves to the White House fence in an ERA protest. In November, they burned effigies and placards with Reagan's anti-ERA statements on them in honor of Abigail Adams's birthday. In early January, carrying banners in the purple and gold colors of the original suffrage movement, the group chained itself to a Mormon temple in Kensington, Virginia, trapping two hundred inside at a wedding as they protested Mormon federal judge Marion Callister's decision that Congress had illegally extended the deadline of the ERA.[143]

These activists were well-organized. Georgia Fuller recalled the intense training involved in being part of the group, including role playing for how different scenarios might pan out. Additionally, everyone involved agreed not to use any mood-altering drugs, including alcohol, on the day of the protest, and to abide by the rules of peaceful resistance. As Fuller remembered, "And it's not just the risk to ourselves, it's the fact that we are presenting our issue. We are presenting the fact that we have worked and worked and worked for the equal rights... in terms of lobbying, in terms of electoral politics, in terms of demonstrating. And this is the only remedy left for us." In fact, they were so organized that, according to Lee Perkins, the activists sought out a chain that could not be cut by traditional police bolt-cutters. They secured the help of one of the husbands, who worked with material scientists, to determine what the heaviest chain they could buy was. Fuller, arrested once in 1981 and three times in 1982, believed the work she and her group were doing was a service for women who could not afford to publicly demonstrate in the same way. The group, originally aligned with the Congressional Union, had to disaffiliate from them after their actions got more radical, perhaps when the group climbed the White House fence on Susan B. Anthony's birthday in 1982 to deliver an ERA petition to Ronald Reagan. Georgia Fuller wrote about this experience in the *Women's Studies International Forum,* describing how she marched to the White House with hundreds of women, scaled the fence with ten of those women, got arrested, and, in her eyes, they were victorious. She said, "We had successfully scaled the forbidding, wrought iron, metaphallic symbol that coils around the White House. We had violated man's world, marching on the inner doors, not just the gates of patriarchal power." Fuller remembered the planning that went into this session. They practiced climbing the fence at a local park, and Mary Ann Beall served as leader of the "street arrest" group with others who did not scale the wall.[144]

Political campaigning and fundraising increased in these years as well, which brought increasing numbers of women into the political process and altered the political landscape in Virginia. NOW had established a PAC in January 1979. NOW-PAC, targeting precincts in Fairfax, Virginia Beach, and Newport News, had raised over thirteen thousand dollars by election season and used the money for mailings, phone banks, and door-to-door canvassing. By 1981, NOW, Virginians for ERA, workers for VERA-PAC, and Virginia Women's Political Caucus, as well as many other pro-ERA groups, were in overdrive, working in the last year of ratification and when all legislators were up for reelection. As they looked to 1982, it appeared that the Virginia Senate was a twenty-twenty vote, so the House of Delegates and statewide races, especially for lieutenant governor, who could break a tie in the Senate, were extremely important. Juanita Sanders of Harrisonburg NOW and Boots Woodyard, ERA coordinator of BPW, recognized the critical nature of Virginia in the ERA struggle and said the focus would be on candidates. When Woodyard asked for money to support the PAC for electoral change at the state BPW meeting, the group raised three thousand dollars in fifteen minutes. Pat Winton of Virginia NOW sent a fundraising letter so appealing that Emily and Fred McCoy of Fairfax borrowed against their savings to provide ten thousand dollars to NOW-PAC. With the money raised, Virginia NOW-PAC and VWPC-PAC flooded voters with flyers endorsing pro-ERA candidates. Volunteers staffed phone banks to galvanize voters. These activities frightened opponents so much that one candidate, Larry Pratt of Springfield, claimed, "The liberals have a list of 25,000 pro-ERA supporters" and the "radical feminists" had a "war chest of 750,000 for Virginia." And a STOP-ERA flyer read, "right now—in Virginia of all states—the vote would be unbelievably close if it were held today. Victory in Virginia could be a political earthquake for the ERA."[145]

To an extent, all of this activity was extremely successful. Virginia elected a full slate of pro-ERA candidates to the state level in 1981, including Chuck Robb as governor. Marianne Fowler was quick to point out that the forty-five thousand Fairfax households targeted, in addition to the ones across the state, yielded results. Ten of twelve of the delegates in the Fairfax area and all in Arlington and Alexandria were now pro-ERA. There were six new vacancies on the House Privileges and Elections Committee. And, in perhaps the most stunning defeat of all, Joan Munford, political newcomer, upset the House Minority leader Jerry Giesler, a notorious anti-ERA candidate, in a district that was overwhelmingly rural and stretched from the Shenandoah Valley to North Carolina. Munford, a Democrat, was elected in a district where no Democrat had been successful since 1965. A Radford University–educated former schoolteacher who ran a chain of nursing homes, Munford said, "I knew the mathematics were against me." ERA proponents "may have had a great deal to do with the fact that I won the election[,]" as hundreds of VWPC and Virginia NOW members worked for her election. As *Washington Post* reporter Judy Mann concluded, "in a state as conservative as Virginia, there is clearly a strong pro-ERA sentiment that galvanized hundreds of volunteers and sent only two anti-ERA people to Richmond from Northern Virginia and sent Joan Munford to Richmond from a rural Republican area."[146]

Of course, the proof is in the pudding, as it were. In the years when pro-ERA PACs were most active, demonstrators were getting more vocal, and the ERA had a clear majority of support in Virginia, how did legislators react? In 1979, the Senate and House Privileges and Elections committees killed the ERA ratification bill. In 1980, while the House Privileges and Elections Committee still held up the amendment, the Senate committee released it to the floor. That's when Virgil Goode of the Southside changed his vote to a "no" and John Chichester of the Fredericksburg area refused to take a vote, citing a Senate rule that one could not vote if one had a "conflict of interest" with the legislation. This led to a twenty-to-nineteen victory, not enough for the supermajority necessary, and not enough to kick it to the pro- ERA lieutenant governor for a vote. In 1981, McDiarmid introduced The ERA in the House, but the committee did not even take a vote on it, and Senator DuVal did not introduce it in the Senate at all in hopes that the House would consider it first.[147]

There was one more crucial year that hung in the balance before the time limit to pass the ERA expired. The General Assembly had changed. Munford had defeated an anti. There were those six seats on the Privileges and Elections Committee up for grabs. ERA activists went into overtime. AAUW, BPW, VWPC, NEA, LWV, and the National Women's Party spent $40,000 on media spots. Vigils continued as usual, with Housewives for ERA providing babysitting. The Virginia Women Attorneys Association was ready to announce its formal support of the ERA and was funding a toll-free information number. ERAmerica provided $40,000 to fund activities in Virginia, although this was less than the organization designated as higher priority received from its

$220,000 budget. In an address to the General Assembly, the newly elected governor, Chuck Robb, said that, while everyone needed to disregard "rhetorical excesses" on both sides, "For me, the issue is one of basic equity. And for a state which played such an essential part in securing freedom for our ancestors centuries ago, it is no less important that we guarantee those same freedoms to *all* Americans today."[148]

A "Dirty Trick"

In 1982, proponents believed they had a chance with the General Assembly. They were suspicious about what might happen if the amendment were released from committee—the Senate was tied, and the lieutenant governor had already said he would break that tie for the supermajority. As the Harrisonburg-Rockingham NOW newsletter told members, "There is a fear on the aprt [sic] of some proponents that one or more Senators may choose to 'take a walk' at the time the vote is called." So each lobbyist was assigned a legislator to track, as Emily McCoy recalled. And follow her senator she did—to the office, to the meeting rooms, to the restroom. So when Bridgewater Senator Nathan Miller (Republican) left for the airport to take a business trip, Marianne Fowler and Pat Winton were there to try to stop him. According to a news report, Fowler said "He looked very sheepish. He finally ducked into the men's room[,]" but he still took the flight. His failure to vote left the tally at twenty to nineteen, not enough to win, but with no way to throw it to the tiebreaking and necessary vote. The House did not have to do anything, as the Senate did not vote to ratify. After this happened, Elise Heinz immediately filed suit in the Virginia Supreme Court trying to overturn the Senate's twenty-one-vote majority rule in favor of a simple majority, but the Supreme Court would not hear the case.[149]

ERA activists were livid. Lulu Meese called Miller's action a "dirty trick" and noted, "ERA died in Virginia on February 16th. It died not from lack of supporters and timeliness but because women continue to be a joke in Virginia." Judy Mann, reporter for the *Washington Post,* chided Miller for not doing his duty: "Ploy or not, Miller is supposed to be working in the state Senate while it is in session, not on private legal business." His response to her, "The world doesn't stop because the General Assembly starts." was less than satisfactory to Mann, who said it was in keeping with his "cavalier" attitude about his office. Even the Waynesboro *News-Virginian,* whose editor had "never endorsed ERA," said that its significance made it deserve at least a vote and that the General Assembly should not have allowed "such an inglorious sequence of events." He concluded by stating that "Washington... has no monopoly on dirty tricks."[150]

Virginia activists were down but not out. VERARC continued to exist, sponsoring a rally with Richmond NOW at the capitol in conjunction with the nationwide protests on the expiration day. It drew a crowd of about fifty, and Lynda Robb, the governor's wife, was in attendance with her four-year-old daughter. Activists continued to target legislators, and the NWPC's list included Virginia's perennial anti-ERA legislator, House Speaker A. L. Philpott. In the Allegheny Highlands, members of a NOW chapter only one year old grilled their delegate, William Wilson, on his anti-ERA stand. Sarah Payne and Stephanie Tyree, the mother-daughter founders of that chapter, recalled how uncomfortable he was in the meeting, and the negative press he garnered. In fact, they believe that their challenge of him led to his ultimate demise at the polls.[151]

And as protesters waved banners saying "ERA Is Not Dead" in the 1980s, they were actually on to something. In 1997, a group of William and Mary law students wrote an article claiming that the passage and inclusion into the Constitution of the Madison, or "Congressional Pay Raise," Amendment over two hundred years after its original introduction set a precedent that could be used to argue against the validity of the time limit on the ERA. Many are using this argument now as they continue to fight for the ERA. The ERA is still introduced in the Virginia General Assembly, as it is in other unratified states. As of 2015, the Senate passed the ERA for a third time, while the House Privileges and Elections Committee refused to even put the amendment on the docket.[152]

Assessing Defeat

Virginia activists spent years, thousands of dollars, and much of their energy on trying to secure the ERA's passage. Although they acknowledged defeat in the short term, they did not think their efforts were in vain. Lulu Meese went to a party at the National Women's Party Headquarters in D.C. right after the deadline was up. She said that the party was "upbeat," and that while they were "devastated," they were not defeated. She wrote, "But from the devastation will grow new strength, new resolve, and ultimately, success." She recapped the reasons for failure, and noted that the Virginia story was so much like that of Oklahoma, Illinois, Florida, and North Carolina. She blamed the ERA's failure on proponents always having to be on the defensive, and the perception that only "militant women" supported the ERA, partly because of media attention on that minority. She also said supporters who tried to lobby with "adversary strategy" backfired, and that "10% of our state coalition members would not cooperate but insisted on following their much broader agenda ... [,]" placing their own desires for members and fundraising above ERA ratification. However, she remembered there was a tremendous amount of cooperation between the ERA supporters, and that lobbyists who acted responsibly "increased visibility and credibility" with legislators.[153]

Georgia Fuller recalled the realities of defeat for so many who worked so hard. She remembered, "After the ERA was defeated, I was sick for about a year and a half. I realized I had been carrying a systemic infection for a long time. But that year we were all tired." Mary Ann Beall had to be hospitalized, as she almost died from a fasting protest in Illinois. Georgia Fuller remembered how Junior Bridge, organizer of the march and other ERA efforts, "had some problems," and that "we all borrowed against some part of our future, whether it was our health, whether it was our career[,]" to try to get the ERA passed. As she remembered her efforts, Fuller explained why the amendment had been so important to her and her colleagues: "it was ten years or more of struggle for us. It was a very, very singular focus ... the struggle for the ERA is what held things together. It held together the work on sexuality and lesbian/gay rights, for reproductive rights, the women in religion, the economic issues, the educational issues, the court issues."[154]

Others had different takeaways from the ERA battle. As Gayle Stoner, coordinator for Virginia Highlands NOW out of far southwest Virginia, said, "the process was one of growth and education for all those involved—and there is no going backwards. Not ratifying now may slow us down, but will not stop us...." She hailed women's ability to change "through introspection, through communication with other women," and by moving into the mainstream of society through political campaigns. She also said women activists "dissolved the stereotype of the female radical because our population includes women of all ages and backgrounds."[155] Pat Winton, who had become NOW's state coordinator, announced the organization had increased its membership to five thousand across the state, and activists learned how to "work the political system."[156]

And it wasn't just an increase in NOW's membership, but in its state reach that signified a change. By the end of the summer in 1975, NOW chapters had been established in Roanoke, Abingdon, Montgomery County, the Shenandoah Valley, and Norton, all in the mountainous western region of Virginia and surrounded by rural counties. By 1983, NOW had chapters in Northern Virginia, and chapters in all urban areas—Charlottesville, Williamsburg, Richmond, Fredericksburg, Tidewater, Hampton–Newport News, as well as in more rural areas like Lynchburg, Rockbridge, Harrisonburg-Rockingham, and Allegheny Highlands. Feminism had extended out beyond urban regions and was making inroads across the commonwealth.[157]

Why did the ERA fail in Virginia? In some ways, Virginia's experience looked much like the failures in other states. While activists did a tremendous job reaching out to diverse geographical regions of the state, they had less success in bringing different kinds of women into the activist fold. LERN rallied labor, which lent tremendous support to the movement, but Mary Ann Bergeron of NOW noted that she did not "recall a lot of women of color participating. There were some. Don't get me wrong... there might have been many, but it was not what I would think could be garnered today." In fact, Rosalind Exum, who had been AAUW state president and took over as coordinator for VERARC, and Ruth Harvey Charity, AAUW's ERA coordinator, were the highest-profile African American Virginians involved in the movement. Bessida White, founder of the NBFO, worked through the VWPC and was often a speaker at ERA conferences. But all in all, the most prominent and dedicated ERA activists tended to be white, middle-class women, much like ERA proponents across the country. Muriel Elizabeth Smith also explained that, while there was geographic diversity, the dominance of Northern Virginia feminists in ERA-supporting organizations was sometimes, in her view, a hindrance to getting things done. As she said, "Northern Virginia was suspect by a lot of people... most of the time it was [that]... the national politics... were not singing the same tune as Virginia politics were singing."

Some feminists blamed powerful conservative forces in Virginia. Smith said the media images hurt activists, and ERA activists were not financially powerful enough to swing votes. Smith concluded, "if you want significant things done, you have to have a moneyed connection. I'm sorry, it's not democratic." Fuller concurred with this opinion, saying that insurance interests and other businesses colluded against the movement. She said that at first activists thought it was about getting enough people educated, but "we learned in the walk to Richmond that there were a lot of... powerful people who were threatened by equality for women and economic interests. Later we realized... that you don't always see who's behind the scenes pulling the strings until the drama is over."[158]

Although other states like Louisiana and North Carolina saw the ERA flounder in committee, Virginia's political system has established committees with such strength that they keep a stranglehold on much legislation. Activists view this as a problem unique to the commonwealth. The committee system enabled a very small group of legislators to stop a floor vote. As VWPC's Sandra Brandt reminded us: "In Virginia what kills us more than anything legislatively on any issue... if you can't get the Equal Rights Amendment... out of the subcommittees, it's gone." For over forty years, the House Privileges and Elections Committee has held up the amendment, not allowing it to go to a vote. And while committees in other places were powerful, as in Louisiana and North Carolina, it seemed that Virginia activists fought an uphill battle for years, just trying to hammer away at a system that would never work for them. In effect, as in other unratified states, legislators did not see the benefit of voting for something that would not prove to be a distinct advantage.[159] What will it take to dislodge the ERA from the Privileges and Elections Committee? Brandt suggests: "Virginia every single year decides it's not something that's important. And I guess if all of the women in the state of Virginia... wrote a letter to their legislator and say sign this or we'll vote you out, maybe it will get passed."[160] As of 2017, Virginia continues to be one of two states in which the ERA has not come up for a floor vote in the House. As Bergeron suggested, "Virginia is a very insular state; it doesn't really care what other states do... regardless of what our lawmakers say, they don't really care."[161]

Forty years later, many activists remember the ERA battle positively. Brinson called it "a pretty heady time on the part of the activists." Emily McCoy pointed out the legislative successes: "a lot of progress had been made in converting legislators... 25 percent of the House was for the ERA.... We were very close to 50 percent when the deadline occurred.... That was a huge thing... roughly twenty-five conversions of people who wouldn't say no in the space of five years of doing political action." Mary Ann Bergeron remembered the ERA's failure as "Horrible, horrible, horrible and horrible." But she believed the defeat galvanized activists to work on other women's issues, where they found more success: "I don't think any effort is ever wasted... we might have gotten farther in Virginia as a result of it not being passed, and getting mad... and getting more active, and more into than maybe if it had been passed." Fuller noted the sense of community that activists built over potlucks and planning sessions at the "Bridge-Beall" house.[162]

ERA was a hard loss for proponents in Virginia. Still, many feminists tried to find positive outcomes in the defeat. The General Assembly may not have passed the ERA, but the work of activists brought more women into the political area and helped to usher in legislative change to benefit women in other areas. It also brought many feminists into the political arena as well as grassroots organizing campaigns. Virginia ERA activists' efforts, like those of their counterparts across the nation in unratified states, made a difference for women.[163]

3

ABORTION RIGHTS AND REPRODUCTIVE JUSTICE

We would have hundreds of people.... It was a huge thing when people would come to the pro-choice lobby day ... it was NOW, it was National Women's Political Caucus, it was AAUW, it was RCAR [Religious Coalition for Abortion Rights], it was other groups in it ... Planned Parenthood, NARAL.... We had buses of people coming.... I would always say to myself, "Wow, the millions of women who live in Virginia, and do you know that it is [only] about forty or fifty of us actually fighting this fight for you every day?"

—DENISE LEE, former legislative co-coordinator, former state coordinator, Virginia NOW

A more controversial, but no less important, issue for which activists fought was to preserve the gains made by the watershed Supreme Court decision *Roe v. Wade,* which in 1973 overturned state bans on first-trimester abortion. Although the decision made abortion more available, it left the door open for the federal and state governments to limit access through statutory restriction. Subsequent rulings, as in the 1977 *Maher v. Roe* case that allowed for Connecticut to withhold public funding of abortions in any case but one that threatened the life of the mother, would continue to erode a woman's right to choose through the twentieth century.

It was this concern that motivated activists. While these women were not successful in staving off anti-choice legislation in Virginia, their efforts, combined with those of other feminists across the country, mattered. Pro-choice advocates secured victory with the 2016 Supreme Court decision *Whole Woman's Health v. Hellerstedt,* striking down Texas law requiring abortion providers to have admitting privileges at nearby hospitals and clinics to have facilities meeting standards for much more complex surgical procedures, part of the TRAP laws (Targeted Regulations Against Abortion Providers). After the decision, Planned Parenthood announced a plan to get TRAP laws off the books in eight states, including Virginia.[1]

Women's rights activists had fought hard to secure access to abortion services, particularly in the decade before *Roe v. Wade*. Abortion was just one plank in an overall platform of women's health matters, which included providing more access to birth control, women's reproductive health services, and sex education in schools. Before *Roe*, members of progressive religious denominations, doctors, lawyers, birth-control advocates, and feminists joined together to demand changes to laws. In many states, laws forced women seeking abortions often had to travel long distances, risk their lives by going through with illegal and very often unsafe and unsanitary abortions, or pull strings with hospital boards to gain access to "therapeutic abortions," those performed legally on women whom medical professionals determined were "at risk" either physically or mentally by being pregnant.[2]

The diversity of abortion-law repeal advocates helped to provide a broad level of support when *Roe* made its way through the courts. However, it also proved challenging in that the ideologies espoused by activists did not always mesh. For example, many feminist activists came to support abortion rights from their work within a larger network that promoted women's rights. These grassroots activists often hailed from the broader women's health movement, and they saw abortion rights as one of many issues related to women's health and autonomy. They saw abortion as an important feminist issue.[3] Sometimes more radical than other groups that worked for repeal of abortion, they found themselves at odds ideologically with the more mainstream organizations like Planned Parenthood, which sought change through electoral politics.[4]

In Virginia, as in the rest of the nation, restrictive abortion laws existed, but were challenged by reproductive rights activists before the *Roe* decision. As early as 1969, a group of women in Virginia got together to organize an effort to reform the commonwealth's laws banning abortion. Under the direction of the Women's Alliance of the First Unitarian Church in Richmond, eighty women attended a panel session and discussed problems with unlicensed abortion providers performing illegal abortions. A temporary spokeswoman for the group, Betty Kenley, told a reporter that the group wanted to end "compulsory pregnancy" and explained that the laws written by men dealt with what was a "woman's problem."[5] The Virginia Women's Political Caucus also included on its legislative program for 1972 a repeal of all abortion and sterilization laws in the commonwealth.[6] The group made plans to lobby the General Assembly.

Activists made some headway prior to the *Roe* decision, as Virginia legislators had changed laws to allow for abortions for maternal health or fetal malformations. Further restrictions included a residency requirement of twenty days for women seeking abortion, and a requirement for the procedure to be "certified" by both a doctor and a hospital board.[7] These laws were not unlike the many that appeared in the late 1960s and early 1970s that had been based on the American Law Institute's model abortion law. Seeking to standardize and liberalize codes, it proposed easing abortion restrictions to allow the procedure in cases of fetal abnormality, rape/incest, or with two doctors' agreements that it was for the health of the mother (therapeutic abortions). In essence, the laws that were passed nationwide, including in Virginia, remained extremely restrictive.[8]

Other national groups began to fight for changes to abortion laws, and those organizations' Virginia chapters would be strong supporters of reproductive freedom in the battle to protect *Roe* in the commonwealth. In 1967, NOW put abortion rights on its national platform. Some NOW members, though, feared that abortion would become associated with feminism to the exclusion of other issues. They had worked diligently to separate the ERA and abortion in the 1970s and early 1980s, and many NOW members, as well as women in other organizations, did not pursue abortion rights with the same vigor as they did the ERA, if they worked on the issue at all.[9] Planned Parenthood also entered the battle for abortion justice from its position as a supporter of birth control. However, Planned Parenthood had been an organization that had in the past argued for eugenics-based birth control, often viewing the problems of the poor as hereditary. Moreover, it was headed by men since its founding by Margaret Sanger in the early twentieth century until the late 1970s.[10] Its reach, support base, and financial situation made it a major player in the struggle for reproductive rights, but it tended to work within the system, rather than supporting a widespread change in the ways society viewed women's autonomy.

Ultimately, in the last quarter of the twentieth century, NOW, Planned Parenthood, and the National Abortion Rights Action League (NARAL, renamed following *Roe*), dominated the abortion rights debate, both nationally and in Virginia. In the commonwealth, several statewide and regional organizations worked to protect abortion access. "Pro-choice" became the rallying cry for those holding the line against legislative attempts to curtail abortion.

Although the focus on providing access to safe and legal abortions was an easier sell to the mainstream population, critics condemned the term as too moderate and exclusionary. Marlene Fried, an activist and scholar, charged activists with trying to "sanitize" abortion rights with choice rather than on affirming women's sexuality. Calling the concept "innocuous and ambiguous," she blamed what she termed "single-issue groups" like Planned Parenthood and NARAL with working in a system of oppressors—police, courts, and legislators—to try to uphold women's rights.[11] Political scientist Rosalind Petchesky argued that, by focusing only on practical aspects of the law and calling for limited government intervention, activists were not necessarily guaranteeing that "good, safe abortions will be provided," and were eliding those broader feminist issues of empowering women.[12] Cherokee activist and professor Andrea Smith charged that the pro-choice argument was so narrow that it failed to address why women might need to have abortions at all. She claimed pro-choice presented a particular burden to women of color and others in marginalized communities because it failed to acknowledge long-standing issues of reproductive justice in their communities.[13] As historian Joyce Berkman explained in a review of reproductive rights historical literature, the concept of pro-choice "seemed hollow to women who have had little choice to have or not have a child."[14]

The pro-choice language was especially limiting because, as Joyce Berkman noted, it assumed women had control over their reproductive lives. First of all, not even birth control was accessible to many women in the late twentieth century because of cost or accessible health clinics.[15] On the other side of the equation, by focusing so much on access to abortion and birth control—that is, the right to not have children—mainstream groups failed to understand state authorities had actively sought to limit the number of children poor women and women of color had. Even Planned Parenthood's "better baby" movement assumed that middle-class families were the ones who were capable of planning when they should have their children and assumed that working-class women were not capable of controlling their reproduction. Because marginalized women fell victim to state eugenics programs forcing them into sterilizations against their will, they often felt alienated by the focus on sterilization and abortion as choices. As African American activist Loretta Ross maintained, black women's fight to control their own bodies dated back to enslavement, and while they desired reproductive autonomy, it meant they had to fight for the right to have or not have children as they chose. Mainstream pro-choice organizations' failure to fully discuss this problematic history limited the willingness of women of color to work with these organizations.[16]

Some Virginia feminists seemed to recognize this problem. Even before the Supreme Court decision, the Virginia Women's Political Caucus (VWPC) met with the African American women's group Women for Political Action and discussed the "possible difference that may arise between black and white women on topics such as abortion." Perhaps this is why the VWPC included a demand to repeal sterilization laws as well as abortion laws in 1972.[17] In addition, Virginia NOW elected Denise Lee, its first African American state coordinator, to lead them in their heated battle to stave off legislative restrictions on abortion in the 1990s.

Nationally, mainstream organizations attempted to expand programming to women of color in the mid-1980s by hosting conferences, and specifically inviting women of color to march for reproductive rights in Washington, D.C., among other initiatives. Faye Wattleton, the first African American president of Planned Parenthood—and first female one since the early twentieth century—used her position as a black woman to press for reproductive justice, but too many women of color were suspicious of the mainstream movement to join those organizations in large numbers.[18] Although some leaders in national reproductive rights–focused movements were African American, few women of color joined. Many were concerned that these organizations concerned themselves with defense of abortion while failing to secure public funding for abortions, and they could not get the momentum to place abortion into a larger women's civil rights framework. They also saw the movement as too conservative and too intent on political lobbying to be attentive to the more complicated needs of poor women or women of color. Instead, across the country, women of color created their own organizations that often were very active with promoting reproductive justice at the grassroots level.[19]

As many scholars of the reproductive rights movement point out, the debate over birth control and abortion in this country is really about what women can and cannot do with their bodies, and serves as an attempt to control women.[20] In the commonwealth, state officials had desired to control society through a vigorous eugenics program which started in the early twentieth century and did not end until the 1970s. Through a program justified by social scientists, health officials, social workers, and doctors, Virginia sought to constrain the effects of poverty and "racial mixing" by passing oppressive miscegenation laws, surveilling and imprisoning women thought to be carrying venereal diseases in the 1930s and 1940s, and engaging in an ambitious sterilization program that targeted the poor, women of color, and the disabled in society. The Virginia Supreme Court asserted the validity of state-mandated sterilization in *Buck v. Bell* in 1927. Between the 1920s and the 1970s, Virginia ranked third behind California and North Carolina in sterilizations performed, at seven thousand. And while many states halted these programs after World War II, Virginia, along with North Carolina and Georgia, expanded their programs, with combined sterilizations comprising 76 percent of the national total.[21] Given the state's history, it is not surprising that Virginia lawmakers would attempt to take back control by regulating abortion almost out of existence after *Roe*.

Many feminists, both in and outside of formal organizations, worked to block legislative changes while simultaneously focusing on education about choice and protection of clinics at the local level. As early as 1973, Virginia women began working to safeguard reproductive rights. The Virginia Organization to Keep Abortion Legal (VOKAL) was the first group organized in Virginia specifically for this purpose. Mary Denyes (Wazlak) led the charge to begin this group, which later formally affiliated with NARAL, out of the Virginia Beach NOW "Our Bodies, Ourselves" Task Force, which was more broadly interested in promoting women's health issues. The organization promoted pro-choice and lobbied the General Assembly and protected clinics with street-level actions. In this, they were joined by the Freedom of Choice Tidewater Coalition, a group of over three hundred members, and organizations like Catholics for a Free Choice, local NOW chapters, and Service Families for Reproductive Freedom.[22]

Although VOKAL publicly focused on "choice" rather than women's rights, its main founder, Denyes (Wazlak), held feminist views about reproductive rights. She remembered, "I'm thinking, 'Who speaks for the woman?' I'm hearing all this stuff about abortion and this fetus or embryo or whatever we have here is a biological beginning [has] now got a higher priority than the woman who is carrying it. Is that fair?" However, she recognized that "the issue had outgrown us as a little committee" and recalled it was time to take the group to the state level—but no further. Wazlak remembered why the Virginians decided to go it on their own. In a state where she recalled, "People don't say the word 'abortion' out loud," she didn't "feel like we could trust [NARAL]" because she did not know their organizers at that time, and so it seemed better to be independent. The name VOKAL reflected where they were at the time, and it was proposed by someone who attended the meeting: "Abortion is a medical procedure. We're trying to keep it legal, which means we're not opposing anybody. We're the state of Virginia, and we're going to be outspoken about it. That's VOKAL."[23]

VOKAL and the Freedom of Choice Tidewater Coalition (later Virginia Pro-Choice Coalition) were only two of myriad organizations supporting abortion rights in the decades following *Roe*. In addition to grassroots organizations, Virginia NOW, the ACLU, and Planned Parenthood battled to keep abortion legal in the commonwealth. These organizations were joined on various efforts by the VWPC as well as the Richmond Lesbian-Feminists. RCAR, headquartered in Annandale, Virginia, also lobbied to protect choice. This group had support in Virginia, including the secretary of the Virginia Baptist General Board's Department of Social Ministries, the Rev. R. Clint Hopkins, and Presbyterian minister Rev. Carol Chase of Hanover Presbytery.[24] The Episcopal Diocese of Virginia joined these and other religious denominations in 1974 as it affirmed a woman's right to abortion, while calling for both medical and pastoral counseling at the time. Although there was some dissension among the 560 delegates, the affirmation passed, along with one calling for the ordination of women.[25] VOICE, Virginians Organized for Community Expression, would join the pro-choice legion in 1980, formed specifically to challenge the homegrown New Right movement. Its goal was to "protect our community institutions by using facts, rather than emotion," against the New Right's attempt to kill choice and sex education in school.[26]

Other women's groups like the AAUW, Virginia Business and Professional Women, and the League of Women Voters determined to support reproductive rights, albeit without taking quite as prominent a stand. As the New Right's assault on reproductive rights became clear in the early 1980s, the League of Women Voters of the United States (LWVUS) asked member chapters to vote on concurrence with the following statement: "The League of Women Voters of the United States believes that public policy in a pluralistic society must affirm the constitutional right of privacy to the individual to make reproductive choices."[27] Across the country, members studied the information provided by LWVUS and debated concurrence. In the Fairfax area, for example, over 260 members showed up at unit meetings. While most supported the statement, some did so with "reservations." These included missives to LWVUS to not join coalitions on this issue. Others wanted LWVUS to use this statement "with restraint."[28] Across the country, units participated at a rate higher than for any other recent study issue, with an 81 percent response rate. Of 984 responses, 912 chapters concurred with the statement, with 5 abstaining. All seventeen of the Virginia chapters concurred. In its analysis, LWVUS noted that many members "expressed overwhelming support for choice for all women[,]" and although members averred abortion as a birth-control choice, they supported its protection based on the right to privacy.[29] LWV Virginia focused most efforts on other issues after ERA, but they did often join with groups to protect abortion in the commonwealth.

Reproductive rights activists focused on two key strategies in the post-*Roe* era: they lobbied the General Assembly and their national representatives to keep legislative restrictions on abortion at bay, and they worked through grassroots organizations to protect clinics and educate the public about abortion. Both efforts highlighted the necessity for maintaining the rights afforded by the Supreme Court. Given the conservative nature of the General Assembly and the fact that Jerry Falwell and Pat Robertson, leaders of the New Right and virulent antiabortion spokesmen, operated out of the east and west quadrants of the commonwealth as the New Right gained steam through the late 1970s through the 1980s, feminists who advocated for access to safe and legal abortions faced an uphill battle.[30]

The majority of reproductive rights activists in Virginia lobbied and mounted educational efforts to protect abortion. They wanted to stand as leaders on choice in the conservative region. These activities centered on several key events, including trying to stop Virginia from rewriting its abortion laws in violation of the *Roe* decision, trying to get federal representatives to vote against the Hyde Amendment to stop Medicaid payments for abortions, and trying to stave off restrictive abortion laws in the wake of Supreme Court decisions enabling states to do so.

Conservative General Assembly members proved willing to consider challenging *Roe,* and activists were there to try to stop that from happening. When some House representatives introduced a bill to allow abortion in a doctor's office through the first trimester and in a hospital up through the twenty-sixth week to reflect *Roe* guidelines, some members balked. Andrew McMurtrie, Democrat from Chesterfield, told a reporter, "If we pass [the bill] ... it puts Virginia on record in support of the Supreme Court's decision on abortion, and that position is tantamount to legally permitting abortion on demand."[31] In response, Virginia Beach NOW mounted an educational campaign. Margaret DeBolt, head of the Reproductive Rights Task Force, told radio listeners that at least 157 women had died from illegal abortions in Virginia the year the General Assembly liberalized the laws. She noted abortion remained restricted to "those with money or special influence" and decried antiabortion activists' use of "emotionally-loaded" language. Comparing antiabortion rhetoric to Hitler's pro-natalist policies, she challenged the General Assembly to abide by the decision, referencing how it had done just the opposite during its massive resistance to civil rights. She concluded: "If the state is set for a new Massive Resistance in Virginia on abortion, it can only keep our energies from more important things, such as the good health of all our citizens."[32]

Ultimately, after intense lobbying, the General Assembly did pass a law that brought Virginia's abortion regulations in line with *Roe*. Over the next several years, anti-abortion forces in the General Assembly were unsuccessful in their attempt to add an anti-abortion amendment to the state constitution, a victory cheered by activists who understood the significance of establishing a beachhead in the South. In 1976, Patricia Harding Clark, chair of the NOW Reproductive Task Force, representatives of ACLU, VWPC, Zero Population Growth, and others testified against the amendment, and it was tabled for a third year in a row, to the surprise of Clark. The majority of those who voted to table the resolution explained that they did so because they were pro-choice, and the rest did so because they believed in minimal government.[33] Through the years, as pro-choice activists lobbied, the calls and letters probably helped—but as Mary (Denyes) Wazlak recalled, the ACLU lobbyist believed Denyes's presence in the committee room, seven months pregnant with her first child, was important. She realized, "There was something to the fact that if you say pro-choice, you're not anti-motherhood."[34] Whatever the ultimate reason, Virginia pro-choice activists had won the early battle, and recognized the significance of that victory.

Even without legal impediments to abortion since the early 1970s and an increase in access, women seeking abortions found it a challenging task. Some providers began clinics to provide outpatient abortions under the care of medical professionals. A clinic serving Northern Virginia opened in Fairfax County under the administration of a registered nurse who had served in a D.C. clinic, staffed by nurses trained in medical and psychiatric care. The $125 cost was significantly lower than in hospitals. In Norfolk, Hillcrest Clinic opened its doors first and quickly became a target of antiabortion picketers, and Peninsula Medical Center began to perform outpatient abortions. In Richmond, Presbyterian minister Robert Bluford teamed up with an obstetrician to found the Richmond Medical Center for women, the first in the central region to perform abortions. The center would expand its operations to open facilities in Charlottesville, Newport News, and Roanoke. Later, Planned Parenthood would make the decision to provide abortions in its clinics as well.[35] All of these clinics offered varied reproductive health services, from pregnancy and venereal disease testing to birth control and exams. But expanding to include legal medical abortions attracted the attention of antiabortion activists. And even though clinics existed, a Planned Parenthood study noted the lack of access women faced a year after the Supreme Court decision. In 1974, in the United States about a third of women who sought abortions could not get them. In Virginia, only about 22 to 31 percent of women could get abortions. Planned Parenthood officials said that abortion was still inaccessible, especially to poor women.[36]

Securing legal abortions became even more challenging after the U.S. Congress and the General Assembly sought restrictions. After attempting to stave off the congressional Hyde Amendment, which restricted the use of Medicaid funds for abortions, Virginia women tried to keep state funds available. Lobbying did not stop the State Board of Health from discontinuing funding except when a woman's life was in danger.[37] VOKAL accused the board of a "change of policy." At its statewide meeting, VOKAL brought together national speakers, representatives of the ACLU, religious leaders, academics, and lawyers and announced plans to testify at statewide hearings on the board's decision.[38]

Virginia feminists recognized that the cutting of public health funding targeted poor women. At one hearing, Denyes spoke in support of education in health and nutrition, pregnancy prevention, and sex education. But she finished with: "To offer coverage for pregnancy costs without providing reimbursement for legal, medical alternatives to pregnancy is not maintaining a neutral position in administration of health care services...." She charged the board with "interference with the rights of low income citizens...."[39] Betsy Brinson, Southern Women's Rights Project director of the ACLU, spoke to the state board in an attempt to get it to reconsider, claiming, "If the earlier decision is upheld, there are Virginia women who will die because they cannot afford an abortion. Most will be young. Many will be black. All will be poor." She argued the policy "punishes pregnant women" and the doctors who deserved compensation for services, in addition to challenging the separation of church and state. She also said sixteen states continued funding the medical procedure, despite the loss of federal funds.[40]

The battle for public funding for abortions dominated lobbying efforts in the General Assembly in the 1970s and early 1980s. When the House of Delegates introduced a bill to end all funding for abortion in any situation, VOKAL, the ACLU, the Virginia Clergy Consultation Service, Women's Equity Action League, Richmond Community Action Program, NOW, Zero Population Growth, doctors from the Medical College of Virginia, Planned Parenthood, and the Virginia Pro-Choice Coalition all stepped forward to lobby against it. Local NOW members provided housing for lobbyists traveling to Richmond, and members of these organizations testified in hearings and met with legislators. Despite their best efforts, the bill passed, and poor women lost all right to state support for abortions for any reason. Looking back at the session, VOKAL's Denyes presented the positive, noting that a parental consent law did not pass, and neither did a call for Congress to pass an antiabortion constitutional amendment.[41] In a postmortem, Denyes said, "We have developed a sense of credibility among the legislators in terms of what we stand for, although we need to work on better cooperation."[42]

This sentiment may have been well-founded. When house bills to support abortion funding came up in 1981 in the case of fetal abnormalities and incest or rape, many more citizens joined the fray. Parents of children dying from genetic disorders, the coordinator of Tidewater Rape Information Services, a doctor, and a Presbyterian minister who also spoke for the Southern Virginia Episcopal Diocese, as well as a representative from NAACP, joined the usual pro-choice lobbyists—Planned Parenthood, VOKAL, NOW, and VOICE. The bills passed, but faced an uncertain future with Governor Dalton, who received visits from a Richmond rabbi, member of the business community, VOICE representatives, and doctors, all of whom pressed him to sign the bills. He did not—although newly elected governor Chuck Robb did when bills passed in the next session.[43]

As conservatives gained control of the U.S. Congress and the White House in 1980, pro-choice activists faced a much greater challenge. This did not stop women from trying to get laws repealed and to halt the passage of other restrictive federal legislation. Virginia women continued to work with the throngs fighting for reproductive justice. They fought against the Human Life Amendment (Hatch Amendment) of 1981 that sought to define life at conception. VOICE held a Tidewater "Rally for 'Real' Life" to educate Tidewater citizens about the implications of the bill. About five hundred women, most of them white, showed up for the rally to hear a law professor from the University of Virginia and a doctor, among others, speak out against the bill. Virginia state NOW officers met with their senators and reported that Byrd would support states' rights over federal mandates and Senator Warner "was enthusiastic about getting a copy of the General Assembly voting record on abortion issues over the past few years in light of the more 'lenient' attitude Virginia has had about abortion restrictions." Lobbying continued the following year, as Charlottesville NOW exhorted its members to write letters to show the importance of the "growing women's voting bloc." Alexandria and Richmond NOW chapters did the same.[44]

On this issue, Virginia feminists could join with other activists across the nation and claim victory. As Jane Wells-Schooley of Richmond NOW rejoiced: "The phone calls... constituent visits, and signature ads which you generated helped keep our friends in the Senate together through three cloture votes and a final critical *tabling motion, killing the Helms HLB* for this year...."[45] A Richmond NOW member credited the "Hundreds of Virginians" who lobbied hard against the Human Life Amendment bill, and called its defeat a "failure of the new right to impose its social agenda upon the country...." The fight, she believed, was far from over.[46]

Restricting state and/or federal funding for abortion and introducing antiabortion amendments were only two planks in the conservative antiabortion platform. The New Right's rise to dominance heralded a push for all kinds of legislation designed to make abortion as inaccessible as possible. From designing health and medical codes to hamstringing clinics and the practitioners who worked in them, to imposing waiting periods, mandatory counseling, and parental notification laws, antiabortion legislators worked with antiabortion activists to create systems that would limit access in all but the most progressive states.

Virginia was no different. As early as 1979, Planned Parenthood determined that its priorities for the General Assembly session would be to stop any sort of parental or spousal consent for abortion, as well as to continue to secure Medicaid funding, support sex education, and oppose the General Assembly call for a constitutional amendment.[47] When the first consent bill came up that year, VOKAL and the ACLU, along with Planned Parenthood, mobilized fifteen member groups to oppose the bill. Denyes traveled to Richmond to speak against the bill, along with twelve people representing Planned Parenthood, Richmond Medical Center for Women, and Eastern Virginia Medical School; a professor of obstetrics and gynecology at Medical College of Virginia; Virginia Public Health Association, and others. According to Denyes, only four testified for the bill, including a physician who "made general charges against the current inadequacies in counseling," an activist with no documentation to support her claims, and a woman who said she was glad her adopted child had "not been killed by her mother." The house committee hearing the testimony voted to kill the bill fifteen to three, which Denyes called a "tremendous victory." On the Senate side, twenty Richmond VOKAL members went to lobby, and succeeded in getting it killed there, too.[48] This would lead to several years of inactivity on the issue.[49]

When activists looked at the decade following the *Roe* decision in Virginia, they could point to two victories—one in securing a modicum of state funding for abortion in limited cases; another, in halting the one legislative attempt to restrict abortion. In addition, they could claim some victory in the federal district court which struck down a law requiring women to go to hospitals for second-trimester abortions as well as a twenty-four-hour waiting period and a requirement for doctors to provide counseling on other options. However, only seven women in Virginia had successfully used the public funding for abortions by 1982, so the Medicaid restrictions were working. And pro-choice activists knew that they faced an increasingly difficult situation as New Right politicians fought in the states to secure serious abortion restrictions.[50]

As the New Right gathered steam across the country, feminists in Virginia would have a harder time trying to stave off antiabortion legislation. Jerry Falwell's Moral Majority had been joined by Pat Robertson's Christian Coalition. Each waged war on feminism and abortion from opposite sides of Virginia. In 1985, reproductive rights supporters knew parental consent would emerge again, this time in the form of H.B. 1364, which did pass. The Association of Virginia Planned Parenthood Affiliates issued a special alert and asked supporters to lobby vigorously against passage, noting talking points about teens seeking illegal abortions, potential suicide, the inappropriateness of judicial bypass, and the precedent in Virginia statutes allowing teens to secure other kinds of medical treatment without parental consent. NOW and VWPC fought against its passage, Virginia LWV President Shirley Taft also issued a press release condemning any antiabortion legislation.[51] In fact, the AAUW, Planned Parenthood, LWVVA, RCAR, Virginia NOW, VOICE, VOKAL, VWPC, Virginia Commission on the Status of Women, and the YWCA went on record together to oppose H.B. 1364.[52]

Activists ramped up efforts to stop the bill's adoption by the Senate when they faced defeat in the House. Edie Harrison, VOICE founder, used her position as former House member and candidate for U.S. Senate to write to senators. She noted, "Very few adults let alone children know how to petition a court...." She also called a bill that treated teens under eighteen as not mature enough to make a decision about their own bodies but capable of raising a child "The saddest irony...."[53] Harrison teamed up with another former delegate and senator from 1982–84, Evelyn Hailey. In a press conference, the two insisted that studies showed 76 percent of teens consulted with their parents about abortion already, and they highlighted the high-school dropout rates of pregnant teens. Turning the tables on antiabortionists who talked about protecting children, the two concluded, "It is time for responsible adults to let their legislators know that they demand protection for the rights of these young women to a safe and legal abortion without state interference."[54] VOKAL joined the two in support, affirming the "mature enough for motherhood/not for abortion" argument and positing the legislation might worsen parental relations in an already bad situation, claiming, "The government can never hope to create a parent-daughter relationship by the mere wave of a legislative wand."[55] Taft reported to Leaguers on the bill's passage, seventy-eight to twenty-one, and asked every member to not only write senators, but also to show up for the hearing.[56]

Many reproductive rights activists swung into action to halt the bill. Former delegate and senator Evelyn Hailey testified for the LWV, arguing that "currently prevailing political pressures should not counteract the Constitution's concern for limited government and individual liberty."[57] NOW's assistant coordinator, Gretchen Roberts, lobbied at the capitol, sent alerts to members asking them to lobby, and coordinated a campaign in which all legislators received a valentine with the message "keep your valentine safe from illegal abortionists...." Emily McCoy and other NOW volunteers kept phone banks going to encourage members to lobby legislators.[58]

Antiabortion activists were out in force as well. Registered nurse and self-described grandmotherly looking Ruth Rouse was at the General Assembly as a pro-choice activist. She claimed: "H.B. 1364 should be recognized as antiabortionist legislation wrapped in the religious morality of a minority group. The anti-abortionist [sic] are once again turning out busloads of Bible toting people into the VA. General Assembly." She was particularly disturbed about students from Christian schools coming en masse on their school buses to confront the legislature "complete in cheerleading uniforms and team jackets."

After being called a "Baby Murderer" by a preteen boy, likely, she thought, because she failed to sport an antiabortion button, she was angry. She asked what court provisions the bill provided so that it could make medical decisions, and pointed out that the men who impregnated women were not addressed in the bill at all.[59]

The Senate passed its own version of parental consent. In it, they substituted a doctor's consent for judicial. When its bill went back to the House for consideration, Joan Munford, who had been elected as part of the pro-ERA push, was one delegate who had taken pro-choice advocates' arguments seriously. According to the *Virginian-Pilot,* Munford said, "Young people view the courts as a place you go for punishment," and the courts had no special medical ability to determine eligibility. Ultimately, the Senate and House could not compromise on a joint bill, and so it did not pass.[60]

The upshot of this close call was that pro-choice advocates came closer together to formalize the Virginia Pro-Choice Alliance. This alliance included Planned Parenthood, the AAUW, the ACLU, RCAR, VOICE, VWPC, NOW, Physicians for Choice, VOKAL, and the YWCA-Richmond. In a press release, the organization announced: "We commend those legislators who had the courage to stand up to the intimidation of those who support the assault on teenage girls through the defeated Parental Consent bill." Members planned for "public education and action" events. It also invited others to take part in the coalition, claiming, "No longer will a small but vocal minority will be able to influence legislation beyond their numerical strength."[61]

Ultimately, the League of Women Voters would join, too, although with reservations. While one board member believed the issue would be controversial, another said that younger people were moving to NOW because of the league's more muted stand on reproductive rights. The group voted nine to five to become a member of the group. Taft said she "felt the other organizations involved are reliable ... and the guidelines adopted by the alliance are very League like." But she also made clear that the League would decide whether and when to "sign on to any specific statement or action."[62]

Into the 1990s

Until 1989, members of these organizations and others successfully worked with pro-choice legislators to kill all new antiabortion legislation.[63] But 1989 was a turning point in the country, signaling a new onslaught of antiabortion initiatives. For it was in this year the Supreme Court determined in *Webster v. Reproductive Health Services* that states could prohibit the use of public funding, employees, and facilities to perform abortions in any cases not related to saving the life of the mother; could prohibit abortion counseling; and could require doctors to do fetal viability tests at twenty weeks. In this ruling, the Supreme Court opened the door to allow for more restrictions on abortion. At this point, nine states had parental notification laws, and six had "trigger laws," which would automatically make abortion illegal should *Roe* be overturned.[64] The gates were now opened for more legislation, like parental consent laws, to be tested, and indeed, these challenges would also move through the court system.

Across the country, antiabortion advocates were making headway. In some cases, they were successful in prompting legislators to focus on fetal rights instead of the pregnant woman's rights.[65] Often, antiabortion activists cast abortion seekers as careless and morally lacking.[66]

Some contemporary scholars faulted reproductive rights activists for failing to see the emergence of the New Right as a threat until regulatory laws were passed and moving through court.[67] Political scientist Rosalind Petchesky essentially accused feminists of leaving the door open for regulation by focusing on privacy as a key issue. In addition, she claimed that naive feminists placed too much stock in government institutions to protect the right to abortion.[68]

But these scholars' critiques were somewhat unfounded, at least in the case of Virginia's activists. Not only had feminists in Virginia been actively fighting against restrictive legislation, but they also renewed their battle with more vigor after *Webster*. Feminists feared anti-choice activists would use *Webster* to launch a renewed assault on women. Georgia Fuller, Virginia NOW state coordinator, said "The patient is alive, but the vultures are circling." She took a different tack in 1989 when she exhorted her members to write many letters, support pro-choice politicians, and attend a national march for women's lives in D.C. in the fall. Ironically, perhaps, Fuller played into the concerns raised by Petchesky about focusing on the issue of privacy as key. Perhaps she knew her audience in the conservative commonwealth would find her message more palatable: "Thanks to years of hard work by Virginia feminists our state is one of the better states for affordable and accessible reproductive health care. In a state with a long tradition of conservatism, many public officials realize that we have the conservative side. *What could be more basic, private, and conservative than the right to make your own medical decisions?*"[69]

Around Virginia, pro-choice activists reacted against what they saw as a dangerous backsliding on the part of the Supreme Court. Many joined feminist organizations. Over 75 women attended a monthly Tidewater NOW meeting, triple the usual number. Statewide, NOW membership went from a historic low of 3,150 before the decision to over 6,570 by April of 1990, with some chapters reporting a doubling in membership. Membership dues filled NOW's treasury, which had amassed twenty thousand dollars by this time The Norfolk chapter of the VWPC, which boasted several hundred members already, increased threefold in the weeks following the decision. A member of the Norfolk YWCA board put it this way to a reporter: "We've been quiet too long. We've been the sleeping bear."[70] Megan McKewan of Roanoke's Planned Parenthood concurred, telling her local paper the decision would cause an increase in lobbying efforts. And a VOKAL representative told a Richmond reporter that the organization would be "working hard in the coming state elections to ensure that a woman's right to decide her own future would not be trampled upon by the state."[71]

The Virginia Pro-Choice Alliance brought in the long-time leader of the National Council for Negro Women, Dorothy Height, to speak at a press conference. Height began: "I am here today to speak for the strong support that exists among African American women for reproductive choice." Talking about African American women's historic demand to control their own bodies, she represented four million women in her organization who would continue to fight for reproductive rights.[72] This press conference may have been part of the calculated effort during a massive electoral campaign in which feminists in Virginia fought hard for choice.

The 1989 electoral campaign would be the first since the ERA battles in which many feminists would throw support squarely and openly behind a single issue. In reality, this campaign began before *Webster*. As early as April 1989, NOW-PAC began fundraising for the election, reminding members their prior political contributions helped Emilie Miller of Fairfax and Ted Harrison of Lynchburg defeat anti-ERA candidates, and assisted in getting pro-ERA candidate Yvonne Harrison elected in Norfolk. A fundraising letter explained: "We use the political organizing tools we learned so well and used so effectively in the past for women...."[73] *Webster* simply fueled the fire.

Abortion politics played a large role in the commonwealth's statewide electoral races that year. Republican J. Marshall Coleman, described by a *Virginian-Pilot* reporter as having a "hard-line stance" against abortion, faced off against Douglas Wilder, whom NOW national president Molly Yard called "wimpy" on abortion for changing his position on parental consent.[74] NOW-PAC supported pro-choice candidates throughout the state, along with Wilder, and appealed for matching funding to National NOW.[75] NOW members held rallies across the state and distributed literature, and worked with NARAL to promote a Freedom Caravan for choice. At designated stops, the caravan showed the movie *Abortion: For Survival*. This thirty-minute documentary, produced in 1989 by Funds for a Feminist Majority and aired by pro-choice Ted Turner on his TBS networks, was designed to be an answer to the antiabortion's *Silent Scream* film of 1985. In addition to casting the antiabortionists as extremists, it defined abortion as a public health issue.[76] NOW and NARAL volunteers staffed phone banks in Rockingham County, Tidewater, and Fairfax, among other places. NOW members demonstrated against an antiabortion congressman in Richmond and held a rally in Charlottesville.[77] In Alexandria, NOW phone bank volunteers made over two thousand pro-choice calls, netted 106 volunteers to work for the cause, and spent eight thousand dollars total on their campaign efforts. And Virginia Republicans for Choice issued a press statement supporting Wilder, Don Beyer for lieutenant governor, and attorney general candidate Mary Sue Terry, as well as local pro-choice candidates.[78]

The most ambitious public relations event of the election may well have been the "Ruler campaign." NOW, Planned Parenthood, and VOKAL/NARAL teamed up to get pro-choice supporters to sign rulers, a symbol of measurements for choice, to legislators and candidates. Planned Parenthood volunteers got thousands of pro-choice voters to sign these rulers at the Virginia State Fair. In addition, ten thousand Virginia households, many of whom were not on membership lists of the sponsoring organizations, received mailings. Wilder campaign operatives were pleased with the number they received, according to Georgia Fuller. NOW was particularly proud of the coordinated effort, she said, because in other states on the national stage pro-choice "allies" did not always work as well together.[79]

But pro-choice supporters also threw their weight in another important way. According to Fuller, when Wilder began running pro-choice ads and came from behind to threaten Coleman, Coleman attacked Wilder on an old vote against a spousal abuse bill. At this point, NOW came to Wilder's defense openly and strongly. Fuller issued a release calling Wilder an "8" and Coleman a "−3" on women's issues. Fuller contended, "We appreciate Coleman's sudden concern for women, but he would do better to change his own platform than muck around in Doug Wilder's past." Fuller explained this release helped Wilder at a time he was under threat because his campaign asked for NOW's open support at this point. She noted that, because he was so much more positive for women, NOW was willing to come out strongly just before the election to make it clear that he was their candidate.[80]

Feminists claimed a victory across the board. NOW board members were elated they were able to change public opinion about lieutenant governor candidate Eddy Dalton, whom they successfully exposed as anti-choice despite 65 percent of the electorate thinking otherwise. Don Beyer was elected instead, and Mary Sue Terry, Virginia's first female attorney general, was reelected. Doug Wilder, who won with a margin of just over sixty-five hundred votes, became the commonwealth's first African American governor. In Northern Virginia, pro-choice candidates Leslie Byrne and Bernie Cohen, both Democrats, gained big victories. In a "State of the State Address," State Coordinator Georgia Fuller claimed the victory as one of two major accomplishments of the organization. NOW's electoral activities also netted them 148 new members and over $4,550 from fundraising appeals, although they spent over $4,500 on election literature alone.[81]

A slate of pro-choice candidates and a spate of friendly legislators in the General Assembly guaranteed against the onslaught of legislation regulating abortion, however. Perhaps they were emboldened by the Webster decision; possibly they sought retaliation for political losses, as had been the case with ERA. Maybe legislators reacted to a poll conducted in Virginia suggesting two-thirds of voters favored notification if only one parent had to be told.[82]

Lobbying in the post-*Webster* era was intense. Planned Parenthood got very serious when the board hired Karen Raschke, a seasoned veteran lobbyist who was, in her own words, "more vocal" and who could "be more of a presence" than her predecessor. She remembered that, from 1990 to 1997, "parental notification for minor's abortion became my work." She remembered, too, having to deal with different lobbying allies once she became the legislative coordinator of Planned Parenthood. Raschke worked in a sometimes conflicted manner with members of organizations like NARAL and NOW, most of whom were volunteers. Raschke recalled: "I was interested in quiet persuasion, realizing that you needed what I called the screamers, but not appreciating them in any group I was associated with."⁸³ So, in the post-*Webster* era, Planned Parenthood worked in an uneasy alliance with NOW and NARAL/VOKAL activists, as well as the entire Pro-Choice Alliance, to try to stop antiabortion laws.

Although five bills went down to defeat in 1990, the parental notification bill was more difficult to kill.⁸⁴ Virginia Planned Parenthood printed and circulated a pamphlet explaining why notification would not lower teen pregnancy rates or protect teen health or family relations. RCAR legislative director Patricia Harding-Clark called on members to lobby hard, especially to committee members, using their "RELIGIOUS principles" to oppose notification. She asked all members to contact at least two senators "IMMEDIATELY" and included RCAR postcards for members to direct to Wilder. Jane Pilley, AAUW's legislative coordinator, also lobbied on behalf of her organization, and many women attended the first Pro-Choice Coalition Lobby Day, representing NOW, Planned Parenthood, NARAL, VOKAL, RCAR, AAUW, and YWCA. NOW also sponsored a signature ad in the *Richmond Times-Dispatch* that included 350 names of pro-choice supporters. Raschke; Judy Castleman, head of the Virginia Nurses' Association; and Edie Harrison, representing VOICE and the Pro-Choice Alliance, testified at the committee hearing. Their efforts worked, and the committee killed the bill.⁸⁵

Perhaps because of their victory, the group developed a "Positive Action Pro-Choice Campaign," which would take a multilayered approach to protecting women's right to abortion. The group, which at this point had formally added the National Council of Negro Women, Catholics for Free Choice, National Council of Jewish Women, and several other organizations, recognized the significance of a large public campaign. The board determined to develop a public information campaign that would include recruitment and petition-signing events; target sympathetic groups which would be likely to vote on pro-choice; and develop a stronger constituent lobbying program. Leaders would identify and call on people with "special influence with the legislators" to fight on its behalf; and promote pro-choice in the media. They reframed parental notification/consent bills as "Teen Endangerment."⁸⁶

In addition, the Pro-Choice Alliance targeted four Virginia Senate districts where they would attempt to get pro-choice candidates elected. NOW also worked through its PAC to support friendly candidates, naming a goal of thirty thousand dollars in its "Dollar$ for Virginia" fundraising campaign. Locally, Northern Virginia NOW members worked a phone bank and distributed literature with other members of the Pro-Choice Alliance to get Jim Moran,

NOW member and Democratic candidate for Congress, elected. In fact, Frances Storey, writing as chair of the NOW PAC, told members they would need to assist the alliance in the face of "far more aggressive" opponents in the General Assembly, and fundraising would assist in paying the few full-time staff members and media campaigns. As part of the campaign, pro-choice activists participated in "Freedom Summer," in which local supporters of choice held events to recruit like-minded feminists and press coverage of the issue. The Positive Action Campaign held events across the state that summer.[87]

In the midst of this intense campaign, the Supreme Court dealt feminists another blow, as they upheld states' rights to parental notification and other restrictions in *Hodgson v. Minnesota* and *Ohio v. Akron Center for Reproductive Health*. In September, the General Assembly moved forward with anti-abortion legislation. In response to a Senate subcommittee's determination to study the parental notification act which had not passed the previous year, co-legislative chairs Denise Lee and Emily McCoy sent an alert to NOW members, asking them to write and visit. In addition, they maintained, "We need to pack this meeting. We need 100 people there! We can be certain our opponents are organizing furiously." And NOW members showed up—from Lynchburg, Amherst, Roanoke, Hampton, Northern Virginia, and Norfolk, in numbers "several times stronger than the antis," according to Lee and McCoy, so much so that the antiabortion lobbyists asked for a continuation of the meeting at a later date.[88] NOW co-coordinators Frances Storey and Joan Taylor composed a letter to Douglas Wilder at this time, informing him the "6500 members" of the organization "rated reproductive rights their Number 1 concern" in a recent poll. Their letter warned him: "As you know, they voted for you based on your PRO-CHOICE platform. In Virginia the *majority* of those are registered to vote and do vote *are women*. Just as you can't be 'a little bit pregnant,' you can't be a little bit PRO-CHOICE in Virginia and survive politically."[89]

As they moved into the 1991 General Assembly session, pro-choice feminists were more active than ever before. They helped secure a victory for Jim Moran, and they had a new poll to use, conducted by Virginia Commonwealth University, which showed that at this point 58 percent of the Virginia population opposed parental notification. Perhaps the education campaigns were indeed making headway in the commonwealth. Activists followed up this good news with a two-day event celebrating the eighteenth anniversary of *Roe v. Wade*. Pro-choice lobbyists descended on the capitol, with NOW directing activities on the first day, following up visitations with a legislative reception at the Valentine Museum, and Raschke and her Planned Parenthood staff organizing the second day, which concluded with an evening vigil at the capitol building.[90] For the first time in ten years, both the House and the Senate rejected all bills targeted at restricting access to abortion.[91]

Pro-choice activists' victory was not long-lasting, however. Some losses in the Senate created a hostile climate, with eight senators now needed to block antiabortion legislation, according to McCoy, and only six supporters left on the Senate Health and Education Committee.[92] When a new parental consent bill was introduced and passed in the House, friendly senators attempted to stave off the legislation. Freshman African American Senator Louise Lucas called parental consent "legislation without compassion." Lucas reiterated many talking points feminists had used for years—that teens couldn't manage a complex legal system for judicial bypass, and that they did not have the resources to travel outside the state to obtain an abortion. She concluded, "No young woman in Virginia should have to lose her life to teach these hard lessons." Dick Saslaw was quoted by a Northern Virginia paper as condemning his Senate colleagues: "The thing I find most nauseating about this bill is that it's the men who introduce it every year, and it's the men who vote for it. . . ." The final attempt to kill the bill came when Don Beyer tried to get it dismissed from the floor as being "non-germane," that is, addressing more than one issue, and he failed. The Senate passed the House notification bill, and it went to Wilder for his signature.[93]

Activists and pro-choice legislators reacted with outrage. Denise Lee, the current NOW state coordinator, said in a press release that parental notification was dangerous: "It could cost you your daughter's life. . . ." Virginia NOW declared a state of emergency, pledging much of its PAC treasury to get out its pro-choice message, urging high-school and college students to write, and using phone banks to galvanize voters to contact Wilder. McCoy reported to NOW members that many pro-choice legislators visited Wilder, and urged members to write and call Wilder and to get ten of their friends to do the same.[94] RCAR provided "Religiously Pro-Choice Postcards" to mail to Wilder. Grace Sparks, director of the Virginia League of Planned Parenthood (VLPP), sent members an alert asking them to write to Wilder as well, and invited all concerned to join Raschke for a letter-writing gathering at Richmond Planned Parenthood. VLPP Executive Board members were also directed to call the governor.[95]

Activists throughout the state worked to make their pro-choice sentiments clear to Wilder. Arlington NOW sent 850 postcards to members within a day of the bill passing, asking people to immediately contact the governor. Fredericksburg pro-choice activists wrote letters and kept a vigil for choice going in the city. Richmond Planned Parenthood supporters set up a table at Virginia Commonwealth University and worked nine-to-five for an entire week securing almost 1,000 signatures for a petition and letters to the governor. The response was so positive, the group decided to start a pro-choice group on campus. Carolyn Corry, a Richmond pro-choice activist, went to the Flood Zone, a nightclub popular with University of Richmond and Virginia Commonwealth University students, and secured several hundred signatures, including from the "House of Freaks" band members playing that evening.[96] When Wilder's office said 65 percent of contacts came from anti-choice activists, pro-choice supporters rallied and got another 19,000 signatures on petitions.[97]

Wilder did not sign the bill, but neither did he veto it. Instead, he sent it back to the General Assembly unsigned. In a letter issued by his office, Wilder said that he supported parental notification, but the bill was "confusing" and "lacking in direction." Prior to sending it back to the General Assembly, he gave a nineteen-point directive explaining the changes the General Assembly could make to secure his signature. He was so clear on how to create a bill he would sign that NOW Executive Council members debated in a meeting whether to publicly thank him for supporting choice (they resolved to do so). Wilder also made no promise that he would sign a bill after the next General Assembly session. Choice was safe for another year—but Raschke told a reporter it was a temporary victory: "We've been trying to protect young women one year at a time."[98] Raschke credited lobbyists with staving off the more conservative tendencies among legislators.[99]

Across the country, pro-choice activists were waging a losing battle. After the close call in Virginia, the Supreme Court upheld the legality of parental consent laws and mandatory waiting periods in *Planned Parenthood v. Casey* (1992). Prior to the ruling, nineteen states had notification/consent laws in place, which included only Alabama, Arkansas, Louisiana, Missouri, West Virginia, and South Carolina in the conservative Sunbelt. Within two years, thirty-four states had either notification or consent laws, with Tennessee, Georgia, and Mississippi joining the other southern states. By this point, only Oregon, Connecticut, New Jersey, and North Carolina had no restrictions on abortions. Virginia had an informed consent law requiring women seeking abortions to sign a detailed form explaining risks. Virginia also had in place a ban on public funds for any abortions not threatening the life of the mother or caused by rape or incest.[100]

Virginia's choice advocates knew what *Planned Parenthood v. Casey* would mean for the commonwealth. Raschke charged that upholding the law "will allow state legislatures to declare 'open hunting season' on women's lives." NOW opined that State Coordinator Denise Lee called the decision a "frontal attack on the rights of women." Blaming the newly nominated Supreme Court Justice Clarence Thomas, and Virginia Senator Chuck Robb for confirming him, she said, "At both the state and federal levels, Virginia voters are actively addressing the appalling lack of leadership truly representative of their views. We are going to respond, in no uncertain terms." Lee also posited a sort of quid pro quo, reminding Wilder of the support he gained from Virginia feminists: "It is apparent that Governor Wilder does not support any legislative measure lending itself to dangerous trends toward the reinstitutionalization of slavery for women. We must continue to insure election of political representatives who will work to defeat any legislation which embodies the intrinsic values of a new Jefferson Davis."[101] Lee's hearkening back to the days of the Confederacy may have been a bit overblown, but perhaps it reflected her understanding of the intersectionality of race and gender, which, given her identity and history, she recognized.

Virginia feminists had continued to lobby the General Assembly to protect abortion rights, but the election of George Allen, conservative Republican, to the governorship of Virginia in 1994 spelled the beginning of the end of pro-choice activists' success. Allen supported a twenty-four-hour waiting period and parental notification. His "point person" on the abortion issue, according to the *Washington Post,* was long-time abortion foe Anne Kincaid, a born-again Christian who had secured an abortion, regretted it, and became a leading activist in the Virginia antiabortion movement.[102]

In his first year as governor, Allen introduced his own parental notification legislation to the legislature. When the General Assembly passed the bill, Allen sent it back with amendments making the legislation more restrictive, and forced a veto when legislators could not compromise on the language. The following year, Senator Houck cast a deciding no vote that killed a notification bill in the Senate Health and Education Committee, explaining that having a teen daughter himself, he could understand the risks and ramifications of forcing teens to notify parents. The same committee killed a bill in 1996 as well, perhaps as a result of hard lobbying from Planned Parenthood that circulated

"Protect Our Daughters" fact sheets about the failures of parental notification/consent in other states. The work of pro-choice legislators like Delegate Vivian Watts and Senator Patsy Ticer, who spoke out against notification on the twenty-third anniversary of *Roe,* most likely contributed to lobbyists' victory as well.[103]

Despite the efforts of reproductive rights activists to the contrary, the Virginia General Assembly passed and Allen signed an extremely restrictive abortion bill in 1997, requiring not only that parents be notified within twenty-four hours of a minor seeking an abortion, but also stating that the parent must give notarized consent before the abortion could be performed. Even if a woman could obtain judicial bypass, the judge must notify parents unless evidence exists to support the contention that a parent is abusive or neglectful. That year, the General Assembly passed what NARAL termed a "biased counseling law," mandating that a provider must give patients materials detailing all agencies and organizations available to assist during pregnancy and enacting a twenty-four-hour waiting period. Two years later, the General Assembly enacted a gag rule banning any agency receiving state funding from providing abortion services or counseling.[104]

Laws in effect in 2016 include the requirement of women under eighteen to provide notarized parental or court consent for an abortion, bans on Medicaid-funded services even related to abortion as well as abortion services, the requirement of doctors to provide written materials about fetal development to all women seeking abortion, and a mandatory ultrasound twenty-four hours before an abortion, as well as a ban on abortion coverage in insurance sold through the insurance marketplace of Virginia.[105] However, in the wake of the 2016 Supreme Court decision in *Whole Woman v. Hellerstedt,* which overturned TRAP (Targeted Regulations for Abortion Providers) laws, the Virginia Board of Health lifted all restrictions requiring the fourteen abortion providers in Virginia to abide by the same regulations as outpatient surgical centers. This it did with the blessing of Democratic Governor Terry McAuliffe, who said in a statement quoted by the *Washington Post,* "This vote demonstrates to the rest of the United States and the world that Virginia is a community where people can live, find employment, and start a family without politicians interfering with decisions that should be made by women and their doctors."[106] Perhaps, this signals a new chapter in the battle for reproductive justice in Virginia. Only time will tell.

Actions on the Ground

While some pro-choice activism focused on laws, other initiatives were part of a nationwide grassroots movement in communities. From participating in demonstrations, to organizing educational events, and even to defending clinics against the harrowing and often violent incursions of antiabortion protestors, women in Virginia worked to maintain public support for abortion rights and to keep abortion available for women of the commonwealth, just as others did across the country. Coupled with lobbying efforts in the General Assembly, these actions demonstrated just how far feminists were willing to go to support choice, and often provided critical assistance to medical practitioners and patients.

Demonstrations were an important way for feminist activists to show support for reproductive rights. They differed from defense, in that these were not intended to protect clinics against antiabortion picketers. Beginning in the 1970s, Virginia women took part in coordinated national efforts. Because of their relatively close proximity to Washington, D.C., feminists could more easily march for reproductive justice.[107] For the national NOW-organized March for Women's Lives in 1986, NOW members from Roanoke, Charlottesville, Fredericksburg, and Alexandria attended the march. Arlington members staked out metro stops to leaflet, and Richmond chartered a bus to the march. Betsy Brinson urged Richmond YWCA members to attend—as the YWCA was a sponsor—and 150 pro-choice supporters, including Tidewater and Peninsula NOW members, chartered a bus from Norfolk. The *Norfolk Journal and Guide* covered the trip, observing that the group may have been dedicated, but was not very diverse, noting that Joseph Millner "was among the few men and few blacks who attended the rally."[108] Students from Sweetbriar, Mary Washington College, and Virginia Commonwealth University went. Arlington NOW members secured pledges via a phone bank to help pay for carpools from around Virginia, and Roanoke's Planned Parenthood chartered buses which transported activists from the extended area, including Clifton Forge and Lexington.[109] Activists continued to march in D.C. well into the twenty-first century, representing NOW, Planned Parenthood, NARAL, and League of Women Voters members, to name a few.[110]

Supporters of reproductive rights also worked to produce local demonstrations in their hometowns. From Richmond, to Tidewater, to Fredericksburg, pro-choice advocates picketed and publicly demonstrated their support. Sometimes rallies turned violent, as in the case of a Prince William NOW-speakout and viewing of *Silent No More*. Based on the case of Paul Galvin, a pro-choice supporter who members believed was unjustly accused of physically harassing an antiabortion activist, the chapter asked NOW's national board to "develop and adopt a policy on the legal defense and support of NOW members involved in NOW reproductive rights actions."[111] In 1991, the Montgomery County NOW, League of Women Voters, and local Planned Parenthood supporters, as well as other pro-choice activists, put a float in the Blacksburg Fourth of July Parade that denounced the Supreme Court ruling allowing for "gag rules" to stand (laws which allowed states and ultimately the federal government to restrict doctors from discussion of abortion in clinics receiving public funding). Walkers handed out informational flyers with contact information for legislators. The float won first prize.[112] Blacksburg, and Montgomery County more broadly, have been known as a progressive spot in a traditionally conservative part of Virginia, probably resulting from the presence of two large universities in the area. The float most likely had a fairly sympathetic reception in the city.

Many activists planned local public responses to the *Casey* decision. Fifty pro-choice supporters in Lynchburg demonstrated for reproductive rights and made front-page news in the local paper, and NOW activists held speakouts and press conferences in Richmond, Fredericksburg, and Northern Virginia. In a move to highlight Virginia's storied history in its support of the Bill of Rights, Planned Parenthood supporters in Richmond raised funds and signatures for an ad to run in the *Free Press* and *Style Weekly*. The ad pictured George Washington, James Madison, Thomas Jefferson, and James Monroe across the top and featured the tag line "Virginians have always stood up for individual freedoms."[113] Virginia feminists would continue to hold actions for choice throughout the twenty-first century, whether or not the General Assembly paid attention.[114]

By organizing the grassroots and participating in large national rallies and demonstrations, feminists for reproductive rights made their presence known in the commonwealth and in the nation's capital. Their presence challenged stereotypes of the South as conservative, even if the General Assembly of Virginia was rolling back the gains made by *Roe*—much like almost all other states had already done by 1997. Moreover, these feminists chose to take their case to the public by showing their own strength in numbers, to counteract the antiabortion campaign, which often appeared more powerful than it was because of the intensity of its members. Feminist activists publicized their willingness to march and demonstrate for choice, even as they lobbied to safeguard abortion from hostile legislators.

These peaceful demonstrations coincided not just with the lobbying efforts, but also with educational campaigns to counter the claims of antiabortionists. The anti-choice side typically relied on emotional appeals to try to reframe abortion to be about "killing babies" rather than women's right to their own bodies. Denyes participated in a midday television program called *Right to Choose*, along with a Planned Parenthood representative and a psychologist. Denyes reported, "Due to the pro-choice tone of the show, irate anti-abortionists besieged the station with hate calls and got [the host] suspended from her own show for the remainder of that series." Although the show was not focused on abortion but pro-choice issues, Denyes noted that the show "conceded to Anti-choice demands" and planned to air a "right-to-life" show. She asked allies to write to the station to support the host.[115]

In addition to television, reproductive rights activists used other venues to educate the public about the pro-choice position. VOKAL members pronounced their appearance at the Arlington County Fair a success, noting, "For those surprised persons who only associate county fairs with home-baked goods and 4-H, seeing their state pro-choice organization present was a revelation worthy of a second glance, and quite often the beginning of a real dialogue with much interest expressed." When Unitarian Universalist Minister David McPherson gave a sermon targeting Jerry Falwell and his anti-choice antics, Richmond NOW chapter members were there after the sermon to meet congregants with newsletters and flyers, and offered to go to other organizations and churches to do the same. Acting in her position as NOW state coordinator in 1985, Emily McCoy discussed holding speakouts around Mother's Day, explaining to a reporter, "One of the things the anti-abortionists have done is completely remove women from the discussion.... It's women's lives that's an issue here."[116]

When feminists learned of Crisis Pregnancy Clinics (CPCs) in their area, they educated their communities about the "false advertising" related to these centers. Disguised as reproductive health clinics, these centers received funding from anti-choice organizations and sought to persuade women to carry fetuses to term. Charlottesville VOKAL ran ads in the paper explaining what the local CPC was doing, and members engaged in letter-writing campaigns alerting the media, sorority chapters, and the public to what they believed were deceptive practices. The Northern Virginia Pro-Choice Alliance protested the Tysons Corner "A Woman's Choice" Center after Planned Parenthood and NOW got complaints about the deceptive practices there. Their methods of choice included a picket and a letter-writing campaign to legislators, but they also planned an education campaign for local high schools and colleges. As spokeswoman Jean Marshall Crawford (formerly Clarke) said, "Women who have visited these centers are justifiably angry...."[117]

These centers continued to pose problems for reproductive rights activists, who continued to respond. In the last decade of the twentieth century, during a Pro-Choice Alliance meeting, Arlington NOW reported that it was discussing the problem, thinking that perhaps they needed to write to the attorney general, lobbying for prohibiting anyone but medical professionals from giving pregnancy tests, and passing out flyers about and picketing these centers.[118] This work continued and came to a head in 2013, when NARAL activists conducted an investigation of these pregnancy centers, which receive state funding through the "Choose Life" license plates. The undercover investigation revealed numerous inaccuracies cited by "counselors" at the centers, including that condoms could not protect against STDs, as well as evasive answers when asked point-blank about abortion as an option for an unwanted pregnancy. Using modern technology, NARAL blasted this information, which included details of the investigation, on its website, and promoted videos on YouTube. The organization directly blamed gubernatorial candidate Ken Cuccinelli for helping these centers receive funding from the state.[119] He was not elected governor.

Ultimately, reproductive rights activists wanted to protect women. This was made clear in the way they stood by clinics and the women who sought abortions there. The act of protecting a clinic, or "counterpicketing," was a serious business. Many antiabortion activists who picketed clinics became increasingly aggressive in the 1980s and 1990s, especially after Randall Terry formed the antiabortion group Operation Rescue in 1986. Operation Rescue saw abortion as murder and vowed to stop it in any way possible. When reproductive rights activists counterpicketed, they never knew what they would face. As antiabortion violence increased in the 1980s, these pro-choice activists put their own lives on the line to protect vulnerable women.

In Virginia, as in the rest of the nation, many abortion providers faced hostility as soon as they opened a clinic. Hillcrest Clinic in Norfolk was picketed by 350 antiabortion protesters in an incident the first year it was open, and these protesters harassed seven women into cancelling appointments. VOKAL swung into action, planning "a coordinated effort to keep Hillcrest Clinic open." One hundred members of Virginia Beach NOW, and other supporters, counterpicketed on the first anniversary of the clinic's opening to counteract the antis who showed up. One pro-choice activist got into a verbal conflagration with an anti-choice picketer.[120]

Tidewater activists were thrown into a defensive position rather quickly. In a letter to a news station, Denyes explained, "The Hillcrest Clinic has unfortunately become a symbol for those who wish to destroy the now legal alternative to criminal abortion." Representing Tidewater Freedom of Choice Coalition at the time, Denyes said its members were not engaging in verbal combat. Instead: "Our members prefer to work quietly rather than exchanging emotional accusations with picketers." When she discussed challenges with the national task force coordinator of NOW, Denyes noted, "The Right to Life people have the money." She also explained that Tidewater pro-choice activists were "not [as] demonstrative."[121]

Norfolk, Richmond, Charlottesville, Northern Virginia—all of these areas saw intense antiabortion activity at local clinics, and in every case, feminist activists stepped forward to defend these clinics and the women who used them. In 1977, the Northern Virginia Women's Medical Clinic in Fairfax suffered two serious breaches when antiabortion activists stormed the place, took over the phones, harassed clients, and destroyed property. They also photographed registered patients, pushed patients and staff to the floor, and injured a clinic worker, as well as threatening arson.[122]

The clinic workers asked the ACLU for assistance in getting an injunction against these protesters, as their claim to be exercising free speech had moved clearly into criminal trespass, even though those arrested were found not guilty by a local court. Betsy Brinson of the SWRP took the case to ACLU lawyers. It was made more complicated by two local judges who ruled that the Virginia statute legalizing abortion was "unconstitutional" and therefore the protestors had a right to "'save innocent life'" through their actions. VOKAL said that the police wouldn't arrest anyone anymore; they were afraid of violating the trespassers' rights because of the judges' prior rulings. The ACLU took the case to federal court in order to determine the constitutionality of the abortion law and to get the attorney general to prosecute trespassers and make police protect the clinic. In the initial phase, judges dismissed a countersuit from trespassers, which in effect upheld the legality of abortion in Virginia. Then, the Eastern District Court issued an injunction against the trespassers, barring entry to the facility or its parking lot, prohibiting them from attempting to restrict clinic traffic, take photographs, verbally abuse patients, or engage in any other destructive behavior. The case received national publicity because, as Brinson said, "The decision is precedent-setting in that it puts anti-abortion trespassers everywhere on notice that the federal courts will not tolerate actions which violate the rights of abortion clinic patients and medical personnel...."[123]

And while the injunction should have set a precedent, by the 1980s, antiabortion tactics had escalated as many activists continued harassing clinic workers, disrupting their business, and even intimidating women into not entering. Many women reported being frightened away from the clinics.[124] In the case of many clinics, women may well have been there to receive other health services like annual exams and birth control pills. So antiabortion activists could well have been stopping women from receiving critical health services. In one case, antiabortion activists purposively stopped the operations of non-abortion-related services. Antiabortion protestors picketed the Fairfax County Hospital, trying to stop people from donating blood to the hospital, for example. Pro-Choice Alliance volunteers held a blood drive in support of the hospital. The blood boycott continued for years, and pro-choice volunteers continued to donate blood through the Fairfax Donor's Center.[125]

Long after the trespass injunction was in place, Georgia Fuller, in her capacity as NOW state coordinator, wrote to the local newspaper: "I watched 500 protestors in Falls Church, many of them from outside the commonwealth, surround and invade the clinic grounds." A police force of only 20 made 238 arrests. She said to NOW members, "We cannot be passive or unconcerned in the face of Operation Rescue. These and related attacks on reproductive freedom are aggressively and persistently about fear, intimidation, and invasion." Fuller spoke about the experience at a national NOW rally against Operation Rescue, as well.[126] When she wrote to the newspaper a second time about a smaller protest at the same clinic, in which 200 people surrounded the clinic and blocked entry before police started making arrests, she said that the police response was inadequate. She called upon authorities to "Stop playing patsy to these fanatics and get tough!" when the protests were not peaceful.[127] In calling upon Virginia feminists to fight outsiders, Fuller called on the same rhetoric used during the ERA campaign—feminism was homegrown and commonwealth-supported, and outsiders threatened the cause. While this rhetoric was not entirely true, it positioned feminists as the Virginia citizens who represented the people of the commonwealth.

Even when they were peaceful, dealing with antiabortion activists could be extremely unnerving. Georgia Fuller recalled: "I was favorably disposed toward anybody who cared enough about their cause to risk arrest. But the more I was out there defending, the more I realized they're not like us." She remembered telling a friend who worked with her at the Quixote Religious Center, "They don't respect people, and they lie." She remembered "the one time my husband almost lost it" on a clinic defense when he was walking the family lab and he heard an anti-choice activist tell her daughter: "See that dog? They feed the aborted babies to that dog." It got to the point where she and her husband would not go to defense actions together, "because we would not want our child orphaned," and they stopped taking their son, who wanted to go, because "the people on the other side of the fence from the clinic heard us call him by name, and started taunting him by name. We never engaged in this kind of behavior. Civil disobedience is supposed to be civil. It's respectful."[128] Richmond NOW described a particularly harrowing event, in which a man, "was practically in the face of one of our members; . . . he screamed at her that she was an abomination before 'their' Lord, a murderer of children, and an instrument of Satan leading others into the sin of murder and that she would pay for her sin. He was shaking with rage. . . ."[129]

These were not isolated incidents. Mary (Denyes) Wazlak ultimately had to step down from actively supporting the group she helped to found because of threats. As VOKAL was just getting organized statewide, she recalled an incident from when she was pregnant with her first child: "I got a phone call from a person I did not know who told me that there would be prayer meetings at their church on a regular basis . . . to pray for the deformity of the fetus I was carrying so that it would [be] forever before me during the course of its life, the result of my sins and representing abortion as an alternative." She remembered that, "In terms [of] what happened to me and the threats that were made, there were threats. There were things that came to me directly and came to me indirectly." While she pulled back from VOKAL by the 1990s partly because her work had demanded so much time as a volunteer, she also noted: "it had gotten personal a couple of times, and I wasn't sure how to protect the kids."[130]

Mary Wazlak's experience shows just how far antiabortion activists were willing to go to intimidate those with whom they disagreed. Wazlak's story is far from unusual. Across the country, the intimidation tactics used by antiabortionists moved from the clinic to the personal lives of clinic workers and others. Workers were threatened by phone, as Wazlak was, and some were followed in non-clinic property. Their efforts took a disastrous toll on pro-choice forces; like Wazlak, many left the movement. Clinics faced an extremely high turnover of workers, and abortion providers closed their doors in the face of continued disruptions.[131]

Feminists' presence at the clinics provided not only a show of strength and support, but also physical protection when needed. When Northern Virginia VOKAL members marched with other pro-choice activists at the Northern Virginia Women's Medical Center in 1980, *VOKAL News* said, "The large turn-out was certainly a tribute to feminist solidarity."[132] Feminist escorts worked to protect women from the antiabortion harassment outside the clinic, providing critical help to vulnerable women. NOVA NOW members served as escorts at a clinic the day before Mother's Day in 1985, when antiabortion activists often came out in full force. They continued this practice "on a rotating basis" after that. The state NOW newspaper reported that northern Virginia NOW chapters had been escorting at Commonwealth Women's Clinic since January 1985.[133] Clinic escorts worked in all major cities in Virginia. In Richmond, the NOW chapter advertised in the LGBT newspaper the *Richmond Pride*, asking volunteers to come out to work each Saturday morning when the antis picketed the Richmond Women's Clinic. In Roanoke, Planned Parenthood clinic director Mary Nottingham was charged with assault and battery and antiabortion picketers were left alone, as they had a permit. Arlington NOW members trained with National NOW's "Project Stand Up for Women" program and learned how to deal with the media and the police.[134]

As escorts continued to protect clinic patients, state leaders went after the antiabortion picketers again, this time in 1989. NOW of Maryland and Virginia teamed up with Planned Parenthood of DC, Commonwealth Women's Clinic, Northern Virginia Medical Center, and Alexandria Women's Health Clinic, Hillcrest, and other clinics in Virginia and Maryland as plaintiffs against Randall Terry and Operation Rescue, seeking a permanent federal injunction against the group to keep them away from clinic property. They were successful, because a U.S. District Court Judge declared that, while barring Operation Rescue volunteers from the property did not limit their free speech, their actions violated the plaintiffs' rights.[135]

Injunctions, however, are only as good as people willing to abide by them and police willing to enforce them. Operation Rescue and other aggressive antiabortion picketers continued their work, so escorts continued their efforts as well. In Richmond, about 140 trained volunteers agreed to defend the local clinic, where Operation Rescue had announced a major offensive. These volunteers had gone through advanced training with the Washington Area Clinic Defense Force and so were prepared for what they would face on site. Police showed up with a "strike force" to arrest injunction violators, and the escorts were able to keep the clinic open all day. Richmond escorts continued to work every Saturday, despite increasing tensions at the clinic. NOW officers welcomed volunteers—"WE NEED YOUR BODY"—but only if the escorts could be peaceful in the face of aggression, because they did not want to incite violence.[136]

Facing down aggressive antiabortion picketers was difficult enough, but reproductive rights activists also had to respond to acts of violence. Incidents ranging from threats that forced workers to alter schedules to bombings, arson, and even murders—hit an all-time high in the United States in the early 1990s. In 1993, an extremist in Pensacola, Florida, murdered a doctor who provided abortions. Since that time, eleven people have been killed and twenty-six wounded, including three killed in a 2015 Colorado clinic attack.[137]

The arson and bombings at Hillcrest illustrated that Virginia was not immune from the violence. And in 1992, an arsonist did twenty-five thousand dollars' worth of damage to the Richmond Medical Center for Women, prompting reproductive justice activists to plan twenty-four-hour-a-day watches outside the facility. As the president of the two-hundred-member Virginia Commonwealth University Delegation for Choice put it, "To set fire to the place is very typical of a reaction by an extremist fundamentalist...." Raschke refused to blame anyone specifically for the arson, but she did say that the "violent rhetoric" of many anti-abortion leaders helped prompt violence. She told a Roanoke reporter, "The anti abortion leaders really ought to look into their hearts to find their parts in the violence."[138] Two years later, an arsonist set fire to the back door of the clinic in Falls Church. Although that incident did little damage, in 1997 a Prince William County man did twenty-five thousand dollars of damage to the clinic in an act of arson.[139]

Hillcrest made the national news in 1995, however, when it was the target of a high-profile attack. After murdering two women and wounding several other people in clinics that provided abortion services in Massachusetts, John Salvi drove to Norfolk and fired twenty-three rounds into Hillcrest Clinic. By chance, no one was hurt there. The shooting showed just how powerful violent antiabortionists were in Virginia; *Boston Globe* reporters quoted a law enforcement official as saying, "You just don't show up in a city and immediately find the local abortion clinic unless you already know something about it."¹⁴⁰ Salvi had been found with notorious Norfolk minister and leader of Pro-Life Virginia Donald Spitz's phone number in his pocket, although there was no direct connection between the two. Still, the *New York Times* described Norfolk as a "hotbed of anti-abortion activity." And while Spitz said that he had no link with Salvi, he did tell the *Times* reporter, "It's not right to go kill people. . . . But when people are involved in killing babies, then it's justified to save the babies." Spitz and several others held a prayer vigil for Salvi outside the Norfolk jail.¹⁴¹

Feminists quickly condemned the incident. Within thirty hours of Salvi's capture, Norfolk NOW members held a candlelight vigil at Hillcrest to show their support, and NOW members peacefully demonstrated at the Norfolk District Court. Brenda Andrews of the *New Journal and Guide* lambasted "so-called religious leaders" for their encouragement of violence: "We are not experiencing a rash of random attacks, but organized guerilla warfare," she said, designed for "intimidating women into submission." She equated their tactics with those of lynch mobs in the early twentieth century that oppressed black men. And Denise Lee called out Governor Allen for his alleged "tough on crime" stance when his reaction to the shooting was noticeably delayed. But then again, as she said, Attorney General James Gilmore had received fifty thousand dollars from Pat Robertson, and Allen had made it clear what he thought about abortion. In response, NOW's national executive vice-president, Kim Gandy, called on U.S. Attorney General Janet Reno to use the FBI to investigate these antiabortion activists, using the domestic terrorism unit.¹⁴² Despite these efforts, clinics around the country—and in Virginia—would continue to experience violence. A Roanoke clinic dealt with an anthrax threat in 2000, and currently there is an open arson case at the Planned Parenthood Virginia Beach Clinic from 2007.¹⁴³

Sometimes feminist programs focused on raising money for different efforts. Some money went to women who could not afford abortions. A popular fundraising effort included the "Pledge-a-Picket" campaign—one pledged a certain amount per every antiabortion picketer who showed up. In Charlottesville, for example, supporters pledged money that went into a fund to assist low-income women seeking abortion services. Chapters across the commonwealth participated to raise money.¹⁴⁴

And after careful study, Virginia League of Planned Parenthood decided in 1992 to provide abortions. This decision hinged on the fact that there were so few providers in Virginia, and it fit with of VLPP's program of "quality care" in reproductive health. Still, the board president assured supporters that *"Prevention is and will remain our goal."* In an article for the state newsletter, Executive Director Grace Sparks explained, "Every day we witness threats to the right to choose—vocal and often violent anti-choice zealots harass and intimidate women seeking abortions[,]" and the board of Planned Parenthood determined "not to be ruled" by challenges, but to help women deal with them. In addition to raising $68,000 for clinic startup costs, Planned Parenthood sought and secured donations for the first clinic in Richmond. Today, Planned Parenthood operates clinics in Blacksburg, Falls Church, Charlottesville, Hampton, Virginia Beach, Richmond, and Roanoke, all of which offer a wide variety of reproductive health services on sliding-scale payments, including abortion.[145]

Lobbyists continued working to roll back restrictions on abortions, and grassroots activists continued protecting choice in their communities, despite major setbacks in Virginia. Raschke left her role as governmental affairs liaison and head lobbyist for Planned Parenthood in 1999 for a position at the Center for Reproductive Law and Policy, and that same year NARAL closed down its Virginia branch, citing the extremely hostile climate in the General Assembly and the lack of volunteers. In 2000, NOW unsuccessfully filed an objection against Attorney General Ken Cuccinelli's decision to give a $170,000 settlement from a lawsuit to the over forty "crisis pregnancy centers" in the commonwealth.[146] As Emily McCoy noted, NOW tried to get these clinics at least regulated, "Because we think they're phony, they're misleading. It's false advertisement.... What are they doing? Is anybody watching them?"[147] Bringing publicity through this attempted lawsuit continued earlier feminist work of educating women about what was happening in these clinics.

If traditional reproductive rights activism appeared on the decline, modern technologies were taking abortion rights to a different place in the commonwealth and across the nation. In 2003, a Richmond resident created the "I'm Not Sorry" blog, website, and later a Facebook page. Unaffiliated with any traditional feminist organization, it published women's own accounts of their abortions in order to challenge beliefs that all women regret having abortions.[148] It was an open internet forum to publicize and educate a new generation about reproductive justice. The internet appears to be the new organizing tool for young activists, as it was through this medium that hundreds of women learned about the transvaginal ultrasound bill, passed by an extremely conservative General Assembly in 2011. With the passage of this bill, the commonwealth became the butt of jokes on the *Daily Show* and *Saturday Night Live*, but for Virginia activist women it was no laughing matter.

Hundreds of activists descended on the legislature, in this case to protest the transvaginal ultrasound law. Drawn to the capitol by Facebook and other social media sites, hundreds of activists descended on the General Assembly, carrying signs like "Private Property: Keep Out" and "Say No to State-Mandated Rape." At its height, the protest had an estimated fourteen hundred protestors. Governor Bob McDonnell signed a mandatory ultrasound bill that had the "transvaginal" portion removed, which was not much of a victory.[149] Still, it demonstrates that reproductive rights activists are working in Virginia, continuing the tradition set by feminists in the late twentieth century. They may use different organizational tools, and they may not always be affiliated with formal groups, but these activists are still fighting for the same ground the founders of reproductive rights groups did in the commonwealth. Although they have been waging a losing battle, these activists, whether on the ground or on the capitol floor, were able to keep antiabortion legislation from passing the General Assembly for years after Supreme Court decisions allowed for restrictions on women's right to choose.

Virginia's story of abortion access has no conclusion at this time. The repeal of several TRAP laws is a significant victory, but mandatory ultrasounds, waiting periods, mandatory consent laws, and other repressive laws threaten women's choice in Virginia. Abortion may be legal but restricted in Virginia, but access continues to be a problem. As of 2011, there were only thirty-five providers in the entire state, a decline from 2008. There were no providers in 92 percent of Virginia's counties, and 78 percent of the commonwealth's women live in those counties. Nationally in 2011, 89 percent of counties had no clinic, but only 35 percent of American women lived in those counties, according to a Guttmacher Institute report. Although Virginia's lack of availability by county looks similar to the rest of the nation, fewer women have local access in the commonwealth.[150]

Reproductive rights activists fought hard to protect women's right to abortion access as part of a larger program of women's health and wellness. The national rise of the New Right, centered in the commonwealth, made their work much harder. The fact that Virginia abortion rights advocates held back the tide of change as long as they did, even when states in regions of the country commonly considered more progressive had rolled back abortion rights, was no small feat. Even in the twenty-first century, activists continue to try to protect what abortion access is left in the commonwealth.

4
ENDING VIOLENCE AGAINST WOMEN

It was just such a diversity in terms of [domestic violence and sexual assault] advocacy and responses... working in a program in Richmond was very different from working in a program in Charlottesville or southwest Virginia. Rural issues, transportation issues, community-response issues.... It was the same state, but culturally, really wide differences.
—KATE MCCORD, communications director, Virginia Sexual and Domestic Violence Action Alliance

In the 1970s feminist work addressing both relational violence and sexual assault altered dramatically the ways in which Americans understood and discussed violence against women. Virginia women, like other activists across the United States, faced antiquated laws, reluctant law enforcement officials and judicial officers, and a total lack of infrastructure to provide aid to survivors of violence. They worked to change laws and the culture of the Old Dominion. As with anti-violence efforts nationwide, activists have achieved legislative successes and can claim to have redefined the way in which citizens and communities respond to survivors. Nevertheless, those involved with the anti-violence movement note that society has a long way to end violence against women.

Anti-rape and domestic-violence campaigns had been around for decades in some fashion, but it took activists in the late twentieth century to effect significant change.[1] In consciousness-raising groups and pamphlets, feminists drew attention to structural issues of power and gender inequality that led to violence against women. One scholar noted that the anti-rape movement gave domestic-violence campaigns a model for how to advocate for survivors, fight on the local level for change, and bring awareness to the issue.[2] At the grassroots level, feminist activists provided support to survivors, challenged the ways in which law enforcement authorities handled domestic violence and rape cases, and founded rape crisis hotlines and domestic-violence shelters, staffed with volunteers.[3] In many places, including Virginia, the campaigns often originated with radical feminists in local efforts and then caught the attention of liberal feminists who sought to lobby for legislative change. Ever at the helm of feminist issues, NOW included anti-rape as part of its official agenda in 1971 and created an anti-rape task force in 1973, headed by Northern Virginia NOW chapter member Mary Ann Largen. From 1973 to 1978, Largen worked with local groups to change state laws and community responses to rape, although the task force was suspended when NOW wanted to focus more efforts on passage of the ERA.[4] This did not stop NOW members from involvement during the ERA period, however.

In the late twentieth century, activists of varying backgrounds focused on legislatures and creating systemic change through local efforts. They demanded reform of state laws in order to better support women who pressed charges against rapists and abusers; they created hotlines, staffed shelters, and educated police and judges. Anti-violence efforts brought women of different socioeconomic backgrounds together ideologically, although they often did not work in the same organizations, partly because of the traditional divide between white feminists and women of color, partly because sometimes feminist activists failed to address the structural inequalities of race that caused women of color to experience violence separately. However, because of the multiplicity of local support groups emerging to fight violence, many women who had not been involved in other efforts worked on this issue.[5]

Scholars explain just how significant this movement was to changing both laws and attitudes about violence against women in the United States. Activists' efforts brought to light domestic violence and rape, enabling people to discuss experiences without shame. Scholars began to address both the causes of and methods for ameliorating violence. Newspapers began running articles about violence. Speakouts, which began in various cities in the early 1970s, led to Take Back the Night (TBTN) marches, which still occur, often on college campuses. Laws changed. Shelters and hotlines began receiving state and federal funding to assist in their programming. But with all of this change, feminists had to make concessions. Violence against women became a legal issue, something to be managed by the police and courts. Shelters professionalized and became as much a realm of social workers as a collective of feminist activists, partly in response to the state money they received. In order to make changes, feminists had to compromise as they found themselves working within state structures dominated by male legislators and law enforcement officers.[6]

In Virginia, activists worked with each other to challenge laws and create safe havens for survivors of violence. As with other women across the country, they sometimes fought an uphill battle to change laws, particularly with regard to marital rape. Just as they did with the ERA and abortion rights, feminist activists took a two-avenue approach to change: they worked for better legislation protecting women, and they became extremely active in grassroots efforts to educate the public and to assist the survivors.

Sexual Assault: Grassroots Activism

Grassroots efforts emerged in the early 1970s as a reaction against increased sexual-assault reporting. Groups of women coalesced to make the public aware of this serious societal problem. They took different approaches to promote awareness. Mary Ann Bergeron remembers the "guerilla tactics" used by an anonymous group of radical women in Richmond. The group went to police stations all over the city to look at crime reports and then used that information: "So every now and then—in fact, a lot of times—people would wake up in Richmond, and there would be spray painted in removable paint, on a wall, or a workplace, or a sidewalk, 'A Rape Occurred Here.'"[7]

Richmond NOW members joined forces with four Virginia Commonwealth University students in the social work program in 1974 to investigate what control/prevention programs were in place, what kinds of training hospitals and police had in dealing with victims, and to better understand how many rapes were going unreported. In a two-month period they had mapped out where reported rapes were happening, and concluded rape was more prevalent in low-income districts where women worked longer hours in the night and had to walk home alone. Eleanor Lawrence, who was in charge of this local task force, explained that the group formed partly in response to the 340 sexual assaults reported in 1972–73, which represented a 300 percent increase. She said, "We feel sure the 340 rapes are just the tip of the iceberg."[8] Lawrence, committed to changing how victims received treatment from police and medical professionals, made media appearances and met with public safety officials.[9]

Joining the NOW activists in Richmond, a group of young women working through the YWCA began Richmond Organized Against Rape (ROAR). This all-volunteer organization began when the Young Women Committed to Action held a seminar on "Women and their Bodies" and could find no experts to talk about sexual assault. As a result they determined they would have to do the job themselves, and, understanding it was an issue demanding much time and energy, split from the original group to do its work.[10]

Norfolk and Virginia Beach NOW chapters started their own task force to help survivors in the Tidewater area. They held workshops and press conferences, and, like ROAR, activists ultimately determined that a specialized response team, Tidewater Rape Information Services (TRIS), would staff a crisis hotline in addition to promoting awareness in the region. As TRIS publicized to state NOW members, "Our approach is a new one for feminist groups, but one whose time has come: complete integration of existing services along two lines—improved victim treatment and education/prevention." TRIS remained independent, but worked with the YWCA and Travelers' Aid, among other organizations, to provide services.[11] TRIS started as a group of volunteers working from their homes and with their own money, conducting awareness campaigns in the media and for organizations. Former Navy signalman and journalist for a Navy publication, Donna Motley, directed TRIS. TRIS workers assisted survivors, trying to encourage them to report crimes to the police, and work for convictions.[12]

TRIS became a major force in sexual-assault reform after receiving a forty-one-thousand-dollar grant of public money. Like other organizations across the country, when TRIS began to work with public money and officials, those involved with the organization tended to sidestep feminist issues. In a response to an editorial in the local paper claiming TRIS should not be publicly funded because it supported abortion, one sexual assault survivor wrote, "I don't know much about NOW, but since TRIS was a task force of NOW that eventually became its own identity I disagree that women at TRIS are a minority group of militant women." Beverly Paulk, who had become head of TRIS, responded that the grant was going only to pay for salaries of four staff members and expenses for the twenty-five volunteers, but that "legal abortion must remain an option for rape victims who feel that a pregnancy is intolerable."[13]

Across the commonwealth, local single-issue groups like TRIS grew organically from meetings of concerned feminists. By August of 1975, volunteers with twenty hours of training were serving bimonthly in Alexandria's Rape Victim Campaign Program, which received sponsorship from the Alexandria Women's Commission. Volunteers worked with police, went to the hospitals to meet survivors, and went through the court system with victims. They also promoted awareness through community education and lobbying for sexual-assault reform at the legislature. One month later, the University of Virginia's Student Council Women's Safety Committee published a pamphlet focusing on how women could protect themselves outside, hitchhiking, in dorms and apartments, and in other scenarios in which "stranger rape" could occur. The next month, the Fairfax League of Women Voters publicized the Northern Virginia Rape Crisis Hotline, which had been organized by the Mount Vernon Mental Health Institute, to provide twenty-four-hour help by a "professionally trained volunteer staff."[14]

These organizations, supported mainly by volunteers, offered help to survivors by acting as advocates from their first trip to the hospital and meeting with police through the court systems. TRIS publicized its hotline, however, by emphasizing it was firmly on the side of the survivor, which meant providing what she needed, rather than what law enforcement might want. As Kathy Powell, TRIS outreach coordinator, told a reporter, "We are more concerned with rebuilding the victim's self-confidence[,]" so volunteers acceded to the wishes of survivors, and were trained to be their confidants rather than their advisors.[15] As the Charlottesville Rape Crisis organization told a local feminist publication: "Our presence has been one of friendship, an information source, a victim advocate, and a person to buffer the victim's contact with 'the system' she must face after the original crime."[16] These early organizers, like those across the country, held fast to feminist ideals of assisting the survivor in navigating a system which, because of the existing laws and police and judicial attitudes towards them, often did more harm than good. All volunteers provided services to anyone in need—and ROAR made this quite clear when it determined it "addresses the major goal of the YWCA—the elimination of racism—by informing a diverse population about rape and rape prevention[,]" seeking to empower women, youth, and "third world people" in their outreach programs.[17]

Survivor services and outreach programs were the two mainstays of these volunteer organizations. In the space of about a calendar year, ROAR recorded educating over four thousand people at community meetings, taught a college class at a community college titled "Avoid Rape," and published a pamphlet on sexual-assault awareness. In the same time frame, TRIS held eighty workshops, to which almost three thousand people had come, took 198 reports of assault, and served as companions for eighty-nine survivors. NOW Richmond secured ten thousand dollars in private donations to publish a pamphlet on rape and posted stickers with the local rape crisis hotline number all over Richmond, particularly in places where women would be working at night. By 1977 the Charlottesville Rape Crisis group had thirty trained volunteers who worked at the University of Virginia emergency room and with police. By 1977 they claimed to have worked with thirty-five clients.[18]

By the late 1970s, demand for these services was so great that volunteers had challenges keeping up with the need. ROAR told members about an upcoming meeting with Richmond Representative Bill Axelle about his rape shield law, the need to attend a rape trial in Richmond, and dates for training sessions in 1975. It concluded, "ROAR is being asked to take on more and more responsibilities in the community—and there are many more ways we could be helping the rape situation in Richmond. But we can only do so much as our membership can handle." TRIS wrote a letter to its members explaining that as of January 1976 it could only focus on holding one workshop a week in the city of Norfolk. It also had to focus on working with educating only the police, because "work with the police takes higher priority and is just beginning to open up." It was receiving thirty calls per day, and hoped to educate the police force "before getting into another problem area."[19] Charlottesville NOW's Task Force on Rape admitted, "All the activities concerning rape are rather mind-boggling." They themselves were involved in trying to get female police officers hired and were contemplating an EEOC complaint.[20]

In 1976, local rape crisis volunteers determined to band together to help each other manage the problem and fight for reform. The first meeting at the Richmond YWCA included representatives from ROAR, TRIS, Charlottesville Rape Crisis Center, Medical College of Virginia School of Nursing Continuing Education, Virginia Commonwealth University Department of Community Services, Virginia Nurses Association, and Northern Virginia Medical Center for Women. Going forward, this group would be known as the Virginia Committee on Sexual Assault Reform (COSAR). It would include organizations and individuals in a coalition to fight for better laws to address rape, as well as better programs to try to end rape and promote awareness of sexual assault.[21] In 1980, Richmonder Pat Tashjian and Roanoke resident Irene Hall called a meeting of rape crisis staff and volunteers. Fifty activists showed up and founded Virginians Allied Against Sexual Assault (VAASA) with the goals to "work toward the elimination of sexual assault in Virginia and to further the public understanding of this multi-faceted problem." They published a newsletter to share information about how to maintain centers, gain funding, and lobby policy makers. By 1983, VAASA had members serving in centers across the commonwealth, from Bristol on the Tennessee line, to Winchester in far Northwest Virginia, in the Southside community of Danville, and in Northern Virginia metropolises like Fairfax, Arlington, and Alexandria. The Tidewater area was well represented, with Avalon Center in Williamsburg, Peninsula Rape Crisis, and TRIS, now renamed Response.[22]

These centers served survivors and their families by providing a range of programs and counseling options. By 1993, the Richmond YWCA reported to members of VAASA that it had two twenty-four-hour hotlines, one in Richmond and one for Chesterfield County, staffed continuously by paid and volunteer workers. They had counselors working through survivor companion programs at hospitals, police stations, and courts. They ran three different support groups, including one for substance abusers and one for survivors of child sexual assault, and they rolled out a new project to be put into direct contact with anyone who reported rape to the local commonwealth attorney's office. In Wytheville, Regina Pack Eller, coordinator of the Sexual Assault Project, noted that in her rural area the lack of public transportation meant volunteers had to drive long distances to help, often needing the use of four-wheel-drive vehicles to get to their clients. The Crisis Center in Bristol, just three blocks from the Tennessee line, assisted women of both states as part of a joint domestic violence/sexual assault response program. While the sexual-assault hotline portion of the center was only eight years old, it had established a local program at Emory & Henry College. These three centers were part of a twenty-two-center consortium which reported helping a total of 5,043 survivors and 2,361 family members and friends of survivors in the commonwealth. These centers were staffed by 78 paid workers and 1,028 volunteers who provided over 190,000 hours of volunteer services. Individuals used 64,879 services, a 64 percent increase from 1991. The centers served a wide range of women, including a disproportionate number of women of color based on the population. While the commonwealth was 18.8 percent African American in 1990, centers' clients were 21 percent African American. And while Virginia had a population of Latin Americans which registered just over 2.5 percent, Latinas comprised 4 percent of the clients at crisis centers.[23]

Grassroots organizations also worked to change law enforcement's handling of sexual assault. TRIS and ROAR, for example, conducted the police-training sessions to help educate law enforcement. ROAR extended beyond city limits and worked with Henrico County, as well as medical personnel in area hospitals. Early on, one ROAR worker reported to the YWCA Board of Directors, "some of the police had been extremely helpful, cooperative, and compassionate. Others had been just the opposite. Working with the police had underscored the need for education of the community at large about the realities of rape."[24]

Activists successfully created awareness about sexual assault in their communities. Groups unaffiliated with rape crisis centers began to discuss the problem. Second Presbyterian Church held a seminar on sexual assault in the Tidewater area, cosponsored by a local group, Contact Peninsula, and the Virginia State Crime Commission. "Women of the Tidewater" sponsored one of the earliest Take Back the Night marches in Virginia in 1980. As Peninsula NOW reported, about two hundred women walked in Norfolk, but there were only about six members of the group present. Others were representatives from the Williamsburg Women's Center, as well as other unaffiliated women from Tidewater feminist groups, including Old Dominion University students and TRIS. A NOW participant wrote, "It is heartening to see so many young women with an interest in feminist issues, ready to take up the cause."[25] Take Back the Night (TBTN) and space-claiming activities continued in Virginia, as they did across the country, through the twentieth and twenty-first centuries. Old Dominion continued to sponsor TBTNs, celebrating their fourth in 1983 by inviting African American lesbian activist Barbara Smith and nationally known Virginia resident and founder of Mormons for the ERA Sonia Johnson.[26] TBTNs would continue across the commonwealth; from Lynchburg to Radford, Charlottesville to Chesterfield, activists brought problems of violence out into the open.[27]

College campuses were important places for activists to make inroads into promoting safe environments. During this period, feminists moved away from focusing on the concept of stranger rape to address the overwhelming problem with acquaintance or "date rape." Considering that a 1988 study noted over 80 percent of rapists were known to their victims, and over 55 percent of rapes happened in dating situations, feminists needed to switch focus and bring awareness to this problem.[28] The YWCA of Richmond reported in 1986 on its "Safe Dating" program, asking the Richmond City Council for a grant of thirteen thousand dollars for educational outreach to teens. Virginians Allied Against Sexual Assault (VAASA), a coalition of rape crisis centers and the feminists who worked in them, as well as antiviolence supporters, sponsored a seminar on "Acquaintance Sexual Assault" the following year.[29]

It would not be until the 1990s when "date rape" became an open topic of conversation across the country, due in part to the efforts of College of William and Mary student Katie Koestner. In 1991, the first-year student was sexually assaulted by another student after a date. She had spurned his advances at least a dozen times, she later wrote. When she went to the campus health center within three days of the assault, she received nothing but a dose of sleeping pills and a recommendation to sleep it off. Koestner then took her complaint to the dean, who referred her only to the college judicial system. During the hearing, she was questioned first by her assailant before being allowed to ask him any questions. And although her attacker was found guilty, his punishment was only to be barred from entering any dormitory or fraternity not his own on campus. She told *Time* magazine, "The hearing officer told me this is an educational institution, not a penitentiary," when she challenged the punishment. The administration's unwillingness to take the issue seriously is reflected in the officer's suggestion to Koestner that perhaps she and her attacker could eventually reunite as a couple.[30] She dropped out of William and Mary for a semester but returned—he eventually dropped out, for an "unrelated incident," according to one news story. Koestner said in a 2001 talk at St. Mary's College in Indiana her assailant was later accused of raping another woman.[31]

After discovering the commonwealth's attorney was reluctant to take her case, Koestner took matters into her own hands by making her case public—very public. As she told a *Washington Post* reporter, "I'm not just some 18-year-old freshman from William and Mary. There's a person and a face and a name."[32] Koestner's story went national to hundreds of news outlets, the cover of *Time* magazine with accompanying cover features about campus sexual assault, and an HBO docudrama. Koestner literally became the face of campus sexual assault, as she later claimed, because she was the "perfect rape victim." She wrote: "my white skin, virginity, Christianity, a prestigious college ... good grades ... an upper-middle-class socioeconomic status, heterosexuality ... youth and innocence" contributed to her dubious status.[33] Her image accompanied the *Time* feature, which explained that fewer than 10 percent of date rapes were reported and fewer than 5 percent were prosecuted successfully. Her name was one of two used to illustrate a *USA Today* story informing Americans that one in four college women would be raped, which equaled approximately one rape every twenty-one hours. The article explained that

90 percent of sexual assaults went unreported, and only one in a hundred was prosecuted. The story noted the inadequacy of the college system for handling these cases and called for campus rapes to go through the traditional criminal-justice system.[34]

While Koestner may have received national support and attention for campaigning for awareness about date rape on campus, she did not face the same reaction at William and Mary. Koestner told a reporter, "People I've never seen will call me 'bitch,' 'whore.' They'll yell it out the car windows. They started throwing cups at my boyfriend." Some questioned her motives and her credibility, especially because of the docudrama deal. The deal did not net her much money at all, and it did not put the name of the school or her attacker in the movie. Others, however, supported her, or at least admitted she brought to light a serious problem. Anne Fullenkamp of Baltimore told a reporter, "During the light of day, people are very well educated and have well-thought-out opinions [about date rape]. But you get to the frats and things change...." The reporter explained that not all attitudes about sexual violence had changed: "Many William and Mary students say they don't think that a woman who gives in to verbal pressure—rather than outright threats—has been raped."[35]

Koestner's outspokenness helped to bring the national spotlight on a problem universities had not been addressing adequately, if at all. And despite the mixed reaction of her efforts at William and Mary, her work did have significant effects on campus. As one reporter noted upon her return to campus in 1996 as a Take Back the Night speaker, "Whatever the truth of the story, the publicity turned a glaring spotlight on William and Mary's quiet, conservative campus." It instituted a sexual-assault task force and new policies and programs. The college hired a coordinator for sexual-assault response and revamped its disciplinary policy regarding sexual assault. By 1993, the Avalon Center had helped the College of William and Mary Police Department to revise its response to assault survivors. After receiving a call, police notified Avalon; a companion team would arrive at the college and be available in an adjacent room if the survivor wanted its support. And reports of campus rape totaled twenty cases a year by 1996, ten times higher than before Koestner spoke up about her experience.[36]

Virginians Allied Against Sexual Assault responded as well, by working to educate members about sexual assault. VAASA reprinted in its newsletter an article by the Richmond YWCA's Becky Weybright on acquaintance rape.

Weybright focused on educating the members of VAASA. She explained that teens often thought they would not be believed if they had been drinking or dressing provocatively. She noted that teens also often failed to see forced sex as rape, and they were known to blame themselves rather than the perpetrator. They were also afraid they would get in trouble, or they did not want to get the perpetrator in trouble.[37]

This would continue to be a problem. Despite the extremely high rate of acquaintance rape, in 1992 only 40 percent of calls to VAASA-allied crisis centers dealt with acquaintance rape.[38] Still, Take Back the Night events continued to be held on college campuses, and student groups worked—and continue to work—to address the problem. And in 1992, President George H. W. Bush signed the Sexual Assault Victims Bill of Rights to address the issues Koestner helped to bring to light. Schools receiving federal funding must assist survivors by notifying them of their options to report to law enforcement, have counseling services, and move living arrangements; allowing them have people present during hearings, and telling them of all results of any disciplinary hearings.[39]

Reforming Sexual-Assault Laws

In Virginia, as in other places, the fact that women fought against poorly designed rape laws caused judges to be hesitant to convict accused attackers and made women fear even coming forward with charges. In 1973, graduate students Wendy Wilson and Kathleen McKinnon, students in Virginia Commonwealth University's School of Social Work posted a flyer titled, "Should Victims Pay the Price for Unjust Laws?" as part of an effort to organize students to lobby for a revision of the criminal code. They suggested revising the law to provide degrees of sexual-assault felony; define rape as "intrusion, however slight," of anyone's body by any means; raise the age of consent; and disallow "Evidence of victim's prior behavior" into testimony. In addition, they called for an addition of marital rape to the code if the husband and wife were legally separated or divorced.[40] They explained in a letter to Meg Williams, a Virginia Commonwealth University student and lobbyist for the Virginia Women's Political Caucus (VWPC), judges were reluctant to pursue rape convictions because they didn't want to commit the perpetrators to life in prison. This was the law of Virginia at the time, and moreover, victims did not want to see their pasts dragged out by the criminal defense team, which explained their desire to see different degrees of sexual assault named.[41] For those unfamiliar with rape law codes, it may seem unusual to try to push for more lenient sentencing. However, as Mary Ann Bergeron remembered, many believed mandated life sentences were "one of the problems with juries convicting." She said there were legislative efforts related to reduced sentencing "that would make it easier for a case to come to trial and actually have a hope of conviction."[42]

Students at Virginia Commonwealth University were not the only ones discussing necessary changes. In fact, a representative from the Fairfax County Board of Supervisors suggested changes to the criminal code in the 1974 state meeting of the Virginia Association of Counties (VAC). After its own task force studied state laws, which had been prompted by the demands of different advocacy groups, including NOW, the Fairfax Commission noted many problems in the code. The representative echoed many of the sentiments of the Virginia Commonwealth University students, asking for different degrees of crime, a shield to prevent victims' past history from being introduced in court, a definition of rape to include both male and female perpetrators, and a suspension of immunity from marital rape if the couple was legally separated. However, while the executive council of the VAC wanted this to be the top priority of the organization for the year, members bumped it down the priority list to third of four.[43]

And just a few months later, the Congress of Women's Organizations in Virginia, representing a diverse group of organizations which included religious groups, League of Women Voters, NOW, and the Virginia Federation of Business and Professional Women's Clubs (BPW), to name just a few, called for a change in state laws as well. A Norfolk NOW representative submitted a resolution demanding the General Assembly study existing rape laws in order to pass better ones, fund development programs for police investigators, add policewomen to rape teams, and provide money for rape crisis centers.[44] The same year, the AAUW passed a Rape Prevention Resolution at its state convention. Different chapters addressed the resolution in many ways, but Springfield-Annandale's sent a speaker to the Fairfax Commission on Women to ask it to propose a resolution to the General Assembly calling for a state study on sexual assault. A group from this chapter went to the House Rules Committee to follow up on the request.[45]

Interest groups made a difference. The 1975 session of the General Assembly saw the introduction of a rape shield law. Representing NOW and VWPC, Zelda Nordlinger spoke at the House Courts of Justice meeting in support of the shield law. Some legislators worried it would hurt the defense's ability to discuss any previous relationship with the victim, which suggests how far legislators still had to come in understanding that forcible rape could happen within the bounds of a relationship.[46] However, legislators did alter the laws somewhat to include the different degrees of rape to provide for a wider range of sentencing in this year.[47]

Anti-rape efforts continued as organizations worked to push the General Assembly further. The Congress of Women's Organizations and NOW formally proposed changes in 1976, including a shield law, having all sexual offenses categorized as assault, and including a provision which would not make a victim have to prove she actively resisted an assault. In Charlottesville, the NOW Task Force worked to get third-year University of Virginia law students to redraft the laws to make the language gender-neutral. And representatives from local anti-rape groups met for the first time in order to form a state organization to lobby for legal reform.[48]

In 1976, the General Assembly listened, to an extent. Representatives passed a law compensating victims for the purchase of rape kits, or providing for support for localities to pay for them. Moreover, in August 1976, legislators created a task force appointed by the State Crime Commission to look at other states' laws. While it's likely pressure from groups lobbying for change helped to prompt the decision, the *Washington Post's* Sara Hansard reported the legislators mandated it partly in response to a 24 percent increase in sexual-assault reporting in a single year. Still, more needed to be done. Task force member Pamela McCoach, also a member of the Fairfax Commission on Women, told Hansard, "I think the biggest problem will be in addressing these issues to the state legislators. . . ." She explained legislators were reluctant to change the laws because they believed the longer sentences protected women, "but when you've got 80 percent of those arrested for the crime going unpunished, something's wrong. . . ."[49]

For a series of successive years, the General Assembly refused to pass Senate Bill 291, which would provide a more comprehensive sex-neutral law that included the degree level of severity as well as a rape shield law. In 1978 the House of Delegates carried it over, and when it came up in 1979 in the Courts of Justice system, the BPW called upon all members to lobby their legislators, asking them to support the bill, but also demanding the spousal exemption be removed. Lynn Valos of Virginia wrote to members: "Again I remind you that with Virginia being 12th in the nation with highest number of reported forcible rapes and 4th among Southeastern States can this be allowed to continue?"⁵⁰

Apparently, legislators believed it should. The bill failed in 1979, which the League of Women Voters–Alexandria chapter discussed at their Conference on Legislative Actions Affecting Women. The issue of sexual assault had become critical to women activists in Virginia, as evidenced by the fact that the conference was keynoted by Virginian Lynda Robb, who served as the chair of the President's Commission on the Status of Women, and attended by shelter and COSAR representatives, including Delegate Mary Marshall, Elise Heinz, and other notables.⁵¹ In 1980 the bill got carried over again because when supporters, who included Democratic delegates Samuel Glasscock of Suffolk and Bernard Cohen of Alexandria, tried to force a vote, Democrat George Allen Jr. of Richmond called for a recess. A long-time supporter of the bill, Democrat Fred Boucher of Washington County, told members, "We've considered this issue for three consecutive sessions, and I submit to you that the time has arrived to act." He told a *Washington Post* reporter, "I'm mad as hell and you can quote me. . . ." Supporters blamed Democrat Theodore Morrison of Newport, who as a defense attorney had concerns about disallowing prior sexual activity as a defense, but others accused the House of simply refusing to take the bill seriously.⁵²

By 1980, thirty-six states had significantly reformed their sexual-assault laws. However, Virginia was not one of them. Because women had to prove they resisted, conviction rates were below 5 percent. Additionally, women appeared reluctant to go to court because Virginia still had no rape shield law. Candy Reuss, a participant in the Fairfax County Court Observer program of the Fairfax Women's Commission, and her cohorts, after observing two hundred hearings, noted, "Again and again we see lawyers find a way to introduce the fact that the woman is on birth control pills, that she is unmarried and living with someone, that she might be an unwed mother." Fred Boucher told the *Post:* "I just don't understand it, after four years there is a continuing insensitivity (in the legislature) to deal with the real problem of rape . . . there's a general feeling that rape trials should proceed the way they have always proceeded—putting victims on the stand. . . ." He noted, "It's as clear as anything I've ever seen" that women should not to be victimized again on the stand in a sexual-assault trial.⁵³

In 1981, continued pressure caused the General Assembly to pass S.B. 158, a sweeping reform which removed the requirement of victims having to prove they tried to resist and instituted a rape shield law of sorts. The law allowed for some "admissible evidence of prior conduct" involving prior acts with the defendant, any history which might show a motive for the victim to "fabricate the story," to show prior proof of sexual activity that may have come from incidents other than the rape, and to rebut any testimony about the sexual history of a witness as brought up by the prosecution. In all of these cases, a judge was empowered to determine if such evidence was relevant before it was admitted to a court. In addition, the criminal code was updated to include forcible sodomy and penetration of foreign objects and sexual battery (no penetration) as crimes punishable as sexual assault. A report by the University of Virginia Institute of Government credited "a seven-year, grassroots citizens' effort to revise Virginia's sexual assault laws" with the 1981 changes. In a letter to women's organizations in Virginia, Delegate Mary Marshall hailed the work of activists, explaining: "For the first time, these bills were carefully monitored and followed by a number of women's organizations." She discussed the work women did in meeting weekly to update each other and follow the bills through the legislature during the session. Marshall also nodded to the diversity of the group which supported the legislation: "Although many shared different points of view, they joined forces to share information.... They attended hearings, interviewed legislators, and testified before committees. This attention was felt." Marshall believed this was the "first time" women were "working together effectively," which spelled success in this case.[54]

This was just the beginning for anti-rape lobbying. Feminist activists' efforts continued to pay off. In 1982, the General Assembly revised the laws again, allowing for people of either gender to be prosecuted for rape, paying for medical fees associated with evidence collection in an assault case, and providing for workers' compensation should a person be sexually assaulted on the job.[55] Prompted by VAASA lobbyists and other feminist advocates for sexual-assault services, the General Assembly provided funding for survivor services. By 1994, it was providing $600,000 to anti-violence programs, the same year it amended sexual-assault laws to allow for prosecution of those who touched victims' genital areas through their clothing.[56]

Domestic Violence—Grassroots Activism

It appeared work on domestic violence got a later start than sexual-assault reform, but once activists began to focus on the issue, they hit the ground running. In Virginia, as elsewhere, those wanting to reform the system dealing with violence faced an uphill battle. Police were not trained to handle relational violence, for one thing. Tidewater-area police officer James Thames worried more "about going to a domestic call than an armed robbery... or anything else.... You never know what to expect with domestic cases." When Portsmouth and Chesterfield got a national grant providing ten to twenty hours of crisis training for area officers, Lieutenant Gene Brooks observed the police were reluctant to deal with the issue: "Maybe we didn't want to become social workers.... With crisis intervention skills, we can still function as police officers and still intervene and help families with their problems...." Gene Brooks and Paul Clark were the directors of this pilot program, which targeted just six cities nationwide with $200,000 grants from the National Institute of Law Enforcement and Criminal Justice. With the money, the departments planned to hire some social workers and psychologists, but the main goal at this time, in 1974, according to Brooks, was "bringing the family back together and try[ing] to reach a solution." Clark told a reporter, police wanted to avoid making "needless arrest[s]."[57] Sergeant Waverly Tanner seemed perplexed about how to handle violent husbands: "Sure, it's a problem.... But, it's a hard thing to put our hands on." Reverend Charlene Linnell of Richmond Unity Center said women often stayed in violent relationships because they had nowhere to go. Afraid of uncertainty, they often believed abusers who told them they would stop.[58]

The problem of intimate violence was inadequately addressed by the police and the courts through the 1970s. Kristi Van Audenhove, current director of Virginia Sexual and Domestic Violence Action Alliance, said in the early days, "there was still this sense of... some things should be off limits to examination by the justice system... 'a man's home is his castle' was not an easy belief to break down."[59] A Richmond NOW Task Force mobilized to learn more about the problem and take action in some way. The group emerged in response to the twelve hundred reported cases of assault in 1974, 90 percent of which were perpetrated by spouses. One judge said in an eleven month period he saw seven hundred battered women on his docket. Judge Max Laster explained his problem with the legal code to the reporter: "There is nothing we can do unless the skin is broken. That constitutes a felony." Richmond NOW Task Force cochair Jane Parsons told the paper: "I think it's a pretty sad commentary that there are facilities for abused animals but no facilities for abused women."[60]

The Charlottesville feminist publication *Blue Lantern* produced a feature on domestic violence. An article related a harrowing story of a woman who was severely beaten for asking to go out with her friends one night. While one million women were battered nationwide, locally, a woman could only receive assistance from Charlottesville's welfare department if she had children or if her husband was previously found guilty of some criminal act. Charlottesville's director of court services admitted most first offenders' cases were dismissed, and one domestic-court judge confirmed men tended to get suspended sentences, which was good enough because incarceration often caused more conflict. The report asserted, "Holding the marriage together rather than providing refuge for the woman whose marriage is destructive to her—is the theme song of the dominant system." Charlottesville judges rarely provided protective orders, and one legal official said, "some women don't mind being beaten...." The article concluded: "In order to make life more bearable for the battered women of Virginia, houses which provide food, shelter, counselling, and employment must be established, and legal challenges to a court system which is far from adequate must be initiated."[61]

Despite its progress on providing assistance for sexual-assault survivors, local groups did not originally focus on helping battered women. Representing the Virginia Women's Political Caucus (VWPC), Meg Williams noted the commonwealth was farther along on addressing rape crisis than providing services for domestic-violence survivors when she testified in front of the Arlington County Commission's hearing on using federal Title XX money to fund rape crisis initiatives. She said: "Right now little attention has been given to this type of crisis. Despite the lack of active publicity and services in the State, I feel that shelters should be created for women who because of brutal treatment cannot live in their homes. Counselors should be trained to deal with this problem."[62] Activists knew getting women out of harmful situations was the priority, especially given the attitudes of law enforcement and courts at the time, so their focus was on providing shelter, wherever it might be.

As activists around the country mobilized to provide services to battered women, feminists in the commonwealth worked to find solutions in their own communities. Originally, concerned citizens mobilized to provide shelter in private homes. This continued for varying lengths of time in different communities, depending on when groups could create more formalized services for survivors. Mary Ann Bergeron was one of a cadre of women in the Richmond/Chesterfield area who housed survivors on an ad hoc basis. She admitted that, in the early years, "there was nothing else to do, I mean, that was the only way." She remembered the women who arrived: "It was very sad. They come with nothing. They come with their children and what's on their backs. Very rarely do they have anything [except] maybe a teddy bear." So activists established funds to pay for toiletries and other necessities. Bergeron explained the challenges of sheltering women in her home: "These women were traumatized. And you had to be kind to them. You had to help them in whatever way possible [to] feel as if they'd done the right thing, because they're being told by society that they have not." Rarely did these women stay more than a night, and they often came in the middle of the night as it was. Bergeron never knew where they went from her house, because "It was better for us not to know." Bergeron remembered women provided shelter in their own homes until the YWCA's temporary shelter opened its doors.[63]

The goal of organizers was to formalize services provided to survivors of domestic violence, which was the same goal they had in assisting survivors of sexual assault. As scholars note, many of the women who established the early shelters worked from an explicitly feminist standpoint. It is not surprising that Bergeron and NOW women were involved in providing shelter to women in the Richmond area, as it is not surprising that in Norfolk a group of "'grass-roots' and 'radical'" feminists who initially met resistance from the YWCA board were also involved. Diane Hall recalled "the work to sell the idea to the board" done by a "core" group of women, including NOW members, a "loosely formed group" titled Woman Space, which used the YWCA as meeting space, and the "Twenty Concerned Women" who involved themselves with fundraising for the effort. After what she called the "initial momentum" provided by these women, the program grew and "became more mainstream."[64]

Like the "core group" of women in Norfolk, feminist groups across the commonwealth mobilized support for women in their communities. Northern Virginia NOW applied for federal funding to expand the Mount Vernon Mental Health Center's services to provide temporary shelter and emergency services to domestic violence victims. NOW's Lois Hunt worked with local police and Fairfax County Social Services to plan services for this shelter, which would include employment counseling for the women in need so they might have a long-term plan to allow them to leave their abusers. After working on rape crisis services and spinning off ROAR as an independent committee, Richmond YWCA's Young Women Committed to Action turned its attention to battered women. Their first efforts included reaching out to individual activists and organizations to see what was happening in the area. The members determined they would contact the Department of Welfare and other community groups to provide at least temporary shelter for women, and then get funding for a permanent shelter. They also discussed beginning a hotline. This committee, working on the mandate of their national resolution to address domestic violence, determined to take a five-month period to educate and train themselves as volunteers and open an operational shelter by December 1977. They wanted to partner with different groups and fund their operations independently from the YWCA, and ultimately turn the project over to the community in some way. After considerable debate, the YWCA Board of Directors decided it would support this effort, but all attempts at fundraising and securing grants would run through the proposed shelter. The YWCA would be listed as a "moral supporter of the group."[65]

As groups formalized and sought both grant funding and social services, more social work professionals joined the team, but not always at the cost of feminist values. When the YWCA Victim Advocacy Program committee discussed hiring a new director, they revealed their preferences. The job description listed requirements as someone with a master's in social work, administrative and supervisory experience, and a "subjectively feminist philosophy."[66]

The Richmond shelter, with its roots in a women's committee of the larger YWCA, is an excellent case study in how an entire community pulled together to provide services. Volunteers, professionals, and money were all required. In 1979, the volunteers from the YWCA determined to open a temporary shelter, with the assistance of funds from the United Way. They were joined by thirty services professionals, volunteers, and clergy across the area who had founded the Domestic Violence Project to assist in setting up services for women. St. Joseph's Villas, a Catholic Charity, provided more permanent housing for up to two months, and applied for a $100,000 Department of Justice grant to secure the personnel support necessary for this move. Volunteers would begin training with the Fairfax County Women's Shelter to assist at intake, in the short-term three-bedroom apartment shelter, and on the crisis hotline, which would run through the YWCA. Funding would come from the United Way in a $40,000 grant, and the Episcopal Women's United Thank You Offering, which donated an additional $20,000.[67]

Finally, the YWCA moved from being a "moral supporter" to becoming intrinsically involved, cutting some programs in order to provide continuous support in the face of a budget shortfall, and creating a new Victim Advocacy

Program for women and children survivors. In its first month, the Y's Victim Advocacy Program assisted 36 battered women and 54 children, as well as 5 rape victims. Six months later, the project had assisted 197 battered women and 328 children, had helped 26 sexual assault survivors, participated in over one hundred media and education events, and were working with two women who killed their husbands in self-defense. In order to purchase a larger shelter, the YWCA moved $10,000 from a fund established in the early twentieth century to help poor women with educational needs and secured a $20,000 grant from Best Products Foundation, a company that also supported ERA efforts.[68]

Community organizations supported the shelter. The Thomas Jefferson Women's Club gave $250 to support the shelter, $250 to stock the pantry, and then promised to continually restock the food for the shelter. The local chapter of the National Council of Jewish Women provided $500 worth of toys and supplies and volunteered their time to work with the children in the shelter as their mothers received counseling. The council did the scheduling and training for the volunteers working on this project. And the twelve men and women who formed the Victim Advisory Board provided the major support for continued service, including LWV's and VERARC's longtime activist Muriel Elizabeth Smith, who volunteered to reach out to numerous church groups to secure extra assistance.[69]

Community volunteers continued to support the shelter's permanent facility. The YWCA members had raised almost $139,000 for the purchase of a house in 1981. Once they found the home on the north side of Richmond, Volunteers of America donated bunkbeds and stored other donations, the Home Builders Association and other volunteers and professionals did the building renovation, and local stores donated supplies. Various organizations like the local AAUW chapter sponsored the furnishing of rooms.[70] In 1982, the Victim Advocacy Program reported it had sheltered 200 women and 282 children, and an average of 42 volunteers per month served 8,347 hours. The hotline fielded over six hundred calls. The group also started a Men's Advisory Council to work with abusers and to create a male support network.[71] The Richmond YWCA shelter is still operating, a testament to community determination and continued support.

What could a community without the resources of a major metropolitan area like Richmond do? In the mountains of Virginia, almost on the border of West Virginia, sits the town of Clifton Forge, about forty-five minutes from the nearest large city, Roanoke. It was here a group of determined NOW members started a shelter because, as Stephanie Tyree remembered, at the first organizational meeting in the early 1980s, dealing with local domestic violence was the "number one priority" of those present. She noted the closest shelters were in Lewisburg and Staunton, and they were "too far, or the shelters at times would be so full," not to mention "the unemployment rate, and the alcoholism rate and everything."

She remembered the time when, as in Richmond, women had to shelter survivors in their homes. When she "lived in this little, teeny town of Glen Wilton," just over the mountain from Clifton Forge, a woman asked for the hotline number for her sister. She recalled giving the woman a number but explaining only a hotel would be available because there was no shelter yet. A few weeks later, Tyree learned: "She had called the police; they said you'll have to come in to Fincastle; she didn't have a car or drive. It was twenty-five miles away.... She was trying to get the [crisis hotline] number; she had put it down in the bottom of the dresser so he wouldn't find it. She was trying to find the number to call. And he took the shotgun and shot her and killed her." She explained a deputy lived next door and "knew what was going on" but did nothing to help.[72]

Like Mary Ann Bergeron, Sarah Payne remembered opening her house as a safe home when there was no shelter for women. She said, "I felt like I was saving their life a lot of times. They had children with them, you know, kids." Tyree remembered housing a blind woman and her two children, and Payne said "you get so attached to them you don't want them to leave." But after a year or so, Sarah Payne said the need for a permanent shelter was clear.

The conveners of the chapter, Sarah Payne and her daughter Stephanie Tyree, started fundraising with the NOW chapter, raising awareness and publicity, with their sister writing articles for the paper as advocates. They asked for donations through a newsletter Melanie Payne-White wrote and distributed. And they received their first grant from the Alleghany Foundation. Once they secured the shelter, all three women worked with NOW members and community supports to paint and renovate the home. Payne-White remembered four churches furnished one bedroom each, just as Richmond organizations did. In the beginning, when Payne-White was the director, she had to live at the shelter due to its lack of funding. She simply took housing as her payment. Ultimately, the shelter became an institution. Sarah Payne sat on the board for ten years, and the shelter celebrated its twenty-seventh anniversary in 2014.[73]

The Payne family brought up something many at the time probably believed, but few would probably acknowledge. These activists tended to be privileged, college educated, and affiliated with organizations, often helping women who were far outside of their social strata. Bergeron mentioned the women who arrived at her house had a difficult time because it was an intrusion, or the women felt as if it were an intrusion, of her domicile, despite Bergeron's best efforts to make them feel at home. Stephanie Tyree discussed the crisis and intervention training they took with the social services workers who assisted in this project. She remembered them telling trainees, "'You are not always going to like these people. They're not always . . . the people you would hang out with or you would like, because quite often they drink or they do drugs or their lifestyle is not what you would condone, so to speak. Get over it. Because this is what you're supposed to be doing. And you deal with it.'" She remembered some of the women seeking asylum "came off kind of tough and rough, like, but they might have had to be that way because of their surroundings or maybe the way they were raised, and they were very good people." Shelter rules often reinforced a behavior standard, as in Richmond YWCA's enforcement of no-alcohol policies. These feminists performed a critical service for survivors—that much is clear—but they often did so from a position of privilege which actually gave them the knowledge and support system to critically examine violence in a way the victims, who were involved in the cycle of violence and were struggling to find resources, could not.[74]

By the late 1970s, so many Virginia groups had organized to protect battered women in so many capacities that services expanded rapidly. Resources included Radford's Wife Abuse Haven and Harrisburg's First Step Program, and Hampton had the Virginia Peninsula Council for Battered Women, to name a few. Still, much work needed to be done, and so local activists joined together to start Virginians Against Domestic Violence (VADV) in 1979 to better standardize counseling techniques, share managerial tips, and secure funding. Chairwoman Cathy Garcia announced meetings in Charlottesville, Richmond, Roanoke, and Williamsburg for 1980.[75]

Organizations continued to stand ready to help the shelters materially and financially, as when the Winchester AAUW furnished and stocked the pantry of the local shelter, or when the Shenrocco chapter of the BPW raised money to help open the Shenandoah County Shelter through bake sales, bazaars, garage sales, and a dried-flower-arrangement sale. Prince William County NOW assisted in the redecorating of the Turning Points Shelter, and Delvia Fisher of the Hampton Roads YWCA said 1983 contributions to their new shelter ranged from 390 volunteer hours to fifteen thousand dollars raised by the community and matched with a fifteen-thousand-dollar Junior League Grant, and chain-link fencing provided and installed by First Presbyterian and Royster Memorial Presbyterian churches. A twenty-five-thousand-dollar DSS grant provided needed money for staffing, and an anonymous donor gave money for an iron in honor of when she had nowhere to go, there was no shelter yet, and a YWCA worker set up a cot for her in the reception area. As this donor said, "It was Heaven to lie down in peace and get a good night's rest." When explaining her desire for an iron, she said, "One's clothing can become quite mussed after being knocked down and kicked." And when Fairfax County's Victim Assistance Network lost grant funding, the local LWV and NOW chapters lobbied hard to get public money to replace it. NOVA NOW celebrated the successful six-month continuation of funding: "In effect our pressure tactics were so successful that not one supervisor voted against [it]." Mary Ann Beall planned to organize a group to fight for permanent funding after this victory.[76]

By the mid-1980s, there were shelters in many areas of the state—seventeen by 1982 alone, with thirty-four programs providing assistance to survivors. Shelters like the ones in Clifton Forge and Bristol, however, served such a large rural population that not all women could get assistance. "The Shelter" in Bristol served women in a hundred-mile radius of the area, and Lynchburg helped Amherst County women, but it wasn't always easy to get to the shelter. Even in urban areas, demand outstripped availability. Carol Tighe, chair of the Virginia Peninsula Council on Battered Women, noted in July of 1982 that the need was so great they were working off of a wait-list and sending emergency cases to Norfolk or Williamsburg. Tidewater's YWCA reported it was "filled to capacity" since it opened its doors in May 1982.[77] Still, in the first half of 1982, Virginia DSS reported that five thousand women sought help, and shelters housed over eighteen hundred women and children throughout the commonwealth.[78]

Support for shelters continued to grow. From Peninsula NOW and Covington Business and Professional Women collecting items and toiletries for their local shelters; to Tidewater and Charlottesville BPWs donating money and sponsoring a Christmas party for shelter children; to BPWs in Culpeper, Fauquier, and Orange counties holding raffles, an auction, and a concert to raise five thousand dollars toward the construction of an area shelter, women's groups did their part. NOW's Arlington chapter held a ten-kilometer walk for several years in a row with proceeds going to the shelter, and a group of thirty-five women in Norfolk held an Annual Women's Musical Extravaganza for several years in the early 1990s to support the shelter. In Richmond, the League of Women Voters sponsored "Once Is Not Enough" events in the 1990s, selling donated used formal dresses to raise money for the YWCA programs.[79] Businesses also sponsored domestic-violence shelters. The Tidewater Builders Association raised ten thousand dollars and renovated a garage for a children's therapeutic center at the Norfolk shelter, and Virginia Power underwrote the costs of the VADV brochure, "Domestic Violence Is a Crime." And ADT teamed up with the YWCA and Chesterfield and Henrico YWCAs to create an "Abused Women's Active Response Emerging Security pendants" program enabling battered women to immediately contact ADT through the push of a button.[80]

Shelters rely on a combination of community support and government funding. The Radford Women's Shelter, for example, reopened after relocating from Christiansburg in 1987. It received a seventy-five-thousand-dollar grant from a Virginia Department of Housing and Community Development Grant, part of the federal HUD program, which was matched by a grant from the Radford Women's Resource Center and a fifteen-thousand-dollar grant from community member Fran Ecker to assist with a job training program. The city of Newport News was able to purchase and renovate a building after receiving a ninety-thousand-dollar Community Development Grant. The shelter, titled SHARE (Shelter and Housing to Alleviate and Resolve Emergencies), would be operated by the Salvation Army and administered by the city's Social Services Department. These funds come in because shelter supporters fund-raise and seek grants, and demand government funding. Their support has been critical, as evidenced in the way in which Alexandria, Dulles Area, and NOVA NOW launched a campaign to save the Fairfax County Shelter and Services after a threatened 30 percent budget cut in 1991, over the Fairfax County Women's Commission assertion that the budget wasn't enough to serve the needs of the community as it was. Working with other concerned women's organizations like the Older Women's League (OWL), feminists collected signatures in a petition drive, distributed flyers, and printed stickers for supporters to wear at meetings. The chapters reported one- to two-thirds of attendees at the meetings in this period sported the stickers. Their efforts worked and saved the shelter's budget.[81] Efforts like these reflect just how a groundswell of activism enables feminist programs to survive.

By the early 1990s, shelters were well enough established to provide significant assistance to women who could avail themselves of the resources. But all of this effort still did not reach all Virginia violence victims. A League of Women Voters study noted that in 1990, Mary Sue Terry, who was the first woman elected attorney general in Virginia, convened a task force to address domestic violence, explaining, "It is long past time when private citizens should have to wage these battles alone, and it is time for their government to enter the battle on their side." The task force suggested a large-scale public education campaign providing information on how to report domestic violence, as well as adult and child education classes, and programming for health care providers. Still, the LWV said that "services and resources are limited and unevenly distributed statewide." The 1992 study, conducted throughout the state, found the average distance between shelters and clients was seventy-five miles. Over half of Virginia counties still had no shelters, and quality of services varied based on the funding available. So in Stanley, Virginia, Choices, Inc., still had volunteer homes opened on an as-needed basis for women. More urban areas had more resources. Turning Point, Inc., in Roanoke was run by the Salvation Army, had forty-five beds, and services including alcohol-abuse programs, self-esteem motivational programs, parenting classes, counseling, and court advocacy.[82] But even urban shelters did not have enough room for women needing their services.

Considering the challenges, VADV highlighted some important achievements on the eve of the 1994 passage of the Violence Against Women Act, a significant piece of federal legislation. In one month alone the Richmond and Chesterfield YWCA shelters helped sixty-eight women and children, sheltering them a total of 529 nights. Statewide, VADV rolled out a toll-free hotline which would route calls to the nearest shelter. A twenty-four-state study in 1993 showed Virginia feminists were doing more with less money than many other states. While the average state funding of domestic-violence programs totaled just over $2,650,000, Virginia came in at $1,041,000. While other states generally received about $1 million more from federal funding, Virginia received about $600,000 more. Virginia had thirty-one shelters, beating the national average of twenty-five. VADV was a major organization with a focus on inclusivity, as evidenced by its Women of Color and Lesbian caucuses, and it held conferences, programming and on-site training for shelters, and educational campaigns.[83] Activists' work was making a difference, even though it was not—and will likely never be—enough.

Educational efforts continued as well. From when Governor Robb signed a declaration of support for National Domestic Violence Awareness Week in 1984, to activities like purple-ribbon projects on campuses like the University of Richmond and Longwood College during Domestic Violence Awareness Month in the 1990s and 2000s, and the many projects facilitated by activists in their communities, the public was becoming increasingly aware of intimate violence. Virginia activists also got involved with the National Clothesline Project, a public display of T-shirts decorated by survivors of rape, incest, domestic violence, or violence directed at the victim because of her sexuality. The Central Virginia chapter first displayed its clothesline in 1993, and other groups would continue to display, add to, or create their own clotheslines.[84]

Domestic-Violence Legislation

As grassroots activists were attempting to shelter battered women and assist in their recovery, they and others were calling for significant changes to the laws to protect women against their abusers. Responding to calls for new legislation, the House of Delegates Committee on Health, Welfare, and Institutions created a Subcommittee to Study Battered Spouses. Committee members held hearings across the state in 1977, hearing testimony about domestic violence and the services provided to survivors. In Falls Church, many came forward to testify, including a father whose daughter could not get help from authorities. A wife who had been hospitalized twice told of how Family Services had offered the family counseling but the husband would not go, and she had no other resources. Legal Aid would not help her because she had not filed for a divorce. Cornelia Suhler of NOVA NOW's Task Force said it received about ten calls a week and, outside of churches and a few underground safe houses, women had nowhere to go.[85]

In Richmond, lawyer Sylvia Clute discussed the problems with women getting support if they sought divorce, as well as the legal classification of assault on a wife being a misdemeanor, one in which officers did not make immediate arrests if they did not witness the violence. Noting that police made arrests for shoplifting misdemeanors they did not witness, she opined, "Wife-beating involves human lives. It, on occasion, becomes a matter of life and death—not a pair of shoes or a piece of costume jewelry."[86]

The committee headed to the Tidewater and heard similar stories. A forty-one-year-old survivor in Norfolk explained to the committee that neighbors called for help after her husband beat her, but the police told her they could not arrest the man without a warrant. When the officers suggested she go somewhere for the night and swear out a warrant tomorrow, she asked: "When your lips are bleeding and you're all beat up, why do you have to get a warrant?" And Caroline Leach, a Presbyterian minister and chair of the Task Force for Battered Wives, said that, of the 8,463 domestic calls the group took from August to November 1976, only 331 women went later to swear out warrants. Observing the YMCA and Salvation Army as shelters for men, she told the committee that if women had somewhere to go for help they would not drop charges.[87]

In their final report, members reported no laws existed to deal specifically with battered spouses, and communities needed help to establish more shelters. The report specifically commended the service organizations which funded and operated these shelters for the most part, and said shelters needed more federal and state funding, especially in rural areas. Members also noted police reluctance to arrest abusers and called for more police training and better laws related to arresting abusers, as well as court-mandated counseling for victims and perpetrators. Citing Clute's testimony, members also suggested a study of existing divorce laws. The report concluded: "Overall, the problems of the battered spouse seem monumental. Certainly, the testimony in the public hearings evidenced that vast numbers of Virginia's citizens are plagued by domestic violence."[88]

Despite the testimony of Virginians and the strong report of the subcommittee, the General Assembly passed only a few half-measures in response. In 1978, the General Assembly passed a resolution to recommend (not require) police training on domestic violence, and to encourage all localities to create shelters using Department of Welfare Title XX money. It did pass a law allowing courts to mandate treatment for one or both spouses "to effect the reconciliation and rehabilitation of the parties." Legislators passed by indefinitely (refused to vote on) bills to have police keep statistics on assaults statewide, to arrest abusers without warrants at the scene, and to allow an unmarried partner to sue another for battery; they carried over a bill to create a pilot program for funding the creation of shelter facilities with grants of up to twenty-five thousand dollars from the Department of Welfare.[89]

Proponents of change denounced recalcitrant legislators. One Democratic delegate, Evelyn Hailey of Norfolk, told a symposium at William and Mary that the laws did not go far enough because some did not believe the problems to be serious and others just could not figure out how to solve them. "I was amazed at the attitude of many male legislators . . . that things have always been this way . . . that we're only going to make it harder for people to live together" by passing laws. Alice Page O'Neal, shelter coordinator for Newport News and Hampton, told the assembly, "you can be half-dead and [a magistrate] will tell you to think about it [swearing out a warrant] for a day or two and come back. . . ." The reporter noted her reluctance to secure help from the system: "I, for one, don't have too much confidence in the court systems, because I've seen them work."[90]

In this way, Virginia feminists were like others throughout the country, whom many scholars defined as having adversarial relationships with the state. Having seen too much damage done to women by problematic law enforcement and court systems, they determined help would come through their counseling and shelter programs.[91] It appears their cynical view of the state was justified in Virginia. No legislation related to violence would come up again until 1980, when the General Assembly passed a law establishing an office for spousal abuse services but refused to fund it. It opened only because the Department of Welfare decided on its own to financially support the initiative.[92]

Perhaps because the newly elected governor, Chuck Robb, was a strong supporter of domestic-violence reform, however, the General Assembly began to work toward providing more assistance to survivors. In 1982, the year Robb took office, and under intense pressure from VADV and NOW members, the General Assembly passed a bill to increase the marriage-license fee from three to ten dollars, using the extra seven dollars for services to abused spouses and children. It also passed a law allowing judges to bar an abuser from the marital home for a period, as well as a law allowing police to make arrests even if they had not witnessed the violence perpetrated. When VADV members cheered Robb's support of the measures, he responded, "I applaud you for bringing it into the open and for your persistence in seeking ways to help solve the problem. . . ."[93] VADV member and director of the Loudon County Victim Witness Program Irene Wodell worked with other anti-crime advocates to lobby for a law allowing victim impact statements in court, a law the General Assembly passed in 1983.[94]

By 1985, the General Assembly had passed a law exempting information about battered-spouse and rape crisis programs from the Freedom of Information (FOIA) act, which the AAUW's lobbyist Suzanne Davis noted had taken up a significant amount of her lobbying time. In 1989–90 the General Assem-

ENDING VIOLENCE AGAINST WOMEN 161

bly increased funding for the battered-women's program after being lobbied by VADV. And two years later, VADV called upon its members to "get in gear" to lobby for a change in the definition of "spouse abuse" to "family abuse," broaden the magistrate's powers to give protective orders, and allow for a history of violence to be introduced in child-custody hearings. In addition, lobbyists fought for a higher classification of felony if abuse happened while a domestic order was in place, as well as a redefinition of the criminal code to include stalking and threatening/intimidation, which NOW also called on its members to support.[95]

All of these bills passed into law with help from activists. As the NOW state newsletter reported, "The bills were amended as requested and slipped through the legislature without being noticed." The House even passed a bill allowing for the "abused spouse" defense as self-defense, although it got held up in the Senate Courts of Justice in 1992. The next year, after intense lobbying by VADV members, the General Assembly increased the marriage-license fee, netting over $540,000 more for survivor and prevention services. Given the state of legislation just ten years before, the laws in Virginia changed dramatically in the decade before VAWA passed Congress. These laws represent the success of many lobbying hours, increased educational efforts, and a change in how the General Assembly determined it would address the serious problem of violence in the commonwealth.[96]

The laws were changing, but even the legal changes were not enough in some places. The 1992 LWV study of Virginia domestic-violence shelters quoted many shelter representatives who claimed laws had not done much to help their clients. Southern Virginia's Family Resource Center, serving areas near the far-west North Carolina border like Galax and Wythe and Smythe counties, had a representative who told them often abusers received nothing more than an order for counseling. She said "In our rural area the police and sheriff's departments are the most conservative. They receive little training." The situation was no different in far-northwest Virginia, where a representative from Choices, Inc., opined "Women in Page County are not protected by the laws like they could/should be." A shelter staff worker in Lexington said women "get second-hand justice," and activists in Culpeper, the Lynchburg shelter which served the city and four rural counties surrounding it, said the police were not cognizant of the new laws. A Purcellville worker in Loudon County observed that only one abuser had actually been sentenced to jail time.[97]

Not all police forces were problematic, however. Melanie Payne-White remembered the local police in Covington/Clifton Forge were willing to learn and listen to the needs as presented by the activists. The LWV study did say other shelters also reported good cooperation, including one where police would come to the shelter if workers suspected an abuser might show up. Arlington police escorted women to the shelter and back to their homes to retrieve belongings, and the LWV called the Alexandria program a model, partly because it had a Domestic Violence Subcommittee of its Victims of Violent Crime Task Force, and partly because it had a local mandatory arrest policy. So Alexandria police were trained to do warrantless arrests, and trial dates were automatically set by the judicial system. The Alexandria model became a focus of study for local and state police forces, and was even held up as an example by the U.S. Department of Justice. Leaguers called for state guidelines establishing a written mandatory arrest procedure and reporting on domestic violence arrests as well as more training of law enforcement and more funding for services and educational programs in general.[98]

After the Federal Government Gets Involved

In 1994, Congress passed the Violence Against Women Act (VAWA), which had far-reaching implications for survivors of sexual assault and intimate violence. Legal Momentum (formerly called NOW's Legal Defense and Education Fund) calls the legislation a "watershed" law, which resulted from the work of women's concerted lobbying efforts at the capitol when they faced roadblocks from recalcitrant state legislators to further reform anti-violence laws. The VAWA enacted stricter federal penalties for repeat offenders, as well as a federal rape shield law. It made states pay for rape kits and protective orders so as to not burden women who could not afford either. It ensured protective orders would be enforced uniformly and carry over to states and tribal nations. Its funding provisions enabled half a million law enforcement officers to be trained on how to better protect women, and money went to local programming and survivor services. Since 1994, VAWA has provided over four billion dollars to these programs. The legislation created a national toll-free violence hotline, which fields about twenty-two thousand calls per month. In addition, it made violence against women a federal crime. Legal Momentum said, "Since the passage of VAWA, from law enforcement to victim services to Capitol Hill, there has been a paradigm shift in how the issue of violence against women is addressed."[99]

Virginia activists found this law helped them in many ways. For one thing, it provided women with a new way to articulate violence against them. As Emily Baker of Alexandria NOW told her members after speaking out at a 1996 Take Back the Night event, "We need to begin talking about these crimes as hate crimes and punishing them as hate crimes. We need to change the law so that we can begin to get the justice that we deserve."[100] Kate McCord, communications director of Virginia Sexual and Domestic Violence Action Alliance (VSDVAA), remembered VAWA as a game-changer. Having just come on board with her local shelter/rape crisis center, Avalon, in Williamsburg, she remembered most the effect VAWA had on law enforcement. In 2018 she wrote, "Prior to [VAWA], many crisis programs considered the criminal/legal system more of a hindrance than helpful." Although she admitted that, even today, rape survivors deal with a lot of victim-blaming and don't often get the response they should from police, VAWA and other federal programs enabled VSDVAA to build statewide training and advocacy programs, including a hotline for sexual-assault survivors. She also explained VAWA changed many people's attitudes about violence: "I think before VAWA it was around legitimacy.... I think we were written off a lot as kind of crazy, man-hating feminists, and ... that probably still exists in some way, folks are less likely to talk about that openly. I think we've gained a lot of legitimacy.... Now we have ... the highest level of government working to address violence against women."[101]

In its original iteration, VAWA included what NOW's Legal Momentum terms a "civil remedy," enabling women to sue their attackers in court.[102] This provision held until the U.S. Supreme Court determined it unconstitutional in 2000. As it took a Virginia college case to bring the issue of campus acquaintance rape to the national stage, perhaps it not surprising that a Virginia college case overturned this portion of the law. In 1994, Christy Brzonkala was allegedly raped by two college football players. For a time, the freshman sports nutrition major and Fairfax native kept the story to herself, staying in her room, failing classes, and ultimately overdosing on pills. She eventually pressed charges through the campus judicial system in the spring of 1995. While one player produced an alibi (but was later expelled for sexual assault), Antonio Morrison claimed the sex was consensual. In the original hearing, he was suspended for two semesters. A subsequent appeal overturned the suspension. When Brzonkala learned he would return the next year, she dropped out of school and with the help of NOW's Legal Defense Fund brought suit against Morrison under the VAWA civil rights provision.[103]

Brzonkala also filed suit against Virginia Tech for violation of Title IX, equity in education, as the university, she claimed, gave male football players preferential treatment. Brzonkala became a spokesperson against campus violence, speaking before a U.S. House subcommittee on campus violence in 1996 as her case made its way through the court system. The judge dismissed the Title IX suit, saying the students, if they did receive preferential treatment, they got it as athletes, not as men, so it was not sex discrimination. A grand jury found insufficient evidence to indict the two in criminal court.[104]

In 2000, in a five-to-four vote, the U.S. Supreme Court determined Congress did not have the authority to impose the civil rights clause of VAWA, as it was not covered under the Interstate Commerce Clause or the Fourteenth Amendment, thus invalidating that section of VAWA.[105] A *New York Times* article quoted the director of NOW's Legal Defense and Education Fund Kathyrn Rogers's critique of the decision as taking "the federal government out of the business of defining civil rights and creating remedies." Delaware Senator Joseph Biden suggested this might be the result of a power struggle between Congress and the judiciary.[106] And while Congress and the judiciary wrestled over who was in power, Brzonkala had moved home and attempted unsuccessfully to attend George Mason University until she began tending bar at a D.C. restaurant.[107] In 2013, in the wake of the Jameis Winston sexual-assault scandal at Florida State University, Brzonkala's case once again made national news as *Mother Jones* ran a story on the problems with football and sexual assault, using her story and twenty-five others dating back to the mid-1970s as evidence of a problem which continues unresolved.[108] Like Koestner, Brzonkala had become another statistic in the struggle against campus sexual assault.

The fight was not over, however. Activists continued to provide support with the assistance of money from state and federal sources. Legislators continued to make improvements in laws relating to violence, including laws mandating that officers make an arrest on a domestic violence call or write a detailed report explaining why not, and requiring judges to file protective orders/all warrants before the batterer is released. Police were also required by law to tell victims about resources, and a subsequent law gave the police power to petition for a protective order for a victim who is incapacitated. Other late-twentieth-century laws included warrantless arrests for stalkers and prohibition of firearms purchase or carrying for anyone under a protection order.[109]

By the end of the century, survivors in Virginia had a range of help available to them. In 1997, over 54,600 people requested services, 11,870 of whom were children. Over 7,275 people were sheltered, but 4,180 were turned away. These numbers were up dramatically from 1995, when just over 41,300 people requested help, 3,464 were sheltered, and 4,351 turned away for lack of space. In 1998, 60 percent of clients were white, 34 percent were African American, and 5 percent were Latina. Eighty-nine percent were between eighteen and forty-four, which suggests that women of childbearing age were the ones who sought services the most.[110]

By 2000, more than fifty-four programs and shelters existed to help survivors of violence throughout the commonwealth. Thanks to a mandate from the government, Virginia was one of the few states to combine state agencies' statistics on sexual assault, family violence, and stalking. Because of this, VADV was able to do an in-depth assessment of programs, clients, and continued needs. Statistics from October 1999 to March 2000 showed anti-violence organizations received a hotline call every four minutes, sheltered a family every four hours, and provided fifteen thousand hours of counseling every four weeks. Between 1999 and 2000, volunteers and paid staff provided almost fifty-seven thousand hours of support to survivors. The racial mix of domestic violence clients remained fairly steady, at 60 percent white, 30 percent African American, and 5 percent Latina, but sexual assault survivors reporting in were 67 percent white, 26 percent African American, 4 percent Latina, and 2 percent American Indian. Stalking was even more skewed in favor of white women reporting, with 77 percent white, 17 percent African American, and 4 percent Latina. Perhaps the numbers reflect the fact that, historically, African American women received little to no help from authorities in prosecuting assaults against them, and so perhaps they were reluctant to report abuse to authorities, fearing they would receive less assistance.[111] But considering that, merely thirty years before, there had been no shelters or rape crisis hotlines in the commonwealth, the progress made by anti-violence activists was stunning.

In the twenty-first century, VADV and VAASA merged to form the Virginia Sexual and Domestic Violence Action Alliance. As Executive Director Kristi Van Audenhove remembered, members of the organizations had been going to retreats for years, and in 2001 famed civil rights activist and singer/songwriter Bernice Johnson Reagon came to speak. Van Audenhove remembered Reagon saying working in coalitions means people who work together do not have to think the same way, "but if the vision you have out there is a common vision, you bring your differences to the table as a strength." Van Audenhove had worked for VADV for decades and had always thought the boards were too different, but "it was a profound moment for them." She said the strength of the new coalition was that activists were able to "create something new that held up both sexual assault and domestic violence as issues.... That we were going to work on both of those issues all the time. And that we were going to do [it] from a social justice framework and articulate very clearly, and it was not [a] social service framework, but a social justice framework that was driving, creating this coalition."[112]

Van Audenhove's statement focusing the coalition's efforts on social justice rather than social services firmly positions the activists as feminists. Despite working with social services, despite having to partner with police and court systems that sometimes work against the best interests of the women who seek assistance, these women know they are working within the system to reform the system. As Van Audenhove also noted, the focus is now far more on prevention than previously. Working in coalition allows everyone to share resources, which she explains helps the sexual-assault response teams. She noted, "The sexual assault coalition always had a higher bar to get over in order to move things forward." People, she believes, have an easier time believing victims of domestic violence and talking about domestic violence than they do about sexual assault, and "people have always rallied around providing shelter to women and children." Historically, she said, "It's much harder to get that same level of support for the services that sexual assault crisis centers provide. It's a hard description of what those services are. It's harder for people to wrap their heads around that as being critical." And this is the case even though more people are affected by sexual assault in some way.[113]

Today the alliance trains over one thousand people a year, keeps detailed statistics on sexual and domestic violence in Virginia, runs a hotline for sexual assault and domestic violence, holds conferences and seminars, provides educational events, and helps advocate for public policy changes. It has a multiracial staff that represents diverse sexual orientations, and it is still firmly rooted in feminist principles. Its website explains its position on intersectionality: "Understanding the great harm that racism has created for individuals, families, and communities in Virginia, we commit to building within the coalition an anti-racist framework from which to address sexual and domestic violence[.]"[114]

* * *

Marital-Rape Law

The most difficult issue with which Virginia legislators wrestled proved to be marital rape. Van Audenhove said marital-rape reform was the single most difficult piece of anti-violence legislation to pass in her long experience, because of "the juxtaposition of the privacy and women lie thing. I couldn't believe some of the things that people were willing to say on the record about why they did not support that legislation."[115] Early attempts focused on getting an acknowledgment that marital rape could happen, but all efforts in the 1970s centered on women separated from their husbands. By 1978, nineteen states had passed explicit marital-rape laws. Virginia was not one of them. COSAR members had testified about marital rape in the 1970s, and some commonwealth attorneys were using the 1981 sexual-assault law against husbands. In eight counties, one man pleaded guilty, three attorneys secured convictions, and one was overturned.[116]

Then two Virginia Supreme Court cases showed just how important law would be to women who faced this sexual abuse. In a Fairfax case, the court upheld the conviction of a separated husband. But in the same year, the Virginia Supreme Court reversed a conviction in a Norfolk case, stating because the woman had delayed filing divorce papers at the request of her husband who was dealing with an ailing father, she had not made her intentions clear. The woman had moved out, the husband was filing custody for the child, and he had broken down the door to get to her. Judges ruled that the delayed divorce papers did indeed prove unclear intent. Perhaps looking to better understand the inconsistencies, the General Assembly passed a resolution to study marital rape in 1985. VAASA called upon its members to testify and show up in support at the public hearings as only two testified in Fairfax and fewer than ten showed up. To assist in drumming up support, VAASA provided the hearing schedule, a copy of its position paper, and a request to contact members of the committee running the hearings.[117]

Exhortations to show up at the meetings must have been successful. Emily McCoy, state coordinator for Virginia NOW, testified: "Too many Virginia women have been the victims of violent sexual assault by their husbands this year and in years past" and called the abusers "criminals who are benefited by a loop hole in the law." The AAUW of Norfolk hosted a meeting with the director of Women in Crisis Center and Response (formerly TRIS) and discussed the "loophole" provided by the Supreme Court decision. They asked all local members to write to their senators and Representative Thomas Moss, who had sponsored the study bill, and to ask AAUW Virginia to pass a state resolution in support of a marital-rape law. Nancy Brock of VAASA told members, "At public hearings across the state, victims of marital rape told of betrayed trust, feelings of guilt, entrapment, anger, and isolation." They explained how police and prosecutors could not respond. One man explained how marital rape affected him as a child.[118]

In response, the House of Delegates passed a marital-rape bill—and the contents divided feminists in the commonwealth. While *Washington Post* reporters said the bill, sponsored by Moss, was "hailed ... as one of the most progressive [laws] in the nation," it left much to be desired. First, it proposed a ten-day limit on reporting the crime to the police. In addition, it provided counseling as an alternative to jail time. It also differentiated punishment based on the status of a couple: living apart, the rapist would see the same punishment as any rapist, but a rapist cohabitating with his wife would see a lighter sentence. In addition, physical harm had to be done in order to prove rape.[119] Marianne Fowler, speaking as state coordinator for the National Women's Political Caucus–Virginia (formerly VWPC), said, "There is good in the bill, ... but it is buried among viciously anti-women provisions."[120] Fowler and Elise Heinz of the VWPC observed that no other crime had a ten-day reporting period, and said the bill did not go far enough to protect women.[121] In contrast, Virginia NOW officially threw its support behind the bill as it stood, explaining to members, "We can't be purest [sic] on this issue—we have to get what we can this year and come back in future years to further change the law...." NOW's co-legislative coordinators urged members to lobby the Senate to bring the bill to the floor, but did note the VWPC's opposition to the bill.[122]

The Senate amended the bill, and the law passed. As the new law stood, with Senate amendments, all restrictions provided by the House remained in place, but sexual crimes beyond sexual assault were now covered under the law. NOW members recorded at their State Council Meeting, "We were very successful on this issue. 'Flawed but helpful' legislation was passed." And NWPC-VA went further, claiming their members were the only ones who refused to support the bill as introduced and that their demands did not fall on deaf ears, writing: "WE SHOULD BE PROUD OF THE CHANGES THAT WERE MADE BECAUSE WE SPOKE OUT!"[123]

However, just because the General Assembly took one step forward, feminist activists were not satisfied, for the law was inadequate. That marital rape continued to be a problem for abused women once again thrust Virginia into the national headlines when Lorena Bobbitt severed her husband's penis after being assaulted in 1994. The case made international news and became the butt of jokes, but the reality of her situation was extremely serious.

Bobbitt had endured abuse throughout the marriage. According to her lawyers, she had been repeatedly abused and sexually assaulted, and her husband threatened to find her and rape her if she left. A native of Ecuador, Bobbitt claimed to live in fear, and on the night in question, her husband had returned home after a "night of drinking" and raped her once again, which proved to be the last straw. In her trial, she talked of her four-year marriage to Bobbitt, and over forty witnesses attested to seeing the bruises on her, as well as witnessing him punching, kicking, and choking her. The defense psychiatrist said her actions stemmed from post-traumatic stress, a symptom of being worn down by abuse for four years. Throughout her trial, supporters sent letters and flowers, and many held a vigil outside the courthouse. Even the commonwealth's attorney admitted to the *Washington Post*: "She's easy to feel sorry for: a little, diminutive woman who obviously had a very terrible marriage at best...." When she was acquitted by reason of insanity, many were relieved, but noted her situation was not unusual. As Stephanie Williams, head of a Latino family support group in the area, said "There are many Lorena Bobbitts. The only difference is that the others have done nothing to retaliate."[124] As Alexandria NOW co-coordinator Susan Hall said, "Instead of blaming Lorena Bobbitt for severing her husband's penis, should we be asking...: What are we doing to ensure accountability of men who violate women?... Men hurt women because they can."[125]

Perhaps spurred on by Bobbitt's experience, feminists set to work reforming the law they reluctantly accepted not ten years before. Virginia NOW announced it would lobby for the elimination of the code determining different punishments for cohabitation or living apart, as well as the ten-day reporting period and proof of physical harm done. Part of this happened during the 1994 General Assembly session, where the General Assembly eliminated the ten-day reporting period.[126]

By 2002, advocates of reform had succeeded in proposing a law to rescind restrictions on cohabitation and the necessity to prove physical injury, essentially defining marital rape as any other type of rape in the criminal code, with the exception of the counseling option. Opposition was strong. As Kate McCord remembered, "it was remarkable what legislators felt like was OK to say in public in terms of what they felt had the right to... sexual activity with their spouses, whether there was consent or not. It was really something."[127]

The bill faced opposition in the House. Republican delegate Dick Black, whose district included Manassas, home of Lorena Bobbitt, was later quoted as saying, "I don't know how on earth you could validly get a conviction of a husband-wife rape, when they're living together, sleeping in the same bed, she's in a nightie, and so forth, there's no injury, there's no separation or anything...."[128] A newspaper reported Republican delegate Robert Marshall asking, "If a wife simply said no and the husband simply wanted to have relations, is that rape?" And many, including a Democratic delegate, Kenneth Melvin of Portsmouth, suggested concern that women could use accusations of rape against husbands in divorce cases. In a floor debate *Washington Post* reporter Lisa Rein described as "wrenching," many delegates illustrated just how equal they thought women should be in the twenty-first century. McCord remembers those who fought the sexist legislators: "Unfortunately, it's only the women delegates that I remember and women senators standing up and saying, 'Are you really saying this? Do you understand what you are actually trying to promote here?'" Despite the concerns of some delegates, this bill did pass as part of a larger domestic-violence reform law, and Virginia became one of eighteen states at the time to have no exemptions on marital rape, with the exception of allowing for a victim to agree that her spouse receive mandatory counseling instead of jail time.[129]

Conclusion

Virginia moved from being a commonwealth with few legal protections for survivors of sexual and relational violence to one with stronger laws, but still much work to do. In addition, feminists established crisis hotlines, shelters, and services in their communities where there were none in 1970, like their counterparts across the country. And students on college campuses in Virginia and around the country have demanded their right to be safe from sexual predators, strangers and acquaintance alike, with some success. Still, the 2010 murder of Yeardley Love, University of Virginia lacrosse player, by her ex-boyfriend, and the 2014 death of University of Virginia student Hannah Graham at the hands of a stranger who then confessed to murdering Virginia Tech student Morgan Harrington, yet again put Virginia colleges in the headlines and revealed that college women are still not entirely safe either on campus or in their surrounding environs.[130] And as Kate McCord explained, the language about sexual assault still needs to change: "all of these victim-blaming comments, and so to counter victim-blaming comments like that or victim-blaming comments about sexual assault ... you just have to stick with basic value statements that anybody should be free from sexual assault, and that a consequence of drinking too much is not abduction, not sexual assault, it's a hangover."[131] McCord stated "slut shaming" is still a big problem, and many have not moved beyond understanding that all women, no matter what they are doing, or wearing, should be safe.

That sexual violence continues to plague college campuses was made clear in 2016, when University of Richmond student Cecilia Carreras posted an essay on the *Huffington Post* website about the university's failure to provide adequate punishment to the male athlete who raped her, and the story caused an uproar among alumni and students. The university's emailed response, which included the statement, "[the] assertions of fact are inaccurate," prompted another student, Whitney Ralston, to come forward and say that her case was also mishandled. After Carreras's story, Richmond's alumni Facebook page was crowded with mostly supportive responses from alumni, as well as alumnae stories of the University of Richmond mishandling their cases, some dating back to the 1990s.[132]

A group of students, assisted by 1993 alumna Melissa Dart, demanded that the university respond to the allegations properly at an "It Ends Now" anti-violence program. The Kappa Alpha Order was later that week suspended from campus when several members sent out an email to almost one hundred students which included the assertion, "we're looking forward to watching that lodge virginity be gobbled up for all y'all. . . . Tonight's the type of night that makes fathers afraid to send their daughters away to school." In response to these incidents and others, University of Richmond students have formed the group Spiders Against Sexual Assault and Violence, a coed organization, which is supported by many UR alumni. They have demonstrated on campus, and a group has met with the president, who assured students and alumni that steps have been taken to address this problem. He has brought in Title IX investigators who are not connected with the men's or women's colleges (Richmond and Westhampton, respectively), and asserts that the university is planning for a Center for Sexual Assault Prevention and Response with a full-time coordinator, and is establishing a Parent's Advisory Committee. Even with as much support as they have received, Carreras and Ralston faced continued harassment and vandalism of their personal property for their efforts.[133]

The University of Richmond was not alone in failing sexual-assault victims. The *Commonwealth Times* reported that, of the 272 universities under Title IX investigation for failing to adequately handle sexual assault cases, 6 are in Virginia. The University of Richmond, Virginia Commonwealth University, College of William and Mary, James Madison University, University of Virginia, and Washington and Lee University had pending cases in 2016.[134] What will happen in these open cases remains to be seen. It is clear, however, that this is one area in which feminists still have a lot of work to do.

The sexual harassment and violence faced by many women on a regular basis are not taken seriously enough, as the above stories suggest. The battle is not over. However, the anti-violence movement had a tremendous impact on women in the commonwealth, and the commonwealth activists have had an impact on the larger national movement. As McCord explained, "The first thing I think about is this safety network... is one major thing that feminists have done in the last thirty years... and so it's saved a lot of lives, adults and children...."[135]

In 2018 McCord wrote that more anti-violence coalitions are moving towards an "intersectional approach" in their work. McCord explained that the VSDVAA examines the racial disparities that lead to different justice outcomes. She also noted, "In cases of family and intimate partner homicide in Virginia, African-American women die at higher rates than any other group." The VSDVAA attempts to understand and address how black women may feel about the police, how their access to services may be more limited, and how "racism is a factor in terms of our institutional responses to domestic violence and sexual assault at every level." This has been an ongoing goal of VSDVAA, as she had argued several years earlier that the organization "will... change the narrative around what equity looks like, what privilege looks like. How other types of oppression interconnect with violence against women."[136]

As someone who has been active in the movement as a career choice since the 1980s, Van Audenhove is the perfect person to reflect on her thirty-five years of work and note where Virginia has gone. She thinks far more needs to be done to provide services for child sexual abuse. But she, too, noted: "There's been massive, massive change in a very short period of time." She concluded: "I work in an organization that we think of ourselves as being very radical, right? But we're really pretty mainstream." They have changed the laws, and they have provided help to women, which often necessitates working in a generally patriarchal structure of the legal and political system to secure change and support.[137]

Before the 1970s, women in the commonwealth, and across the country, had little recourse as survivors of violence. But the work of grassroots activists and lobbyists made a difference. Feminists changed the laws as they created support structures from the ground up, shared information, and founded institutions that now respond to violence against women in myriad supportive ways. It is not enough, however. Continued issues with relational violence and sexual assault plague women, and until we change the rape culture that normalizes aggression towards women, feminists will not easily resolve these problems. Recent developments in 2017, including women coming forward to accuse high-profile celebrities and politicians of sexual misconduct ranging from harassment to rape, perhaps reflect the end result of decades' worth of activist efforts to bring violence to light, support survivors, and punish the offenders. The #metoo Twitter campaign, begun by African American activist Tarana Burke to assist women of color who were survivors and co-opted more broadly in 2017 on Twitter and Facebook as a way to combat ignorance about assault and harassment, shows just how widespread sexual violations against women are. Time will tell if this new campaign, built on the work of countless women in previous decades, is effective.

Conclusion

ASSESSING PROGRESS AND EVALUATING THE PATH FORWARD

So... feminism truly has changed the construct of woman in America, but in the South, definitely where the demure, voiceless belle could find her voice. And then, on the flip side of that, the silent, black woman could find her voice.
—TERRIE PENDLETON, founder, Lesbian Womyn of Color

Virginia feminists believed that their work has made a difference for women of the commonwealth, despite the failure of ERA ratification, rollbacks on abortion rights, and the failure of society to adequately address violence against women. While many acknowledged that the commonwealth—and society— have a long way to go, twentieth-century Virginia has changed politically, and women have made important gains. Activists recognized the work they did as significant, even as they accepted their failure to achieve success on all fronts.

The ERA

Feminists interviewed took ERA ratification's failure hard. Stephanie Tyree explained, "My biggest disappointment is I was born and raised in Virginia, and... they wouldn't even [ratify ERA]. And it wasn't even taking away anything, and that just, I will never get over that."[1] Mary Coulling claimed ERA, along with better subsidies for child care and stronger family leave policies and access to better medical facilities in rural areas are still necessary for Virginia women to achieve equality.[2] Lee Perkins admitted that "Unless we're in the Constitution" reproductive rights and other freedoms are at threat, especially since "Virginia has been an example of... essentially limiting rights... especially with reproductive rights."[3]

But the ERA continues to be introduced in the General Assembly. In 2015, the Virginia ERA network, now working under the auspices of Virginia NOW, rallied supporters to get the amendment passed. Their online campaign included Twitter hashtags and cut-and-paste email addresses, reflecting how much easier it is to lobby for change with twenty-first century technology.[4]

As it had in days past, the ERA fell prey to General Assembly machinations. The Virginia Senate passed—and then rescinded—the amendment in a partisan battle over a separate issue. The Senate majority leader, Tommy Norment, declared to a reporter that the vote was "absolutely" in retribution for a revote on a secret ballot measure, saying, "I prefer to refer to it as a quid pro quo." The Democratic Caucus leader, Don McEachin, reportedly answered, "If [Norment is] going to be for equal rights today but not tomorrow, it's a great headline for you."[5] Amid pressure, the Senate again revisited and passed the vote, but the House refused to docket the amendment, killing it for the year. The following year, the Senate again passed the ERA, marking its fifth pro-ERA vote in a row, but again the House refused to hear the amendment, despite being met outside the committee by a number of pro-ERA lobbyists. Eileen Davis of Richmond-based ERA-lobbying organization Women Matter vowed that her group would continue to try to dislodge the amendment from the House committee: "At what point are you simply obstructing the democratic process? We're not giving up."[6]

What will it take to ratify the ERA? The Virginia Women's Political Caucus president, Sandra Brandt, explained: "each year we get [ERA] almost there and then you know... I don't understand why this is an issue anymore."[7] In 2018, the battle continued, waged by AAUW, NOW, and other groups working to get ERA ratified. Whether it will ever get to a House floor vote remains to be seen.[8] In the commonwealth, the battle to ratify the ERA will continue, as activists continue to make known just how important they believe it is.

Abortion Rights

Many activists cite the continued assault on reproductive choice as an ongoing problem, but some even find success in the failure. Emily McCoy recalled that "holding off the assault on reproductive rights was big." Denise Lee agreed: "keeping us as pro-choice as purely as you could for as long as you could" was a victory, albeit a dubious one. Because activists fought to make abortion available, women growing up after *Roe* have not lived in a world completely devoid of options. Sandra Brandt noticed that young women are "not fighting for those issues like we did... how we marched for it, and how we were at bell towers, on lobby day, and... dropped off literature to all our legislators and everything... none of them have concepts of that." She partially blamed younger women who never lived without choice for failing to really fight against bills like TRAP laws, but Perkins also called out the General Assembly's persistence on this issue: "you shouldn't have to lobby against, say, ultrasound."

Pro-choice activists continue to be concerned about the direction in which reproductive rights are moving. Linking abortion rights to larger issues of reproductive justice and choice, Georgia Fuller asked rhetorically, "Wouldn't it be great if no women ever had an abortion because no woman ever needed an abortion?" Kate McCord linked reproductive rights to larger issues, explaining: "remember we were talking about transvaginal ultrasounds, and... feeling as though legislators have the right to dictate what happens to the bodies of other people is something that continues today, unfortunately." Karen Raschke also expressed concern over social justice and reproductive rights: "Going forward, I think we're going to go to the olden days when any intelligent [woman], or woman with money, is going to be able to get an abortion if she needs one," but she fears that poor and rural women will "especially" lose their access if laws continue to get more restrictive.

Many activists cited the growing legal impediments in the commonwealth. But Denise Lee worried that "it's not going to be over until [abortion is] outlawed," explaining just why abortion rights are still at the forefront of the choice campaign. On the topic of abortion rights, Mary Ann Bergeron has her own personal views on abortion but explained that she is entirely pro-choice. She fears that TRAP laws and other restrictions are threatening choice "Because of legislative maneuvering, and because of the ideology of political parties in Virginia." As Lynn Bradford discussed the red-herring issue of the partial-birth-abortion law, she noted: "we're not going to need laws against abortion, there['s] not going to be anybody to do them." Sandra Brandt also said that she sees a problem with access in simply trying to keep clinics open in Virginia. Raschke believes that nothing less than a changeover of the Supreme Court and getting pro-choice voters out en masse will stop the continued attack on choice.

* * *

Violence

McCord discussed reproductive rights in the context of ongoing problems with violence against women, explaining: "We're kind of... losing ground on reproductive justice.... And there are so many ways that reproductive coercion plays into the violence against women that I would like to see us broaden our work on that." She noted that, not too long ago, debates on marital rape exposed ongoing problems: "This is what rape culture looks like. Is that these men, who are legislators on the floor, feel like it is ok to say this without any repercussions, and not even understand... the actions they're describing...."[9] The persistence of rape culture, slut shaming, and victim blaming explains why sexual and intimate-partner violence is still a big problem.

Ongoing problems in Virginia colleges mirror those across the country. McCord explained that colleges still don't work closely enough with sexual-assault response groups, which is important because, "(A) somebody who has been traumatized needs all the support they can get, right, and (B) there's no such thing as too many resources, and in terms of responding to... you get a confidential response from a local crisis center that you may not be able to guarantee on campus now, so they serve different purposes and complementary purposes." McCord cited a 2011 letter from the Department of Education that, in her words, "clarified that all forms of sexual violence—including sexual harassment—can constitute a violation of Title IX because it interferes with the rights of students to receive education free from discrimination." The 2013 Campus SaVe Act is also evidence, she says, of how national support affects survivors. Colleges and institutions determine who can be mandated reporters of violence, which was a provision of the Clery Act. Often, they name professors and administrators as reporters, who then must provide a woman's name and details to a centralized office. This can wrest control from the survivor. But Title IX offices are there as a safety net for survivors, whatever their faults. President Trump's education secretary, Betsy DeVos, created a firestorm in 2017 when she announced at a talk at George Mason University that she planned to rescind the Department of Education 2011 guidelines that she believes unfairly target the accused by requiring a lower burden of proof. What will happen in the future remains to be seen on campus, but activists are already gearing up to fight this change.[10]

It is not just guidelines and legislation that need to be addressed, however. Laws do not necessarily end violence against women. Kristi Van Audenhove discussed the ways in which we need to reconceptualize violence against women—it's not just assault, but the "tremendous amount of sexual violence that takes place within the negotiation of sexual relationships. And we have to talk about that. And the solution to that is maybe not in the criminal justice system."

Although we have a long way to go to end violence against women, how we address the violence changed as a result of the feminist movement. Van Audenhove explained that the fifty-three agencies addressing domestic and sexual violence, employing seven hundred paid staff members and countless volunteers, show progress in Virginia. She warns, however, that centers and shelters continue to suffer from a lack of financial and material support. Too many survivors are turned away from shelters for lack of space.

Activists helped to change the laws, but existing laws continued to be inadequate in addressing violence against women. Melanie Payne-White and Beth Marschak both cited changes to laws addressing violence as evidence of feminist victories. However, in 2014, the House of Delegates refused to pass a bill keeping guns out of the hands of domestic abusers, despite overwhelming support in the Senate and Virginia's dubious rank as sixteenth worst in the country for intimate homicide by gun.[11]

Some feminists believed that attitudes towards violence changed as well, because feminists worked hard to dislodge them—but again, there is more work to be done. Bonnie Atwood argued that "we're headed in the right direction as far as awareness of violence toward women[,]" and Mary Ann Bergeron cited changed attitudes about domestic violence, child abuse, and sexual assault as a direct result of feminists' publicizing and discussing these issues. McCord said: "people now understand that it is a choice to commit violence," but there is not a "huge turnaround" in people believing they can or should "step in when we see more violence."

And while legislation has changed, attitudes, particularly about sexual violence, have not necessarily caught up. Van Audenhove explained that she would be hard-pressed to find anyone trying to justify intimate violence as they did forty years ago, beyond some still asking why women stayed in the face of problems, but that some people still question women's behavior when it comes to sexual assaults. When one in five women is assaulted during her college career and reporting of sexual assaults has increased by 50 percent as other crime reporting has been on the decline across college campuses, it's indicative of a serious problem.[12] Increased university efforts, prompted in large part by the Obama administration's task force to address this problem, account for some of the increase in reporting.[13] But recent scandals involving sexual assault by athletes at major universities like Florida State and Baylor suggest just how pervasive this problem is, and that it is an issue that reaches far beyond the boundaries of the commonwealth.

This problem, rape culture, is ongoing. In the fall of 2017, women stepped forward to demand recognition of sexual violence, from microaggressions to physical harassment and rape. The "Me Too" campaign, actually conceived in 2007 by Brooklyn African American activist and founder of Girls for Gender Equality Tarana Burke to empower women of color to speak out against assault, went viral after actress Alyssa Milano tweeted a suggestion for survivors to use it. Since October 2017, over 825,000 have posted #metoo on Twitter and Facebook.[14] In Virginia and across the world, survivors spoke their truths with the simple hashtag, showing the pervasiveness of the problem.

Having learned the hard way what kinds of legislation did not resolve the issue, the movement is shifting strategies. Even officials from the Virginia Sexual and Domestic Violence Action Alliance (VSDVAA) noted that good intentions can often backfire when it comes to addressing violence against women. Van Audenhove said now that many legislators want to put a domestic-violence law in their "portfolio" of legislation; sometimes VSDVAA needs to explain ramifications—like what might happen if the General Assembly passes a law that would arrest women for "allowing" their children to witness them being abused. Kate McCord sees VSDVAA as one of a group of coalitions "conducting anti-violence [work] . . . through a racial justice lens," and the goal is to change "the narrative around what equity looks like, what privilege looks like. How other types of oppression interconnect with gender-based violence . . . ." It's a lofty goal that has not been realized to its fullest yet, as McCord recently admitted after participating in a national conference. She explained why the women's movement focused on criminalization of violence as its priority, including the desire to end violence, and the need to be taken seriously, but she also acknowledged the repercussions:

> Through this focus on criminalization, we have created our own world in which accountability is equated with punishment. We have contributed to the building of the prison nation. In return for legitimacy, funding, and influence at certain tables, we have sold out our own dream of liberation for all. . . .

A few of the ideas that coalitions are willing to try: shift policy work away from carceral strategies toward racial and economic justice; divest from criminal legal system in all work; shut down the school to prison pipeline; build and pilot restorative justice models; repeal mandatory minimum sentences; build ways to reintegrate formerly incarcerated people into our communities; advocate for incarcerated survivors; partner with other groups working to disrupt state violence and reduce state control over communities of color.[15]

VSDVAA has joined other anti-violence coalitions in once again moving the conversation forward in new and progressive ways. The impact of this will have to be determined as they work on initiatives to address this issue.

Failures

Ever the realists, feminists acknowledge many ways in which their movement failed to achieve progress for many Virginia women. Some believe women's own attitudes and behavior caused problems. Bonnie Atwood and Boots Woodyard argued that young women were, in Atwood's words, "degrading themselves" by claiming "freedom" in ways not intended by older feminists. While Atwood decried some women's jump to "online nudity... and so-called sex positive feminism," Woodyard said, "Well I think one thing right now is to teach our women that [she] must respect herself... 'Cause they can't go around here being a prostitute, or they can't come around here cussin' or carrying on." Mary Wazlak and Emily McCoy cited a hostile media climate for perpetuating problems. McCoy explained: "they're fighting some very different battles now. I mean this sexism and TV and movies and the misogyny is awful." And she believes young women don't "recognize it because it permeates the air." Bergeron concurred with this, and said that on many issues, including the way women are savaged by media images, "I see women losing ground, and not even realizing that they're losing ground."

Some feminists talked about the necessity for women to recognize their own worth. Wazlak couched it in terms of "women's need to feel safe" and not exploited or told they are lacking by the media. She said, "We need to go back to *Our Bodies, Ourselves*. Learning who we are and how our bodies limit us and allow us the capabilities for enjoyment." (Muriel) Elizabeth Smith said that feminists still need to help people reach their own full personal potential as they work on themselves, which "sounds like a simple answer but it's very complicated...."

Many also defined challenges that kept women from being economic powerhouses. Inadequate childcare, unequal pay, and not enough political or economic opportunities for women to advance came up in many interviews with feminists. Lynn Bradford admitted that men do more to help around the home than they used to, but "some of them still have the mentality that they're helping out." Holly Farris noted that unequal credit practices still prevailed and harmed potential women home buyers, something she saw in her work with a nonprofit organization dedicated to assisting first-time buyers. McCoy said that, while feminists had great success in changing divorce laws to make property distribution more equitable, more work needs to be done on providing alimony for former spouses, and Bonnie Atwood also pointed out that divorced women still did not receive enough support and assistance. Although Virginia allows for permanent alimony, that occurs mainly in cases of long-term marriages when the spouses are at or close to retirement age. The courts can determine length of time for other cases.[16]

Some feminists, like Atwood, Wazlak, and Bergeron, explained that gender difference—the incredible work women do as mothers—should be acknowledged and appreciated more. But, as Bergeron said, honoring women's capacity for motherhood "without being patronized, and without being protected," is critical in promoting equality. Holly Farris suggested that more focus on women's thoughts, ideas, and work would go a long way in creating a more socially just society. Issues related to motherhood, property, and income equality are particularly salient issues for young feminists today, but so much progress has been made since the 1970s that perhaps younger feminists believe they have nothing left for which to fight. It may also be that white women think that these problems automatically resolved themselves and are no longer a problem.

Others cited feminism's failure to promote long-term inclusion of diverse points of view or diverse people. Terrie Pendleton claimed that, while feminism "brought people together" from many different walks of like, "we're still divided in our ways of looking at each other." Lisa Beckman explained feminism's failure to provide cohesiveness: "it's not always a clearly defined, easily embraceable ... united front." Denise Lee said providing the LGBT community with full rights is one of the issues around which "I think there's a lot to be done,..." although others did note how far society has moved on issues of rights for those who identify as LGBTQ. Wazlak said, "I hope we'll get eventually to all states on acceptance, for equality, for diversity."

As Wazlak pointed out, these issues go well beyond gender equality. The fact that a majority of white women voted for Donald Trump, who allowed his supporters to antagonize and demean people of color, over a qualified progressive woman candidate suggests that there is still a serious racial divide in this country that feminism has not resolved. The feminists who fought for the ERA, abortion rights, and anti-violence initiatives sometimes recognized their own racial and class privilege, but not always, and not enough to resolve the problems by including more voices outside of their own, even when they knew it was a challenge that needed to be met.

Some blame larger societal forces for the failure of feminism to achieve all of its ambitious goals. Suzanne Keller posited this theory: while feminism "has had a tremendous impact . . . it is limited by the kind of society that we live in that is so individualistic and so capitalist and so countervailing towards really integrating the feminine. . . ." She explained "we haven't . . . dismantled . . . the structures of oppression . . . including sexism and institutionalized racism" to produce real social change. Georgia Fuller also cited the challenges to holistic change that plagued—and continue to create problems for—women: "patriarchy is so ingrained and it's so systemic that . . . maybe we need a hundred years to sift all that out, and to also to bring about a balance." Mary Dean Carter put it this way: "I feel like there are some factions within society that still want to put their thumb on women, still want to put them in their place and keep them in a certain role." As Denise Lee said, it's not like feminists didn't try to address all of these issues, "But now that I'm kind of getting older and thinking . . . 'My God, that's the same arguments that we made back in 1989, 1990.' It's the same thing." And Stephanie Tyree saw the general nature of the problem as "it's still a white male–dominated society, and it's not just Virginia."

Others put the blame for lack of progress, or rollbacks, on a new political climate. Melanie Payne-White said, "What scares me now, mostly, is that we're going to go back. Because of these Tea Partiers and these stubborn men, that . . . we're going to end up back where we were, and that's frightening." Mary Ann Bergeron claimed, "I have never seen so much intensity over these very dumb social issues." She opined that some of the reactions she sees to issues like gay marriage and choice constitute "an absolute circus." The "circus" came to Virginia in 2017, as the fallout from the 2016 election emboldened white supremacists. In August, white supremacists, mainly male, demonstrated against the removal of a statue in Charlottesville. The demonstration was meant to intimidate, and violence broke out, leading to the death of Virginian Heather Heyer, who was murdered as a white supremacist plowed his car through a parade of peaceful counterdemonstrators.

The General Assembly

Many Virginia feminists cited the distinct problems they face because of a hostile General Assembly, created when the Republican-dominated legislature redistricted so dramatically after its 2010 electoral victory that Virginia became the fifth most gerrymandered state in the country.[17] Lynn Bradford explained that gerrymandering has created "safe districts." Stephanie Tyree posited, "Virginia has a long way to go ... it's very patriarchal. It's run by very conservative men who feel like they know better than women what women need." Bergeron said, despite more women in the legislature, "we still have a very white, male leadership conglomeration within the General Assembly. And they're the ones ... who are making the decisions, and it is becoming weird." She explained that it is "weird" when conservative politicians cite Thomas Jefferson and claim to not want big government but "government is intruding ... in every part of life you can imagine."

Some pointed to the dearth of women in the commonwealth's General Assembly as ongoing problems. Lynn Bradford cited this and a lack of women in managerial positions as places where feminism did not achieve as much success, although she would not vote for a woman just because she was a woman. Bonnie Atwood recently retired from lobbying in the General Assembly. She believed she was not "treated as important" by some of the male legislators as her male colleagues were, because "It was a man's world. A lot of people don't agree with me on that. I say it was a man's world. I say it still is." Some, she said, were "disrespectful" and "They act like frat boys...." Although she had not been harassed, like Karen Raschke, she knew women who were. Suzanne Keller remembered that engaging with the legislature allowed women to see legislators in action: "It was very interesting because it was lifting the veil on these remnants of the Confederacy and patriarchy." She argued women's activism revealed not only what happened in the past, but also showed there is "more work to be done." Bergeron gave credit to governors for putting more women on executive and administrative committees and appointing them as agency heads and in cabinet positions, "And you would never have seen that back in the day. Never."

Some see women as having made gains in the General Assembly as a result of feminism—gains that have not gone far enough. Sandra Brandt, who now sits on the Democratic National Committee, said that she sees more women active in different roles at the General Assembly. She also said that "women have been more now in the forefront, they were before, but they are really there and talking to legislators about the issues that are important to not only them but to society, or you know, to different groups they represent...." Brandt believes, "I think women have gotten a lot more respect in the General Assembly of Virginia now." However, like Atwood, she recognized that "We still have some ways to go, but we also need to get more women in the General Assembly."

Recent statistics supported these women's assertions about how far women had to go—in 2015, a year after these women were interviewed, there were sixteen women in the House and eight in the Senate, comprising 17 percent of the total legislature. Nationally, women averaged just over 24 percent of legislative seats. And the commonwealth was not ahead in the South, either—North Carolina, Georgia, Florida, Missouri, and Arkansas ranked higher at that time.[18]

Still, women have worked, and continue to work, to make inroads into political avenues of power. Sandra Brandt discussed the ways in which feminists are attempting to get women elected—first Mary Sue Terry gathered a group of women to start a "Farm Team" created to assist women Democrats in getting elected. Now, Emerge Virginia works toward the same goal as part of a fourteen-state network across the country that includes California, Oregon, and Massachusetts. The only other participating southern state was Kentucky several years ago, but now North and South Carolina have Emerge programs.[19] Kristi Van Audenhove says for more change to happen, "It requires there not be public bodies that are 75 and 80 percent male or 75 or 80 percent white... so that's the long game." Given these historic challenges, Beth Marschak made clear just how important feminist work was: "These men were ... in what they considered to be powerful positions; they were not ready to give up their power. And they didn't want things like we did. Some of the things actually did get through, you know... they were kicking and screaming the whole way on that stuff. That was not what they wanted. Those things they ended up going for ... because public opinion and public attention made it harder for them to oppose...."

Achievements

When asked what feminism achieved, some activists reflect on the concrete gains made. Some cited the changes in domestic-violence and sexual-assault laws, or more equitable divorce laws, as Emily McCoy, Mary Ann Bergeron, and Beth Marschak remember. Some, including Bessida White, Kristi Van Audenhove, and Mary Dean Carter pointed to the increase in LGBTQ rights. White said the election of Barack Obama indicates how far we have come in society.

Others viewed increased opportunity for women as signs of feminist success. Bonnie Atwood said, "Equal pay is starting to be a respected idea even though it's not really a reality yet," and Kristi Van Audenhove pointed to pay equity as a feminist achievement as well. Sarah Payne explained that nursing is far more lucrative and respected than it was when she was working; Stephanie Tyree reminded us that more women are entering the STEM fields; and Bergeron and Lynn Bradford also saw women's success in diverse workplaces as evidence of concrete change created by feminism. Bradford maintained that women "think it's their birthright that they have the same opportunities that men have..." because of the earlier efforts of women activists. Elizabeth Smith believed so much progress was made that "[people] are beneficiaries of it, I think without knowing what it was that made it possible for them to have a better development of their potential." Betsy Brinson also viewed the presence of so many more women in college was a sign that "we have made more progress than we had before when we started this," but cautioned against too much optimism, explaining that schools still ignore Title IX and workplace inequity continues to plague women. She opined, "I would never say 'no, [the feminist movement]'s been a dismal failure,' but...."

Others, however, believe that, even though feminism didn't achieve all of its concrete goals, as Bessida White said, feminism "laid the groundwork for... some of the things that have changed and evolved." She claimed feminist activism showed that women could be friends and work together towards common goals. Holly Farris also thought that feminists are "not as fragmented" now as they were in the past, which is a success of the movement itself. Beth Marschak noted that feminists "laid a very important groundwork" in the 1970s for many changes to come, and established long-standing networks that continue to work on justice issues today. NOW, Richmond Lesbian-Feminists, and National Women's Political Caucus–Virginia are still active in promoting women's issues, and the growth of shelters, advocates, and crisis programming for women reveals the power in anti-violence networks. As Karen Raschke explained, "there was feminism and active feminism before I got here and became active. There was active feminism all the time I was here and have been active, and there's feminism continuing to this day."

Some activists argued that feminism's greatest success was in making issues visible and enabling women to simply talk about their problems. In a sense, these activists were arguing the feminist line, "the personal is the political." As Terrie Pendleton said, "I think feminism is the key that opened ... Pandora's Box ... opened up the opportunity for women to really speak and do and create, so the box that it opened was all the voices of women that were not able to shine through." Beth Marschak agreed: "I think that to me part of what we were able to do was, it had to do with ... visibility and discussion and conversation. We were able to make those different components of what feminism was about, those different ideas, something that people knew and heard about." She explained that feminism introduced people to ideas that they had never considered before: "There's just so many things that are rooted in that experience of women's liberation in the seventies.... Once you see something, you can't not see it. In a way we ... made things visible that people had not seen before." Lee Perkins thought that activists introduced feminism in a way that it became "part of the national conversation. I mean you can't ... pick up a magazine, *Washington Post,* or watch something on television which doesn't have something related to our issues." Mary Dean Carter concurred: "groups like RLF, NOW, and Women's Political Caucus, all of those groups kept putting these issues in people's faces and they weren't going to go away.... Over time, people just started to become more aware."

Several focused on feminism's success in transforming individuals. Elizabeth Smith credited feminism with "Consciousness raising. Which has now I think seeped into people's general consciousness of who they are[,]" even if they do not realize it. Georgia Fuller believed feminism affected her: "What I know is I'm a better person. I'm a better person for all the risks I've taken. For all the amazing, amazing people I've met."

Time and again, feminists noted that so much progress has happened, sometimes people forget that it took the efforts of many, many activists to achieve progress. Lee Perkins explained that NOW membership in Virginia dropped "when most of the goals of ERA had been realized." She also believes so much progress has been made that many people think we *do* have the ERA. In fact, she had to convince a cousin's daughter—a lawyer—that the amendment did not, in fact, pass. Lynn Bradford saw the "sea change" in American society that has provided women with so much more than they had just forty years ago, but says, "it's taken for granted that they can participate in sports and run for office and run a company...." While Emily McCoy was positive about women thinking it has always been the way they have it, because she wanted them to think it has always been this way, others were not so sanguine. When asked what she would say to today's feminists, Mary Ann Bergeron opined, "I would remind them that they're standing on the shoulders of people who have done so much grunt and groundwork. And never, never forget what it took to get where we are today." Georgia Fuller explained, "How does change happen, you know, real change kind of happens at the grass roots and then suddenly the top topples and the change is there and you wonder what took so long. Or you think it's always been there."

To those who may be skeptical of activists' optimism about how much feminism has changed Virginia, and American society as a whole, it is important to again consider the concrete gains achieved by the hard work of many. From Virginia Military Institute opening its doors to women after losing a federal lawsuit in 1996, to the ERA being ratified by Virginia's Senate year after year through 2017, and shelters and crisis centers still operating despite budget challenges, change has happened. Mary Dean Carter said, "Sometimes now it's hard for me to look back on the way it was then. . . . So much has happened, even in the last ten years." The goals set forth by feminists have made a difference, even if, as many of them acknowledge, they do still have a long way to go.

Virginia has also experienced dramatic political change, in part because of feminist activism. A 2013 *New York Times* article posited that Virginia's becoming a blue state resulted from more than demographic changes. Acknowledging that the scandal-ridden administration of Bob McDonnell didn't help Republicans, the article projected that for the first time in over thirty-five years a Democratic gubernatorial candidate (Terry McAuliffe) would win while a Democrat was in the White House—a Democratic presidential candidate who has also won Virginia twice. And indeed, Terry McAuliffe was elected governor. Reporter John Harwood said the demographic shift was not as significant a factor as others, noting the percentage of white voters was down to 75 percent from 78 percent in 2009. Instead, he maintained, "The mix of white voters has also changed, because of rapid growth among college-educated suburban moderates who have proven receptive to Democratic stances on social issues."

Could it be that feminists' fight to foreground issues of equality, access, and social justice had an impact on the hearts and minds of Virginia's electorate? Virginia political historian and Republican advisor Frank Atkinson told Harwood, "I've been saying for 20 years we're a purple state.... It's a very different electorate." Given the work of grassroots feminist activists, it is entirely possible that their education efforts helped to shift Virginia to the left.[20]

Gerrymandering has the General Assembly far more conservative than the average population in Virginia, and until that changes, feminist legislative goals may well go unachieved. Gerrymandering has recently presented to a commonwealth a political system that is in opposition to the will of the majority of Virginians, and it enables the more conservative rural areas to be overrepresented at the state level.

Movement forward took the hard work of many activists against entrenched systems of power. Mary Ann Bergeron acknowledged it this way: "There were thousands of people... thousands of women in Virginia who participated and helped that movement along, and they are going to be unknown; they are going to be unsung." The odds against them were, and continue to be, great, and change slow in coming. Georgia Fuller credited her anthropology background with her understanding of the challenges posed by patriarchy and racism: "it's so ingrained in the culture, sometimes people don't even think about it.... And my philosophy tended to be that you couldn't just pick one thing and go with it. You had to have a multiplicity of actions, of challenges, against the patriarchy because it's a many-headed monster. Or whack-a-mole. Bonk, bonk, bonk and three more pop up, right?"

As some explained, the odds seem to be even more challenging in Virginia. Both Mary Ann Bergeron and Lynn Bradford referenced a quote often attributed to Mark Twain, "When the end of the world comes, I want to be in —— because it's always twenty years behind the times,"[21] when discussing the commonwealth. But Mary Dean Carter also provided encouragement: "Change doesn't happen overnight, it happens over a period of time.... Forty years, and we were starting to see some real concrete change, but it didn't happen overnight." Mary Ann Bergeron saw Virginia itself as part of the problem. She believed that, even as the commonwealth has been changed by people moving in with new talents and ideas, "Virginia lets every other state try it before it adopts anything. Every other state."

That a shift to the left happened at all, and is still happening, is something some feminist activists point to as evidence of their work. Having spent most of her life in the commonwealth, Lisa Beckman did not concur with Bergeron's characterization of Virginia. Instead, she sees the Old Dominion as a place rife with possibility. She stated, "Virginia could not have escaped feminism. It's a done deal, the way I think about it . . . and maybe it's because it's the middle between the North and the South. . . . Where there's convention and then there's . . . growth, new ways of thinking." She described the state in which she grew up as special, and different: "And you know, . . . it doesn't surprise me that this is the little pot that's bubbling, that Virginia is setting standards in a lot of ways." Thinking back on the changes she has seen in Virginia since she moved to the commonwealth in sixth grade, Suzanne Keller viewed continued progress as well: "I still think radical feminists have a lot to offer. And in ways that . . . no one else does. . . . In my view, we are in the last gasp of patriarchy. I love to say this. This is the last gasp of patriarchy and it is so violent and so reactionary because it is the last gasp."

Her comment could be extrapolated to the country in 2018. Many feminists are pointing to the misogynistic statements women activists now garner online when they write blogs, challenge white male privilege in any way, or point out continued inequality. The chauvinist reactions Hillary Clinton faced as the first female candidate for president certainly suggests that patriarchal oppression is not limited to Virginia.

Where Is Feminism Going?

Looking back on their own activities, feminists noted the work that remains to be done. Mary Wazlak concluded: "It's been an amazing journey. A lot of this is still being lived out today. I would love to say that all the work we've put into all of this stuff was decided, over, done with, and now we can move forward from there, but it looks like we're not done yet."

Speaking to a new generation of activists, these feminist veterans have some advice. Denise Lee exhorted young feminists to be aware and active at every level of government, including the school board: "Don't take anything for granted. You have to fight for it. You have to stay in tune." Sandra Brandt asked young activists to join organizations that make a difference and "be passionate about the issues that make a difference to them." Lee and Brandt also believed that young feminists need to lobby for change. Suzanne Keller also said, "I think direct action is where it's at as well as this inside work of being conscious about what you are doing." Betsy Brinson would tell young feminists not to "be afraid to use the word feminist, for heaven's sake, you know."

Many feminists wanted young women to know that achieving change means hard work and not to shy away from those issues that matter. Many talked about being brave, fighting and not giving up, standing up for themselves and their beliefs, and as Elizabeth Smith put it, "Keep your hand on the plow, hold on. Hold on. That a lot of it is quite very nitty gritty work. And one needs to do the nitty gritty work as well as dreaming in the clouds." Mary Coulling reminded women, "keep on keeping on. I mean, look back at how things have changed. And I know that it isn't always fun, because you want things to change and you want things to change faster.... So we've come a long way. But there are still a lot of inequities." She also said that young women should focus on solving the problems in their own communities as a way to make change because trying to solve the world's problems is overwhelming. Holly Farris asked activists to consider the work done before them: "Educate yourself about the history. You don't have to know us... go through our struggle," but they do need to "Get out, get cooking on something."

The feminist activists of Virginia were part of a larger movement—they changed the world as they joined the movement of feminist activists fighting patriarchal oppression across the globe, but they did so, as Coulling suggested, by working on their own community, the commonwealth, to effect change. The groundwork laid by thousands of activists in countless lobbying, education, and grassroots activist campaigns in Virginia made a real difference in the lives of many women, and the ramifications of their efforts continue to this day as activists struggle to maintain the progressive momentum created by these earlier efforts. Southern feminism was a force that demanded and achieved change, despite challenges posed by legislators, conservative countermovements, and a more oppressive racial and gender hierarchy.

As they themselves admit, their work, as well as the story of feminism in Virginia, is not over. That the struggle is ongoing and is carried forward by longtime activists who are still active with organizations they have been members of since the 1970s, and are joined by new activists challenging many of the same attempts to restore oppressive gender norms, is a testament to the significance of southern feminists and their role in advancing change. Even in the face of Hillary Clinton's loss in the presidential election, Virginia stood at the forefront of change in the South. The commonwealth's voters elected Clinton, continuing their trend of supporting the party and revealing their political inclinations to be more liberal than upper-midwestern states. Clinton won by a larger margin in Virginia than did Obama, suggesting that progressivism in the commonwealth is on the rise.[22]

Additionally, Emerge Virginia had a tremendous victory, even in the face of Hillary Clinton's loss. Emerge Virginia, the organization that trains Democratic women to run for office, could celebrate the fact that its alumnae candidates won 75 percent of their races. Across the country, Emerge programs' alumnae won 70 percent. Women made gains in electoral office in 2016, thanks to this program that trains and assists them in running for office.[23]

And if 2016 was a win for forces of progressivism in Virginia, 2017 was an electoral earthquake. Democrats swept the governor, lieutenant governor, and commonwealth attorney slots, but the big story was in the House, all of which was up for reelection. Democrats picked up fourteen seats. Eleven of those were won by women. The House now has twenty-seven female delegates (four Republican), up from seventeen. Republicans lost their supermajority, despite the gerrymandered nature of the districts, and almost had to enter a power-sharing agreement with the Democrats. That possibility ended when a Democratic candidate tied with her incumbent Republican male opponent and lost when his name was pulled out of a bowl in the court-determined tiebreaker.[24]

The story does not end with the Democratic victories, however. It is not just in how many won, but where. Henrico County and the surrounding district, a traditional conservative powerhouse that saw Tea Party candidate Dave Brat beat more moderate Republican Eric Cantor in a U.S. House race, saw a Democratic sweep in all local and state races, and elected political newcomer and history teacher Schuyler VanValkenburg as new delegate. He wrote his MA thesis on Richmond NOW. The district that includes Chesterfield County, to the south of Richmond, has been known as a stalwart of conservatism. It now has a female commissioner of revenue, Jennifer Hughes, and a female delegate, Dawn Adams. Adams ran as openly lesbian and beat a male incumbent, and signaled the first time a Democratic delegate has won the district since the late 1950s. In what could be considered the biggest upset of the election, Danica Roem, a transgendered candidate, beat Delegate Bob Marshall. Marshall, who had held his seat for almost three decades, was the opponent of marital-rape bills and self-described "'chief homophobe'" of the General

Assembly. Pundits were quick to credit backlash against President Trump for this historic victory.[25]

But perhaps the victory is more than just anti-Trump backlash. For decades, Virginia feminists have worked to promote issues of import to women, battling with legislators and building grassroots support for progressive issues. Virginia voted for Hillary Clinton. This "historic" election of 2017 could may well be a sign that Virginia feminists' work has borne fruit. As Kristi Van Audenhove put it, "feminism is achieving things every freakin' day." When change comes, it comes because dedicated people choose to fight at the local level, and are willing to take their battles to the highest levels of government. Feminism has dramatically changed Virginia, the South, and the nation, and will continue to do so, so long as there are grassroots activists fighting for the cause.

NOTES

List of Abbreviations

Carlton	Mary Holt Woolfolk Carlton Papers, M 11
Carlton W&M	Mary Holt Carlton Papers, College of William and Mary
Harrison	Papers of Edythe C. Harrison
Hellmuth	Jean D. Hellmuth Papers
LWV Fairfax	League of Women Voters of the Fairfax Area Records
LWV Montgomery	League of Women Voters of Montgomery County, Virginia, Records
LWV Richmond	League of Women Voters of the Richmond Area Records
LWVVA	League of Women Voters of Virginia Records, 1920–2011
Marburg	Jean Marburg League of Women Voters Collection
McClenehan	Records of Mary Tyler Freeman Cheek McClenehan
Miller	Emilie F. Miller Papers
Norfolk AAUW	Papers of the Norfolk Branch of the American Association of University Women
NOWVA	Virginia Chapter of the National Organization for Women Records
OOCP	*Our Own Community Press*
Raschke	Records of Karen Raschke
RNL	*Richmond News Leader*
RTD	*Richmond Times-Dispatch*
Shackelford	Carroll Kem Shackelford Papers
Smith	Elizabeth Smith Collection
SWRP	ACLU Southern Women's Rights Project Records
VABPW	Virginia Federation of Business and Professional Women's Clubs Records
VERARC	Virginia Equal Rights Amendment Ratification Council Papers
VLPP	Virginia League of Planned Parenthood
VOKAL	Records of the Virginia Organization to Keep Abortion Legal
VSDV	Records of the Virginia Sexual and Domestic Violence Action Alliance

White	Juanita White Papers, 1970–1997
Williams	Margaret Williams Papers, 1970–1985
WP	*Washington Post*
YWCA	Richmond YWCA Records
YWCA Hampton Roads	Papers of the YWCA of Hampton Roads
ZNLVA	Zelda Kingoff Nordlinger Papers, 1970–2007
ZNWM	Papers of Zelda Nordlinger, 1969 (1970–1977)

Introduction

1. For a history of how women have sought to claim power in Virginia from the 1600s to the present, see Cynthia Kierner et al., *Changing History*.

2. Ruth Rosen, *The World Split Open: How the Modern Women's Movement Changed America*, and Sara Evans, *Tidal Wave: How Women Changed America at Century's End*, provide detailed and inclusive overviews of the feminist movement, although they do not pay attention to southern politics. Alice Echols, *Daring to Be Bad: Radical Feminism in America, 1967–1975*, examines radical feminist ideologies and strategies for change, focusing much of her work on California and New York. Amy Erdman, *Yours in Sisterhood: Ms. Magazine and the Promise of Popular Feminism*, writes about how the magazine brought ideologies of feminism to mainstream readers. Jane Gerhard, *Desiring Revolution: Second-Wave Feminism and the Rewriting of American Sexual Thought, 1920–1982*; Flora Davis, *Moving the Mountain: The Women's Movement in America Since 1960*; and Barbara Ryan, *Feminism and the Women's Movement: Dynamics of Change in Social Movement Ideology and Activism*, examine in detail feminist thought, divisions, and philosophies. These books tend to narrowly conceptualize the women's movement as emerging in the 1960s and focus mainly on college-educated white women involved in the movement. The first book-length study of a southern feminist issue is Donald G. Mathews's and Jane Sherron De Hart's study of ERA activism in North Carolina, *Sex, Gender, and the Politics of the ERA: A State and a Nation*. Temma Kaplan's chapter "Generation X, Southern Style," in *Crazy for Democracy: Women in Grassroots Movements*, chronicles the experiences of women in the civil rights organizations Leadership Initiative Project and Youth Task Force in North Carolina. Janet Allured's study of the feminist movement in Louisiana, *Remapping Second-Wave Feminism: The Long Women's Rights Movement in Louisiana, 1950–1997*, is one of the first comprehensive study of feminism in a single southern state, examining the origins of the movement as well as key issues addressed by the feminists. Katarina Keane's dissertation, "Second-Wave Feminism in the American South" also addresses feminist activity in Dallas, Chapel Hill–Durham, and Atlanta. She argues that, although many of the feminist movement leaders hailed from the South, problems related to historical race/class hierarchies, limitations on women's power, and history of resisting outside power affected the development of feminism (4, 9, 337).

3. Allured's work corrects the northern-centric work of feminist scholars. Her study of the long feminist movement in Louisiana brings in labor women, women of color, as well as those traditionally defined as feminists—middle-class white women—in her study of women's activism and change in the state. Her book examines the long feminist movement in Louisiana, from its inception with women's organizations like the YWCA and League of Women Voters, to civil rights

activists getting involved, to labor and religious groups who fought for the ERA, anti-violence measures, and the right to safe abortions prior to *Roe*. She also explores in-depth the identities of southern feminists, from lesbian activists, to African American women, to members of formal religious organizations, thus highlighting the complex interplay of positions within the larger feminist movement. She argues that "the South had a vigorous, defiant, and persistent cadre of committed feminists who supplied national organizations with both ideas and personnel" (*Remapping Second-Wave Feminism*, 3). As such, it was not a branch of the northern feminist movement—it was homegrown and had its own look, including one that might have appeared more conservative than those in northern urban areas, partly because of what they had to fight against (5–6). Allured's introduction contains impressive historiographical discussions that address all of the recent work in late-twentieth-century feminism (4–5, 12–19). Stephanie Gilmore's *Groundswell: Grassroots Feminism in Postwar America*, a study of NOW activities in Memphis; San Francisco; and Columbus, Ohio, persuasively argues that NOW chapters in each region had different levels of access to power, different participants, and thus different approaches to change—often reflecting local interests and initiatives over the issues proposed by the NOW national officials. Melissa Estes Blair's study of organizational women, most notably the League of Women Voters, NOW, and YWCA boards and members, in Durham, Denver, and Indianapolis complicates the narrative of what kinds of women were feminists, what the goals of feminists were, and how wide the range of women's activism was in the late twentieth century. Like Gilmore, she contends that different political landscapes in each region, as well as different reactions to these organizations, tended to dictate how these groups addressed important feminist issues.

Others are working to examine southern feminism, including Joey Fink in her work on southern textile laborers and their fight for equity in the mills, and Jesse Wilkerson, who explores the work of women activists in mining towns in Appalachia, both of whom presented their work at a roundtable at the Tenth Southern Conference on Women's History. Katarina Keane's dissertation convincingly argues that urban southern feminists succeeded from the 1960s to 1980 in using historical networks like the Business and Professional Women, League of Women Voters, and YWCA, as well as NOW and other newer organizations, to fight for the ERA, reproductive justice, workplace equality, welfare rights, and the creation of lesbian space. In "Stealth in the Political Arsenal of Southern Women: A Retrospective for the Millennium," Sarah Wilkerson-Freeman cautions us to look for "stealth feminism" in southern places, as southern women fighting for public health initiatives, educational opportunities, civil rights, and equality often "*masked* and *coded* their efforts to influence politics and conditions in the public realm" (44). Anna Zajicek et al. determine that the university and the agrarian movement collectives in the region converged to prompt the creation of a Women's Center, a Rape Crisis Project, and other Fayetteville, Arkansas, feminist initiatives in "The Emergence and First Years of a Grassroots Women's Movement." Stephanie Gilmore and Elizabeth Kaminski explore the ways in which lesbian and straight feminists negotiated for space in the Memphis NOW and worked on many initiatives, including antirape and -violence campaigns and the ERA in "A Part and Apart: Lesbian and Straight Feminist Activists Negotiate Identity in a Second-Wave Organization."

Nancy Baker's work on Hermine Tobalowsky and her successful effort to get the ERA passed in Texas, "Hermine Tobalowsky: A Feminist's Fight for Equal Rights," challenges any monolithic view of Texas as entirely conservative. Marjorie Spruill's study of South Carolina feminists, "Victoria Eslinger, Keller Bumgardner Barron, Mary Heriot, Tootsie Holland, and Pat Callair: Champions of Women's Rights in South Carolina," finds that, despite South Carolina being "profoundly conservative and wary of social change" (375), women were active in NOW, LWV, and other organizations for equal opportunities, abortion rights, the ERA, and other feminist issues. These feminists, she argues, found most of their success in making sure that South Carolina adhered to new federal laws that were beneficial to women, but they risked their jobs, their friendships, and even their personal safety to do so. Janine Parry's "'What Women Wanted': Arkansas Women's Commissions and the ERA," explores the ways in which the Women's Commission of Arkansas advanced the ERA and the reasons it failed in the state, particularly when faced with strong and organized opposition, and Janet Allured compares Arkansas Baptists and Methodists and the denominations' national stands and local views on the ERA in "Arkansas Baptists and Methodists and the Equal Rights Amendment." Florida ERA studies contribute to our understanding of regional southern challenges, including Joan Carver's "The ERA and the Florida Legislature," and Kimberly Wilmot Voss's "The Florida Fight for Equality: The Equal Rights Amendment, Senator Lori Wilson, and Mediated Catfights in the 1970s." There are also many oral histories of southern feminists in archives throughout the South, including Virginia. One such collection is the Virginia Foremothers project, sponsored by Virginia NOW and conducted by Dr. Simone Roberts and Ms. Hadley Elizabeth Hunter Hawks. They are available here: https://www.youtube.com/user/vanowforemothers.

Some of these historians and others use case studies to challenge the conceptualization of feminism as a movement that came in waves, with the first being woman suffrage and the second the battles that erupted in the 1960s and continued through the 1980s. The term "second wave," discussed by Nancy Hewitt in the 2010 introduction to *No Permanent Waves: Recasting Histories of U.S. Feminism* as one used by feminists themselves in the 1960s but in the historical context of wave metaphors used as early as the nineteenth century, has become a term hotly contested by historians (1–2). In 1987, Verta Taylor and Leila Rupp contended in *Survival in the Doldrums: The American Women's Movement 1945 to the 1960s* that elite women maintained the movement by working through institutions like the National Women's Party and at federal levels of government administration. Susan Hartmann's 1998 study of women activists in liberal organizations like the ACLU, National Council of Churches, and the labor movement illustrates that feminist activism had not died with the failure of ERA to pass in the 1920s. She argued in *The Other Feminists: Activists in the Liberal Establishment* that these organizations continued to fight for equal employment opportunities, equal rights, and other feminist causes. The contributors to *Feminist Coalitions: Historical Perspectives on Second-Wave Feminism in the United States*, ed. Stephanie Gilmore; *No Permanent Waves*, ed. Hewitt; and *Breaking the Wave: Women, Their Organizations, and Feminism, 1945–1985*, ed. Kathleen Laughlin and Jacqueline Castledine, noted the ways in which organizations like the League of Women Voters, Lesbian Feminists, the National Council of Negro Women, and labor and welfare rights activists kept women's issues alive in the twentieth century. As Allured explained, while the wave movement elides the work done by women prior to the late twentieth century, it was in the 1960s and beyond in which feminists gained traction for the concept of "wave" to be useful (*Remapping Second-Wave Feminism*, 3). The wave concept also often ignores the work done by activist women of color and working-class women by privileging the periods in which middle-class white women were most active, as posited by Kathleen Laughlin et al. in the 2010 article "Is It Time to Jump Ship? Historians Rethink the Waves Metaphor."

I avoid the term "wave," but in focusing on late-twentieth-century activism and direct political engagement, I am not able to delve deeply into organizational histories.

4. For more on Lost Cause ideology, specifically about the women who were instrumental in crafting, displaying, and disseminating it through the educational system, as well as the United Daughters of the Confederacy chapter that founded the Museum of the Confederacy and placed the monuments on Monument Avenue in Richmond, see Karen Cox, *Dixie's Daughters: The United Daughters of the Confederacy and the Preservation of Confederate Culture*.

5. Benjamin Muse, *Virginia's Massive Resistance*, 28–32; James Howard Hershman Jr., "A Rumbling in the Museum: The Opponents of Virginia's Massive Resistance," 187–88. For more on massive resistance and the ways in which black and white women responded to integration in Virginia, see Kierner et al., *Changing History*, 302–12.

6. For more information, see Kierner et al., *Changing History*, 243–45; J. Douglas Smith, *Managing White Supremacy: Race, Politics, and Citizenship in Jim Crow Virginia*, and Gregory Michael Dorr, *Segregation's Science: Eugenics and Society in Virginia*, as well as Peter Wallenstein, *Blue Laws and Black Codes: Conflict, Courts, and Change in Twentieth Century Virginia*, and *Tell the Court I Love My Wife: Race, Marriage, and Law—An American History*. This is not to say that violent action against desegregation did *not* occur. Civil rights violence erupted throughout the commonwealth, and Danville was the site of terrible police brutality in 1963, as described in Len Holt's *An Act of Conscience*.

7. For an overview of Virginia women's activism, see Kierner et al., *Changing History*.

8. William Martin, *With God on Our Side: The Rise of the Religious Right in America*, 55–72, 163–64, 201–4, 213.

9. Ruth Murray Brown, *For a "Christian America": A History of the Religious Right*, 183–84; Martin, *With God on Our Side*, 301–5, 309.

10. In "Trying to Be Good: Lessons in Oral History and Performance," from *Remembering: Oral History Performance*, ed. Dena Pollock and Jacquelyn Dowd Hall, Alicia Rouverol says that life-review questions are meant to elicit life stories, to help the teller fashion narratives of their experiences, understanding pivotal points and influences, but oral histories are more general, in that they collect information and memories about events in the recent past (25–26).

11. Sherna Berger Gluck argues that "Women's oral history is a feminist encounter" because it facilitates cross-generational discussion, creates "a new kind type of material about women[,]" and it legitimizes the importance of women's lives and experiences (5). I tried to follow her advice to balance what I believed was important with what the activists addressed as significant in their own lives, which she cautioned for in "What's So Special about Women?" in the 2002 collection *Women's Oral History: The Frontiers Reader*. In "Our Remembered Selves: Oral History and Feminist Memory" Julie Stephens argues that oral histories can challenge more "fixed versions" of feminist history to create more complex narratives. They can explore the "role of emotions" in the movement, as well as avoid a score-keeping focus on wins/losses in the movement that is often seen in memoirs and scholarship. Stories reveal a much more complex story and resist the "binary logic" of that conceptualization (81, 82). While I asked the activists I interviewed about successes and failures, often their answers suggested that even in failure, like with the ERA, they found aspects of success. When they talked about heartbreak and remembered other incidents with humor, I brought those stories to the narrative. However, I did have to fit the stories into an analytical framework, as Marie Francoise Chanfrault-Duchet urged in "Narrative Structures, Social Models and Symbolic Representation," in the 1991 collection *Women's Words: The Feminist Practice of Oral History*. She argued that oral history serves not just to assert the importance of the women's experiences or raise consciousness but to better understand these women as sig-

nificant historical actors whose stories are part of the actors' life patterns and informed by their own subjectivities. In "Telling Our Stories: Feminist Debates and the Use of Oral History" (1994) Jean Sangster posited that "Asking why and how women explain, rationalise, and make sense of their past offers insight into the social and material framework within which they operated, the perceived choices and cultural patterns they faced, and the complex relationship between individual consciousness and culture" (6). She also reminds us that historians must recognize "our *own* influence on the shape of the interview" (10). Still, she suggests it is historians' responsibility to use their "insights" and knowledge to interpret oral histories (12).

12. Allured, *Remapping Second-Wave Feminism*, 11.

Chapter One

1. Studies that document the change that occurred in the last seven decades of twentieth-century Virginia include Peter Wallenstein, *Tell the Court I Love My Wife*, and *Cradle of America: Four Centuries of Virginia History*; Ronald Heinemann, *Depression and New Deal in Virginia: The Enduring Dominion*; Evan Bennett, *When Tobacco Was King: Families, Farm Labor, and Federal Policy in the Piedmont*; Ronald Heinemann et al., *Old Dominion, New Commonwealth: A History of Virginia, 1607–2007*; Pippa Holloway, *Sexuality, Politics, and Social Control in Virginia, 1920–1945*; Megan Shockley, *"We, Too, Are Americans": African American Women in Detroit and Richmond, 1940–1954*; Kierner et al., *Changing History*.

2. Brent Tarter's *The Grandees of Government: The Origins and Persistence of Undemocratic Politics in Virginia* illustrates vividly just how much of an old boy's club Virginia politics had been and continues to be. His sweeping history of the government from the colonial period to the present singles out Byrd's political system as being one of the worst offenders in Virginia's history. He writes that "advocates of alternatives were systematically and deliberately excluded from the political process to such an extent that their voices could not be heard and their alternative proposals never got seriously considered." He claims the regime left "an undemocratic legacy of exclusiveness, arrogance, and bitterness" (302, 3). Allured notes that Louisiana's legislature resembled the commonwealth's, with men employing "locker-room humor" when dealing with issues related to sexuality, where there were very few female legislators, and where the men were clearly in charge (*Remapping Second-Wave Feminism*, 126). Janet Boles in *The Politics of the Equal Rights Amendment* said: "One problem faced by women's groups in their attempt to influence legislators may stem from their exclusion from the common socio-occupational pool from which legislators and lobbyists are drawn" (113). Because most lawyers and business professionals at the time were men, and those were the people who generally went into the legislature, women had little chance to participate. In *Why We Lost the ERA*, Jane Mansbridge says legislators were "overwhelmingly male" in Florida, North Carolina, Oklahoma, and Illinois (150), and Mathews and DeHart assert that "females were part of the accoutrement of power" in the North Carolina legislature (*Sex, Gender, and the Politics of the ERA*, 201).

3. "Miller Spoofs Rights Movement," *Harrison Daily News-Record*, 11 July 1979, 28, clipping in Box 15, Folder 13, NOWVA.

4. "Miller Talk Assailed," 7 July 1979, clipping in Box 15, Folder 13, NOWVA.

5. Kathryn Baker and Pat Bauer, "Sexism Imposes Special Burden, Women at Virginia General Assembly Say," *Washington Post*, 1980, clipping, Box 9, Folder 3, NOWVA. I also discuss these incidents in Kierner et al., *Changing History*, 341.

6. Kathryn Baker and Pat Bauer, "Sexism Imposes Special Burden, Women at Virginia General Assembly Say," *Washington Post*, 1980, clipping, Box 9, Folder 3, NOWVA.

7. Ibid.

8. Ibid. And while that may have been true for them, Virginia's legislature was not alone in this kind of behavior. Mathews and DeHart found an article about this in the *Durham Morning-Herald* and explained, "Interaction between male legislators and women who were not their colleagues was that of 'superficial flirtation' or the casual categorization of women by calling out 'hello sweetheart'" (*Sex, Gender, and the Politics of the ERA*, 201).

9. Baker and Bauer, "Sexism Imposes Special Burden, Women at Virginia General Assembly Say," *Washington Post*, 1980, clipping, Box 9, Folder 3, NOWVA.

10. Ibid.

11. Ibid.; Pat Bauer, "Virginia Delegates Indignant at Sex Harassment Story," *Washington Post* 26 February 1980, C1, 6.

12. Tom Sherwood, "Nearly Nude Females to Dance for Va. Speaker, All-Male Luncheon Is Charity Roast," *Washington Post*, C5, 10 October 1994; Tom Sherwood, "400 Attend Charity 'Roast' of Va. Philpott Featuring Strippers," *Washington Post*, 12 October 1984, C1.

13. Clipping from *Virginian-Pilot* and response from Goldberg, November 1984, Box 9, Folder 6, NOWVA.

14. Interview with Karen Raschke.

15. For African American women's activism during World War II, see Shockley, *"We, Too, Are Americans."* For a contemporary account of massive resistance, see Muse's *Virginia's Massive Resistance*. Holt provides a contemporary account of the Danville civil rights protest and its aftermath in *An Act of Conscience*. Many historians have discussed many facets of the civil rights movement in Virginia. Their studies include Wallenstein, *Tell the Court I Love My Wife*; Earl Lewis, *In Their Own Interests: Race, Class, and Power in Twentieth-Century Norfolk, Virginia*; Kathleen Murphy Dierenfield, "One 'Desegregated Heart': Sarah Patton Boyle and the Crusade for Civil Rights in Virginia"; William G. Thomas III, "Television News and the Civil Rights Struggle: The Views in Mississippi and Virginia"; Wallenstein, *Blue Laws and Black Codes*; Simon Hall, "Civil Rights Activism in 1960s Virginia"; Phyl Newbeck, *Virginia Hasn't Always Been for Lovers: Interracial Marriage Bans and the Case of Richard and Mildred Loving*.

16. For histories of school desegregation, see Jill Ogline Titus, *Brown's Battleground: Students, Segregationists, and the Struggle for Justice in Prince Edward County, Virginia*; Matthew Lassiter and Andrew Lewis, eds., *The Moderates' Dilemma: Massive Resistance to School Desegregation in Virginia*; Lauranett Lee, *Making the American Dream Work: A Cultural History of African Americans in Hopewell, Virginia*; Robert Pratt, *The Color of Their Skin: Race and Education in Richmond, Virginia, 1954–1989*. There were white women who challenged the shutting down of schools, and Andrew Lewis's "Emergency Mothers, Basement Schools, and the Preservation of Public Education in Charlottesville" discusses how they did this in Charlottesville.

17. For more information on how Prince Edward County shut down its schools and what happened when it did, see Titus, *Brown's Battleground*, and Amy Murrell, "The 'Impossible' Prince Edward Case: The Endurance of Resistance in a Southside County, 1959–1964." For more on the *Loving* case, see Newbeck, *Virginia Hasn't Always Been for Lovers,* and Wallenstein, *Tell the Court I Love My Wife*. Virginia continues to be a site of significant Supreme Court decisions related to family and marriage. Sharon Bottoms, the Virginia lesbian who lost custody of her child to her mother, and Sharon Kaufman, the lesbian mother who successfully sued Virginia to adopt a second child, brought tremendous national attention to LGBT parenting issues. And it was a

Virginia case that overturned the Defense of Marriage Law in 2015. See Megan Shockley, "Sharon Bottoms and Linda Kaufman: Legal Rights and Lesbian Mothers."

18. All material from the women interviewed is attributable to them. The oral histories are available at Virginia Commonwealth University.

19. Interview with Beth Marschak. The University of Virginia did not begin accepting residential women undergraduate students until 1970. For more information on the history of women at UVA, see Phyllis Leffler, "Mr. Jefferson's University: Women in the Village!"

20. Interview with Mary Dean Carter.

21. Interview with Elizabeth Smith.

22. Interview with Mary Coulling.

23. Countless historians have written about the role of African American women in the civil rights movement, documenting their activities and their impact. Belinda Robnett's *How Long? How Long? African American Women in the Struggle for Civil Rights* interprets the ways in which women acted as bridge leaders between national leaders and grassroots communities. Danielle McGuire's *At the Dark End of the Street: Black Women, Rape, and Resistance—A New History of Civil Rights from Rosa Parks to the Rise of Black Power* explains the ways in which African American women's daily struggle to escape sexual harassment and sexual assault informed their struggle for civil rights. Annelise Orleck's *Storming Caesar's Palace* highlights the ways in which poor African American women mixed their battle for civil rights with a war against marginalization in the workforce and by the unfriendly welfare state. Shannon Frystak's *Our Minds on Freedom: Women and the Struggle for Black Equality in Louisiana, 1924–1967* documents the role of women and civil rights in Louisiana, and the contributors to Bruce Glasrud and Merline Pitre, eds., *Southern Black Women in the Modern Civil Rights Movement: African American Women in the Civil Rights-Black Power Movement,* and Bettye Collier-Thomas and V. P. Franklin, eds., *Sisters in the Struggle,* relate the myriad ways women engaged in the civil rights struggle across the nation. Individual biographies of African American women in the civil rights movement include Barbara Ransby, *Ella Baker and the Black Freedom Movement: A Radical Democratic Vision*; Katherine Mellen Charron, *Freedom's Teacher: The Life of Septima Clark*; and Chana Kai Lee, *For Freedom's Sake: The Life of Fannie Lou Hamer.*

24. Susan Hartmann noted that some African American women came to the feminist movement because of the discrimination they experienced in the civil rights movement (*The Other Feminists,* 179). Ula Taylor discusses the fact that many black feminists organized in reaction to what they perceived as chauvinism in the movement in "Black Feminisms and Human Agency," 66–67; Kristen Anderson-Bricker argues in "Triple Jeopardy: Black Women and the Development of Feminist Consciousness in SNCC, 1964–1975," that it was African American women's experiences with discrimination that they discussed in the Black Women's Liberation Committee and then moved beyond their personal experience to demand equality for all women as a critical component to black liberation (58–59). From this committee, dedicated feminists formed the Black Women's Alliance to reach out to membership beyond SNCC, and then created the Third World Women's Alliance to battle exploitation on a more global scale, drawing attention to inequalities faced by all women of color, according to Anderson-Bricker. Kimberly Springer's *Living for the Revolution: Black Feminist Organizations, 1968–1980,* explores the ways in which black feminist organizations articulated their own version of empowerment and activism. Having found themselves marginalized by male civil rights activists and white feminists, these women created their own networks like the National Black Feminist Organization, the Combahee River

Collective, and the Third World Women's Network to battle racial, gender, and class inequities.

25. In *Daring to Be Bad,* Echols argues that many radical feminists were influenced by the New Left movement and more particularly the antiwar, anti-establishment Students for a Democratic Society as they learned how to articulate their personal experiences as coming from a lack of power and how to name their alienation. While they disagreed over whether to work within the SDS or split to form a new movement, their experience in the movement was formative for them (17, 51–101). Anita Shreve argued in *Women Together, Women Alone: The Legacy of the Consciousness Raising Movement* that the consciousness-raising movement, a critical component of women's liberation, tended to be dominated by middle-class white women because they had more leisure time and they "often tended to spring up... on college campuses" (12); Ruth Rosen argues in *The World Split Open* that many women were extremely influenced by their participation and challenges they faced within civil rights and student-protest organizations. While these groups helped women build networks of activists and hone their political skills, she contends, they had to break with the groups when it came to their views on women's liberation (94). Sara Evans and Linda Gordon also document large numbers of young women moving from civil rights and student-protest organizing to the feminist movement, sometimes having experienced gender oppression when working on behalf of these groups (Evans, *Tidal Wave*, 21–23, 42; Gordon, "The Feminist Movement," in Dorothy Sue Cobble et al., *Feminism Unfinished: A Short, Surprising History of American Women's Movements*, 104–5). In *Moving the Mountain,* Flora Davis defined many feminists as "movement veterans" and documented their trajectory into women's rights (70–71, 70–93). And Sara Evans in *Personal Politics: The Roots of Women's Liberation in the Civil Rights Movement and the New Left* also documented the movement of women from civil rights to feminism, citing black women activists as role models for these feminists.

26. While Atwood may not have experienced discrimination within her peer group, Judith Ezekiel argues that many women in Dayton became active in the feminist movement because of the "feminist-left split" (*Feminism in the Heartland,* 23). After a debate of working within the left to change the culture or removing themselves from the movement, many did move more toward feminist action as a result of the sexism they saw (22–26); Harold Smith describes in "Casey Hayden: Gender and the Origins of SNCC, SDS, and the Women's Liberation Movement" the way in which Casey Hayden's increasingly ambivalent attitude within SDS and her alienation from SNCC prompted her to circulate the "Sex and Caste" memo, which blew open the issue of sexism within the student-leftist movement. He explains how this memo electrified white women in the movement (it had little impact on black women activists in SNCC) and articulated the experience of so many women in SDS. Smith explains why the memo prompted so many women to move into liberationist efforts.

27. Many scholars argue that employed women of all socioeconomic classes worked to advance equal opportunity in the workplace, even if those women did not view themselves as feminist activists. These historians include Dorothy Sue Cobble, *The Other Women's Movement: Workplace Justice and Social Rights in Modern America*; Alice Kessler-Harris, *In Pursuit of Equity: Women, Men, and the Quest for Economic Citizenship in Twentieth-Century America*; Hartmann, *The Other Feminists*; Dorothy Sue Cobble, "More Sex than Equality" in Cobble et al., *Feminism Unfinished*; and Virginia Seitz, "Class, Gender, and Resistance in the Appalachian Coalfields," in *Community Activism and Feminist Politics: Organizing Across Race, Class, and Gender,* ed. Nancy Naples.

28. Scholars have long noted that women who self-identified as feminists tended to be educated white women. Davis, Rosen, Evans, Echols, and others have cited the preponderance of

evidence that those who were active in feminist organizations, from NOW to grassroots radical feminist organizations, were white. Although scholars cited in footnote 24, above, complicate this narrative by studying the activities of the National Black Feminist Organization as well as black activists working for women's issues who may not have self-identified as feminists, the sheer number of middle-class white women in the formal movement cannot be overstated. And interestingly enough, in *Remapping Feminism* Allured noted that, although the relationship between black and white feminists was "rocky," Louisiana had a rich black feminist tradition. She explains interracial activism as possibly owing to the rich racial complexity of Louisiana's history, as well as labor activism in the state (10, 19, 236–45). Sherna Berger Gluck et al. in "Whose Feminism, Whose History? Reflections on Excavating (the) U.S. Women's Movement(s)" argue that women of color, working-class women, and lesbian feminists were active organizing for economic and social equity in neighborhood-based grassroots organizations.

At the grassroots level the lack of diversity could be quite clear. Even radical collectives like the Califia Women of Los Angeles had problems; they tried to integrate and focus on anti-racist initiatives, but it remained white-dominated throughout its heyday, as Clark Pomerleau argues in *Califia Women: Feminism against Sexism, Classism, and Racism*, 123–45. Judith Ezekiel explains in *Feminism in the Heartland* that "Dayton Women's Liberation's limited connections with black women activists" were clear in its failure to attract black members, and that their lack of African American members did not seem to be much of a problem for most of the membership (58–59). She did find that they fought for racial justice, as when they called the plan to pay women on welfare to have abortions "racist" and "genocidal," but they still did not attract an inclusive membership (42).

29. Zelda Nordlinger to Louise Prechtl, 8 January 1973 Box 1, Folder 4, ZNLVA.

30. Examples can be found in *Northern Virginia Equal Times,* Box 16, Folder 6, NOWVA; "Tentative Chapter Development Plan, 1982-3," Box 2, Folder 15, NOWVA; Emily McCoy, acting Co-Chair, Minority Issues Task Force, to Joyce Johnson, Minority Issues Staffperson, NOW, 24 Nov 1984, Box 9, Folder 6, NOWVA; AAUW Branch Report Form, 1985–86, Box 4, Folder 9, Norfolk AAUW. I discuss these issues in Kierner et al., *Changing History*, 335–36.

31. Annual Report 1990, Arlington NOW, Box 15, Folder 1, NOWVA; Annual Report 1995, Montgomery County NOW, Box 15, Folder 19, NOWVA.

32. NOW 2004 program, Box 13, Folder 8, NOWVA.

33. Many scholars examining women of color who were activists fighting for women's rights, whether they self-identified as feminist or not, provide a much broader picture of feminist activism in the late twentieth century. These scholars include Benita Roth; Susan Hartmann; Janet Weaver, "Barrio Women: Community and Coalition in the Heartland," in *Breaking the Wave,* ed. Laughlin and Castledine. Becky Thompson, "Multiracial Feminism: Recasting the Chronology of Second Wave Feminism"; Ula Taylor, "Black Feminisms and Human Agency"; Marisela Chavez, "'We Have a Long, Beautiful History': Chicana Feminist Trajectories and Legacies"; Premilla Nadasen, "Expanding the Boundaries of the Women's Movement: Black Feminism and the Struggle for Welfare Rights"; and Judy Tzu-Chun Wu, "Living a Feminist Lifestyle: Peace Activism and Women's Orientalism," are all in *No Permanent Waves,* ed. Hewitt. Benita Roth follows the development of African American, Chicana, and white feminist ideologies and activist strategies in *Separate Roads to Feminism: Black, Chicana, and White Feminist Movements in America's Second Wave.* Kimberly Springer, Benita Roth, and Ula Taylor, as well as Anne Valk in *Radical Sisters: Second-Wave Feminism and Black Liberation in Washington, D.C.,* and Kristen Anderson-Bricker

argue specifically that African American women's feminism did not develop in response to white women's, but from their understanding of themselves as oppressed by their gender and race, and in the knowledge that advancing women's rights and the rights of people of color would be the only way to achieve equality. The contributors to *Community Activism and Feminist Politics*, ed. Naples, also provide a very clear illustration of just how very diverse women activists were.

34. In "The Making of the Vanguard Center: Black Feminist Emergence in the 1960s and 1970s," Benita Roth argues that black feminists formed a critical front of the feminist movement by identifying multiple oppressions. They challenged black men who led the civil rights movement and white women who could not see beyond their own privilege, but Roth claims that these women were the real revolutionaries who understood that the move to change society would come from their fight against racism, sexism, and classism. Winifred Breines argues in *The Trouble Between Us: An Uneasy History of Black and White Women in The Feminist Movement* that, although the black feminist movement never became as large a grassroots movement as the radical feminist white movement, the work done by the National Black Feminist Organization and the Combahee River Collective, among other groups, to identify and challenge multiple oppressions and to work at the grassroots level for change, was significant. Breines argues that in Boston the Combahee River Collective not only produced nationally significant black feminist theory but also worked to create a local domestic-violence shelter and battle against oppression interconnect with [gender-based violence] and for reproductive rights, often working in coalition with white women's groups.

Kimberly Springer contends in *Living for the Revolution* that black feminists and their organizations worked within the "cracks" of the white feminist movement and the civil rights movement to articulate positions against oppression. They embraced diversity in their own organization and used consciousness raising to help women see interlocking oppressions. They held conferences, retreats, and public forums to reach each other and articulate their concerns to a wider public. And she too found evidence that black feminists would work in coalition with white feminists on important issues.

Becky Thompson points out that histories of second-wave feminism create a kind of "white-led" hegemony. As she argues, "Hegemonic feminism deemphasizes or ignores a class or race analysis, generally sees equality with men as the goal of feminism, and has an individual rights-based, rather than a justice-based vision for social change" (337). It was women of color who were at the center of feminism, really, and their work deeply influenced the "white antiracist feminism" that emerged. In fact, it was women of color who drove antiracist feminism ("Multiracial Feminism," 337). Thompson argues that women of color focused on three key areas: developing their own organizations, creating caucuses within mixed-gender racial advocacy groups, and working on issues with white-dominated women's groups (338). Often, though, feminists of color were caught between the mixed-gender groups to whom they had to explain their ideology and white feminists "whose politics they considered narrow at best and frivolous at worst" (342). To address multiracial feminism, she argues, is to reperiodize the feminist movement, as multiracial feminist groups were extremely active in the 1980s, despite the conservative turn taken by the country (344–45).

35. Deborah K. King, "Multiple Jeopardy, Multiple Consciousness: The Context of a Black Feminist Ideology," 57.

36. Ibid., 57, 58.

37. Ibid., 63.

38. Del Dobbins, "On Recruitment of Minority Women," *Northern Virginia Equal Times* 5, no. 10 (December 1975): 2, Box 16, Folder 6, NOWVA.

39. "Black Women Plan Seminar on Wednesday," *RTD*, 4 July 1975, B7; Douglas Durden, "Feminism, Its Impact on Blacks Discussed," *RTD*, 21 November 1975, B9.

40. Douglas Durden, "Feminism, Its Impact on Blacks Discussed," *RTD*, 21 November 1975, B9.

41. Cindy Creasy, "While ERA stole the headlines, far-reaching goals become reality: activists say fairness issue," *RTD*, 13 January 1985, 1, 15, quote on 15.

42. Carole Marcoux, "The Start of a Dialogue Between Black and White Women," *NOVA NOW Newsletter*, August 1982, pp. 1–2, Box 16, Folder 9, NOWVA.

43. Liz Wheaton, "ERA: Black Women Ask 'What's in It for US?'" *ACLU Women's Rights Report* 1, no. 3 (Fall 1979): 3, Box 34, Women's Rights Project Folder, YWCA M 177.

44. Ibid. Draft article in folder has final quote.

45. In "Second-Wave Feminism in the American South," Katarina Keane argues that southern feminists breached the color line only "sporadically" (143). She claims that creating multiracial organizations in the South was challenging because of the South's history as a deeply segregated society, and so women worked in "multiple movements, overlapping at times, if only in limited ways, and moving along parallel tracks at others" (16–25, quote on 19).

46. Jerry Turner, "Panelists disagree on focus for black feminists," *Richmond Afro-American*, 18 June 1983, 5.

47. A. Finn Enke argues, "The lack of interracial queer space meant that many white lesbians doubted the existence of black lesbian communities altogether." As a result, many black lesbians would not or could not identify with white feminists. She discusses the fact that black women often felt uncomfortable at white-dominated bars in *Finding the Movement: Sexuality, Contested Space, and Feminist Activism* (36–37).

48. Betsy Brinson, "Opinion," *ACLU Women's Rights Report* 1, no. 3 (Fall 1979): 2, 7, Box 34, Women's Rights Project Folder, YWCA M 177. Quote on 7.

49. Patricia Hill Collins, "From Civil Rights to Black Lives Matter: Gender, Sexuality, and Black Social Movements," 2 March 2016, video, tv.clemson.edu/distinguished_author_speaks_at_clemson/ (accessed 27 June 2016).

50. Allured's chapter on lesbian feminism highlights the many ways that lesbian feminists crafted their identities. She also explains the significance of lesbians to providing radical critiques of violence in rape-awareness and domestic-violence campaigns (*Remapping Second-Wave Feminism*, 120–21).

51. Verta Taylor and Leila Rupp posit that lesbian committees in feminist groups were the lifeblood of the movement, preserving radical impulses at critical times and providing an engine for change at critical junctures in "Women's Culture and Lesbian Feminist Activism: A Reconsideration of Cultural Feminism," in *Community Activism and Feminist Politics*, ed. Naples. Enke also argues in *Finding the Movement* that, as lesbians carved out space in bars and on softball fields, they were advancing feminist goals and politicizing space.

52. For a review of Virginia marriage laws and how Sharon Bottoms became the national face of discrimination against same-sex couples, see Shockley, "Sharon Bottoms and Linda Kaufman."

53. Mike D'Orso, "What N.O.W.? new state officer Watches women's group struggle," *Virginian-Pilot*, 6 July 1986, clipping in Box 3, Folder 10, ZNLVA.

54. Annual Report 1997, Richmond Chapter, Box 17, Folder 14, NOWVA.

55. Information about these activities can be found in the VSDV records, as well as in the newsletters of the Richmond Lesbian-Feminists, the *Richmond Lesbian-Feminist Flyers* which are found in many different collections at VCU, most notably in the Central Virginia Gay and Lesbian Publications Collection, M 334, Special Collections and Archives, James Branch Cabell Library, VCU. Studying Baltimore's group of "mostly white, middle-class" lesbian feminists who partnered with other organizations to further projects like the Women's Health Center Collective, Laurel Clark cautions us to see the limits of such partnerships. She argues "The homophobia that feminists exhibited toward each other and toward gay and lesbian people outside of the movement should not be erased in order to highlight the cooperation that managed to overcome it" ("Beyond the Gay/Straight Split: Social Feminists in Baltimore," 1, 4).

56. The most comprehensive study of radical feminism and its actions is Echols's *Daring to Be Bad*, which explains these "zap actions" that took place across the country in great detail. As is the case with most scholarship on feminist action, she focuses on actions in large northern-based cities.

57. Interview with Bonnie Atwood. Echols's *Daring to Be Bad* is a classic comprehensive account of the backgrounds, philosophies, and actions of radical feminists. Jane Gerhard focuses on how radical feminists rethought sexuality, gender, and power in *Desiring Revolution*.

58. In "Stealth in the Political Arsenal of Southern Women," Sarah Wilkerson-Freeman argued, "In the southern woman's arsenal of political tactics, *stealth* was a critical feature. Women's ability to leverage power was severely limited by social and cultural norms and legal and political structures designed to advantage men" (45). Janet Allured argues that, in Louisiana, feminists "tended to behave with decorum" when faced with extremely conservative political powers (*Remapping Second-Wave Feminism*, 5). She explained that feminists "had a tendency to glove their defiance in respectability" (6). And Katarina Keane says that, not only did women present themselves as conservative, but they often tried to use stereotypes to their advantage, as when they fought for the ERA (283). She argued, though, that such a move was fraught with problems. Calling upon stereotypes attributed to "white, upper-class Southern womanhood ... suggested an ignorance of both real and symbolic uses of white womanhood to restrict the rights of women of color and poor women" ("Second-Wave Feminism in the American South," 284).

59. Michael Braun, "NOW Waits and Watches," *Richmond Mercury*, 14 November 1973, 1, 3–5, clipping, Box 1, Folder 11, ZNLVA.

60. Madeline Havelick, "36 At NOW Session," *Potomac News*, 7 October 1974, clipping, Box 7, Folder 7, NOWVA; Joan Mower, "NOW Gets County Chapter," *Journal Messenger*, 17 September 1974, clipping, Box 7, Folder 7, NOWVA.

61. Emma Livingstone, "No 'Instant Revolution' Is Planned for Richmond," *RTD*, 20 August 1970, 1–2.

62. "Meet Zelda Nordlinger: Women's Lib, You Know!" (partial title), *Chesterfield News-Journal*, 10 August 1972, 1, 17; Michael Braun, "NOW Waits and Watches," *Richmond Mercury*, 14 November 1973.

63. D'Orso, "What N.O.W.?" *Virginian-Pilot*, 6 July 1986, clipping, Box 3, Folder 10, ZNLVA.

64. Interview with Georgia Fuller; Michael Braun, "NOW Waits and Watches, *Richmond Mercury*, 14 November 1973; Douglas Durden, "Feminism Here: Small, Dedicated," *RTD*, 19 December 1976, G 1, 15. Quote on 15.

Chapter Two

1. Historians of the ERA in the South, including Mathews and De Hart and Nancy Baker (cited in note 2, below) assert that southern ERA activists were more diverse than their opponents. As Janet Allured notes in *Remapping Second-Wave Feminism*, "supporters of the ERA were more diverse ethnically, socioeconomically, and 'religiously' than antiratificationists..." (216).

2. Flora Davis references "Crater's Raiders" in *Moving the Mountain*, 129. Discussions of how feminists decided on the ERA as an issue in the 1960s and the ERA's passage in Congress can be found in Davis, 46–49, 67–68, 123–26; and Mathews and De Hart, *Sex, Gender, and the Politics of the ERA*, 34–35, 42–53. Mansbridge's *Why We Lost the ERA* provides a discussion of the legal, cultural, and political issues surrounding the amendment at the national level. Mary Frances Berry's *Why ERA Failed: Politics, Women's Rights, and the Amending Process of the Constitution* provides a strong overview of ERA's history from the 1920s and argues that supporters organized "too late" for ratification, and that divisions among women caused problems in the states that didn't ratify (69). In *Divided We Stand: The Battle Over Women's Rights and Family Values that Polarized American Politics*, Marjorie Spruill explains that by the time of ERA's passage in Congress, feminism had become the establishment position in Washington, D.C. Betty Ford lobbied hard for the ERA, to the dismay of anti-ERA activists (42–50, 63–67). Spruill argues, "The women's movement was powerful and entrenched" (75). Catherine Rymph points out in *Republican Women: Feminism and Conservatism from Suffrage Through the Rise of the New Right* that many Republicans populated the National Women's Political Caucus, which strongly supported the ERA, and that the National Federation of Republican Women officially supported the ERA, although there was dissension in the ranks over the issue (198, 216–22).

Several scholars have addressed the ratification movement in the South, including Nancy Baker in "Hermine Tobolowsky: A Feminist's Fight for Equal Rights," showing just how critical local efforts were in state lobbying efforts in Texas, the only southern state that passed and did not rescind the ERA. Tobolowsky had been deeply involved in securing a state ERA in the 1950s and 1960s, prior to passage of the federal amendment, which Baker argues made it easier to get the amendment through the legislature very quickly. Baker also argued convincingly in "Integrating Women into Modern Kentucky History: The Equal Rights Debate (1972–1978) as a Case Study" that "Local politics and local people shaped the course of events in every state that considered rescission, and state has its own story to tell" (485). Spruill's study of feminists in South Carolina, "Victoria Eslinger, Keller Bumgardner Barron, Mary Heriot, Tootsie Holland, and Pat Callair," finds that the ERA activists in the state teamed up, headed by NOW and LWV as well as other organizations like the ACLU and AAUW. These groups formed the South Carolina Coalition for the ERA, which was "formidable" (384). Still, they could not succeed in the face of legislative opposition. Other scholars who study the ERA in the South include Janet Allured, *Remapping Second-Wave Feminism*, Janine Parry, "What Women Wanted"; Joan Carver, "The Equal Rights Amendment and the Florida Legislature"; Katarina Keane, "Second-Wave Feminism in the American South"; and Janet Boles, *The Politics of the Equal Rights Amendment* (which includes Georgia as a case study). I provide an overview of ERA ratification in Virginia in Kierner et al., *Changing History*, 323–30.

3. Spruill's *Divided We Stand* explains that "What finally moved conservative women from anger to action was Congressional approval of the Equal Rights Amendment..." (75). She examines the emergence of Phyllis Schlafly as the leader of STOP-ERA, from how she chose and

trained her state leaders, to how she drew together unlikely coalitions to defeat the amendment. She also notes that religion, concerns over the loss of traditional families, and concepts of morality affected ERA activists, who often worked within their Mormon, Baptist, or other conservative church denominations to spread their message (71–127). Spruill explains, "Religion was at the core of the anti-ERA movement" (90). She also analyzes their fear: anti-ERA activists believed, "Instead of simply extending women's rights, feminists seemed intent on taking rights and privileges away" (75). Erin Kempker in "Battling 'Big Sister' Government: Hoosier Women and the Politics of International Women's Year" says "The ERA ratification had the ironic effect of fostering a burgeoning conservative movement" while dividing Indiana's "liberal coalition" of women's groups that tried to come together to support the ERA (150). For more information about anti-ERA activists, see Val Burris, "Who Opposed the ERA? An Analysis of the Social Bases of Antifeminism"; David Brady and Kent Tedin, "Ladies in Pink: Religion and Political Ideology in the Anti-ERA Movement"; Rymph, *Republican Women*, 213–29; O. Kendall White Jr., "Overt and Covert Politics: The Mormon Church's Anti-ERA Campaign in Virginia"; and Brown, *For a "Christian America,"* 45–98. Donald Critchlow's *Phyllis Schlafly and Grassroots Conservatism: A Woman's Crusade* explores Schlafly's biography and explains her central role in the ERA ratification battle. Allured noted that many Louisiana Baptists and other evangelicals, as well as many Catholics, opposed the ERA as they "opposed many of the other changes associated with the modern women's movement: abortion, premarital sex, easy divorce, wives working outside the home, and equality in marriage" (*Remapping Second-Wave Feminism*, 220). These, she posits, were issues that galvanized anti-ERA forces across the country and mobilized women to fight against the amendment (218–21).

Mathews and De Hart argue that "Antiratificationists skillfully wove the symbols of ERA, 'women's lib,' and 'family' into a web of apprehension, defensiveness, and anger. The result was to enmesh the ERA in a psychic trap that separated liberation from obligation: wanting to be free meant no longer wanting to be female" (*Sex, Gender, and the Politics of the ERA*, 152). Mathews and De Hart's chapter 6 analyzes the thoughts and ideologies of the anti-ERA activists in North Carolina.

4. In "The Equal Rights Amendment and the Florida Legislature," Joan Carver pointed out "clear regional divisions" in the way the ERA ratification played out. Of the fifteen states that had not passed or rescinded by 1982, eleven were in the South. Three, she explained, were states with heavy Mormon presence (456). Val Burris explains what kinds of people opposed ERA in "Who Opposed the ERA?"

5. Mathews and De Hart explain the gains made in North Carolina during ERA passage, and as Mansbridge notes, women made so many legislative gains from 1972 to 1982 that the ERA would not really have addressed as many problems as proponents claimed. Mansbridge argues that it would have been more of a symbolic gain, as well as a way to move constitutional law forward. Mathews and De Hart also conclude that the ERA would have advanced equality in a more symbolic, less concrete way because of the gains made through legislation.

6. Donald Critchlaw and Cynthia Stacheski, "The Equal Rights Amendment Reconsidered," argues that, while anti-ERA forces were more successful in mobilizing populations in states because of their "more determined, more politically active, and more knowledgeable" stand and their better organization, it was still the action at the local level, not just Schlafly, that made the difference (160–71). I believe that pro-ERA forces were just as active in Virginia, but as in North Carolina, they lacked what Mathews and De Hart called "access and credibility" that more moneyed

interests had (*Sex, Gender, and the Politics of the ERA*, 181). Mary Bezbatchenko's excellent thesis, "Virginia and the Equal Rights Amendment," goes into great detail about how Virginia General Assembly committees worked, what the ERA Task Force created by the Senate wrote, how interest groups testified in front of the Privileges and Elections Committee year after year, and what kinds of maneuvering occurred on the Senate and House floors to try to dislodge the amendment from committees. It is extremely useful for understanding exactly how committees could hold up legislation.

7. Mathews and De Hart note that activists believed the ERA could essentially help to reshape gender stereotypes and structures, which could transform society (*Sex, Gender, and the Politics of the ERA*, 129–34). Mansbridge claims that the real change ERA would effect would be completely ideological, with the exception of altering constitutional law in the years to come. Carver notes that, in Florida, "the issue had been transformed from one primarily about the rights of women to one about federalism and broad social trends" ("The Equal Rights Amendment and the Florida Legislature," 480). Mathews and De Hart point out a distinctively southern nature to the defeat in North Carolina; many there, "like other Southerners, have historically defended elite male power by appeal to the myth of the dependent woman.... Southerners are traditionalists, and ERA challenged tradition. They are provincials opposed to cosmopolitan values and antistatists suspicious of federal authority" (*Sex, Gender, and the Politics of the ERA*, 181). Not *all* southerners were this way, and certainly this view of southernness applies to white southerners, but there was definitely a belief among Virginia activists that this was a problem. As Bezbatchenko pointed out, in testimony from 1973 a Washington and Lee professor complained of federal intervention in the forty years preceding the ERA, and she explained that several other ERA opponents discussed the danger of loss of state control over family matters, or intrusion of the Supreme Court in issues like busing ("Virginia and the Equal Rights Amendment," 28, 24–27). Janet Allured argues that "Antis recycled states' rights arguments developed in their battle against civil rights, contending that the amendment constituted a power grab by the federal government" (*Remapping Second-Wave Feminism*, 219).

8. Eileen Shanahan, "The ERA Is Approved by Congress," www.nytimes.com/learning/general/onthisday/big/0322.html (accessed 3 November 2017); Bezbatchenko, "Virginia and the Equal Rights Amendment," 17.

9. Audrey Capone, "Women's Rights," *Federation Notes*, April 1972, 9, Box 7, Folder 2, VABPW.

10. "NCJW Virginia State Public Affairs Committee Press Release," March 1973, Box 5 Lobby History of the ERA Folder, Smith; "Resolutions Adopted by the Congress of Women's Organizations," 1–2 June 1973, Box 1 Folder 5, Williams; "Women's Groups Organize Lobbying," *Richmond Times Dispatch*, 8 December 1973, Box 1 Folder 5, Williams; "VWPC Quarterly Report," 11 January 1973, Box 1, Folder 6, Williams.

11. Doris Kearn, "Some Guideposts on Ratification of the E.R.A.," and Mary Holt Carlton, "The Equal Rights Amendment: A Brave New ERA," *The Virginia Club Woman* 45, no. 1 (September 1972): 16–17 and 20–21, in Box 1, Carlton.

12. Interview with Muriel Elizabeth Smith.

13. Bezbatchenko has an excellent analysis of this first ERA hearing, as well as the import of the Privileges and Elections Committee. She discusses the committee and Thomson's role ("Virginia and the Equal Rights Amendment," 8, 49–51).

14. Bezbatchenko explains who spoke and what the issues were in the September hearings ("Virginia and the Equal Rights Amendment," 20–30).

15. Betty Booker Luce, "Women Argue Rights Bill," *RTD*, 2 February 1973, A12; Anne Smith and Linda Waller, "Assemblymen Given Equal Rights Earful," *Virginian-Pilot*, 2 February 1973, D1; "Chronology of ERA in Virginia State Legislature," VERARC, Box 7, ERA Legislators Kit Folder, Hellmuth.

16. Mathews and De Hart note that because NC Senator Sam Ervin was passionately against the ERA, he was able to work closely with Phyllis Schlafly to provide ammunition for the STOP-ERA movement. The STOP-ERA movement was also very active in Illinois, as Mansbridge explains. Anywhere that ERA was up for contestation over a long period of time—places where the amendment had a chance of ratification, like Illinois and North Carolina—and Virginia, the STOP-ERA forces battled hard, generally to maintain what they viewed as privileges granted to them because of their status as traditional homemakers and mothers.

17. Bezbatchenko, "Virginia and the Equal Rights Amendment," 43.

18. Ibid., 42–44; Neil Young, "'The ERA Is a Moral Issue': The Mormon Church, LDS Women, and the Defeat of the Equal Rights Amendment," 629; White, "Overt and Covert Politics," 13–16.

19. Bezbatchenko, "Virginia and the Equal Rights Amendment," 43.

20. As quoted in Bezbatchenko, "Virginia and the Equal Rights Amendment," 44.

21. Berry discusses the way in which opponents were able to claim the safer, more "traditional" stereotype of womanhood, despite their political sophistication, to put proponents on the defensive (*Why ERA Failed*, 85). In North Carolina, Mathews and De Hart discuss the ways in which negative stereotypes were so ingrained that they were hard to dislodge (*Sex, Gender, and the Politics of the ERA*, 202–3).

22. Betty Booker Luce, "Women Argue Rights Bill," *RTD*, 2 February 1973, A12.

23. Memo to local LWV presidents, ERA Coordinators, State Board, Subject: ERA Perspective and Planning, from Buffie Scott, ERA coordinator, Box 43, Folder 5, LWVVA. Please note: this collection has been reprocessed. Please check the new finding guide for subject titles to find new box/folder numbers.

24. "Everything You Already Know About the ERA—Plus," *Fairfax Area League of Women Voters Bulletin*, October 1973, pp. 8–10, Box 10, Folder 3, LWV Fairfax. Quote on 8.

25. "NJCW State Public Affairs Committee Press Release," March 1973, Box 5, Lobby History of the ERA Folder, Smith; "Resolutions Adopted by the Congress of Women's Organizations," 1–2 June 1973, Box 1, Folder 5, Williams; "Women to Escalate Rights Measure Fight," *RTD*, 12 August 1973, B9.

26. Natalie Cooper, Testimony for ERA Hearing, 18 September 1973, Box 43, Folder 8, LWVVA.

27. Virginia Churn, "Effect of ERA on Law Debated," *RTD*, 19 September 1973, A8; Faye Ehrenstamm, "Woman Lawyer Stumps for ERA," *RTD*, 14 September 1973, B3; Anne Smith and Laura White, "ERA Testimony Heard Once Again," *Virginian-Pilot*, 19 September 1973, A10–11, Box 3 Folder 4, ZNWM.

28. Memo to Members of BPW et al. from ERA Central, Box 12, Misc. ERA clippings 1972–79, SWRP.

29. LWV Memo, 11 October 1973, Box 43, Folder 5, LWVVA.

30. Frieda Stanley to Mr. Bryan, 16 January 1974, Box 6 Folder 3, AAUW.

31. Mathews and De Hart as well as Mansbridge argued that, although the ERA would have ultimately made little real changes to the lives of American women, especially since so much pro-woman legislation passed in the decade between congressional ratification and the ERA's ultimate defeat in the states, activists perceived that the amendment would ameliorate wage in-

equities, help women claim property in divorce cases, and equalize educational and employment opportunities. But women also recognized that the ERA was actually more of a symbolic, or ideological, issue—that it would help women's status in the country by ending negative stereotypes and assisting in the refashioning of traditional gender roles.

32. Nancy Joyner, "The Commonwealth's Approach to the Equal Rights Amendment," *University of Virginia Newsletter* 50, no. 9 (15 May 1974): 33–34, in Box 1, Folder 19, Williams.

33. Ibid., 33.

34. Virginia Wives and Mothers for the Equal Rights Amendment, Press Release, 31 January 1973, 1–3, Box 2, Housewives for ERA Folder, Smith. Quote on 1.

35. "Women of Virginia: Rights You Are Denied," n.d., Box 3, Correspondence 1974–82 Folder, Hellmuth.

36. Sylvia Clute, "The Women's Movement: Why Does It Exist?" 17 December 1975, p. 5, Box 14, Constitution-ERA Folder, VERARC.

37. "Equal Rights Amendment," *Fairfax Area League of Women Voters Bulletin*, September 1976, p. 7, Box 10, Folder 3, LWV Fairfax.

38. See note 7, above, for more information on southern stereotypes and the ERA.

39. Marinelle Duggan, "Debate on Rights Goes On and On," *RNL*, 6 February 1973, 11.

40. Ehrenstamm, Woman Lawyer Stumps for ERA," *RTD*, 14 September 1973, B3.

41. "Mind Your Manners," *Legislative Bulletin*, no. 1 (25 January 1974): 3, Box 1, Folder 5, Williams.

42. Ibid., and "Antis Attack NOW," *Legislative Bulletin*, no. 1 (25 January 1974): 3, 4–5, Box 1, Folder 5, Williams.

43. Letter from Mrs. Stanley Neustadt, 10 January 1974, Box 43, Folder 5, LWVVA.

44. Virginia activists used this term in correspondence and in interviews, but it was a term bandied about in other places at the time. Morton Kondrake cited the term in "End of an ERA," *New Republic*, 30 April 1977, 14–16.

45. Spruill, *Divided We Stand*, 94, 83.

46. Letter from Mrs. Stanley Neustadt, 10 January 1974, Box 43, Folder 5, LWVVA; Betty Booker Luce, "It's a Womanly Battle of Principle and Words," *RTD*, 11 February 1974, A12–13. Quote on A13.

47. Lela Spitz, Update on Equal Rights Amendment, 1974 Summary, Box 43, Folder 5, LWVVA; Betty Booker Luce, "Opening of General Assembly Holds Promise for Women," *RTD*, 6 January 1974, G1.

48. "Bouquets and Brickbats," 2, and "Breakfast a Success," 4, Virginia ERA Central, *Legislative Bulletin* #1 (25 January 1974), Box 1, Folder 5, Williams; Betty Booker Luce, "Group Seeks ERA Support," *RTD*, 18 January 1974, A11; Zelda Nordlinger to Meg Williams, 10 January 1974, Box 1, Folder 11, Williams.

49. Bezbatchenko, "Virginia and the Equal Rights Amendment," 57–58.

50. Betty Booker Luce, "ERA Would Bring Few Changes," *RTD*, 9 January 1974, A7; "Chronology of ERA in Virginia State Legislature," VERARC, Box 7, ERA Legislators Kit Folder, Hellmuth. For a detailed analysis of the Task Force Report, see Bezbatchenko, "Virginia and the Equal Rights Amendment," 34–41.

51. Betty Booker Luce, "Audience of about 600 at ERA Hearing Proves Vocal," *RTD*, 13 February 1974, B1, 3; Lela Spitz, "Update on the Equal Rights Amendment: ERA in Virginia, 1974 Summary," p. 1, Box 43, Folder 5, LWVVA.

52. Spitz, "Update on the Equal Rights Amendment," p. 1, Box 43, Folder 5, LWVVA; Helen

Dewar, "Women's Rights Loses in Virginia," *WP,* 28 February 1974, B1–2; "Mystery Memo," *Virginia ERA Supporter's Handbook,* September 1974, p. 17, Box 3, Equal Rights Amendment Handbook Folder, Hellmuth.

53. Flora Crater, "Democracy in Virginia: For Men Only," *The Woman Activist: Virginia Edition* 4, no. 3 (March 15, 1974), in Box 12, ERA–Misc. Clippings Folder, SWRP; Stephen Fleming, "Battle Erupts in House on Rights Bill's Death," *RTD,* 1 March 1974, B1, 8 (quote on B8); Spitz, Spitz, "Update on the Equal Rights Amendment," Box 43, Folder 5, LWVVA; Stephen Fleming, "ERA Innocence Pleaded by Miller," *RTD,* 2 March 1974, B3; James Latimer, "House Group Seeking to Quiet ERA 'Noise,'" *RTD,* 7 March 1974, C1.

54. "Unethical Tactics Charged," *Daily Progress,* 7 March 1974, clipping, Box 1, Folder 19, Williams; James Latimer, "House Group Seeking to Quiet ERA 'Noise,'" *RTD,* 7 March 1974, C1.

55. Latimer, "House Group Seeking to Quiet ERA 'Noise,'" *RTD,* 7 March 1974, C1.

56. Virginia Women's Political Caucus Letter, 6 March 1974, Box 1, Folder 19, Williams.

57. Flora Crater to Edna, 30 August 1974, Box 1, Folder 2, Smith.

58. "Women's Club 'NOW' to Meet Nov. 21 at YW," *Norfolk Journal and Guide,* 16 November 1974, 9.

59. *Virginia ERA Supporter's Handbook,* 39, 41, 37, 38, Box 3, Equal Rights Amendment Handbook Folder, Hellmuth.

60. Ibid., 41, list on 37.

61. "The Equal Rights in Virginia: The 1975 Legislative Story," Box 5, Misc. Minutes, Notes, Correspondence, Hellmuth.

62. "ERA Can Succeed In Virginia If Each Believer Wins Over One More Person," *Virginia Voter* 21, no. 7 (September–October 1974), 1, Box 64, Folder 16, LWVVA.

63. Betty Pettinger, "ERA Backers Are Seeking a Floor Vote," *RTD,* 15 November 1975, A5; "The Equal Rights in Virginia: The 1975 Legislative Story," Box 5, Misc. Minutes, Notes, Correspondence, Hellmuth.

64. Mary Parsiani, "Re: Past Efforts (ERA) And Future Directions," *NOW Notes* 3, no. 2 (February 1975): 2, Box 1, Folder 18a, White.

65. Ward Sinclair, "Political Consultants: The New Kingmakers Work Their Magic," *WP,* 5 June 1982, www.washingtonpost.com/archive/politics/1982/06/05/political-consultants-the-new-kingmakers-work-their-magic/c80142ee-d602-4f41-9a4c-9107b36f6928/?utm_term=.b68264eabe5e (accessed 14 November 2017). If this is the Joe Rothstein of Rothstein & Company, he was a high-powered political consultant who worked on many successful Democratic campaigns. Mike McLister was also listed in Meese's notes.

66. "Mini Report to the State Board on ERA Campaign Management and Planning," 17 October 1975, Box 5, Misc. Minutes, Notes, Correspondence Folder, Hellmuth.

67. "Film Set by NOW," *RTD,* 29 October 1975, Box 3, Folder 7, ZNWM; *Charlottesville NOW Newsletter,* June 1975, 1, Box 15, Folder 4, NOWVA; Ellen Griffee, "ERA #1 Issue to VA AAUW," *Virginia Division AAUW Bulletin* 50, no. 1 (Fall 1975): 1–2, Box 11, Folder 6, AAUW; *VWPC Newsletter,* October 1975, Box 13, ERA Women's Rights Folder, SWRP.

68. Anne Lunde, "Legislative Committee Report," *Federation Notes* 24, no. 1 (Summer 1975): 16, 27. Quote on 27.

69. *Virginia Women's Political Caucus Newsletter,* October 1975, 1, Box 13, ERA Women's Rights 1975-8 Folder, SWRP; VERARC "October Meeting," 17 October 1975, Box 1, Folder 5, Smith, 1; VERARC News Release, 4 October 1975, Box 1, Folder 19, White.

70. "How to Discharge a Committee," *VWPC Newsletter,* October 1975, Box 13, ERA Women's Rights 1975-8 Folder, SWRP; VERARC "October Meeting," 17 October 1975, Box 1, Folder 5, Smith, 1; VERARC News Release, 4 October 1975, Box 1, Folder 19, White.

71. Minutes, 19 March 1975, 8, Box 4, Folder 4, LWVVA.

72. News Release, 5 November 1975, Box 1, Folder 1, Smith.

73. *VERARC Bulletin,* 22 August 1975, Box 1, Folder 5, Smith; "ERA Activities Planned," *Equal Times* 5, no. 7 (August 1975): 12, Box 16, Folder 6, NOWVA.

74. "To All ERA Supporters," *Equal Times* 5, no. 9 (October 1975): 11, Box 16, Folder 6, NOWVA.

75. "VERARC Minutes," 8 November 1975, Box 1, Folder 4, Smith; "VERARC November Meeting," 28 November 1975, Box 1, Folder 4, Smith; "December Meeting," VERARC, 24 December 1975, Box 1, Folder 4, Smith; "Action Is Everybody's Business," *Fairfax Area League of Women Voters Bulletin,* January 1976, 3, Box 21, Folder 4, LWV Fairfax.

76. Robin Gallaher, "March Starts for ERA," *RTD,* 10 January 1976, B1; "NOW Press Release: 100 Mile Walk for Equality to Begin January 9, 1976," 2 January 1976, Box 7, Folder 10, NOWVA; Douglas Durden, "ERA Backers Reach City after 5 Days," *RTD,* 14 January 1976, B1, 5.

77. Bezbatchenko, "Virginia and the Equal Rights Amendment," 71–72.

78. "Press Release—News from the National Organization for Women: Local N.O.W. Chapter to Raley [sic] in Richmond," Box 18, Folder 1, NOWVA; Suzanne Freeman, "ERA Supporters Rally," *Charlottesville Daily Progress,* Box 15, VERARC Press Coverage Folder, VERARC; *Equal Times* 5, no. 10 (February 1976): 3, Box 16, Folder 7, NOWVA; "Ordering Our Priorities," 18a, Virginia AAUW, Box 7, Folder 2, Norfolk AAUW.

79. Douglas Durden, "Virginia Is Out of Step, Ms. Heinz Tells Marchers," *RTD,* 15 January 1976, D1; Statement of Heinz for Monroe Park Delivery, 14 January 1976, Box 7, Folder 10, NOWVA.

80. Durden, "ERA Backers Reach City"; "March pamphlet," n.d., p. 7, Box 6, Projects 1976 Folder, Hellmuth; Durden, "Virginia Is Out of Step," *RTD,* 15 January 1976, D1.

81. "Action Is Everybody's Business," *Fairfax Area League of Women Voters Bulletin,* January 1976, 3, Box 21, Folder 4, LWV Fairfax; *League of Women Voters Montgomery County Bulletin* 5, no. 7 (March 1976): 5, Box 5, Folder 34, LWV Montgomery; "Minutes of Virginia ERA Ratification Council," 10 January 1976, Box 1, Folder 7, Smith; "Information Flyer," Box 11, Catholic Women for the ERA, Folder 7, Smith; "What Happened in Richmond," VERARC, 27 February 1976, Box 1, Folder 7, Smith.

82. As Janet Allured explains in her study of Louisiana feminists, the committee system actually enabled legislators to get away with appearing to support a measure *or* refusing to take a stand on a measure without actually having to record a vote on it. What Happened in Richmond," VERARC, 27 February 1976, Box 1, Folder 7, Smith; "Summary of What Happened on General Assembly 1976," Box 2, Chronology Folder, Hellmuth; Jane Malone, "Senate Kills Move to Resurrect ERA," *RTD,* 7 February 1976, A1–2. For a detailed description of what went on in the 1976 session see Bezbatchenko, "Virginia and the Equal Rights Amendment," 73–74.

83. "Brickbats and Bouquets," *Charlottesville NOW Newsletter,* February 1976, 1, Box 15, Folder 4, NOWVA; Flora Crater, "Strategy for ratification of the ERA by the General Assembly," ERA Action Plan, 1 March 1976, 5–7, Box 1, Folder 7, Smith; "Pre-Council Board Meeting Minutes," 20 April 1976, 6, and "Minutes of the LWVVA Board of Directors Meeting," 20 May 1976, 8, both in Box 4, Folder 5, LWVVA; Ordering Our Priorities," p. 18b, Virginia AAUW, Box 7, Folder 2, Norfolk AAUW.

84. Margaret Bond, "Chisholm, 'Do Your Thing,'" *Norfolk Journal and Guide,* 6 March 1976, 1,

2; *NOW What?* 4, no. 6 (June 1976), Box 1, Folder 18a, White; *Charlottesville NOW Newsletter*, June and July 1976, 1, Box 15, Folder 4, NOWVA; *Charlottesville NOW Newsletter*, August 1976, 1, Box 15, Folder 4, NOWVA; *NOW What?* 4, no. 10 (October 1976), Box 1, Folder 3, Carlton.

85. Bezbatchenko, "Virginia and the Equal Rights Amendment," 76–77.

86. *NOW What?* 4, no. 10 (October 1976), Box 1, Folder 3, Carlton; Jean Hellmuth and Jeanie DeLassus, "Equal Rights Amendment," *The Leaguer*, September 1976, p. 6, Box 6, Newsletters 1976 Folder, LWV Richmond; Judy Harris, "Wanted: ERA Lobbyist," 1 October 1976, Box 7, Folder 10, NOWVA; Pat Jensen to Local League Presidents, ERA Coordinators, Acting Chairman, State Board, 13 January 1977, Box 43, Folder 5, LWVVA.

87. Pat Jensen, "The Equal Rights Amendment," *The Virginia Voter*, Piggyback Edition, vol. 13 (January 1977): 1–2, Box 64, Folder 19, LWVVA.

88. LWVVA Board of Directors Meeting Minutes, 4–5 January 1977, p. 6, Box 4, Folder 6, LWVVA; Flyer for Speakout, Box 7, Folder 11, NOWVA; "ERA Facts for Action: A Teach-in," Box 7, Folder 11, NOWVA; "ERA FFA Schedule," Box 5. Misc. Minutes, Notes, Correspondence Folder, Hellmuth; Jean Hellmuth, "Equal Rights Amendment Committee," *The Leaguer*, January 1977, 6, Box 6, Newsletters 1977–79 Folder, LWV Richmond. Bezbatchenko also discusses the many actors involved in ERA week ("Virginia and the Equal Rights Amendment," 76–79).

89. Flyer, Richmond ERA Week, in Box 12, ERA Groups—Local ERA Coalitions Folder, VERARC.

90. Toba Singer, Open Letter to Richmond Ratification Council, 20 March 1977, Box 12, Local Coalitions Folder, VERARC; Toba Singer, "Red-Baiting in the ERA Movement," *The Militant*, 25 February 1977, 13, clipping in Box 12, Local Coalitions Folder, VERARC.

91. "The Equal Rights Amendment," Box 21, Folder 5, LWV Fairfax. For a detailed analysis of the debate on the Senate floor and the fallout from the vote, see Bezbatchenko, "Virginia and the Equal Rights Amendment," 79–81.

92. Singer, "Red-Baiting in the ERA Movement," *The Militant*, 25 February 1977, 13.

93. Ibid.

94. Singer, "Open Letter," Juanita White to Evelyn Marr Glazier, 11 April 1977, Box 1, Folder 1, White; Zelda Nordlinger to Richmond ERA Ratification Council, 31 March 1977, Box 7, SWP 1977 Folder, Hellmuth; Zelda Nordlinger to *ERA Monitor*, 31 March 1977, Box 7, SWP 1977 Folder, Hellmuth.

95. Interview with Mary Wazlak; for more information about the ties anti-ERA activists made with abortion, see Spruill, *Divided We Stand*, 104, and Rymph, *Republican Women*, 213–14. A full explanation of their beliefs can be found in note 30 of chapter 3, below.

96. Interview with Beth Marschak.

97. Pat Watt to Ruth Clusen, 18 July 1977, Box 44, Folder 5, LWV Fairfax.

98. Interview with Beth Marschak.

99. Bezbatchenko, "Virginia and the Equal Rights Amendment," 81–82. She argues that the years had "taken a toll" on organizers, and that this episode is a clear indication of fatigue.

100. Marjorie Spruill's *Divided We Stand* provides a clear synopsis and analysis of how the IWY came to be, as well as the ramifications from it.

101. "The ERA Strategy for Virginia (And the Nation)," Box 10, ERA 1977 Folder, SWRP.

102. Ibid.

103. "ERA Strategy for Virginia (And the Nation)," Box 10, ERA 1977 Folder, SWRP; *VERARC Newsletter*, July 1977, Box 11, ERA Educational Materials Folder, SWRP; "Assembly Faces

ERA," *E.R.A. Time,* 11 January 1978, 3–4, Box 4, VERARC Folder, Smith; "NOW and ERA Caravan," *The Blue Lantern* 1, no. 5 (May 1977), Box 2, Folder 2, White.

104. "ERA Pledge," 19 May 1977, Box 44, Folder 4, LWVVA; Vivian Watts to Lulu Meese, 27 May 1977, Box 44, Folder 21, LWV Fairfax; "National Council Debates Leagues' Role in ERA Campaign," *Virginia Voter,* Piggyback Edition, vol. 17 (June 1977): 2, Box 64, Folder 19, LWVVA; Pat Jensen, " Virginia Leagues Accept Challenge, Begin ERA Fundraising Efforts," *Virginia Voter,* Piggyback Edition, vol. 19 (October 1977): 1–2, LWVVA B 64, F 19; "3-2-1-Go ERA," *The Leaguer,* October 1977, 6, LWV Richmond, Box 6, Newsletters 1977–79 Folder; *The Virginia Voter,* Piggyback Edition, vol. 21 (December 1977): 1, Box 2, Folder 5, LWV Fairfax.

105. Lulu Meese, "Closing Remarks to State LWV Convention," *The Leaguer,* May 1977, 7–8, Box 6, Newsletters 1977–79 Folder, LWV Richmond; "Plans for 1977-8, VERARC," Box 6, Projects 1976–77 Folder, Hellmuth; Muriel Smith to Crystal Perry, 10 May 1977, and Barbara Haga to Muriel Smith, 10 May 1977, both in Box 1, Folder 10, Smith; *The Leaguer,* 77 February 1977, p. 8, Box 6, Newsletters 1977–79 Folder, LWV Richmond; "Action in the Districts," *Go ERA!* 1, no. 2 (13 October 1977): 1, Box 17, Common Cause Folder, VERARC; *Go ERA!* 1, no. 5 (3 November 1977): 5, Box 17, Common Cause Folder, VERARC.

106. "Action in the Districts," *Go ERA!* 1, no. 2; "Action in the Districts," *Go ERA!* 1, no. 3 (20 October 1977): 3; "Action in the Districts," *Go ERA!* 1, no. 5 (4 November 1977): 3–5; "Action in the Districts," *Go ERA!* 1, no. 6 (10 November 1977): 4, all from Box 17, Common Cause Folder, VERARC. "Action in the Districts," *Go ERA!* 1, no. 4 (27 October 1977), Box 2, Common Cause Folder, Smith; "Action in the Districts," *Go ERA!* 1, no. 5.

107. "Action in the Districts," *Go ERA!* 1, no. 2; "From Your Editor," *VERARC Newsletter,* ACLU Box 10, ERA 1977 Folder, SWRP; "Equality March," *Federation Notes* 26, no. 2 (Fall 1977): 11, Box 7, Folder 5, BPWVA; "Action Is Everybody's Business" and "Thanks to the Marchers," *Fairfax Area League of Women Voters Bulletin,* October 1977, pp. 3, 13, Box 21, Folder 5, LWV Fairfax; "ERA 3-2-1 Go!" *The Leaguer,* October 1977, Box 6, Newsletters 1977–79 Folder, LWV Richmond; Coordinator of Charlottesville NOW to Walker, 7 October 1977, Box 15, Folder 4, NOWVA. Critchlow explained in *Phyllis Schlafly* that NOW Walkathons were a major national initiative and that by 1981 NOW had raised one million dollars (250).

108. Douglas Durden, "ERA Backers Prevail in Votes in Parley Here," *RTD,* 12 June 1977, C6; "To Form a More Perfect Commonwealth," *Charlottesville NOW Newsletter,* July 1977, 2–3 Box 15, Folder 4, NOWVA. For a detailed analysis of how Congress designated 1975 the International Year of the Woman, funded the conference, and what happened at the Houston conference in 1977, as well as the way the conference prompted a surge in anti-feminist activities, see Spruill, *Divided We Stand.*

109. *Charlottesville NOW Newsletter,* July 1977; Durden, "ERA Backers Prevail"; Douglas Durden, "ERA Backers Elect National Meeting Slate," *RTD,* 15 June 1977, B7; Jean Marshall Clarke to Virginia NOW Chapters, 15 June 1977, Box 3, NOW 1977–86 Folder, Smith.

110. Labor interests did not always step up to the plate to provide ERA assistance. Mary Frances Berry argues that labor didn't help in Illinois much at all (*Why ERA Failed,* 67), but Janet Allured finds that the Louisiana AFL-CIO strongly supported the ERA and other feminist measures. She notes that as labor lost influence over the course of the late 1970s and early 1980s, though, it lost the power to convince the House committee that held the amendment hostage to discharge it (*Remapping Second-Wave Feminism,* 294–304).

111. Hartmann, *The Other Feminists,* and Dorothy Sue Cobble, *The Other Women's Movement,* discuss this shift in policy.

112. "Resolution #6," Box 11, Telephone Fundraising Campaign Folder, SWRP; Jan Neber to Mary, 13 September 1977, Box 11, Telephone Fundraising Campaign Folder, SWRP; Lizzie Corbin to Betsy Brinson, 23 November 1977, Box 11, Educational Materials Folder, SWRP.

113. "Action in the Districts," *Go ERA!* 1, no. 4, 5; Eduardo Coe, "ERA Foe's Defeat Cheered," *WP,* 10 November 1977, clipping, Box 10, ERA 1977 Folder, SWRP; Virginians for the Equal Rights Amendment to Alexandria Voter, 17 October 1977, Box 16, Folder 8, NOWVA; *Equal Times,* October 1977, 13, Box 16, Folder 8, NOWVA; Eduardo Coe, "Delegate Is Target of ERA Supporters; ERA Is Issue in Alexandria," *WP,* 6 November 1977, B1.

114. "Reflections on the Recent Election," *Go ERA!* 1, no. 6 (November 10, 1977): 13, Box 17, Common Cause Folder, VERARC; Virginia NOW Proposal for Funding of ERA Lobbying Effort, 27 November 1977, Box 12, ERA Misc. Clippings, SWRP; Coe, "ERA Foe's Defeat Cheered," *WP,* 10 November 1977, clipping, Box 10, ERA 1977 Folder, SWRP; Ozzie Osborne, "Defeated ERA Foe Gives Women Partial Credit," *Roanoke Times and World News,* 24 November 1977, B1.

115. "Reflections on the Recent Election," *Go ERA!* 1, no. 6 (November 10, 1977): 3, Box 17, Common Cause Folder, VERARC; "What We Did for ERA in October and November," *Go ERA!* 1, no. 6 (November 10, 1977): 1, Box 17, Common Cause Folder, VERARC.

116. Memo to Marie Bass from Paul Lutzker, 15 November 1977, Box 12, ERA Misc. Clippings 1972–79, SWRP.

117. Virginia NOW Proposal for Funding of ERA Lobbying Effort, 27 November 1977, Box 12, ERA Misc. Clippings, SWRP; "Issues," *Charlottesville NOW Newsletter,* January 1978, Box 15, Folder 4, NOWVA.

118. "Update," and "From the Editor's Desk: Why Economic Boycotts?" *E.R.A. Time,* 18 January 1978, p. 1, 4, 2 Box 4, VERA PAC Folder, Smith.

119. Endorsers List for January 22 (Partial), Box 3, LERN Folder, Smith; LERN Flyer, Box 3, LERN Folder, Smith; *Virginia Division Bulletin* 52, no. 2 (Winter 1978): 5, Box 6, Folder 11, AAUW Norfolk; "Virginians of All Walks March for ERA," *E.R.A. Time,* 23 January 1978, 2, Box 4, VERA-PAC F, Smith; Georgia Fuller, "Giving the Sabbath to the ERA," *E.R.A. Time,* 23 January 1978, pp. 4–5, Box 4, VERA-PAC Folder, Smith; "Labor-Sponsored Rally," *E.R.A. Time,* January 18, 1978, 2, Box 2, ERA Extension Folder, Hellmuth.

120. Pat Jensen, "ERA—A Time for Action," *Virginia Voter,* Piggyback Edition, vol. 22 (January 1978): 1, 2 (quote on 2), Box 6, Newsletters 1977–79 Folder, LWV Richmond.

121. "Top Priority: The Equal Rights Amendment," *Montgomery County LWV Newsletter* 7, no. 6 (January 1978): 7–8, Box 7, Folder 1, LWV Montgomery; Board of Directors Meeting Minutes, LWV Richmond, 31 January 1978, Box 5, Minutes 1975–78 Folder, LWV Richmond; "ERA Symposium at Old Dominion University," *Our Own Community Press* 2, no. 6 (January 1978): 1; Ad for ERA, *RTD,* 17 January 1978, A12, Box 2, Advertisements Folder, Smith.

122. "From the Editor's Desk: The State Seal," *E.R.A. Time,* 30 January 1978, 2, Box 4, VERA-PAC Folder, Smith. Winton noted in the article that a NOW member from Chesapeake reworked the seal, but in an email to Emily McCoy dated 7 February 2018 she remembered it may have been two members from Harrisonburg.

123. Interview with Emily McCoy.

124. Deborah Woodward, "Who Killed the ERA?" *Richmond Magazine,* April 1978, 42, Box 13, ERA Women's Rights Folder, SWRP.

125. Ibid.

126. Lulu Meese, Report on ERA Action to Local League Presidents, February 1978, Box 9, LWV Folder, VERARC; Statements of ERA proponents, 8 February 1978, Box 5, Lobby History of

ERA Folder, Smith; Woodward, "Who Killed the ERA?" *Richmond Magazine,* April 1978, 45, Box 13, ERA Women's Rights Folder, SWRP; Patricia Winton Goodman, "The ERA in Virginia: A Power Playground," 11, Box 13, ERA Women's Rights Folder, SWRP. This was a typed version of an article that later appeared in *Southern Exposure* in 1978. Please note that Pat Winton will be cited sometimes in the notes as Pat Winton Goodman, She prefers to be called Pat Winton in the text.

127. Goodman, "The ERA in Virginia," 12, Box 13, ERA Women's Rights Folder, SWRP; "Virginia ERA Leaders Appeal Conviction for 'Trespassing,'" *Women's Agenda* 3, no. 8 (October 1978): 11, Box 11, ERA Arrests Publicity Folder, SWRP.

128. "Arrested!" *E.R.A. Time,* 10 February 1978, 1, B4, VERA-PAC Folder, Smith; "Richmond Judge Fines ERA Lobbyists," clipping, Box 11, ERA Arrests Publicity Folder, SWRP; Alan Cooper, "2 ERA Activists Convicted," *RNL,* 12 September 1978, 7; Memorandum from Liz Wheaton to Southern Affiliate Directors, 8 January 1979, Box 6, 1979 Affiliate Memos, SWRP.

129. Memorandum from Liz Wheaton to Southern Affiliate Directors, 8 January 1979, Box 6, 1979 Affiliate Memos, SWRP; "ERA Legal Defense Fund," Betsy Brinson to Ms. Editor, 25 April 1978, Box 11, ERA Arrests Publicity Folder, SWRP; *VERARC Newsletter,* n.d., 3, Box 1, Legal Strategies Folder, Smith; Goodman, "The ERA in Virginia," 8, Box 13, ERA Women's Rights Folder, SWRP; "ERA Killed in Committee, Virginia Leaders Arrested: Virginia Defeats ERA," in Box 11, ERA Arrests Publicity Folder, SWRP Woodward; "Who Killed the ERA?" *Richmond Magazine,* April 1978, 41, Box 13, ERA Women's Rights Folder, SWRP.

130. "ERA Killed in Committee, Virginia Leaders Arrested: Virginia Defeats ERA," in Box 11, ERA Arrests Publicity Folder, SWRP Woodward, "Who Killed the ERA?" *Richmond Magazine,* April 1978, 49, Box 13, ERA Women's Rights Folder, SWRP.

131. Executive Committee Minutes 1979, Box 5, Miscellenous Notes, Correspondence n.d.–1970s–80s Folder, Hellmuth.

132. Lulu Meese, Report on ERA Action; Dorothy Spinks to Delegate, 10 February 1978, Box 9, National Association of BPW Folder, VERARC; "Virginia and the ERA," *Norfolk Journal and Guide,* 17 February 1978, 8; Woodward, "Who Killed the ERA?" *Richmond Magazine,* April 1978, 48, Box 13, ERA Women's Rights Folder, SWRP.

133. Ray McAllister, "Pair's Last Charge is Dropped," *RTD,* 11 December 1978, Box 11, ERA Arrests Publicity Folder, SWRP; "ACLU Press Release, 11 December 1978, Box 11, ERA Arrests Publicity Folder, SWRP; ACLU Press Notice, 14 December 1978, Box 11, ERA Arrests Publicity Folder, SWRP; "Ms. Clarke Lost Prize, Won Goal," 15 September 1978, Box 11, ERA Arrests Publicity Folder, SWRP.

134. Woodward, "Who Killed the ERA?" *Richmond Magazine,* April 1978, 43, Box 13, ERA Women's Rights Folder, SWRP.

135. "Pig Roast Fattens N.O.W.'s ERA Fund," *Montgomery NOW Newsletter* 3, Fall 1980, Box 15, Folder 8, NOWVA; "Run for Equality" Flyer, Box 17, Folder 12, NOWVA; *NOVA NOW Newsletter,* April 1981, Box 8, Folder 3, NOWVA; "Run for Equality," *Be Counted N.O.W.* 9, no. 9 (September 1981), Box 17, Folder 13, NOWVA; "What Has Been Happening in Virginia," *VERARC Newsletter* 4 (July 1981), Box 1, VERARC Folder, Smith; Ruth Ferrer, "ERA Walkers Raise $4,500," *Charlottesville Observer* 4, no. 35 (27 August–2 September 1981): 1, 31; clippings from *RTD* and *RNL,* 3 February 1982, Box 5, Miscellaneous Folder, Hellmuth; Barbara Bomfalk, "ERA Annual Report," AAUW Annual Convention Program, May 1981, Box 7, Folder 4, AAUW Norfolk; Virginia NOW State Policy Council Meeting Minutes, 22 November 1980, Box 2, Folder 13, NOWVA; Flora Crater, "Report on the Election Day Petition Drive," *VERARC Newsletter,* Box 6, Publications 1974–89 Folder, Hellmuth.

136. "Increased Support for ERA Tied to Perception of Backers," *RNL*, 17 July 1978, Box 5, Newsclippings Folder, Smith.

137. Betsy Brinson, Memo to VERARC Re: New Directions, 1 March 1978, Box 12, ERA Ratification Council 1977–78 F, SWRP.

138. Jerry Gordon and Suzanne Kelly, "Resolution for an Education/Action Program," p. 2, Box 8, Folder 1, NOWVA; "ERA Extension," *Charlottesville NOW Newsletter*, 1, Box 15, Folder 4, NOWVA; Memo to Southern Chapters from Betsy and Liz, Box 19, Regular Communications 1977–79 Folder, SWRP; Muriel Smith to Nancy Newman, 11 July 1978, Box 1, Correspondence 1978 F, Smith; "Summer Greetings," and "White House Vigil," Box 5, Miscellaneous Folder, Hellmuth.

139. "Virginians Organize for ERA Amendment," *Norfolk Journal & Guide*, 20 July 1979, 4; "Newport News Local Steelwomen Say 'Unite for ERA,'" *United Labor Action* 9, no. 8 (August 1979), Box 3, LERN Folder, Smith.

140. "Virginia Labor Giving ERA Major Push," *RNL*, 13 August 1979, Box 8, Folder 1, NOWVA; Gordon and Kelly, "Resolution for an Education/Action Program," 3–5, Box 8, Folder 1, NOWVA.

141. Estelle Jackson, "Almost 7,500 March in Support of ERA," *RTD*, Box 11, ERA Articles Folder, SWRP; LERN Rally Flyer, Box 5, LERN Folder, Smith.

142. "Sixty Picket Falwell Church," *RTD*, 1 May 1981, Box 19, ERA Supporters Folder, VERARC; "The ERA Rallies," *NOW Harrisonburg-Rockingham Chapter Newsletter*, February 1981, 2, Box 15, Folder 13, NOWVA; "The ERA Rally in Charlottesville," Box 15, Folder 5, NOWVA.

143. Interview with Lee Perkins, "Feminists Arrested in Washington," *New York Times*, 27 August 1981, A14; Michel McQueen, "ERA Supporters Protest Outside Mormon Temple," *WP*, 10 January 1982, A10; Michel McQueen, "ERA's Triumph: Activists, Gaining Strength in Defeat, Continue the Fight," *WP*, 7 July 1982, Virginia Weekly section, 1.

144. Interviews with Georgia Fuller and Lee Perkins; Georgia Elaine Fuller, "Climbing the President's Fence," quote from 112.

145. *Virginia Division Bulletin AAUW* 55, no. 4 (Summer 1981): 1, Box 11, Folder 6, AAUW Norfolk; Ellen Layman, "Virginia Could Swing ERA Vote," *Daily News-Record*, Box 6, Newspapers 1981 Folder, Smith; Pat Winton to Ellie Smeal, Box 8, Folder 3, NOWVA; Emily McCoy to Ellie Smeal, 16 August 1981, Box 8, Folder 3, NOWVA; "If You Vote for E.R.A. Now, We Will Ratify in 1982," Box 8, Folder 3, NOWVA; Fundraising Letter from Larry Pratt, Box 8, Folder 3, NOWVA; STOP-ERA letter, 28 December 1981, Box 8, Folder 3, NOWVA.

146. Judy Mann. "Yes, Virginia, There's Still an ERA," *WP*, 6 November 1981, B1.

147. "The Virginia General Assembly and the Equal Rights Amendment," *Virginia Voter*, Piggyback Edition, vol. 31 (March 1979): 1, Box 64, Folder 21, LWVVA; "Senator Uses Trick Against ERA," *Peninsula NOW Times* 2, no. 3 (March 1980): 1, Box 17, Folder 7, NOWVA; Rosalind Exum, Memo to Member Organizations, 17 March 1980, Box 4, Minutes Folder, Hellmuth; "Chronology of Virginia State Legislature," Box 5, Miscellaneous Folder, Hellmuth. More detail on the 1980 legislative session can be found in Bezbatchenko, "Virginia and the Equal Rights Amendment," 97–98.

148. VERARC Council Meeting, 10 January 1982, Box 2, VERARC Folder, Smith. Information on the ERAmerica budget can be found on Bezbatchenko, "Virginia and the Equal Rights Amendment," 100; Address of Charles S. Robb to the General Assembly, Monday, 18 January 1982, Senate Document no. 2B, 6, Box 1, Folder 1, Office of the Governor—Charles Robb Speeches, Library of Virginia.

149. "First Procedural Vote Falls Short," *E.R.A. Time,* 2 February 1982, 1, 3, Box 2, VERARC 1982 Folder, Smith; *NOW Harrisonburg/Rockingham Newsletter,* February 1982, p. 1, Box 15, Folder 13, NOWVA; Interview with Emily McCoy; "Political Ploy Blamed for the Rejection of ERA," 17 February 1982, Box 8, Folder 5, NOWVA; "Report from the President," *Richmond NOW Newsletter,* February 1982, 3, Box 3, NOW Richmond Chapter 1977–82 Folder, Smith.

150. Lulu Meese address, *VERARC Newsletter* 5, 1982, Box 2, VERARC Folder, Smith; Judy Mann, "Obstruction," *Washington Post,* 19 February 1982, Box 19, ERA in Virginia (and other legislatures) Folder, VERARC; Editorial in *News-Virginian,* 18 February 1982, Box 8, Folder 5, NOWVA.

151. "ERA Supporters Keep Fighting," *RNL,* 2 July 1982, and "Virginia ERA Ratification Council Continues Activity," *Woman's Press,* September–October 1982, in Box 5, Miscellaneous Folder, Hellmuth; Sandra Gregg and Bill Peterson, "Backers, Foes Mark End of ERA Battle: Both Sides Agree Fight Will Continue," *WP,* 1 July 1982, B1; Stephany Hall, "Wilson Answers Questions From NOW Chapter Members," *Daily Review,* 10 March 1983, Box 14, Folder 1, NOWVA; Interview with Sarah Payne, Stephanie Tyree, and Melanie Payne-White.

152. Allison Held et al., "The Equal Rights Amendment"; Updates on ERA in Virginia can be found at Virginia ERA Network, run by Virginia NOW, at http://virginiaeranet.com. (Last accessed 26 February 2018).

153. Memo to Local League Presidents, ERA Chairs, and State Board from Lulu Meese, 1 August 1982, Box 3, Folder 16, LWV Montgomery.

154. Interview with Georgia Fuller.

155. Gayle Stoner, "Women Are Here to Stay," *Virginia Highlands Chapter Newsletter,* July 1982, 1–2, NOWVA, Box 19, Folder 10.

156. Pat Winton to NOW Members, 31 March 1982, Box 4, Women's Round Table Folder, Smith.

157. Pat Matheny, "Grass Roots Digging May Reap Equal Rights, Some Say," *Roanoke Times and World-News,* 21 August, 1975, Box 18, Folder 1, NOWVA. Evidence of these chapters exists in the NOWVA records at the Library of Virginia, attesting to newsletters from these organizations.

158. Interviews with Mary Ann Bergeron, Muriel Elizabeth Smith, and Georgia Fuller.

159. Legislators do not see this issue as one that is important enough to draw votes either way. As Berenice Carroll explained in "Direct Action and Constitutional Rights," "the predominantly male legislatures and executive offices of the nonratified states did not see the ERA as a priority sufficiently compelling to brook the opposition and risk its political costs" (65). Mathews and De Hart explain that state legislatures also tended to avoid large ideological conflicts, like the ERA, which "became a conflict based on gender differences," and ultimately, "It failed because of political opposition to applying the principle of equality in public policy and the racism this resistance implied" (*Sex, Gender, and the Politics of the ERA,* 225).

160. Interview with Sandra Brandt; Allured, *Remapping Second-Wave Feminism,* 304.

161. Interview with Mary Ann Bergeron.

162. Interviews with Betsy Brinson, Emily McCoy, Mary Ann Bergeron, and Georgia Fuller.

163. Mansbridge argued that the ERA "focused public attention on women's disadvantage in the workplace, the home, and the streets" which would ultimately help women (*Why We Lost the ERA,* 188). While Mathews and De Hart claim that ERA failed in North Carolina because it became associated with feminism and increasing activism, the General Assembly changed divorce laws, sexual assault, and other laws friendly to women. They also claimed that the "ratification process was consciousness raising" (*Sex, Gender, and the Politics of the ERA,* 208–10, 144).

Chapter Three

1. Julie Rovner, "5 Things to Consider About the Supreme Court's Decision on Texas Abortion Law," 1 July 2016, National Public Radio, www.npr.org/sections/health-shots/2016/07/01/4843328 07/5-things-to-consider-about-the-supreme-court-s-decision-on-texas-abortion-law (accessed 19 November 2016).

2. There are numerous works that deal with the history of abortion reform and reproductive rights. For example, Leslie Reagan's *When Abortion Was a Crime: Women, Medicine, and Law in the United States, 1867–1973* tracks changes in attitudes about and laws regarding abortion from the mid-1800s to the landmark Supreme Court decision, focusing on Chicago. She argues that the movement to secure changes in abortion laws moved from a grassroots movement to one in which feminists finally convinced professional organizations that repealing laws was the only way to deal with the reality of illegal and unsafe abortions (216–33). Patricia Miller's *The Worst of Times: Illegal Abortion: Survivors, Practitioners, Coroners, Cops, and Children Who Died Talk About Its Horrors* provides detailed oral histories from the mid-Atlantic region of abortion practitioners, activists, and clients to explain just how difficult, dangerous, and widespread abortion was before *Roe*. David Cline's *Creating Choice* oral-history collection focuses on the Pioneer Valley of western Massachusetts and shows that many organizations came together locally to fight for change, including doctors and the Clergy Consultation on Abortion Service, which had forty chapters across the country, including in the Pioneer Valley (6, 65–66, 114–16).

Ultimately, according to Suzanne Staggenborg in *The Pro-Choice Movement: Organization and Activism in the Abortion Conflict*, Zero Population Growth had paid lobbyists in Washington and NOW had volunteers from local chapters trying to push Congress for changes to the law in 1973, to little avail, and the National Association for the Repeal of Abortion Laws was designing plans to try to dislodge abortion restrictions (13–16, 17–21). Rosalind Petchesky claims that "Feminists and abortion repeal activists in liberal church, political, legal, and medical circles provided the critical material and human network through which old laws could be exposed, challenged, and, for the first time, openly and collectively defied" (*Abortion and Woman's Choice: The State, Sexuality, and Reproductive Freedom*, 103). And Janet Allured provides a comprehensive analysis of how Louisiana feminists expanded access to birth control prior to *Roe* in *Remapping Second-Wave Feminism* (149–81). Judith Ezekiel also explains in *Feminism in the Heartland* how feminists in Dayton, Ohio, came together to provide secure access to abortion services, and then after *Roe* formed the Freedom of Choice coalition that demonstrated, circulated petitions, and fought against ordinances. The coalition included groups like NOW and Planned Parenthood (121–27, 215–41). I discuss abortion rights in Virginia in Kierner et al., *Changing History*, 330-32, 336, 342–43, 359–60.

Rickie Solinger provides an excellent overview of changes that took place leading up to and through *Roe* in her introduction to *The Abortion Wars: A Half-Century of Struggle*, as well as in her review article "Layering the Lenses." Joyce Berkman provides a review of literature on the reproductive rights movement in "The Fertility of Scholarship on the History of Reproductive Rights in the United States." Solinger's *Pregnancy and Power: A Short History of Reproductive Politics in America* also provides an excellent synthesis of the reproductive rights movement. More recently, Johanna Schoen's *Abortion After Roe: Abortion After Legalization* provides a history of the clinic workers and activists who fought to keep abortion available and provide services to women across the nation. Using oral histories and records from local clinics and the National Abortion Federation, Schoen documents the ways in which clinics were established, the tensions that emerged between physicians and feminist activists over standards and practices in medical clinics and counseling care, and the ways in which they have responded to anti-choice activists and legal challenges to their existence.

3. Linda Gordon claims in *Woman's Body, Woman's Right: Birth Control in America* that feminists conceptualized abortion as part of a broader women's health movement (439–41). In "Beyond Safe and Legal: The Lessons of Jane," Laura Kaplan argues that many feminists began working in the broader health movement in Chicago, and then moved into work with abortion counseling and ultimately to providing abortion services before *Roe* through the Jane network, as part of a larger program of empowering women (33–41). And Solinger posited that feminists succeeded in defining abortion as a "women's issue" rather than an individual problem (*Pregnancy and Power*, 214).

4. Marlene Fried, Introduction to *From Abortion to Reproductive Freedom: Transforming a Movement*, 9.

5. "Abortion Reform Unit Organized in Virginia," *RTD*, 26 October 1969, B13.

6. VWPC Policy Council Minutes, 4 December 1971, Box 1, Folder 7, Williams.

7. "Legislators Ponder Abortion Upset," *RNL* 23 January 1973, Box 3, Folder 3, ZNWM.

8. Johanna Schoen addresses state movements to adopt the ALI code in *Abortion After Roe* (9–10), and Marcy Wilder details the full scale of the model law proposed and its narrowly defined allowances in "The Rule of Law, the Rise of Violence, and the Role of Mortality: Reframing America's Abortion Debate," 77.

9. Faye Ginsburg, *Contested Lives: The Abortion Debate in the American Community*, 39–40. Stephanie Tyree remembered that many in her own NOW chapter were lukewarm about supporting abortion rights, which may have been a carryover from when Mary (Denyes) Wazlak had to separate from her friends when exiting the NOW buses to Richmond so legislators would not mix up the activists and their causes. Many groups like LWV reported divides in their membership, and other groups simply did not work to support abortion rights as they had ERA.

10. Gordon, *Woman's Body, Woman's Right*, 339–49; Reagan, *When Abortion Was a Crime*, 230–31.

11. Fried, Introduction to *From Abortion to Reproductive Freedom*, 6, 8, 12.

12. Petchesky, *Abortion and Women's Choice*, 130–31.

13. Andrea Smith, "Beyond Pro-Choice vs. Pro-Life," 129. Smith's entire argument focused on the need to move beyond, and not expand, the pro-choice "paradigm" because it was too narrow and reified the white-supremacist, capitalist, system of power.

14. Berkman, "The Fertility of Scholarship," 435.

15. Solinger, *Pregnancy and Power*, 172.

16. Gordon, *Woman's Body, Woman's Right*, 339–49; Jael Silliman et al., *Undivided Rights: Women of Color Organizing for Reproductive Justice*, xx, 5; Loretta Ross, "African American Women and Abortion," 163–77. Jennifer Nelson, *Women of Color and the Reproductive Rights Movement*, 1–5. Angela Davis maintains in "Racism, Birth Control, and Reproductive Rights" that white feminists were not cognizant of black women's history and the need to fight for control of their own bodies, which made them suspicious of mainstream feminism's attempts to address reproductive issues (16–21). Sherie Randolph's study of Florynce Kennedy and her leadership in overturning abortion in the New York courts, "Not to Rely Completely on the Courts: Florynce 'Flo' Kennedy and Black Feminist Leadership in the Reproductive Rights Battle, 1969–1971," posits

that Kennedy had given up on NOW when it failed to make racism and sexism priorities, and challenged male black power activists' stance on abortion (140, 146–48). Kennedy believed that reproductive rights were critical to helping advance black women's autonomy and that rights and should be supported in public and through court battles. She turned legal proceedings into open protests as she brought in women to testify about their own experiences, bridging the public and the court system in the era before *Roe* (140–45). In *Feminism in the Heartland*, Ezekiel claims the Dayton Women's Liberation group called a plan to pay women on welfare to secure abortions "racist" and "genocidal," and this sentiment was coming from a group that was entirely white (42, 59). In fact, the Freedom of Choice coalition that emerged to protect abortion rights in the post-*Roe* world was also almost entirely white, with the exception of some representative members from the YWCA and the Urban League (224–25).

17. VWPC Policy Council Minutes, 4 December 1971, and Proposed Legislative Program of the Virginia Women's Political Caucus for the Virginia Legislative Assembly Convening, January 12, 1972, both in Box 1, Folder 1, Williams.

18. Silliman et al., *Undivided Rights*, 36–39, 78–92, 57.

19. Ibid., 30–33. *Undivided Rights* details extensively the reproductive justice organizations that emerged to specifically address the more complex issues women of color had with abortion and birth control, as well as maternal health and access to healthcare in general. Silliman et al. contend that these groups, like the National Black Women's Health Project, in addressing the multiple oppressions women of color faced, weren't interested in joining mainstream women's movements (16). Jennifer Nelson argues that women of color often had to challenge their own nationalist organizations and white feminist concepts of choice while explaining the important issues they faced regarding power and economics in their battle for reproductive freedom (76–83, 121–32).

20. Solinger makes this claim and provides an interesting overview of the issue in *Pregnancy and Power*, 9–11.

21. Peter Wallenstein discusses the ways in which Virginia and other states passed and instituted eugenics-based miscegenation laws in *Blue Laws and Black Codes* and *Tell the Court I Love My Wife*, and Dorr's *Segregation's Science* examines the ways scientists and officials created the framework of eugenics and oppressive policies in Virginia during the first half of the twentieth century. Holloway's *Sexuality, Politics, and Social Control in Virginia* argues that women's bodies became the battleground of debates over sexual behavior and social control in mid-twentieth-century Virginia. Information about sterilization is from Schoen, *Choice and Coercion: Birth Control, Sterilization, and Abortion in Public Health and Welfare*, 82, 105–6. Schoen argues that women had to negotiate the desire to maintain control with the state officials who wanted to wrest it (3–6).

22. Call-to-meeting letter, Mary Denyes, 30 June 1977; letter to William Gietz, 13 October 1974, both in VOKAL. Information about member organizations in Freedom of Choice Coalition from 9 October 1974 Press Release, "Freedom of Choice Coalition," VOKAL.

23. Interview with Mary Wazlak.

24. Ed Briggs, "Antiabortion Bid Countered by Coalition," *RTD*, 22 October 1977, B8.

25. Ed Briggs, "Stance Eased on Abortion," *RTD*, 3 February 1974, B1, 2.

26. "Rationale for Informed Community Expression," Box 70, Folder 18, Harrison.

27. "Public Policy on Reproductive Choices," *League of Women Voters Montgomery County Newsletter* 12, no. 4 (January 1983): 6, Box 9, Folder 32, LWV Montgomery.

28. "Discussion Report," League of Women Voters Fairfax Area Executive Board Minutes, 7 December 1982, Box 1, Folder 13, Marburg.

29. Memo to State League Presidents, 18 January 1983, Box 43, Folder 15, LWVVA.

30. The New Right was galvanized by the *Roe* decision, and even linked it directly with the ERA. As Rymph argues in *Republican Women*, "For antifeminists, *Roe* and the ERA were fundamentally linked, because they were both endorsed by feminists" and because both appeared to threaten their ideas of family (213–14). Spruill explains in *Divided We Stand* that antiabortion activists after *Roe* actually helped to strengthen the anti-ERA battle (104). In 1977, many of these activists came together to challenge what was happening at the International Women's Year Conference, holding a competing "Pro-Life, Pro-Family," rally that drew thousands of conservative women and heralded the beginning of a new movement (260–61).

Leaders in the movement like Falwell built their following focusing on anti-ERA, anti-homosexuality, antiabortion, and anti-pornography rallies. In *With God on Our Side*, William Martin describes how Falwell's "I Love America" rallies mobilized money for his Moral Majority, and Falwell often traveled 300,000 miles in a year to support these rallies (202–4). Using images of "aborted fetuses in bloody hospital pans," images of the sex industry in Times Square, pictures of Charles Manson and nuclear explosions, and using anti-Communist rhetoric, he had a talent for "stirring his crowds" to action (218). Martin also explores the rise of the antiabortion movement and Randall Terry (332–33).

31. "Abortion Changes Again Rejected," *RTD*, 14 February 1973, B6.

32. Margaret Debolt, radio transcript, 11 March 1973, VOKAL.

33. Jan Lieberman and Ann Scott, Reproduction and Legislation Task Forces memo, 15 August 1973, in *The Woman Activist* 3, no. 9 (September 1973), Box 1, Folder 3, LWV Montgomery; Patricia Harding Clark to Patricia Daluiso, 1 May 1976, VOKAL; NOW Reproductive Rights Task Force Memo, 21 March 1976, VOKAL; "Abortion Constitutional Resolutions Defeated in Virginia Legislature," 1976, VOKAL.

34. Interview with Mary Wazlak.

35. "Abortion Clinic Tries to Relieve Anxiety," *RTD*, 24 June 1973, C1, 2; "Abortion Clinic Picketed by 350," *RTD*, 12 October 1973, B1; "Center Deals with Unwanted Pregnancy," www.richmondmedctrforwomen.com/ (accessed 9 November 2015); *Norfolk Journal and Guide*, 23 October 1976, 4; "Abortion Clinic Due in North Richmond," *RTD*, 8 August 1973, A1.

36. Victor Cohn, "33% Wanting Abortions Can't Get Them," *Washington Post*, 7 October 1975, VOKAL.

37. "Entire Virginia Delegation Votes Against Anti-Abortion Amendment," *VWPC August Newsletter,*1974, Box 1, Folder 7, Williams; "Abortion Rights," *Charlottesville NOW Newsletter*, April 1977, Box 15, Folder 4, NOWVA; Letter from VOKAL, 31 July 1977, VOKAL.

38. *VOKAL Newsletter*, September 1977, VOKAL; *VOKAL Newsletter*, October 1977, VOKAL; Pamphlet, *Keeping Abortion Legal Conference*, 1977, Box 5, Abortion 1977–86 Folder, SWRP; Jerry Lazarus, "Dr. Edelein Is Alarmed at Anti-Abortion Group Tactics," *RTD*, 9 October 1977, C13.

39. Mary Denyes, Testimony on Draft of Systems Health Plan for Northern Virginia, 9 November 1977, VOKAL.

40. Betsy Brinson, Testimony for the State Board of Health, 15 November 1977, Box 5, Abortion (VA) 1977–86 Folder, SWRP.

41. VOKAL Update, March 1978, VOKAL; Testimony of VOKAL, 28 February 1978, Box 7, Abortion 1977–86 Folder, SWRP; "Effect," VOKAL Update, March 1978, VOKAL.

42. Lobbying Report to NARAL and VOKAL Board of Directors, 14 March 1978, Box 5, Abortion (VA) 1977–86 Folder, SWRP. Quote on 2.

43. Testimony on HB 1576&7, 29 January 1981, Box 71, Folder 9, Harrison; HEW and Institutes Hearing, Medicaid Funded Abortion, 29 January 1981, VOKAL; News Flash, Medicaid Funding for Abortion, HB1576&7, 16 March 1981, Box 70, Folder 23, Harrison; "Virginia General Assembly Votes on Women's Issues," 1982, Box 71, Folder 22, Harrison.

44. "Rally for 'Real' Life" Publicity Flyer, Box 70, Folder 22, Harrison; Sandy Baksys and Ida Kay Jordan, "Anti-abortion bills draw fire at rally," *Ledger-Star* 8 July 1981, D2; Board of Directors Meeting Minutes, VOICE, 18 August 1981, Box 70, Folder 8, Harrison; "Senate Activity," *Be Counted N.O.W.* 10, no. 7 (September 1982), Box 1, Folder 18b, White; *Charlottesville NOW News*, November 1981, Box 15, Folder 14, NOWVA; Charlottesville NOW Alert, 1 March 1982, Box 15, Folder 4, NOWVA; "Pro-Choice Alert," *Alexandria NOW Newsletter*, August 1982, Box 13, Folder 10, NOWVA.

45. Jane Wells-Schooley, "Double V for Women's Reproductive Rights," *Be Counted N.O.W.* 10, no. 8 (October 1982): 1, Box 1, Folder 18b, White.

46. "Contact Senators Warner and Trible NOW," *Be Counted N.O.W.* 10, no. 10 (January–February 1983): 3, Box 1, Folder 18b, White.

47. "Priorities for the 1979 Session of the Virginia General Assembly," Box 17, Medicaid Funding Folder, SWRP.

48. Lobbying Report 1979, VOKAL.

49. "Report from VOKAL's president," *VOKAL News*, 3, Box 5, Abortion 1977–86 Folder, SWRP; "June Minutes," *Peninsula NOW Times* 2, no. 7 (July 1980): 3, Box 17, Folder 7, NOWVA.

50. "Reproductive Rights," *Do It NOW*, July 1983, Box 17, Folder 16, NOWVA; "Group Seeks Funds for Abortions," *Norfolk Journal and Guide*, 11 July 1984, 4; "A Decade of Choice," and "Supreme Court Hears Abortion Regulation Cases, in *Be Counted N.O.W.* 10, no. 10 (January–February 1983): 1–3, Box 1, Folder 18b, White; *The NOW and Then Times* 2, no. 12 (January 1983): 1, Box 17, Folder 10, NOWVA; "Roe v Wade Anniversary Ad," *Harrisonburg Rockingham NOW News*, December 1983, 1, Box 15, Folder 13; NOWVA.

51. *Women's Political Caucus Third District Newsletter*, January 1985, Box 3, VWPC 1983–86 Folder, Smith; "Virginia NOW State Council Minutes," 26 January 1985, Box 3, Folder 4, NOWVA; Virginia Planned Parenthood legislative alert, 21 January 1985, Box 68, Folder 12, Harrison; LWVVA Press Release, 28 January 1985, Box 43, Folder 15, LWVVA.

52. Statement on H.B. 1364, n.d., Box 68, Folder 12, Harrison.

53. Letter to members of the Virginia General Assembly Senators, n.d., Box 68, Folder 12, Harrison.

54. Press conference, Harrison and Hailey, 1 February 1985, Box 68, Folder 12, Harrison.

55. "VOKAL's policy statement on minors' access," Box 68, Folder 12, Harrison.

56. LWV Action Alert, 8 February 1985, LWVVA, Box 43, Folder 15, LWVVA.

57. Testimony in opposition to H.B. 1364, 11 February 1985, Box 43, Folder 15, LWVVA.

58. Virginia NOW State Council Minutes, 9 March 1985, 1, Box 3, Folder 4, NOWVA.

59. "Virginia House Bill 1364 in Senate," Box 68, Folder 12, Harrison.

60. Kent Jenkins Jr, "House Renews Support for Teen-Abortion Bill," *Virginian-Pilot*, 22 February 1985, clipping, Box 68, Folder 12, Harrison; Kitty Johnson, "1985 General Assembly Bills of Interest to Women," *The Leaguer*, March 1985, 10–11, Box 6, Newsletters 1983–86 Folder, LWV Richmond.

61. Press Release, Virginia Political Action Alliance, 7 March 1985, Box 69, Folder 4, Harrison.

62. President's Briefing, 24 June 1985, 2, Box 6, Folder 7, LWVVA.

63. Virginia Forum Press Release, "'Parental Consent' Measure Called 'Teen Suicide Bill,'" Box 69, Folder 2, Harrison; General Assembly Update, 15 February 1986, 1–2, Box 3, Folder 8, NOWVA; *Vokalizer,* Winter 1987, Box 8, Folder 33, Miller; "Summary of 1988 General Assembly Accomplishments for Women," Box 11, Folder 3, NOWVA; Celia Barteau and Emily McCoy, "Legislative Alert," 26 January 1989, Box 11, Folder 9, NOWVA; Celia Barteau and Emily McCoy, "NOW Legislative Action," 26 February 1989, Box 11, Folder 9, NOWVA; "Minutes of the State Organizing Council," 4 March 1989, Box 5, Folder 2, NOWVA; "Reproductive Rights Task Force," *Richmond NOW Newsletter* 17, no. 2 (April–June 1989), Box 5, Folder 17, ZNLVA; "Draft Presentation to the Courts of Justice," 2 February 1989, Box 69, Folder 3, Harrison.

64. "Current analysis of political status of abortion in the fifty states," 27 April 1989, Box 11, Folder 6, NOWVA.

65. Gordon, *Woman's Body, Woman's Right,* 409–10; Melody Rose, *Safe, Legal, and Unavailable? Abortion Politics in the United States,* 15.

66. In *Pregnancy and Power,* Rickie Solinger says that this focus effected several problems for women—first, it enabled "public policies to enforce distinct reproductive experiences for distinct groups of women," by creating a situation in which abortion was constrained and available only to advantaged women. Also, it allowed for the Supreme Court to fail to take into account the "undue burdens" faced by these women, who again, were cast as morally lacking (231, 232).

67. Staggenborg, *The Pro-Choice Movement,* 4, 129–31, 134–35. Petchesky provides a detailed account of the rise of the antiabortion New Right in *Abortion and Women's Choice,* linking its antiabortion stand to its overall anti-feminist agenda (241–76).

68. Petchesky, *Abortion and Women's Choice,* 131–32, quote from 241.

69. Georgia Fuller, Alert, July 1989, Box 1, Folder 8, NOWVA, emphasis in original quote.

70. Jim Morrison, "Area Groups Amass for Abortion Fight," *Virginian-Pilot,* D1, D5, clipping in Box 70, Folder 4, Harrison; Georgia Fuller, "State of the State," Box 5, Folder 8, NOWVA.

71. Jim Stratton, "Sides weigh ramifications of decision," *News and Daily Advocate,* 4 July 1989; Anna Barron Billingsley, "State legislators expect efforts to restrict abortion law," *RNL,* 4 July 1989, both clippings in Box 1, Folder 1, Miller.

72. Press conference with Dorothy Height, 7 September 1989. Box 69, Folder 17, Harrison.

73. "Fundraising PAC Letter," April 1989, Box 4, Folder 28, Miller; "Abortion Rights Reinstated," *NOW or Never,* July 1989, Box 69, Folder 10, Harrison; "Women's Political Caucus Backs Choice," 3 July 1989, Box 69, Folder 10, Harrison.

74. Bill Byrd, "Abortion Nabs Center Stage in Governor Race: Court Ruling Creates Instant, Divisive Issue," *Virginian-Pilot,* 9 July 1989, A1–2.

75. Letters from Georgia Fuller to Molly Yard, 7 September 1989, Box 11, Folder 4, NOWVA; Letters from Georgia Fuller to various candidates, 3 October and 12 October 1989, Box 11, Folders 4–5, NOWVA; "Letters to the Editor for Choice," Memo to Virginia NOW Chapter leaders from Alexandria NOW Letters Subcommittee, September 1989, Box 1, Folder 7, NOWVA.

76. Harold Rosenberg, "Ted Turner Has His Say with 'Abortion: For Survival,'" *Los Angeles Times,* 20 July 1989, articles.latimes.com/1989-07-20/entertainment/ca-5125_1_ted-turner (accessed 14 December 2017).

77. "Volunteer and Rally for Reproductive Choice NOW," *Virginia NOW Choices* October–November 1989, Box 20, Folder 2, NOWVA; "Pro-Choice Action Campaign Report," 18 Novem-

ber 1989, Box 1, Folder 15, NOWVA; "Actions to Hook Up With or Plan for Your Area," Box 11, Folder 4, NOWVA; "Press Release," Lynn Bradford, 13 October 1989, Box 11, Folder 8, NOWVA; "Attached is a copy of the first speech I gave," Georgia Fuller, 22 February 1990, Box 1, Folder 8, NOWVA.

78. "Alexandria NOW Electoral Phone Bank," 17 November 1989, Box 1, Folder 7, NOWVA; "Statement of Virginia Republicans for Choice," 30 October 1989, Box 30, Folder 3, Harrison.

79. "Pro-Choice Action Campaign Report," 18 November 1989, Box 1, Folder 5, NOWVA.

80. "Copy of our last release," 22 February 1990, Box 1, Folder 8, NOWVA; Georgia Fuller Press Release, 30 October 1989, Box 11, Folder 4, NOWVA.

81. "Pro-Choice Action Campaign Report," 18 November 1989, Box 1, Folder 5, NOWVA; Georgia Fuller, "In 1989 State-Wide Races Virginia Women Win," and Emily McCoy, "Election Results," *Virginia NOW Choices* 1, no. 4 (December 1989–January 1990): 1, Box 20, Folder 2, NOWVA; Georgia Fuller, "State of the State" address, Box 5, Folder 8, NOWVA.

82. Thomas Boyer, "Poll Shows Virginia Voters Favor Parental Notification of Abortion," *Virginian-Pilot,* 12 January 1990, A2.

83. Interview with Karen Raschke.

84. Karen Raschke, report to Friends of Planned Parenthood, 17 February 1990, and House Bill 1119, both in Box 69, Folder 6, Harrison.

85. "3 Reasons to Oppose Parental Notification," Box 16, Planned Parenthood 1990 Folder, McClenehan; Memo to RCAR, Patricia Harding-Clark, n.d., Box 11, Folder 9, NOWVA; "Board Meeting," 23 January 1990, Box 3, Folder 10, AAUW Norfolk; Memo from Grace Sparks, 23 January 1990, Box 16, Planned Parenthood 1990 Folder, McClenehan; Pro-Choice Signature Ad, *RTD,* 29 January 1990, A8; House Bill 1119, Box 69, Folder 6, Harrison; NOW Legislative Mailing, 90-5, 23 February 1990, Box 11, Folder 9, NOWVA.

86. List of Pro-Choice Alliance Members and Pro-Choice Positive Action Campaign, Box 69, Folder 16, Harrison; Pat Kibler to Pro-Choice Alliance Members, 27 April 1990, Box 1, Folder 8, NOWVA; Denise Lee and Emily McCoy to Virginia NOW Leaders, 30 August 1990, Re: Virginia Pro-Choice Positive Action Campaign, Box 1, Folder 8, NOWVA.

87. "Dollars for Virginia," *Arlington NOW Newsbreaks,* November 1990, Box 15, Folder 2, NOWVA; Frances Storey, "NOW Political Involvement: What We Can Do," 13 July 1990, Box 1, Folder 11, NOWVA; "NOW Legislative Action," 90/1–5, 10 November 1990, Box 1, Folder 10, NOWVA; "Election Project—Virginia 8th Congressional District," Box 11, Folder 7, NOWVA; "Pro-Choice Positive Action Campaign," Minutes of the Virginia NOW Council, 14 July 1990, 1, Box 6, Folder 1, NOWVA.

88. Emily McCoy and Denise Lee, Legislative Action Alert, 1 September 1990, 90/1–3, p. 1, Box 1, Folder 11, NOWVA; Emily McCoy and Denise Lee, Legislative Action, 90/1–5, 10 November 1990, Box 1, Folder 10, NOWVA.

89. Frances Storey and Joan Taylor to Douglas Wilder, September 1990, Box 5, Folder 8, NOWVA.

90. Press Release, 8 January 1991, Pro-Choice Alliance, Box 69, Folder 23, Harrison; "The Virginia Pro-Choice Alliance Invites You to Participate in Two Days of Lobbying Activity," Box 69, Folder 23, Harrison; Virginia State NOW Meeting Minutes, 27 July 1991, 3, Box 6, Folder 5, NOWVA.

91. Pro-Choice Alliance Release, n.d., Box 69, Folder 11, Harrison.

92. Virginia NOW Council Minutes, 23 November 1991, Box 6, Folder 5, NOWVA.

93. "Notification: Legislation Without Compassion," n.d., Box 12, Senator Lucas Notification Folder, Raschke; Norman Gomlak, "Pro-Choice Lobbies Wilder 'not to turn clock back," *Fairfax Journal,* 3 March 1992, 1, clipping in Box 40, Folder 4, Miller; NOW Legislative Action, 18 March 1992, Box 12, Folder 1, NOWVA.

94. Gomlak, "Pro-Choice Lobbies Wilder," *Fairfax Journal,* 3 March 1992, 1, clipping in Box 40, Folder 4, Miller; Denise Lee Press Release, n.d., Box 2, Folder 2, NOWVA; Minutes from NOW Council Emergency Meeting Concerning Teen Endangerment, Box 6, Folder 7, NOWVA; Emily McCoy, NOW Legislative Action 92–98, 18 March 1992, Box 12, Folder 1, NOWVA.

95. "Prayerfully Pro-Choice," Box 4, Abortion Folder, Smith; Grace Sparks to Alert List, 18 February 1992, Box 17, Planned Parenthood 1992 Folder, McClenehan; Minutes of the Monthly Meeting of the Board of Directors, VLPP, 17 March 1992, Box 17, Planned Parenthood 1992 Folder, McClenehan.

96. Minutes of the Virginia NOW Council, 11 April 1992, Box 6, Folder 7, NOWVA; Executive Director's Report, VLPP, 15 April 1992, Box 17, Planned Parenthood 1992 Folder, McClenehan; Mike Allen, "Proposal Drew Most Comment," 6 April 1992, Box 24, KAL in News '92 Folder, Raschke.

97. Allen, "Proposal Drew Most Comment," 6 April 1992, Box 24, KAL in News '92 Folder, Raschke.

98. Michael Hardy and Mike Allen, "Governor Sends Abortion-limits Bill Back Unsigned," 6 April 1992, clipping, Box 24, KAL in News '92 Folder, Raschke; Minutes of the State Council Meeting, 1 August 1992, Box 6, Folder 7, NOWVA.

99. "An Effective Voice for Progress," *Progress* 3, no. 2 (Summer 1992), Box 24, KAL in News '92 Folder, Raschke.

100. Summary, Parental Notification Abortion Laws, by Brenda Edwards, Box 40, Folder 4, Miller; "Abortion State Laws," *Public Policy on Reproductive Choice: Community Action Guide,* p. 13, addition to *The Leaguer,* February 1994, Box 6, January 1993–May 1995 Newsletters Folder, LWV Richmond.

101. "An Effective Voice For Choice," *Progress* 3, no. 2, Box 24, KAL in the News Folder, Raschke; Denise Lee to Editor, Press Release, 29 June 1992, Box 2, Folder 2, NOWVA.

102. "Reproductive Choice: The Law of the Land v. the Lie of the Land," *Virginia Women's Network Newsletter,* 13 February 1994, 2, Box 5, Publications, Mostly ERA-Related Folder, Hellmuth; Ellen Nakashima and Spencer Hsu, "Focus, Fortitude on Both Sides of Abortion Fight," *Washington Post,* 3 March 1996, clipping, Red Folder on top of Box 34, Raschke.

103. Pro-choice activists continued their lobby days, as well as their efforts to contact legislators: "Incentives for Every Branch to Attend CFC Lobby Day, January 18," *Virginia Vision* 68, no. 2 (Winter 1992–93), Box 11, Folder 10, AAUW Norfolk; "Notes from the Chair," *Virginia Women's Political Caucus Newsletter,* January 1994, Box 12, Folder 4, NOWVA; "Legislative Update," *NOW or Never,* March 1995, Box 18, Folder 14, NOWVA. Information about Houck in Flora Crater, "Annual Report of Action Coordinator," *Virginia Women's Network* 17 (January 1995), Box 3, Virginia Women's Network Folder, Smith; Ted Byrd, "Houck's vote aborts parental notification bill," *The Free-Lance Star,* 3 February 1995, C3; "Senate again rejects abortion notification bill," *RTD,* 2 February 1996, A8; "Pro-Choice Lobby Day" *NOW or Never,* January 1996, Box 19, Folder 1, NOWVA; "Protect Our Daughters" Fact Sheets, Box 3, 1996 Fact Sheet "POD" Folder, Raschke; "23rd Anniversary of Roe v Wade: Speaking Points for Delegate Vivian Watts," and "Floor Speech on Notification, Senator Patsy Ticer," Box 12, Del Watts–RVW Anniversary 1996 Folder, Raschke.

104. NARAL abortion-laws summary, Virginia, www.prochoiceamerica.org/government-and-you/state-governments/state-profiles/virginia.html (accessed 18 December 2015).

105. "Timeline of Abortion Laws in Virginia," NARAL, www.naralva.org/assets/bin/pdfs/VA%20Timeline.PDF (accessed 29 October 2016).

106. Laura Vozzella, "Virginia Rolls Back Restrictions on Abortion Clinics," *WP,* 24 October 2016, www.washingtonpost.com/local/virginia-politics/virginia-rolls-back-restrictions-on-abortion-clinics/2016/10/24/9f3fb3e8–99fd-11e6-9980-50913d68eacb_story.html (accessed 29 October 2016).

107. "Pro-Choice Banner," and "Vigil" in *VOKAL News,* April 1980, Box 5, Abortion (VA) 1977–88 Folder, SWRP; "Pulsepoint," *NOVA NOW Equal Times* 5, no. 5 (May 1975): 3, Box 16, Folder 6, NOWVA; "Reproductive Rights Commemoration," *Alexandria NOW Newsletter,* January 1983, Box 13, Folder 10, NOWVA; "Roe v. Wade: Virginia NOW Commemorates 10th Anniversary of Choice," *Virginia NOW Newsletter,* March 1983, 102, Box 19, Folder 14, NOWVA.

108. Virginia NOW Council Meeting, 16 February 1986, Box 8, Folder 3, NOWVA; Memo Re: March for Women's Lives, Box 5, Folder 21, YWCA M373; "Legislative Report," Box 8, Folder 67, Miller; T. L. Smith, "Tidewater and Peninsula NOW members join fight to keep abortion safe and legal," *Norfolk Journal and Guide,* 12 March 1986, 9.

109. NOW State Council Minutes, 6 May 1989, Box 5, Folder 1, NOWVA.

110. "Virginia NOW Chapters Rev Up for April March," 26 February 1992, Box 2, Folder 2, NOWVA; "News from LWVUS," *Fairfax Area League of Women Voters Bulletin,* April 1992, 8, Box 24, Folder 3, LWV Fairfax; "A Call to Act," *NOW Is the Time* 1, no. 2 (May–June 2001), Box 18, Folder 5, NOWVA; "March for Women's Lives," *Chapter News,* March–April 2001, Box 13, Folder 11, NOWVA; "March for Women's Lives," *Fairfax Area League of Women Voters Bulletin* 56, no. 10 (June 2004): 7, Box 25, Folder 12, LWV Fairfax; "March for Women's Lives" *CNOW,* Box 18, Folder 6, NOWVA.

111. "Anti-Abortionist Is Picketed Here," *RTD,* 24 April 1977, clipping, Box 3, Folder 11, ZNWM; "Calendar," *KNOW NOW* 5, no. 4 (April 1977), Box 1, Folder 1a, White; "Woman's Body, Woman's Right" flyer and information pamphlet, Box 70, Folder 24, Harrison; NOW Council Meeting, 3 August 1985, 2, Box 3, Folder 4, NOWVA.

112. Memo to NOW Leadership from Joan Taylor, 29 June 1990, Box 1, Folder 16, NOWVA; "Chapter Actions," *Virginia NOW Choices,* Summer 1991, 4, Box 20, Folder 2, NOWVA.

113. Minutes of NOW State Council, 4 August 1992, Box 6, Folder 7, NOWVA; Letter from Richard Grier and Grace Sparks, 7 July 1992, Box 17, Planned Parenthood 1992 Folder, McClenehan.

114. NOW newsletters from around the state, as well as minutes into the twenty-first century, show that chapters remained active, sponsoring campus events, holding annual pro-choice lobby days, and keeping choice at the forefront of the feminist agenda. The import of this became clear when the Transvaginal Ultrasound Bill was introduced, causing an outpouring of feminist activity in the state.

115. *Control of Our Bodies Task Force Newsletter,* 13 January 1976, Control of Our Bodies Minutes 1974–Present Folder, VOKAL.

116. "Local News," *VOKAL News,* April 1980, 5, Box 5, Abortion 1977–86 Folder, SWRP; *Be Counted N.O.W.* 2 (October 1981): 9, Box 1, Folder 4, Carlton; Cindy Creasy, "Abortion clinic escorts set," *RTD,* 10 May 1985, B12.

117. "Chapter Reports," *The VOKALIZER,* Winter 1987, Box 8, Folder 33, Miller; Pro-Choice Alliance Announces Protest Campaign press release, 24 April 1987, Box 1, Folder 3, NOWVA.

118. "Fake Clinics," *Arlington NOW Newsbreaks*, May 1991, Box 15, Folder 2, NOWVA.

119. Crisis Pregnancy Centers Revealed Updated Report, www.naralva.org/what-is-choice/cpc/revealed.shtml (accessed 21 December 2015).

120. "Abortion Clinic Picketed by 350," *RTD*, 12 October 1973, B1; "The Picketers Picket Each Other," *Virginian-Pilot*, clipping, scrapbook, VOKAL.

121. Denyes to William Gietz, 13 October 1974, "Control of Our Bodies" Correspondence/Info Folder, VOKAL; Denyes to NOW Information Office, 27 September 1974, VOKAL; Denyes to Jan Liebman, 14 October 1974, VOKAL.

122. Memo to ACLU from Brinson re: proposed lawsuit against Right to Life demonstrators, 17 November 1977, Box 3, Virginia Correspondence 1977–81 Folder, SWRP; VOKAL update, March 1978 and May 1978, VOKAL.

123. News Statement, 15 February 1978; Civil Action 78–94—A Permanent Injunction in *Northern Virginia Women's Medical Center et al. v. Protestors Horan Jr. Esq. et al.*; Memo to ACLU from Brinson re: proposed lawsuit against Right to Life demonstrators, 17 November 1977; Janet Benshoof and Judy Levin to Chan Kendrick, 5 January 1978; all in Box 18, Northern Virginia Women's Medical Center Folder, SWRP. Press Release, 15 June 1978, Box 21, Southern Projects Press Releases 1979 Folder, SWRP.

124. Schoen, *Abortion After Roe*, 170–74.

125. Clipping, *Fairfax Journal*, Box 14, Folder 1, LWV Fairfax; Virginia NOW Council Meeting, 8 December 1985, Box 3, Folder 4, NOWVA; "Celebrate Roe v. Wade Anniversary at Fairfax Hospital," *Virginia NOW Choices* 4, no. 4 (December–January 1990): 1, Box 20, Folder 2, NOWVA.

126. Georgia Fuller, "Protests Threaten Women's Freedom," *Fairfax Journal*, 4 November 1988, A8; Virginia NOW State Coordinator's Report, 12 December 1988, Box 4, Folder 6, NOWVA.

127. Georgia Fuller, "Clinic not getting protection it needs," *Fairfax Journal*, 9 December 1988, clipping, Box 1, Folder 6, NOWVA.

128. Interview with Georgia Fuller.

129. "Abortion Clinic Defense," *Richmond NOW Newsletter* 18, no. 7 (September 1990): 1, Box 5, Folder 17, ZNLVA.

130. Interview with Mary Wazlak.

131. Schoen, *Abortion After Roe*, 194–95.

132. "An Evidence of Support," *VOKAL News*, April 1980, 2, Box 5, Abortion (VA) 1977–88 Folder, SWRP.

133. Creasy, "Abortion Clinic Escorts Set," *RTD*, 10 May 1985, B12; Minutes of the NOW State Council Meeting, 19 May 1985, Box 4, Folder 4, NOWVA; "Happy New Year," *NOVA NOW Newsletter*, 1988, Box 4, Folder 28, Miller; "Safeguarding our Reproduction," *NOW Choices* 3, no. 4 (December–January 1989): 1, Box 20, Folder 1, NOWVA.

134. "Pro-Choice Demonstrations," *Richmond Pride* 12 (July 1989): 3, 12, Newspapers can be found at the Virginia Historical Society, Richmond, Virginia; Planned Parenthood Sponsored Picketing Meeting, 1 August 1989, Box 1, Folder 6, NOWVA; "Project Stand Up for Women and Clinic Defense," *Arlington NOW Newsbreaks*, November 1989, Box 15, Folder 2, NOWVA.

135. *NOW et al. v. Operation Rescue*, Civil Act 89–1558-A, Box 11, Folder 6, NOWVA.

136. Lynn Bradford, "Richmond NOW keeps clinics open," *Virginia NOW Choices* 4, no. 6 (May–August 1990): 1, Box 20, Folder 2, NOWVA; "Abortion Clinic Defense," *Richmond NOW Newsletter* 18, no. 7 (September 1990): 1, Box 15, Folder 17, ZNLVA; "Clinic Defense Volunteers Needed for Friday, March 29," *Arlington NOW Newsbreaks*, March 1991, 2, Box 15, Folder 2, NOWVA; Letter to Clinic Defenders, December 1991, Box 17, Folder 14, NOWVA.

137. In "The Rule of Law, the Rise of Violence, and the Role of Morality," Marcy Wilder notes that the number of bombings and other violent acts rose precipitously in the early 1980s as anti-abortionists found that they were not able to secure laws banning abortion outright. After Reagan was elected as president, violence rose 450 percent nationwide (74, 82). In *Safe, Legal, and Unavailable*, Melody Rose argued that the violence spiked in 1992–93 and 2001–2 with 450 incidents and 750 incidents, respectively, and she attributed a decline in abortion providers partially to this rise in violence (94–98). Linda Gordon notes in *Woman's Body, Woman's Right* that, in 1985, 80 percent of clinics across the country reported some kind of harassment, and by 1986 there were an average of 400 incidents a year (412). Rickie Solinger concurs with the rise in violence leading to a decline in doctors willing to perform abortion (*Pregnancy and Power*, 225). See also "Clinic Violence Statistics," National Abortion Federation, prochoice.org/education-and-advocacy/violence/violence-statistics-and-history/ (accessed 22 December 2015).

138. Peter Bacque, "Fire Mars Clinic," *RTD*, 7 September 1992, clipping, Box 4, Folder 6, ZNLVA; "Uncivilized Act in Richmond," *Roanoke Times and World News*, 21 September 1992, B6.

139. "Arsons/Attempted Arsons," *Anti-Abortion Violence Watch* 7 (July 1997): 2, www.feminist.org/rrights/pdf/aavw2.pdf (accessed 22 December 2015).

140. Daniel Golden and Brian McGrory, "Clinic Shooting Suspect John Salvi Captured," *Boston Globe*, www.bostonglobe.com/metro/1995/01/01/clinic-shooting-suspect-john-salvi-captured/5xfDlnGIUssY3LSnPp5xwO/story.html (accessed 22 December 2015). Information about the crime itself can be found in the *Washington Post*: www.washingtonpost.com/wp-srv/national/longterm/abortviolence/stories/salvi3.htm (accessed 22 December 2015).

141. Robert Pear, "Authorities Seeking Motives for Attacks at Abortion Clinics," *New York Times*, www.nytimes.com/1995/01/02/us/authorities-seeking-motive-for-attacks-at-abortion-clinics.html (accessed 3 February 2018).

142. "A Note from the President," *NOW or Never*, December 1994–January 1995, 1, Box 18, Folder 13, NOWVA; Brenda Andrews, "Publisher's Topic: Anti-Abortion Vigilantes: War against Women Must be Stopped," *New Journal and Guide*, 4 January 1995, 2; "Lee Speaks Out," *NOW or Never*, March 1995, Box 18, Folder 14, NOWVA; "Statement on the Clinic Shootings," *NOW or Never*, December 1994–January 1995, 2, Box 18, Folder 13, NOWVA.

143. "Anthrax Treat to Planned Parenthood Clinic Follows Threats," 4 January 2000, www.newson6.com/story/7670028/anthrax-threat-to-planned-parenthood-clinic-follows-threats (accessed 22 December 2015). Statistics on clinic violence from Daily Kos, www.dailykos.com/stories/864356/full_content (accessed 22 December 2015).

144. "Abortion Assistance Fund," *Charlottesville NOW Newsletter* 3, no. 3 (March 1991), Box 15, Folder 5, NOWVA; "Safeguarding our Reproduction," *NOW Choices* 3, no. 4 (December–January 1989): 1, Box 20, Folder 1, NOWVA; Virginia NOW State Coordinator's Report, 12 December 1988, Box 4, Folder 6, NOWVA; Virginia NOW Council Minutes, 23 November 1991, Box 6, Folder 5, NOWVA.

145. President Brewster to Friends of Planned Parenthood, 17 January 1992; Grace Sparks, "VLPP Board Makes Decision to Provide Abortion Services," *Progress* 3, no. 1 (Winter 1992); and "VLPP Offers First-Trimester Abortion Services," all in Box 17, 1992 Planned Parenthood Folder, McClenehan; Planned Parenthood Health Centers, Virginia, www.plannedparenthood.org/health-center/VA (accessed 22 December 2015).

146. Statement of Karen A Raschke, 11 January 1999, Box 1, Planned Parenthood Public Policy Folder, Raschke; Letter to VA NARAL members and friends, 22 December 1999, Box 14, Board Meeting 1999 Folder, LWV Richmond; "Truth About Crisis Pregnancy Centers," *NOW Is the Time* 1, no. 4 (September–October 2001), Box 19, Folder 5, NOWVA.

147. Interview with Emily McCoy..

148. "I'm Not Sorry," www.facebook.com/ImNotSorrynet-232796755203/ (accessed 15 September 2017).

149. "Virginia Signs Pre-Abortion Ultrasound Bill," *USA Today*, usatoday30.usatoday.com/news/nation/story/2012-03-07/virginia-abortion-ultrasound-bill/53401720/1; "Virginia Women Gain Revision of Anti-Abortion Legislation," nvdatabase.swarthmore.edu/content/virginia-women-gain-revision-anti-abortion-legislation-2012.

150. "State Facts About Abortion," Guttmacher Institute, www.guttmacher.org/fact-sheet/state-facts-about-abortion-virginia?gclid=CIadtYqrg9ACFdgDgQodFQcJbQ (accessed 30 October 2016).

Chapter Four

1. There are excellent works addressing the history of violence against women in America. Sharon Block's *Rape and Sexual Power in Early America* argues that gendered constructions of men as powerful and women as sexually available made rape difficult for white women to prosecute and pursue, and for black women almost impossible. She traces the history of black-on-white rape as more prosecutable to this era, because societal assumptions were that if you knew your attacker then it wasn't rape—and white women would not move in the same social circles as black men. Conversely, because of racial prejudice and structural inequality, black women could not begin to seek redress on any level for rape. Elizabeth Pleck's *Domestic Tyranny: The Making of American Social Policy against Family Violence from Colonial Times to the Present* notes that, while Massachusetts passed a domestic-violence law in 1641, domestic abuse, including marital rape, was tolerated in society through the late twentieth century. Courts did not want to deal with spousal abuse, and in fact child abuse was the first focus of violence-prevention organizations in the late nineteenth century.

Pleck documents cases of women being sent home to violent husbands in the early twentieth century, as does Linda Gordon in *Heroes of Their Own Lives: The Politics and History of Family Violence in Boston, 1880–1960*, which documents the ways in which women attempted to seek help from social services and the courts in the face of violent husbands in Boston during the first half of the twentieth century. As Pleck notes, temperance reformers in the mid-nineteenth century attempted to address violence in marriage, to little effect, except that marital rape became one of the few grounds for divorce granted by late-nineteenth-century judges. Many of these early reform efforts were meant to protect and preserve a more stable family (*Domestic Tyranny*, 92–93). In "'In the Marriage Bed Women's Sex Has Been Enslaved and Abused': Defining And Exposing Marital Rape in Late-Nineteenth Century America," Jesse Battan found critiques of marital rape in temperance activists' work, as well as in the marriage critiques of free-love advocates (207–21). Jill Hasday found the roots of marital-rape reform in prescriptive literature trying to "convince husbands to voluntarily cede discretion over sex to their wives" ("Choice and Consent: A Legal History of Marital Rape," 1379). Elizabeth Cady Stanton, Lucy Stone, and Paulina Wright Davis all discussed marital rape either in private writings or at women's rights conventions ("Choice and Consent," 1424–27). As Hasday noted, free-love advocates "condemned" marriage in general, so it was not surprising that they fought against marital rape (1444–46).

As many of these scholars point out, for women of color, racial and gender oppression affected them in a way that white women did not have to address. Historians of enslaved women point out the rampant rape of slaves in their many works. Debra Gray White, *Ar'n't I a Woman*; Stephanie Camp, *Closer to Freedom: Enslaved Women and Everyday Resistance in the Plantation South*; and Nell Irvin Painter, "Soul Murder: Toward a Fully Loaded Cost Accounting," are just a few of these. After freedom, definitions of black men as predators of white women and the continued sexual harassment of black women meant that, for African American women, issues of sexual violence could not be extricated from racial prejudice. For more information on the racialized definitions of rape in the nineteenth and twentieth centuries, see Diane Sommerville, *Rape and Race in the Nineteenth-Century South*, and Lisa Lindquist Dorr, *White Women, Rape, and the Power of Race in Virginia, 1900–1960*. Crystal Feimster addresses the ways in which black and white women addressed this racialized system of violence in *Southern Horrors: Women and the Politics of Rape and Lynching*, and Jacquelyn Dowd Hall argues in *Revolt Against Chivalry: Jesse Daniel Ames and the Women's Campaign Against Lynching* that the privileged white women who started the Anti-Lynching Society with Jessie Daniel Ames challenged men's excuses of lynching black men to "protect" white women. Danielle McGuire argues in *At the Dark End of the Street* that much of the civil rights movement was prompted by the actions of African American women who had suffered sexual violence ranging from harassment to rape. In *Redefining Rape: Sexual Violence in the Era of Suffrage and Segregation,* Estelle Freedman explores the ways in which rape was racialized and class-based in the nineteenth and early twentieth centuries. She details the ways in which African American club women, the NAACP, and other activists fought for protections for African American women and to redefine rape as a black-on-white crime. She also examines the institution of protections for poor white women, and she details the changes wrought in the 1970s (278–89). For a short history of sexual violence in Virginia before the twentieth century, see Kierner et al., *Changing History*, 11–13, 16, 35–36, 71–72, 108, 111–12, 166, 179.

2. Pleck, *Domestic Tyranny*, 185.

3. Janet Allured explains in *Remapping Second-Wave Feminism* that southern violence was a big problem, and that women engaged in consciousness-raising groups, scholars from the University of New Orleans examined the culture in which rape violence emerged, and radical feminists there "stressed female strength and agency and sought to counter the image of women as helpless victims" (109–12, 117). Many Louisiana lesbian feminists were involved in activism and awareness campaigns, and hotlines were available and used by a wide range of women across racial and economic barriers (120–22). Allured also discusses the religious diversity of those who started shelters and the way activists had to deal with a hostile legislature when they moved to change laws, much like in Virginia (142–44, 123–27). Judith Ezekiel also discusses the ways in which activists banded together to provide services for survivors in Dayton, and the run-ins the Victimization Project and Women Against Rape had with the medical institutions (*Feminism in the Heartland*, 128–41). Carol E. Jordan's comprehensive study *Violence against Women in Kentucky* provides stories of the victims to illustrate domestic and sexual violence in the state, and examines the ways in which advocates lobbied the state legislature to change domestic and sexual violence laws from the 1970s through the twenty-first century, through the Kentucky Coalition Against Rape and Sexual Assault, founded in the late 1970s with five hundred members, to other groups working to create better legislation (147). I address violence against women in Kierner et al., *Changing History*, 346–49.

4. Maria Bevacqua, *Rape on the Public Agenda: Feminism and the Politics of Sexual Assault*, 36–37.

5. In "Reconsidering Violence Against Women," Maria Bevacqua argues that violence was a "bridge issue" bringing women together to work to eradicate violence, but in coalitions—not necessarily in the same groups (164–67). She notes that women of color tended to avoid work with mainstream groups because of those group's failure to address structural inequality (170–71). Nancy Matthews's study of rape crisis hotlines in California, *Confronting Rape: The Feminist Anti-Rape Movement and the State,* examines just how many neighborhood groups formed to create the support system to address different women.

6. Bevacqua's *Rape on the Public Agenda* is an excellent and comprehensive study of the issue in the late twentieth century. Bevacqua examines the ways in which responses to rape changed over time, and how statewide organizations emerged to address rape during this time. She also notes: "Indeed, it cannot be disputed that the activities of the women's movement and its organizations have had a marked impact on U.S. policy making, even when outcomes have fallen short of stated goals" (111). But she does explain that the achievements they made moved anti-rape language away from feminist critiques to policy issues, which allows for reform without the accompanying structural critique (121). However, in terms of rape, the work done has somewhat dislodged—somewhat—the concept that women's behavior or dress invites assault (58–65). Matthews's *Confronting Rape* explains the ways in which hotlines and anti-rape activists were realm of feminist reformers—often radical feminist reformers, who often had an adversarial relationship with law enforcement (9–12, 21–22). Matthews also argues that those who came to anti-rape work, particularly women of color, often developed a feminist consciousness through this work: "Involvement in anti-rape work contributed to the development of a feminist perspective among these activists who were initially motivated by the need for services, but only as they gained confidence to define 'feminist' on their own terms" (36). But state funding, as well as the involvement of police and medical personnel, challenged the ways in which hotlines operated, forcing them to become more bureaucratic in some ways, working through social services, and professionalizing (73–126). Because of this, Matthews considers the impact of the anti-rape movement limited, because there is still inaction and a failure to stop the violence altogether (166). Clark Pomerleau's *Califia Women* explains that the feminist collective which had worked with rape crisis centers to help with counseling and staffing hotlines, worked in coalitions with others. But the Valley Hotline, which it dominated, retained its feminist outlook to the point where staffers would not apply for state funding (78–79). They had been fighting issues of sexual violence by speaking about it publicly and ultimately even promoting an anti-pornography movement (79–81).

As Nichola Gavey argues in *Just Sex? The Cultural Scaffolding of Rape,* while the past thirty years have seen a massive change in how we view rape legally, culturally, and psychologically, it is still happening and is often still tolerated, although now such tolerance faces challenges on many fronts (17).

This happened in the domestic violence movement too, as in its early years it was explicitly feminist. As Claire Reinelt argues in "Moving onto the Terrain of the State: The Battered Women's Movement and the Politics of Engagement," "The battered women's movement in its early years drew its political strength and energy from defining itself in opposition to patriarchal and hierarchical institutions" (91). Judith Wittner states in "Reconceptualizing Agency in Domestic Violence Court," it was the women's activists who forced the hand of legislators, judges, police, and even lawyers as they pushed to seek redress. Women who found themselves in the court, often poor women, or women of color, worked with feminist advocates to push for remedies that had been unimaginable before the feminist movement (81, 83, 87, 99). As Julie Blackman argued in *Intimate*

Violence: A Study of Injustice, groups like NOW and other organized activists changed how people discussed and viewed violence, and moved it from being a personal problem to a public reflection of patriarchal power (10–11). And these activists had a "profound and tangible effect," in the words of David Del Mar in *What Trouble I Have Seen: A History of Violence Against Wives,* both at the local level (he studied Oregon), and nationally, as we see with the passage of the Violence Against Women Act (147). But again, to get these changes, feminists had to compromise and drop some of the most salient critiques about male prerogative, according to Pleck (*Domestic Tyranny,* 199).

7. Interview with Mary Ann Bergeron.
8. "Rape-Crisis Center Slated by NOW Group," *RTD,* 4 June 1974, A7.
9. Zelda Nordlinger to Meg Williams, 5 June 1974, Box 1, Folder 3, Williams.
10. Program Plan, ROAR, Box 1, ROAR Folder, YWCA M 177.
11. "One Area's Approach to the Criminal Sexual Assault Program," Box 8, Folder 10, NOWVA.
12. Deborah deSchewett, "TRIS Helps Ease Trauma of Rape," *The Beacon,* 13 August 1975. "They Offer Help to Rape Victims"; "Women's Equality Day Celebration," *Virginian-Pilot,* 26 August 1975. "Rape to Be Topic of WHRO-TV Show," 8 November 1975, *Norfolk Journal and Guide,* 11 November 1975. All in TRIS Scrapbook, Box 24, YWCA Hampton Roads.
13. "42,000 Granted Rape Information Group," *Virginian-Pilot,* 14 November 1975, D1; "Achievement Award Given to TRIS Director"; Editorial in *Ledger-Star,* 17 January 1975, "TRIS Role," 28 December 1975, and "TRIS Listened," 17 January 1975, *Ledger-Star.* All in TRIS Scrapbook, Box 24, YWCA Hampton Roads. According to the article, the public money came from a grant the city of Norfolk received from a federal revenue-sharing program.
14. City of Alexandria Commission on the Status of Women Report on Programs, Box 1, Folder 13, Williams; UVA Pamphlet, Box 1, Folder 13, Williams; Fairfax Area League of Women Voters *Bulletin,* October 1975, 19, Box 21, Folder 3, LWV Fairfax.
15. City of Alexandria Commission report gives examples of services provided; "Rape Prevention Goal of TRIS," *Norfolk Journal and Guide,* 29 November 1975, 14.
16. "Earbenders," *Blue Lantern* 1, no. 2 (February 1977): 3, Box 7, Battered Women Speakers and Articles Folder, SWRP.
17. ROAR Program Plan, Box 1, Executive Director Associated Agencies Richmond Organized Against Rape Folder, YWCA M 177.
18. Ibid.; Ann Hall, "TRIS," Norfolk Department of Human Resources, *Resources* 1, no. 8 (December 1976), TRIS Scrapbook; "NOW Publishes Pamphlet on Rape," *RTD,* 9 October 1975, D5; "Earbenders," *Blue Lantern* 1, no. 2 (February 1977): 3, Box 7, Battered Women Speakers and Articles Folder, SWRP.
19. "November ROAR dates," Box 1, ROAR Folder, Richmond YWCA M 177; Letter to TRIS members, Box 1, Folder 14, Williams.
20. "Anti-Rape Activities," *Charlottesville NOW Newsletter,* February 1976, Box 15, Folder 4, NOWVA.
21. Minutes of the YWCA Board of Directors, 18 February 1976, p. 2, Box 5, Folder 8, Richmond YWCA M 373.
22. "Efforts in Virginia, 1970s–1980s," and "Coalition," in *Advocate* 1, no. 1 (September 1983): 2, VSDV, unprocessed. Note: "unprocessed" means that the material was still at the VSDVAA office when I used it. That material has since been taken to VCU. All box/folder numbers listed for VSDV material may now be in different boxes at VCU, as more material has come in and the collection has been processed.

23. "Chapter News," *Advocate* 9, no. 3 (Spring 1993): 6, VSDV, unprocessed; "What's New with Richmond YWCA Outreach Program?" *Advocate* 9, no. 3 (Spring 1993): 7, VSDV, unprocessed; "Sexual Assault Crisis Centers in Southwest Virginia, *Advocate* 10, no. 3 (Winter 1994): 1, 2, VSDV, unprocessed; Fiscal Year 1993 Annual Statement, VAASA, in VSDV, unprocessed; Domenico Montanaro, "Demographics Are Destiny in Virginia," NBC News, 4 November 2013, www.nbcnews.com/news/other/demographics-are-destiny-virginia-f8C11525607 (accessed 13 April 2016).

24. Letter to TRIS members, Box 1, Folder 14, Williams; YWCA Board of Directors Minutes, 19 November 1975, Box 5, Folder 7, YWCA M 373; YWCA Board of Directors Minutes, 18 February 1976, 2, Box 5, Folder 8, YWCA M 373.

25. "Presbyterian Women to Sponsor Seminar on Criminal Sexual Assault," *Norfolk Journal and Guide*, 11 August 1978, 18. "Take Back the Night," *Peninsula NOW Times* 2, no. 9 (September 1980), and "Take Back the Night," *Peninsula NOW Times* 2, no. 10 (October 1980), both in Box 17, Folder 7, NOWVA. Quote from October 1980, 2.

26. "Prominent Feminists Will Help 'Take Back the Night,'" *OOCP* 7, no 13(October 1983): 2, 13.

27. Virginia NOW Council Minutes, 9 March 1985, Box 3, Folder 4, NOWVA; State Policy Council Minutes, 6 December 1986, Box 3, Folder 8, NOWVA; State Policy Council Minutes, 6 May 1989, Box 5, Folder 1, NOWVA; "Local," *Richmond Lesbian-Feminist Flyer* 14, no. 9 (October 1987), Mary Dean Carter's personal collection; "Center News," *Advocate* 9, no. 3 (Spring 1993): 3, VSDV, unprocessed; "Center News," *Advocate* 10, no. 1 (Summer 1993): 8–10 VSDV, unprocessed. Take Back the Night and other events promoting awareness of sexual and domestic violence occurred at Longwood College when I was women's studies director from 2000 to 2003, often organized by SAFE (Students Advocating a Fearless Environment) and WILL (Women Involved in Learning and Leadership).

28. "Basic Sexual Assault Facts," University of Alaska–Fairbanks, uaf.edu/uafwomen/empower/sexualassault/justfacts/ (accessed 13 April 2016).

29. YWCA Executive Council Minutes, 15 April 1986, Box 5, Folder 21, Richmond YWCA M 373; "VAASA Sponsors Seminar in September," *Norfolk Journal and Guide*, 1 July 1987, 7.

30. Nancy Gibbs, "The Clamor on Campus," *Time* 137, no. 22 (3 June 1991): 54; Judy Mann, "Women's Empowerment Wins a Pulitzer Prize," *WP,* 12 April 1991, D3; Brooke Masters, "Alleged Date Rape Is College's Topic A: William and Mary Campus Is Divided on Student's Public Accusation," *WP,* 27 April 1992, B1; Katie Koestner, "The Perfect Rape Victim," in *Just Sex? Students Rewrite the Rules on Sex, Violence, Equality, and Activism,* eds. Gold and Villari, 32.

31. Margaret Fosane, "Date Rape Survivor Sees Awareness Slowly Growing," *South Bend Tribune*, 6 December 2001, D1.

32. Mann, "Women's Empowerment Wins a Pulitzer Prize," *WP,* 12 April 1991, D3

33. Koestner, "The Perfect Rape Victim," 30, 33.

34. "Campus Rapes Should Go to Court," *USA Today,* 12 June 1991.

35. Masters, "Alleged Date Rape Is College's Topic A," *WP,* 27 April 1992, B1.

36. Ibid.; Donald Baker, "Talk of Sexual Violence Stirs Campus: Speaker Put William and Mary at Center of Date Rape Debate in 1990," *WP,* 20 April 1996, C3; "Chapter News," *Advocate* 9, no. 3 (Spring 1993): 6, VSDV, unprocessed.

37. Becky Weybright, "Why Teenagers Don't Tell," *Advocate* 8, no. 2 (Winter 1992): 8–9. VSDV, unprocessed.

38. Fiscal Year 1993 Annual Report, VAASA, VSDV, unprocessed.

39. Sexual Assault Victims Bill of Rights, 1992, clerycenter.org/federal-campus-sexual-assault-victims%E2%80%99-bill-rights (accessed 22 April 1992).

40. "Should Victims Pay the Price for Unjust Laws," and attached legislative proposal, Box 1, Folder 13, Williams.

41. McKinnon and Wilson to Meg Williams, 16 October 1974, Box 1, Folder 13, Williams.

42. Interview with Mary Ann Bergeron.

43. Lawrence Hilliard, "Rape, Sunday Sales are Topics at County Association's Talks," *RTD,* 21 November 1974, C6.

44. "BPW Well Represented at Third Congress," *Federation Notes* 24, no. 1 (January 1975): 10 Box 7, Folder 2, BPWVA.

45. "Virginia Division Community Representative Report," Program of the 1976 Annual Convention of the Virginia Division of the AAUW10, Box 7, Folder 2, AAUW Norfolk.

46. "Rape Case Bill Would Aid Victim," *RTD,* 25 January 1975, B3.

47. Lora Mackie, "Changes in Laws on Rape Said to Come Slowly," *RTD,* 25 August 1975, B9, quote in "Living Today" section of the article.

48. Katherine Calos, "Women's Groups Limit Legislative Aims," *RNL,* 7 January 1976, 27; "Anti-Rape Activities," *Charlottesville NOW Newsletter,* February 1976, Box 15, Folder 4, NOWVA.

49. Sara Hansard, "Commission named to study Virginia laws on sexual assault," *Washington Post,* 26 August 1976, Virginia 3, clipping in Box 3, Folder 10, ZNWM.

50. Lynn Valos, "Senate Bill 291—Sexual Assault Laws," *Federation Notes* 27, no. 1 (Summer 1978): 9, 11, Box 7, Folder 5, BPWVA.

51. "Conference on Legal Issues Affecting Women," 27 October 1979, Box 2, Folder 7, Marburg.

52. Karlyn Baker, "Sexual Assault Bill a Casualty of Closing Rush," *WP,* 6 March 1980, B5.

53. Elsa Walsh, "Rape: A Push for Legal Reforms," *WP,* 12 February 1981, Va. 1, 4. Quotes on 4.

54. H. Lane Kneedler, "Sexual Assault Reform in Virginia: An Overview," *UVA Institute of Government Newsletter* 58, no. 5 (January 1982), Box 13, Folder 12, LWV Fairfax. Quote from 22; "Summary of S.B. 158: Criminal Sexual Assault; Letter to Women's Organizations from Del Mary Marshall," Box 10, Folder 9, NOWVA.

55. "1982 Legislative Report," Box 10, Folder 10, NOWVA.

56. Ingrid Olson, "Summary of the 1984 Virginia General Assembly," *Advocate* 10, no. 4 (Spring 1994): 1–2VSDV, unprocessed.

57. Faye Ehrenstamm, "Police Train for 'Domestics,'" *RTD,* 16 July 1974, A1, 8.

58. Lora Mackie, "Victims Keep Hoping Husbands Will Keep Promises to Stop," *RTD,* 4 January 1976, G1.

59. Interview with Kristi Van Audenhove.

60. Jill Melichar, "NOW Task Force Tackles Problems of Battered Wives," *RNL,* 18 March 1977, Box 3, Folder 11, ZNLVA.

61. "Domestic Abuse: Women Fighting Back," *Blue Lantern,* 1977, 6–7, clipping, Box 7, Battered Women Speeches and Articles Folder, SWRP.

62. "Virginia Women's Political Caucus Testifies for Title XX Money for Rape Counseling," *The Virginia Woman Activist,* June 1976, Box 1, Folder 14, Williams.

63. Interview with Mary Ann Bergeron.

64. Letter from Diane Hall to Alice, 31 December 1987, Box 2, Folder 29, Hampton Roads YWCA.

65. "NOVA NOW Originates Program for Battered Women," *Equal Times,* August 1976, Box 16, Folder 7, NOWVA; Young Women Committed to Action Minutes, 25 October 1976, and Board of Directors Meeting Minutes, 17 November 1976, both in Box 6, Board of Directors 1976 Folder, YWCA M 177.

66. Committee Meeting Minutes, 11 May 1981, 2, Box 1, Folder 20, YWCA M 373.

67. Mary Ann Pikrone, "Shelter for Battered Women Planned," *RNL*, 18 July 1978, Box 5, Newsclippings Folder 1, Smith; Dawn Chase, "Women to Focus on Abuse," *RNL*, 7 October 1978, Box 5, Newsclippings Folder 2, Smith. Board of Directors Minutes, 21 August 1979, and 16 October 1979, both in Box 5, Folder 11, YWCA M 373.

68. Quote from Pikrone, "Shelter for Battered Women Planned," *RNL*, 18 July 1978, Box 5, Newsclippings Folder 1, Smith. YWCA Board of Directors Minutes, 21 August 1979; Board of Directors Minutes, 18 November 1979 and 15 January 1980, both in Box 5, Folder 12, YWCA M 373.

69. Board of Directors Minutes, 15 January 1980; WVAP Advisory Board Meeting, 11 August 1980, Box 1, Folder 18, YWCA M 373; VAP Advisory Board Meeting Minutes, 11 February 1980, Box 1, Folder 17, YWCA M 373.

70. VAP Committee Report in Board of Directors Meeting Minutes 20 January 1991, Box 5, Folder 13, YWCA M 373; VAP Shelter Minutes, 6 April 1981, Box 1, Folder 20, YWCA M 373; Committee Meeting Minutes, 11 May 1981, Box 1, Folder 20, YWCA M 373; "Committee on Women Report, 1980–1," 15–15c, AAUW Virginia Division 56th Anniversary Convention, 27–29 March 1981, Box 7, Folder 4, AAUW Norfolk; "Victim Advocacy Program," *Be Counted N.O.W.* 2, no. 10 (October 1981), Box 1, Folder 4, Carlton W&M.

71. WVAP Summary 1982, Box 5, Folder 17, YWCA M 373.

72. Interview with Sarah Payne, Stephanie Tyree, and Melanie Payne-White; Chase, "Women to Focus on Abuse," *RNL*, 7 October 1978, Box 5, Newsclippings Folder 2, Smith.

73. Interview with Sarah Payne, Stephanie Tyree, and Melanie Payne-White.

74. Ibid.; Chase, "Women to Focus on Abuse," *RNL*, 7 October 1978, Box 5, Newsclippings Folder 2, Smith.

75. Sharon Neuner, "Annual Report of Community Representative," April 1980, Box 7, Folder 3, AAUW Norfolk; VADV Meeting Minutes, 19 January 1980, Box 20, Roanoke 1978 Folder, SWRP.

76. "Committee on Women Report," AAUW 1980–81; "Shenrocco BPW Club Report," 29, BPW Annual Reports, 1980–81, State Convention Report, 22–24 May 1981, Box 1, Folder 1, BPWVA. "Domestic Violence: More Common Than You Think," *The NOW and Then Times* 2, no. 15 (April 1983): 2 Box 17, Folder 10, NOWVA; Delvia Fisher, "Community Need: Individual and Collective Efforts," *YWCA Report*, June, July, August 1983, Box 2, Folder 6, Hampton Roads YWCA; Anonymous Letter to "Shelter," 8 May 1983, Box 2, Folder 7, Hampton Roads YWCA; Letter to Board of Supervisors from Mary Treadwell, President, 27 May 1981, Box 14, Folder 1, LWVFA; "Thanks to you VAN lives," 5, *NOVA NOW*, July 1981, Box 16, Folder 9, NOWVA.

77. "Group Against Domestic Violence Praises Governor Robb for Support," 21 July 1982; Meg Hibbert, "Help Available for Spouse Abuse Victims," 16 September 1982; "Domestic-Violence Awareness Day Set," 10 July 1982; Sally Price, "Battered Women Fill Shelter to Capacity," 22 July 1982, all in Box 7, 1982 news clippings, VSDV; Jerry Alley, "A Haven Awaits Battered Women," *The Beacon*, 15 May 1983, Box 3, Folder 11, Hampton Roads YWCA.

78. "Domestic Violence Awareness Week," *Rappahannock Record*, 4 October 1982, Box 7, 1982 Clippings Folder, VSDV.

79. "Chapter News," *Do it NOW*, February 1983, 2, Box 17, Folder 6, NOWVA; Annual Report, Tidewater BPW, 5 February 1993, Box 1, Folder 4, BPWVA; Connie Carver, "Western Region Coordinator," *Federation Notes* 42, no. 2 (Fall 1993): 15–16 Box 8, Folder 2, BPWVA; BPW Local Organizations Annual Reports, 1993–94, Box 1, Folder 4, BPWVA; "Network News and Announcements,"

Virginia Women's Network Bulletin 8 (November 1992), Box 3, Virginia Women's Network Folder, Smith; "Please support the Annual Women's Musical Extravaganza," *NOW or Never,* March 1994, Box 18, Folder 13, NOWVA; letters, promotional materials, and newspaper clippings (including a flyer from 1996) in Box 13a, Adult Domestic Violence Dress Fundraiser 1993 Folder, Richmond LWV.

80. Cindy Crofford, "YWCA's Women-In-Crisis Shelter Gets Children's Center from Tidewater Builders Association," Promotional Supplement, *The Ledger-Star,* 20 February 1984, and *Virginian-Pilot,* 1 March 1984, E7, E8; letter to Tom Hogg from Judy Gundy, 30 August 1988, Box 3, Fundraising Appeals Folder, VSDV; Susan Winiecki, "ADT, YWCA two counties plan alarm program for women," *RTD,* 28 January 1994, clipping in Box 4, Folder 11, ZNLVA.

81. "Women's Shelter Re-Opens in Radford" and "Spouse Abuse," Box 8, Folder 10, LWV Montgomery; "City of Radford Receives Grant for New Women's Resource Center Shelter," *Advocate* 8, no. 2 (Winter 1992): 8, VSDV, unprocessed; "Action on Fairfax Co. Battered Women's Shelter Continues," *Alexandria NOW Newsletter,* April 1991, 1–2, Box 13, Folder 11, NOWVA; Amy Tracy, "President's Corner," *Alexandria NOW Newsletter,* May 1991, 1, Box 13, Folder 11, NOWVA.

82. "Adult Domestic Violence," League of Women Voters Study of Domestic Violence in Virginia, 20 February 1992, quotes on 17, 19, Box 8, Folder 4, LWVVA.

83. YWCA Executive Director Report, February 1993, Box 6, Folder 3, YWCA M 373; "Did You Know?" and "Statewide Toll-Free Hotline," *Taking Action Bulletin, July 1993,* 2, 6, Box 3, Folder 2, VSDV.

84. "National Domestic Violence Week," 7–13 October 1984, reported to YWCA board meeting, 1 November 1984, Box 5, Folder 18, YWCA M 373; I participated in or witnessed some of these projects at both universities, first as an undergraduate, then as a professor and director of women's studies; "Richmond NOW Spearheads Project on Domestic Violence," *Richmond NOW Newsletter* 21, no. 3 (August 1993), Box 17, Folder 14, NOWVA; "Center News," *Advocate* 10, no. 4 (Spring 1994): 8–9, VSDV, unprocessed.

85. Liz Wheaton, 15 October 1977 Testimony; Mr. X, Mrs. X, Cornelia Souther, from Virginia House of Delegates Committee on Health, Welfare, Institutions—Subcommittee to Study Battered Spouses, 3 October 1977, all in Box 7, Battered Women Speakers and Articles Folder, SWRP. Note: Cornelia Suhler's name was spelled Souther in the testimony transcript—newsletters from her chapter attest to the correct spelling.

86. Sylvia Clute, 14 October 1977 testimony, Box 7, Battered Women Speakers and Articles Folder, SWRP. Quote on p. 2.

87. Paula Squires, "Battered Wives: The Fearful Plead for Help, Home," *Virginian-Pilot* 15 October 1977, A6.

88. "Report of the Subcommittee to Study Battered Spouses," 15 November 1977, Box 5, Folder 47, Shackelford.

89. "Legislation Introduced in the 1978 Session of the Virginia General Assembly Regarding Battered Spouses," Box 7, Battered Women Speakers and Articles Folder, SWRP.

90. Sam Barnes, "Aid Urged for Abused Wives," *RTD,* clipping, Box 5, Folder 47, Shackelford.

91. See reference to Nancy Matthews in note 5, above.

92. "Legislative Agenda," *Virginia Division Bulletin* 54, no. 4, Box 11, Folder 6, AAUW Norfolk.

93. "Virginia General Assembly: Votes on Women's Issues, 1982," Box 5, Miscellaneous—Minutes, Notes, Correspondence Folder, Hellmuth; 1982 Legislative Report, Box 10, Folder 10, NOWVA; "Group Against Domestic Violence Praises Governor Robb for Support," 21 July 1982, Box 7, 1982 Newsclippings Folder, VSDV.

94. "Victim Impact Statement," *VADV News* 2, no. 6 (March 1983): 2 Box 4, Sexual Assault/Domestic Violence Folder, Smith.

95. "Legislative Session," prepared by Elsa Levy and Elaine Kramer for National Women's Political Caucus–Virginia, Box 71, Folder 23, Harrison; "State Legislation, 1984–5," 60th Virginia AAUW Annual Convention, April 26–28 1985, p. 19, Box 7, Folder 7, AAUW Norfolk; Fundraising appeal letter from Deborah Simmons, n.d., Box 3, Fundraising Appeals Folder, VSDV; "Taking Action! A Bi-Monthly Bulletin for Advocates," January 1992, VSDV, unprocessed.

96. "Chapter Actions," *Virginia NOW Choices*, July–August 1992, 3, Box 20, Folder 3, NOWVA; "Achievements in 1993," VADV Administrative Report, January–December 1993, 8, Box 1, Folder 2, VSDV.

97. "Adult Domestic Violence," LWV Study of Domestic Violence in Virginia, 20 February 1992, 7, Box 8, Folder 4, LWVVA.

98. Ibid., 7, 14–15; "Adult Domestic Violence," *The Leaguer*, November 1992, Box 6, Newsletters 1990–92 Folder, LWV Richmond.

99. VAWA Fact Sheet, www.whitehouse.gov/sites/default/files/docs/vawa_factsheet.pdf (accessed 22 April 2016); "History of VAWA," www.legalmomentum.org/history-vawa#sthash.cFUiHmmN.pdf (accessed 22 April 2016).

100. Emily Baker, "Take Back the Night," *Chapter News*, November and December 1996, 2, Box 13, Folder 11, NOWVA.

101. Interview with Kate McCord. Some of these quotes came from the original interview, and some from a written clarification and update sent by McCord, 12 February 2018. This document with the updated quotations can be found in the oral history collection.

102. "History of VAWA," www.legalmomentum.org/history-vawa#sthash.cFUiHmmN.pdf.

103. Brooke Masters, "'No Winners,' In Rape Lawsuit," *Washington Post*, 19 May 2000, posted on Center for Individual Rights, www.cir-usa.org/2000/05/no-winners-in-rape-lawsuit/ (accessed 22 April 2016).

104. Nina Bernstein, "Virginia Tech Wins Dismissal of a Rape Suit," *New York Times*, 8 May 1996, www.nytimes.com/1996/05/08/us/virginia-tech-wins-dismissal-of-a-rape-suit.html (accessed 22 April 2016); Testimony before House Subcommittee, Campus Crime Initiatives, 6 June 1996, C-Span, www.c-span.org/video/?72765-1/campus-crime-initiatives (accessed 22 April 2016).

105. *United States v. Morrison,* Oyez.com, www.oyez.org/cases/1999/99-5 (accessed 22 April 2016).

106. Linda Greenhouse, "The Supreme Court: The Court on Federalism; Women Lose Right to Sue Attackers in Federal Court," *New York Times,* 16 May 2000, www.nytimes.com/2000/05/16/us/supreme-court-court-federalism-women-lose-right-sue-attackers-federal-court.html?ref=topics&pagewanted=1 (accessed 17 December 2017).

107. Masters, "'No Winners,' In Rape Lawsuit," *Washington Post,* 19 May 2000, www.cir-usa.org/2000/05/no-winners-in-rape-lawsuit/.

108. Tim Murphy, "Forty Years of College Football's Sexual-Assault Problem," *Mother Jones,* 5 December 2013, www.motherjones.com/media/2013/12/college-football-sexual-assualt-jameis-winston (accessed 22 April 2016).

109. Sarah Jane Brady, "July 1, 1997—New Virginia State Laws Go Into Effect," *Chapter News,* July–August 1997, Box 13, Folder 11, NOWVA; Ann Crittenten, "Legislative Update," *Taking Action,* April 1998, 1–2, VSDV, unprocessed.

110. "It's A Fact," Box 1, "Facts About Domestic Violence Services in Virginia Handout and Statistics" Folder, VSDV.

111. Report from Virginia's Domestic Violence Programs and Sexual Assault Centers from October 1999 to March 2000, Box 3, "A Report from Centers" Folder, VSDV.

112. Interview with Kristi Van Audenhove.

113. Ibid.

114. VDSVA website, www.vsdvalliance.org/#/aboutcontact-us/mission-and-principles (accessed 3 February 2018).

115. Interview with Kristi Van Audenhove.

116. Betty Ardus and Anne Dawson, "On Marital Rape," *Advocate* 2, no. 6 (August 1985): 2–3,VSDV, unprocessed; "Marital Rape," *Advocate* 2, no. 2 (January 1985):3, VSDV, unprocessed.

117. "Virginia Supreme Court Hears Marital Rape Case," *Advocate* 2, no. 2 (March 1984), VSDV, unprocessed; "Marital Rape," *Advocate* 2, no. 2 ; News Release, 12 February 1986, VWPC, Box 71, Folder 25, Harrison; Ardus and Dawson, "On Marital Rape," , VSDV, unprocessed; "Summary of Major Bills from the 1985 Legislative Session," prepared by Elsa Levy and Elaine Kramer for VWPC, Box 71, Folder 23, Harrison; Memo to Supporters of Women's Issues from VAASA, 28 August 1985, Box 4, Sexual Assault/Domestic Violence Folder, Smith.

118. Testimony of McCoy, 19 September 1985, Box 6, NOW-VA 1977–86 Folder, Smith; AAUW General Meeting Minutes, 8 October 1985, Box 3, Folder 6, AAUW Norfolk; Nancy Brock, "General Assembly Outlaws Martial Rape," (reprinted from *Responseline) Advocate* 3, no. 4 (April–May 1986): 2,VSDV, unprocessed.

119. Tom Sherwood and Donald Baker, "Feminist Group Assails Va. Spousal Rape Bill as 'Atrocity,'" *WP,* 13 February 1986, D1, D5 (quote on D1); Memo to NOW Leadership, and "Weekly Legislative Update" by co-coordinators Celia Barteau, Jean Marshall Crawford, Marilyn Summerford, 15 February 1986, Box 3, Folder 8, NOWVA; Dale Eisman, "Panel Likely to Clear 'marital rape' bill," *RTD,* 20 February 1986, A6.

120. News Release, NWPC-VA, 12 February 1986, Box 71, Folder 25, Harrison.

121. Sherwood and Baker, "Feminist Group Assails Va. Spousal Rape Bill as 'Atrocity,'" *WP,* 13 February 1986.

122. Memo to NOW leadership, 15 February 1986, Box 3, Folder 8, NOWVA.

123. Brock, "General Assembly Outlaws Martial Rape";; NOW State Council Meeting, 6 April 1986, Box 3, Folder 8, NOWVA; "1986 General Assembly Review," *WPC News,* April 1986, 2, Box 71, Folder 23, Harrison.

124. "Lorena Bobbitt Not Guilty: Knife-Wielding Wife Pushed Issue of Abuse," *St. Louis Dispatch,* 22 January 1994, 1A; Marylou Tousignant, Bill Miller, "Tale Of Two Lorenas: Bobbitt Trial Doctors Detail States of Mind," *WP,* 19 January 1994, D1; Bill Miller, Marylou Tousignant, "Bobbitt Acquitted in Attack on Husband; Woman Is Found Not Guilty by Reason of Insanity," *WP,* 22 January 1994, A1. I discuss the Bobbitt case in Kierner et al., *Changing History,* 348.

125. Susan Hall, "Co-Coordinator Notes," *Alexandria NOW Newsletter,* November 1993, 1, Box 13, Folder 11, NOWVA.

126. "Virginia NOW Legislative Agenda," Box 12, Folder 4, NOWVA; Ingrid Olson, "Summary of 1994 Virginia General Assembly."

127. Brian Carnell, "Is Virginia's Proposed Marital Rape Statute a Good Idea?" brian.carnell.com/articles/2002/is-virginias-proposed-marital-rape-statute-a-good-idea/ (accessed 22 April 2016); interview with Kate McCord.

128. Rebecca Leber, "Congressional Candidate Who Justified Marital Rape Has Dropped Out," *Think Progress*, 23 January 2014, thinkprogress.org/justice/2014/01/23/3198411/congressional-candidate-justified-marital-rape-dropped/.

129. Lisa Rein, "Virginia House Backs Bill to Outlaw Wife Rape," *Washington Post*, 8 February 2002, www.washingtonpost.com/archive/local/2002/02/08/va-house-backs-bill-to-outlaw-wife-rape/30280d7f-b8d4-4967-adf1-ea15d4a85182/; interview with Kate McCord.

130. Steve Helber, "Former UVA Lacrosse Player Huguely Gets 23 Years in Death of Ex-Girlfriend Yeardley Love," usnews.nbcnews.com/_news/2012/08/30/13571569-former-uva-lacrosse-player-huguely-gets-23-years-in-death-of-ex-girlfriend-yeardley-love?lite (accessed 22 April 2016); Meghan Keneally, "Hannah Graham's Accused Killer May Face Death Penalty," abcnews.go.com/US/hannah-grahams-alleged-abductor-now-faces-death-penalty/story?id=30828027 (accessed 22 April 2016).

131. Interview with Kate McCord.

132. Much of this information can be found on the "Spiders Against Sexual Assault and Violence" Facebook page, www.facebook.com/groups/210758632673331/permalink/226855461063648/ and on the University of Richmond Alumni Facebook page, of which I am a member. For more information, see Stassa Edwards, "After Richmond Student Writes Viral Essay About Her Rape Case, the University Calls Her a Liar," Jezebel website, 9 September 2016, jezebel.com/after-richmond-student-writes-viral-essay-about-her-rap-1786444075; Charlie Broaddus and Lindsey Schneider, "University of Richmond Student Files Complaint with DOE Over Title IX Case," *The Collegian*, 6 September 2016, www.thecollegianur.com/article/2016/09/richmond-student-speaks-about-title-ix-case; Karin Kapsidelis, "Second University of Richmond Student Alleges Mishandling of Sexual Assault Complaint," *RTD*, 9 September 2016, www.richmond.com/news/article_dd353b34-d44b-55b7-b50a-96d7349f4dda.html.

133. Missy Schrott, "It Ends Now: Students Walk Out on Discussion About Mishandled Rape Case," *The Collegian*, 9 September 2016, www.thecollegianur.com/article/2016/09/it-ends-now-students-walk-out-on-discussion-about-mishandled-rape-case; Kayla Solsbak, "Kappa Alpha Order Chapter Suspended After Sexist Email," *The Collegian*, 12 September 2016, www.thecollegianur.com/article/2016/09/breaking-richmonds-kappa-alpha-order-chapter-suspended-after-sexist-email; Tyler Kingkade, "Why Don't Sexual Assault Victims Report? Ask These Women," *Buzzfeed*, 5 November 2016, www.buzzfeed.com/tylerkingkade/retaliation-reporting-sexual-assault?bffbmain&ref=bffbmain&utm_term=.tvAbxOVQz#.lnWdlgYoM. (All of these sites were accessed 19 November 2016.)

134. "U of R, VCU among 272 schools facing federal Title IX investigation," *Commonwealth Times*, 12 September 2016, www.commonwealthtimes.org/2016/09/12/51168/ (accessed 19 November 2016).

135. Interview with Kate McCord. McCord has altered the language of this quote to make it gender-neutral in an update sent 12 February 2018, which can be found in the oral history collection,

136. Ibid. and update, details above. Thanks to McCord for this citation: http://www.vdh.virginia.gov/content/uploads/sites/18/2016/04/2014-FIPS-Report-FINAL.pdf and her information is taken from page 9.

137. Interview with Kristi Van Audenhove.

Conclusion

1. Interview with Sarah Payne, Melanie Payne-White, and Stephanie Tyree.
2. Interview with Mary Coulling.
3. Interview with Lee Perkins.
4. "ERA Passed One Vote, With Moderate Enthusiasm," virginiaeranetwork.wordpress.com/2015/01/27/era-passed-one-vote-with-moderate-enthusiasm/ (accessed 10 May 2016).
5. Travis Fain, "Equal Rights Amendment Passes, Then Doesn't, in Virginia Senate," *Daily Progress*, 3 February 2015, www.dailypress.com/news/politics/dp-nws-ga-era-shenanigans-20150203-story.html (accessed 10 May 2016).
6. Greg Hambrick, "Virginia House Panel Blocks Equal Rights Amendment," *Fredericksburg Patch*, 6 March 2016, patch.com/virginia/fredericksburg/va-house-panel-blocks-equal-rights-amendment-0 (accessed 10 May 2016).
7. Interview with Sandra Brandt.
8. "Women's Rights Groups Urge Virginia to Ratify ERA," wtvr.com/2018/01/15/womens-rights-groups-urge-virginia-to-ratify-era/ (accessed 3 February 2018).
9. Interview with Kate McCord.
10. Thanks to McCord for the citation of the "Dear Colleague" letter: https://obamawhitehouse.archives.gov/sites/default/files/dear_colleague_sexual_violence.pdf. Sophie Tatum, "Education Department Withdraws Obama-era Sexual Assault Guidance," CNN News, 22 September 2017, www.cnn.com/2017/09/22/politics/betsy-devos-title-ix/index.html (accessed 14 November 2017).
11. Chelsea Parsons, Tim Daly, and Eugenio Vargas, "Virginia Under the Gun," Center for American Progress, 27 October 2015, www.americanprogress.org/issues/guns-crime/report/2015/10/27/124132/virginia-under-the-gun/ (accessed 19 May 2016).
12. Sexual assault on campus statistics, www.edsmart.org/college-sexual-assault-statistics-top-ranked-schools/ (accessed 19 May 2016).
13. Joe Shapiro, "Campus Rape Reports Are Up, and Assaults Aren't the Only Reason," National Public Radio, www.npr.org/2014/04/30/308276181/campus-rape-reports-are-up-and-there-might-be-some-good-in-that (accessed 19 May 2016).
14. Cassandra Santiago and Doug Criss, "An Activist, a Little Girl, and the Heartbreaking Origin of 'Me Too,'" CNN, 17 October 2017, www.cnn.com/2017/10/17/us/me-too-tarana-burke-origin-trnd/index.html (accessed 14 November 2017).
15. Kate McCord, Facebook post, 7 May 2016.(accessed 3 February 2018). The contents of this post is included with the editorial notes in the oral history collection at Virginia Commonwealth University.
16. "Alimony laws," divorce.laws.com/alimony/alimony-in-virginia (accessed 18 November 2016).
17. One Virginia 2021, www.onevirginia2021.org/redistricting (accessed 19 May 2016).
18. "Women in State Legislatures for 2015," National Conference of State Legislatures, www.ncsl.org-staff/legislators/womens-legislative-net (accessed 24 May 2016).
19. "About Emerge Virginia," www.emergeva.org/about (accessed 24 May 2016).
20. John Harwood, "Democratic Shifts May Help Virginia Democrats," *New York Times*, 23 August 2013, www.nytimes.com/2013/08/23/us/politics/in-virginia-demographic-shifts-may-help-democrats.html (accessed 17 May 2016).

21. This quote (quoteinvestigator.com/2012/03/20/end-of-world-time-lag/) has been attributed to many, but the fact that two Virginia feminists used it to illustrate the particular challenges they see in Virginia is telling.

22. "Virginia Election Results," *New York Times,* www.nytimes.com/elections/results/virginia (accessed 18 November 2016).

23. Emerge Virginia, Facebook post, 11 November 2016, www.facebook.com/EmergeVirginia/ (accessed 19 November 2016).

24. Jack Moore, "Why women won big in Va. House of Delegate races," WTOP.com news story, 8 November 2017, wtop.com/virginia/2017/11/women-won-big-va-house-delegate-races/ (accessed 14 November 2017); Seth McLaughlin, "David Yancey wins in tie-breaker over Shelley Simonds, Republicans retain control of House by luck of the draw," *Washington Times,* 4 January 2018, www.washingtontimes.com/news/2018/jan/4/david-yancey-wins-house-delegates-tie-breaker-over/ (accessed 3 February 2018).

25. Jack Moore, "Why women won big in Va. House of Delegate races," WTOP.com news story, 8 November 2017, wtop.com/virginia/2017/11/women-won-big-va-house-delegate-races/ (accessed 14 November 2017); Greg Sargent, "Virginia Bloodbath: Trump Is Exorcising the Democrats' Midterm Curse," *WP,* 8 November 2017, www.washingtonpost.com/blogs/plum-line/wp/2017/11/08/virginia-bloodbath-trump-is-exorcising-the-democrats-midterm-curse/?utm_term=.f3ee798aef09; Brittany Levine Beckman, "Danica Roem Beats 'Chief Homophobe' Bob Marshall in Historic Virginia Race," Mashable, 8 November 2017, hwww.aol.com/article/news/2017/11/08/trans-woman-danica-roem-beats-chief-homophobe-bob-marshall-in-historic-virginia-race/23270498/. (All accessed 14 November 2017.)

BIBLIOGRAPHY

Manuscript Collections

American Civil Liberties Union—Southern Women's Rights Project, M 178. Special Collections and Archives, James Branch Cabell Library, Virginia Commonwealth University.
Carroll Kem Shackelford Papers, 1954–1985. Accession 32577. Personal Papers Collection, Library of Virginia, Richmond.
Elizabeth Smith Collection of Virginia ERA Ratification Council Records, M 425. Special Collections and Archives, James Branch Cabell Library, Virginia Commonwealth University.
Emilie F. Miller Papers, Collection #C0048. Special Collections and Archives, George Mason University.
Jean D. Hellmuth Papers, M 304. Special Collections and Archives, James Branch Cabell Library, Virginia Commonwealth University.
Jean Marburg League of Women Voters Collection, Collection #C0039. Special Collections and Archives, George Mason University.
Juanita White Papers, 1970–1997, Collection Number M 354. Special Collections and Archives, James Branch Cabell Library, Virginia Commonwealth University.
Karen Raschke Papers, 1982–2003, M 348. Special Collections and Archives, James Branch Cabell Library, Virginia Commonwealth University, Richmond. (Unprocessed.)
League of Women Voters of Montgomery County, Virginia Records, Mss. 1997-016. Special Collections, Virginia Polytechnic Institute and State University, Blacksburg, Virginia.
League of Women Voters of the Fairfax Area Records, Collection #C0031. Special Collections Research Center, George Mason University.
League of Women Voters of the Richmond Area Records, M 18. Special Collections and Archives, James Branch Cabell Library, Virginia Commonwealth University.
League of Women Voters of Virginia Records, 1920–2011. Accession 39487. Organization Records Collection, Library of Virginia, Richmond.

Margaret Williams Papers, 1970–1985. Accession 32504. Personal Papers Collection, Library of Virginia, Richmond.
Mary Holt Carlton Papers. Special Collections Research Center, Swem Library, College of William and Mary.
Mary Holt Woolfolk Carlton Papers, M 11. Special Collections and Archives, James Branch Cabell Library, Virginia Commonwealth University.
Mary Tyler Freeman Cheek McClenehan Papers, M 302. Special Collection and Archives, James Branch Cabell Library, Virginia Commonwealth University.
Papers of Edythe C. Harrison. Special Collections and University Archives, Patricia W. and J. Douglas Perry Library, Old Dominion University Libraries, Norfolk, Virginia.
Papers of the Norfolk Branch of the American Association of University Women. Special Collections and University Archives, Patricia W. and J. Douglas Perry Library, Old Dominion University Libraries, Norfolk, Virginia.
Papers of the YWCA of Hampton Roads, Special Collections and University Archives, Patricia W. and J. Douglas Perry Library, Old Dominion University Libraries, Norfolk, Virginia.
Richmond YWCA Archives, M 177. Special Collections and Archives, James Branch Cabell Library, Virginia Commonwealth University.
Richmond YWCA Records, M 373. Special Collections and Archives, James Branch Cabell Library, Virginia Commonwealth University, Richmond.
Speeches of Governor Charles S. Robb, 1982–1984, Accession 51882. State Government Records Collection, Library of Virginia, Richmond.
Virginia Chapter of the National Organization for Women Records, 1971–2004, 2011. Accession 43458. Organization Records Collection, Library of Virginia, Richmond.
Virginia Equal Rights Amendment Ratification Council. Papers, 1970–1982. Accession 31486. Organization Records Collection, Library of Virginia, Richmond.
Virginia Federation of Business and Professional Women's Clubs. Records, 1921–2009. Accession 44419. Organization Records Collection, Library of Virginia, Richmond.
Virginia Feminist Oral History Project, 2013–2014, Collection #M 541. Special Collections and Archives, James Branch Cabell Library, Virginia Commonwealth University, Richmond.
Virginia Organization to Keep Abortion Legal. Special Collections and Archives, James Branch Cabell Library, Virginia Commonwealth University. (Unprocessed.)
Virginia Sexual and Domestic Violence Action Alliance Records, M 432. James Branch Cabell Library, Virginia Commonwealth University.
Zelda Kingoff Nordlinger Papers, 1970–2007. Accession 31719, 44035. Personal Papers Collection, Library of Virginia, Richmond.
Zelda Nordlinger Papers, Special Collections Research Center, Swem Library, College of William and Mary.

Newspapers

New Journal and Guide.
Norfolk Journal and Guide.
Our Own Community Press.
Richmond Pride.
Richmond News Leader.
Richmond Times-Dispatch.
Roanoke Times and World News.
Virginian-Pilot.
Washington Post.

Interviews

Bonnie Atwood, Richmond, 28 October 2014.
Lisa Beckman, Portsmouth, 2 October 2014.
Mary Ann Bergeron, Richmond, 30 October 2014.
Lynn Bradford, Richmond, 27 October 2014.
Sandra Brandt, Virginia Beach, 2 October 2014.
Betsy Brinson, Richmond, 2 June 2013.
Mary Dean Carter, Richmond, 29 May 2013.
Mary Coulling, Lexington, 4 September 2014.
Holly Farris, Draper, 6 September 2014.
Georgia Fuller, Falls Church, 18 March 2014.
Suzanne Keller, Richmond, 27 May 2013.
Denise Lee, Chesapeake, 27 September 2014.
Beth Marschak, Richmond, 30 May 2013.
Kate McCord, Williamsburg, 9 September 2014.
Emily McCoy, Alexandria, 29 May 2014.
Sarah Payne, Stephanie Tyree, and Melanie Payne-White, Iron Gate, 7 September 2014.
Terrie Pendleton, Richmond. 28 November 2014.
Lee Perkins, Alexandria, 11 March 2014.
Karen Raschke, Richmond, 1 June 2014.
(Muriel) Elizabeth Smith, Richmond, 1 May 2014.
Kristi Van Audenhove, Richmond, 29 October 2014.
Mary Wazlak, Virginia Beach, 3 October 2014.
Bessida White, Jamaica, 1 June 2014.
Boots Woodyard, Berryville, 3 September 2014.

Books

Allured, Janet. *Remapping Second-Wave Feminism: The Long Women's Rights Movement in Louisiana, 1950–1997*. Athens: University of Georgia Press, 2016.

Bennett, Evan. *When Tobacco Was King: Families, Farm Labor, and Federal Policy in the Piedmont*. Gainesville: University Press of Florida, 2014.

Berry, Mary Frances. *Why ERA Failed: Politics, Women's Rights, and the Amending Process of the Constitution*. Bloomington: Indiana University Press, 1988.

Bevacqua, Maria. *Rape on the Public Agenda: Feminism and the Politics of Sexual Assault*. Boston: Northeastern University Press, 2000.

Blackman, Julie. *Intimate Violence: A Study of Injustice*. New York: Columbia University Press, 1989.

Blair, Melissa. *Revolutionizing Expectations: Women's Organizations, Feminism, and American Politics, 1965–1980*. Athens: University of Georgia Press, 2014.

Block, Sharon. *Rape and Sexual Power in Early America*. Chapel Hill: University of North Carolina Press, 2006.

Boles, Janet. *The Politics of the Equal Rights Amendment*. New York: Longman, 1979.

Breines, Winifred. *The Trouble Between Us: An Uneasy History of Black and White Women in The Feminist Movement*. New York: Oxford University Press, 2006.

Brown, Ruth Murray. *For a "Christian America": A History of the Religious Right*. New York: Prometheus Books, 2002.

Camp, Stephanie. *Closer to Freedom: Enslaved Women and Everyday Resistance in the Plantation South*. Chapel Hill: University of North Carolina Press, 2004.

Charron, Katherine Mellen. *Freedom's Teacher: The Life of Septima Clark*. Chapel Hill: University of North Carolina Press, 2009.

Cline, David. *Creating Choice: A Community Responds to the Need for Abortion and Birth Control, 1961–1973*. New York: Palgrave, 2006.

Cobble, Dorothy Sue. *The Other Women's Movement: Workplace Justice and Social Rights in Modern America*. Princeton, N.J.: Princeton University Press, 2005.

———, Linda Gordon, and Astrid Henry. *Feminism Unfinished: A Short, Surprising History of American Women's Movements*. New York: Liveright Press, 2015.

Collier-Thomas, Bettye, and V. P. Franklin, eds. *Sisters in the Struggle: African American Women in the Civil Rights-Black Power Movement*. New York: New York University Press, 2001.

Cox, Karen. *Dixie's Daughters: The United Daughters of the Confederacy and the Preservation of Confederate Culture*. Gainesville: University of Florida Press, 2003.

Critchlow, Donald. *Phyllis Schlafly and Grassroots Conservatism: A Woman's Crusade*. Princeton, N.J.: Princeton University Press, 2005.

Davis, Flora. *Moving the Mountain: The Women's Movement in America Since 1960*. New York: Prentice Hall, 1991.

Del Mar, David Peterson. *What Trouble I Have Seen: A History of Violence Against Wives.* Cambridge, Mass.: Harvard University Press, 1996.

Dorr, Gregory Michael. *Segregation's Science: Eugenics and Society in Virginia.* Charlottesville: University of Virginia Press, 2008.

Dorr, Lisa Lindquist. *White Women, Race, and the Power of Rape in Virginia, 1900–1960.* Chapel Hill: University of North Carolina Press, 2004.

Echols, Alice. *Daring to Be Bad: Radical Feminism in America, 1967–1975.* Minneapolis: University of Minnesota Press, 1989.

Enke, A. Finn. *Finding the Movement: Sexuality, Contested Space, and Feminist Activism.* Durham, N.C.: Duke University Press, 2007.

Erdman, Amy. *Yours in Sisterhood: Ms. Magazine and the Promise of Popular Feminism.* Chapel Hill: University of North Carolina Press, 1998.

Evans, Sara. *Personal Politics: The Roots of Women's Liberation in the Civil Rights Movement and the New Left.* New York: Vintage, 1980.

———. *Tidal Wave: How Women Changed America at Century's End.* New York: Free Press, 2004.

Ezekiel, Judith. *Feminism in the Heartland.* Columbus: Ohio State University Press, 2002.

Feimster, Crystal. *Southern Horrors: Women and the Politics of Rape and Lynching.* Cambridge, Mass.: Harvard University Press, 2011.

Freedman, Estelle. *Redefining Rape: Sexual Violence in the Era of Suffrage and Segregation.* Cambridge, Mass.: Harvard University Press, 2013.

Fried, Marlene Gerber, ed. *From Abortion to Reproductive Freedom: Transforming a Movement.* Boston: South End Press, 1990.

Frystak, Shannon. *Our Minds on Freedom: Women and the Struggle for Black Equality in Louisiana, 1924–1967.* Baton Rouge: Louisiana State University Press, 2009.

Gavey, Nichola. *Just Sex? The Cultural Scaffolding of Rape.* New York: Routledge, 2005.

Gerhard, Jane. *Desiring Revolution: Second-Wave Feminism and the Rewriting of American Sexual Thought, 1920–1982.* New York: Columbia University Press, 2001.

Gilmore, Stephanie. *Groundswell: Grassroots Feminism in Postwar America.* New York: Routledge Press, 2012.

———, ed. *Feminist Coalitions: Historical Perspectives on Second-Wave Feminism in the United States.* Champaign: University of Illinois Press, 2008.

Ginsburg, Faye. *Contested Lives: The Abortion Debate in the American Community.* Updated ed. Berkeley: University of California Press, 1998.

Glasrud, Bruce, and Merline Pitre, eds. *Southern Black Women in the Modern Civil Rights Movement.* College Station: Texas A&M University Press, 2013.

Gordon, Linda. *Heroes of Their Own Lives: The Politics and History of Family Violence in Boston, 1880–1960.* Rpt. Champaign: University of Illinois Press, 2002.

———. *Woman's Body, Woman's Right: Birth Control in America.* New York: Penguin Books, 1990.

Hall, Jacquelyn Dowd. *Revolt Against Chivalry: Jesse Daniel Ames and the Women's Campaign Against Lynching.* Rev. ed. New York: Columbia University Press, 1993.

Hartmann, Susan. *The Other Feminists: Activists in the Liberal Establishment.* 1998. New Haven, CT: Yale University Press, 2013.

Heinemann, Ronald. *Depression and New Deal in Virginia: The Enduring Dominion.* Charlottesville: University of Virginia Press, 1988.

——, John Kolp, Anthony Parent, and William Shade. *Old Dominion, New Commonwealth: A History of Virginia, 1607–2007.* Charlottesville: University of Virginia Press, 2008.

Hewitt, Nancy, ed. *No Permanent Waves: Recasting Histories of U.S. Feminism.* New Brunswick, N.J.: Rutgers University Press, 2010.

Hoff-Wilson, Joan. Ed. *Rights of Passage: The Past and Future of the Equal Rights Amendment.* Bloomington: Indiana University Press, 1986.

Holloway, Pippa. *Sexuality, Politics, and Social Control in Virginia, 1920–1945.* Chapel Hill: University of North Carolina Press, 2006.

Holt, Len. *An Act of Conscience.* Boston: Beacon Press, 1965.

Jordan, Carol E. *Violence against Women in Kentucky: A History of U.S. and State Legislative Reform.* Lexington: University Press of Kentucky, 2014.

Kaplan, Temma. *Crazy for Democracy: Women in Grassroots Movements.* New York: Routledge, 1997.

Kessler-Harris, Alice. *In Pursuit of Equity: Women, Men, and the Quest for Economic Citizenship in Twentieth-Century America.* New York: Oxford University Press, 2003.

Kierner, Cynthia, Jennifer Loux, and Megan Shockley. *Changing History: Virginia Women Through Four Centuries.* Richmond: Library of Virginia Press, 2013.

Lassiter, Matthew, and Andrew B. Lewis, eds. *The Moderates' Dilemma: Massive Resistance to School Desegregation in Virginia.* Charlottesville: University of Virginia Press, 1998.

Laughlin, Kathleen, and Jacqueline Castledine, eds. *Breaking the Wave: Women, Their Organizations, and Feminism, 1945–1985.* New York: Routledge, 2011.

Lee, Chana Kai. *For Freedom's Sake: The Life of Fannie Lou Hamer.* Champaign: University of Illinois Press, 2000.

Lee, Lauranett. *Making the American Dream Work: A Cultural History of African Americans in Hopewell, Virginia.* Morgan James Publishing, 2008.

Lewis, Earl. *In Their Own Interests: Race, Class, and Power in Twentieth-Century Norfolk, Virginia.* Berkeley: University of California Press, 1993.

Mansbridge, Jane. *Why We Lost the ERA.* Chicago: University of Chicago Press, 1986.

Martin, William. *With God on Our Side: The Rise of the Religious Right in America.* New York: Broadway Books, 1996.

Mathews, Donald G., and Jane Sherron De Hart. *Sex, Gender, and the Politics of the ERA: A State and a Nation.* New York: Oxford University Press, 1990.

Matthews, Nancy. *Confronting Rape: The Feminist Anti-Rape Movement and the State.* New York: Routledge, 1994.

McGuire, Danielle. *At the Dark End of the Street: Black Women, Rape, and Resistance—A New History of Civil Rights from Rosa Parks to the Rise of Black Power.* Rpt. New York: Vintage Press, 2011.

Miller, Patricia. *The Worst of Times: Illegal Abortion: Survivors, Practitioners, Coroners, Cops, and Children Who Died Talk About Its Horrors.* New York: HarperCollins, 1993.

Muse, Benjamin. *Virginia's Massive Resistance.* Bloomington: University of Indiana Press, 1961.

Naples, Nancy, ed. *Community Activism and Feminist Politics: Organizing Across Race, Class, and Gender.* New York: Routledge, 1998.

Nelson, Jennifer. *Women of Color and the Reproductive Rights Movement.* New York: New York University Press, 2003.

Newbeck, Phyl. *Virginia Hasn't Always Been for Lovers: Interracial Marriage Bans and the Case of Richard and Mildred Loving.* Carbondale: Southern Illinois University Press, 2004.

Orleck, Annelise. *Storming Caesar's Palace: How Black Mothers Fought Their Own War on Poverty.* Boston: Beacon Press, 2006.

Petchesky, Rosalind. *Abortion and Women's Choice: The State, Sexuality, and Reproductive Freedom.* Boston: Northeastern University Press, 1990.

Pleck, Elizabeth. *Domestic Tyranny: The Making of American Social Policy against Family Violence from Colonial Times to the Present.* Champaign: University of Illinois Press, 2004.

Pomerleau, Clark. *Califia Women: Feminism against Sexism, Classism, and Racism.* Arlington: University of Texas Press, 2013.

Pratt, Robert. *The Color of Their Skin: Education and Race in Richmond, Virginia, 1954–1989.* Charlottesville: University of Virginia Press, 1993.

Ransby, Barbara. *Ella Baker and the Black Freedom Movement: A Radical Democratic Vision.* Chapel Hill: University of North Carolina Press, 2005.

Reagan, Leslie. *When Abortion Was a Crime: Women, Medicine, and Law in the United States, 1867–1973.* Berkeley: University of California Press, 1998.

Robnett, Belinda. *How Long? How Long? African American Women in the Struggle for Civil Rights.* New York: Oxford University Press, 2000.

Rose, Melody. *Safe, Legal, and Unavailable? Abortion Politics in the United States.* Washington, D.C.: CQ Press, 2006.

Rosen, Ruth. *The World Split Open: How the Modern Women's Movement Changed America.* New York: Penguin Books, 2000.

Roth, Benita. *Separate Roads to Feminism: Black, Chicana, and White Feminist Movements in America's Second Wave.* New York: Cambridge University Press, 2003.

Rupp, Leila, and Verta Taylor. *Survival in the Doldrums: The American Women's Movement 1945 to the 1960s.* New York: Oxford University Press, 1987.

Ryan, Barbara. *Feminism and the Women's Movement: Dynamics of Change in Social Movement Ideology and Activism.* New York: Routledge, 1992.

Rymph, Catherine. *Republican Women: Feminism and Conservatism from Suffrage Through the Rise of the New Right.* Chapel Hill: University of North Carolina Press, 2006.

Schoen, Johanna. *Abortion After Roe: Abortion After Legalization.* Chapel Hill: University of North Carolina Press, 2015.

———. *Choice and Coercion: Birth Control, Sterilization, and Abortion in Public Health and Welfare.* Chapel Hill: University of North Carolina Press, 2005.

Shockley, Megan Taylor. *"We, Too, Are Americans": African American Women in Detroit and Richmond, 1940–1954.* Champaign: University of Illinois Press, 2003.

Shreve, Anita. *Women Together, Women Alone: The Legacy of the Consciousness-Raising Movement.* New York: Viking Press, 1989.

Silliman, Jael, Marlene Gerber Fried, Loretta Ross, and Elaine Gutierrez. *Undivided Rights: Women of Color Organizing for Reproductive Justice.* Cambridge, Mass.: South End Press, 2004.

Sokoloff, Natalie with Christina Pratt. Eds. *Domestic Violence at the Margins: Readings on Race, Class, Gender, and Culture.* New Brunswick: Rutgers University Press, 2005.

Solinger, Rickie, ed. *The Abortion Wars: A Half-Century of Struggle.* Berkeley: University of California Press, 1998.

———. *Pregnancy and Power: A Short History of Reproductive Politics in America.* New York: New York University Press, 2007.

Sommerville, Diane. *Rape and Race in the Nineteenth-Century South.* Chapel Hill: University of North Carolina Press, 2004.

Smith, J. Douglas. *Managing White Supremacy: Race, Politics, and Citizenship in Jim Crow Virginia.* Chapel Hill: University of North Carolina Press, 2002.

Springer, Kimberly. *Living for the Revolution: Black Feminist Organizations, 1968–1980.* Durham, N.C.: Duke University Press, 2005.

Spruill, Marjorie. *Divided We Stand: The Battle Over Women's Rights and Family Values that Polarized American Politics.* New York: Bloomsburg Press, 2017.

Staggenborg, Suzanne. *The Pro-Choice Movement: Organization and Activism in the Abortion Conflict.* Rev. ed. New York: Oxford University Press, 1994.

Tarter, Brent. *The Grandees of Government: The Origins and Persistence of Undemocratic Politics in Virginia.* Charlottesville: University of Virginia Press, 2013.

Titus, Jill Ogline. *Brown's Battleground: Students, Segregationists, and the Struggle for Justice in Prince Edward County, Virginia.* Chapel Hill: University of North Carolina Press, 2011.

Valk, Anne. *Radical Sisters: Second-Wave Feminism and Black Liberation in Washington, D.C.* Champaign: University of Illinois Press, 2010.

Wallenstein, Peter. *Blue Laws and Black Codes: Conflict, Courts, and Change in Twentieth Century Virginia.* Charlottesville: University of Virginia Press, 2004.

———. *Cradle of America: Four Centuries of Virginia History.* Lawrence: University Press of Kansas, 2007.

———. *Tell the Court I Love My Wife: Race, Marriage, and Law—An American History.* New York: St. Martin's Press, 2004.

White, Debra Gray. *Ar'n't I a Woman: Female Slaves in the Plantation South.* New York: W. W. Norton, 1985.

Articles

Allured, Janet. "Arkansas Baptists and Methodists and the Equal Rights Amendment." *Arkansas Historical Quarterly* 43, no. 1 (Spring 1984): 55–66.

Anderson-Bricker, Kristen. "Triple Jeopardy: Black Women and the Growth of Feminist Consciousness in SNCC, 1964–1975." In *Still Lifting, Still Climbing: African American Women's Contemporary Activism.* Ed. Kimberly Springer. 49–70. New York: New York University Press, 1999.

Baker, Nancy. "Hermine Tobolowsky: A Feminist's Fight for Equal Rights." In *Texas Women: Their Histories, Their Lives.* Ed. Stephanie Cole and Rebecca Sharpless. 434–56. Athens: University of Georgia Press, 2015.

———. "Integrating Women into Modern Kentucky History: The Equal Rights Debate (1972–1978) as a Case Study." *Register of the Kentucky Historical Society* 113, no. 2–3 (Summer 2015): 477–508.

Battan, Jesse. "'In the Marriage Bed Women's Sex Has Been Enslaved and Abused': Defining And Exposing Marital Rape in Late-Nineteenth Century America." In *Sex Without Consent: Rape and Sexual Coercion in America.* 204–29. New York: New York University Press, 2001.

Berkman, Joyce. "The Fertility of Scholarship on the History of Reproductive Rights in the United States." *History Compass* 9, no. 5 (2011): 433–47.

Bevacqua, Maria. "Reconsidering Violence Against Women: Coalition Politics in the Antirape Movement." In *Feminist Coalitions,* ed. Gilmore. 163–77.

Brady, David, and Kent Tedin. "Ladies in Pink: Religion and Political Ideology in the Anti-ERA Movement." *Social Science Quarterly* 56, no. 4 (March 1976): 564–75.

Brauer, Carl. "Women Activists, Southern Conservatives, and the Prohibition of Sex Discrimination in Title VII of the 1964 Civil Rights Amendment." *Journal of Southern History* 49, no. 1 (February 1983): 37–56.

Burris, Val. "Who Opposed the ERA? An Analysis of the Social Bases of Antifeminism." *Social Science Quarterly* 64, no. 2 (June 1983): 305–17.

Carroll, Berenice. "Direct Action and Constitutional Rights: The Case of the ERA." In *Rights of Passage: The Past and Future of the ERA.* Ed. Joan Hoff-Wilson. 63–75. Bloomington: Indiana University Press, 1986.

Carver, Joan. "The Equal Rights Amendment and the Florida Legislature." *Florida Historical Quarterly* 60, no. 4 (April 1982): 455–81.

Chanfrault-Duchet, Francoise. "Narrative Structures, Social Models and Symbolic Representation." In *Women's Words: The Feminist Practice of Oral History*. Ed. Sherna Berger Gluck and Daphne Patai. 77–92. New York: Routledge, 1991.

Chavez, Marisela. "'We Have a Long, Beautiful History': Chicana Feminist Trajectories and Legacies." In *No Permanent Waves*, ed. Hewitt. 77–97.

Clark, Laurel. "Beyond the Gay/Straight Split: Social Feminists in Baltimore." *NWSA Journal* 19, no. 2 (Summer 2007): 1–31.

Cobble, Dorothy Sue. "Labor Feminists and President Kennedy's Commission on Women." In *No Permanent Waves*, ed. Hewitt. 144–168.

Critchlaw, Donald and Cynthia Stacheski, "The Equal Rights Amendment Reconsidered: Politics, Policy, and Social Mobilization in a Democracy," *Journal of Policy History* 20, no. 1 (January 2008): 157–76.

Davis, Angela. "Racism, Birth Control, and Reproductive Rights." In *From Abortion to Reproductive Freedom: Transforming a Movement*. Ed. Marlene Gerber Fried. 15–26. Boston: South End Press, 1990.

Dierenfield, Kathleen Murphy. "One 'Desegregated Heart': Sarah Patton Boyle and the Crusade for Civil Rights in Virginia." *Virginia Magazine of History and Biography* 104, no. 2 (1996): 251–84.

Fuller, Georgia Elaine. "Climbing the President's Fence." *Women's Studies International Forum*. 12, no. 1 (1989): 107–12.

Gilmore, Stephanie and Elizabeth Kaminski. "A Part and Apart: Lesbian and Straight Feminist Activists Negotiate Identity in a Second-Wave Organization." *Journal of the History of Sexuality* 16, no. 1 (January 2007): 95–113.

Gluck, Sherna Berger. "What's So Special About Women?" In *Women's Oral History: The Frontiers Reader*. Ed. Susan Armitage et al. 27–42. Lincoln: University of Nebraska Press, 2002.

———, in conjunction with Maylei Blackwell, Sharon Cotrell, and Karen S. Harper. "Whose Feminism, Whose History? Reflections on Excavating (the) U.S. Women's Movement(s)." In *Community Activism and Feminist Politics*, ed. Naples. 31–56.

Hall, Simon. "Civil Rights Activism in 1960s Virginia." *Journal of Black Studies* 38, no. 2 (2007): 251–67.

Hasday, Jill. "Choice and Consent: A Legal History of Marital Rape." *California Law Review* 88, no. 5 (2000): 1373–1505.

Held, Allison, Sheryl Herndon, and Danielle Stager. "The Equal Rights Amendment: Why the ERA Remains Legally Viable and Properly Before the States." *William and Mary Journal of Women and the Law* 3, no. 113 (1997): 113–36.

Jackson, Shirley. "'Something About the Word: African American Women and Feminism.'" In *No Middle Ground: Women and Radical Protest*. Ed. Kathleen Blee. 38–50. New York: New York University Press, 1998.

Kaplan, Laura. "Beyond Safe and Legal: The Lessons of Jane." In Solinger, ed., *The Abortion Wars*, 33–41.

Kempker, Ellen. "Battling 'Big Sister' Government: Hoosier Women and the Politics of International Women's Year." *Journal of Women's History* 24, no. 2 (Summer 2012): 144–70.

King, Deborah. "Multiple Jeopardy, Multiple Consciousness: The Context of a Black Feminist Ideology." *Signs* 14, no. 1 (Autumn 1988): 42–72.

Koestner, Katie. "The Perfect Rape Victim." In *Just Sex? Students Rewrite the Rules on Sex, Violence, Equality, and Activism*. Ed. Jodi Gold and Susan Villari. 30–38. New York: Rowman & Littlefield, 1999.

Laughlin, Kathleen, Julie Gallagher, Dorothy Sue Cobble, Eileen Boris, Premilla Nadasen, Stephanie Gilmore, Leandra Zarnow. "Is It Time to Jump Ship? Historians Rethink the Waves Metaphor." *Feminist Formations* 22, no. 1 (Spring 2010): 76–135.

Leffler, Phyllis. "Mr. Jefferson's University: Women in the Village!" *Virginia Magazine of History and Biography* 115, no. 1 (2007): 56–107.

Lewis, Andrew B. "Emergency Mothers, Basement Schools, and the Preservation of Public Education in Charlottesville." In *The Moderates' Dilemma*, ed. Lassiter and Lewis. 72–103.

Maclean, Nancy. "Gender Is Powerful: The Long Reach of Feminism." *The OAH Magazine of History* 20, no. 5 (October 2006): 19–23.

Murrell, Amy. "The 'Impossible' Prince Edward Case: The Endurance of Resistance in a Southside County, 1959–1964." In *The Moderate's Dilemma*, ed. Lassiter and Lewis. 134–67.

Nadasen, Premilla. "Expanding the Boundaries of the Women's Movement: Black Feminism and the Struggle for Welfare Rights." In *No Permanent Waves*, ed. Hewitt. 168–192.

Painter, Nell Irvin. "Soul Murder: Toward a Fully Loaded Cost Accounting." In *U.S. History as Women's History: New Feminist Essays*. Ed. Linda Kerber, Alice Kessler-Harris, and Kathryn Kish Sklar. 125–46. Chapel Hill: University of North Carolina Press, 1995.

Parry, Janine. "'What Women Wanted': Arkansas Women's Commissions and the ERA." *Arkansas Historical Quarterly* 59, no. 3 (Fall 2000): 265–98.

Randolph, Sherie. "Not to Rely Completely on the Courts: Florynce 'Flo' Kennedy and Black Feminist Leadership in the Reproductive Rights Battle, 1969–1971." *Journal of Women's History* 27, no. 1 (Spring 2015): 136–60.

Reger, Jo. "Organizational Dynamics and the Construct of Multiple Feminist Identities in the National Organization for Women." *Gender and Society* 16, no. 5 (October 2002): 710–27.

Reinelt, Claire. "Moving onto the Terrain of the State: The Battered Women's Movement and the Politics of Engagement." In *Feminist Organizations: Harvest of the*

New Women's Movement. Ed. Myra Max Ferree and Patricia Yancy Martin. 84–104. Philadelphia: Temple University Press, 1995.

Ross, Loretta. "African American Women and Abortion." In Solinger, ed., *The Abortion Wars,* 161–206.

Roth, Benita. "The Making of the Vanguard Center: Black Feminist Emergence in the 1960s and 1970s." In *Still Lifting, Still Climbing: Contemporary African American Women's Activism.* Ed. Kimberly Springer. 70–90. New York: New York University Press, 1999.

Rouverol, Alicia. "Trying to Be Good: Lessons in Oral History and Performance." In *Remembering: Oral History and Performance.* Ed. Dena Pollock and Jacquelyn Dowd Hall. 19–44. New York: Palgrave Macmillan, 2005.

Sangster, Jean. "Telling Our Stories: Feminist Debates and the Use of Oral History." *Women's History Review* 3, no. 1 (1994): 5–28.

Seitz, Virginia Rinaldo. "Class, Gender, And Resistance in the Appalachian Coalfields." In *Community Activism and Feminist Politics,* ed. Naples. 213–36.

Shockley, Megan Taylor. "Sharon Bottoms and Linda Kaufman: Legal Rights and Lesbian Mothers." In *Virginia Women: Their Lives and Times.* Vol. 2. Ed. Cynthia Kierner and Sandra Treadway. 354–76. Athens: University of Georgia Press, 2016.

Smith, Andrea. "Beyond Pro-Choice vs. Pro-Life: Women of Color and Reproductive Justice." *National Women's Studies Association Journal* 17, no. 1 (Spring 2005): 119–40.

Smith, Harold. "Casey Hayden: Gender and the Origins of SNCC, SDS, and the Women's Liberation Movement." In *Texas Women: Their Lives and Times.* Vol. 2. Ed. Elizabeth Turner, Stephanie Cole, and Rebecca Sharpless. 296–318. Athens: University of Georgia Press, 2015.

Solinger, Rickie. "Layering the Lenses: Toward Understanding Reproductive Politics in the United States." *Journal of Women's History* 25, no. 4 (Winter 2013): 101–12.

Spruill, Marjorie. "Victoria Eslinger, Keller Bumgardner Barron, Mary Heriot, Tootsie Holland, and Pat Callair: Champions of Women's Rights in South Carolina." In *South Carolina Women: Their Lives and Times.* Vol. 3. Ed. Joan Johnson, Valinda Littlefield, and Marjorie Spruill. 373–408. Athens: University of Georgia Press, 2012.

Stephens, Julie. "Our Remembered Selves: Oral History and Feminist Memory." *Oral History* 38, no. 1 (Spring 2010): 81–90.

Taylor, Ula. "Black Feminisms and Human Agency." In *No Permanent Waves: Recasting Histories of U.S. Feminism.* 61–76. New Brunswick, N.J.: Rutgers University Press, 2010.

Taylor, Verta, and Leila Rupp. "Women's Culture and Lesbian Feminist Activism: A Reconsideration of Cultural Feminism." In *Community Activism and Feminist Politics,* ed. Naples. 57–80.

Thomas, William G., III. "Television News and the Civil Rights Struggle: The Views in Virginia and Mississippi." *Southern Spaces,* 3 November 2004. southernspaces.org /2004/television-news-and-civil-rights-struggle-views-virginia-and-mississippi.

Thompson, Becky. "Multiracial Feminism: Recasting the Chronology of Second Wave Feminism." In *No Permanent Waves,* ed. Hewitt. 39–60.

Tzu-Chun Wu, Judy. "Living a Feminist Lifestyle: Peace Activism and Women's Orientalism." In *No Permanent Waves,* ed. Hewitt. 193–220.

Voss, Kimberly Wilmot. "The Florida Fight for Equality: The Equal Rights Amendment, Senator Lori Wilson, and Mediated Catfights in the 1970s." *Florida Historical Quarterly* 88, no. 2 (Fall 2009): 173–208.

Weaver, Janet. "Barrio Women: Community and Coalition in the Heartland." In *Breaking the Wave: Women, Their Organizations, and Feminism, 1945–1985.* Ed. Kathleen Laughlin and Jacqueline Castledine. 173–87. New York: Routledge, 2011.

White, O. Kendall, Jr. "Overt and Covert Politics: The Mormon Church's Anti-ERA Campaign in Virginia." *Virginia Social Sciences Journal* 19 (Winter 1984): 11–16.

Wilder, Marcy. "The Rule of Law, the Rise of Violence, and the Role of Mortality: Reframing America's Abortion Debate." In Solinger, ed., *The Abortion Wars,* 73–94.

Wilkerson-Freeman, Sarah. "Stealth in the Political Arsenal of Southern Women: A Retrospective for the Millennium." In *Southern Women at the Millennium: A Historical Perspective.* Ed. Melissa Walker, Jeannette Dunn, and Joe Dunn. 42–82. Columbia: University of Missouri Press, 2003.

Wittner, Judith. "Reconceptualizing Agency in Domestic Violence Court." In *Community Activism and Feminist Politics,* ed. Naples. 81–106.

Young, Neil. "'The ERA Is a Moral Issue': The Mormon Church, LDS Women, and the Defeat of the Equal Rights Amendment." *American Quarterly* 59, no. 3 (September 2007): 623–44.

Zajicek, Anna, Allyn Lord, and Lori Holyfield. "The Emergence and First Years of a Grassroots Women's Movement in Northwest Arkansas, 1970–1980." *Arkansas Historical Quarterly* 62, no. 2 (Summer 2003): 153–81.

Unpublished

Allured, Janet, Melissa Blair, Hannah Dudley-Shotwell, Joey Fink, Samantha Rodriguez, Jesse Wilkerson, and Keira Williams. "Finding Southern Feminism—Oral History, Archives, and the Challenges of Researching Feminism in the South: A Roundtable Discussion." Tenth Southern Conference on Women's History, Charleston, SC, 2015.

Bezbatchenko, Mary. "Virginia and the Equal Rights Amendment." MA thesis, Virginia Commonwealth University, 2007.

Collins, Patricia Hill. "From Civil Rights to Black Lives Matter: Gender, Sexuality, and Black Social Movements," 2 March 2016. Video at http://tv.clemson.edu/distinguished_author_speaks_at_clemson/. Last accessed 27 June 2016.

Hershman, James Howard Jr. "A Rumbling in the Museum: The Opponents of Virginia's Massive Resistance." PhD diss., University of Virginia, 1978.
Keane, Katarina. "Second-Wave Feminism in the American South, 1965–1980." PhD diss. University of Maryland, 2009.
Van Valkenburg, Schuyler. "Defying Labels: Richmond NOW's Multigenerational Dynamism." MA thesis, Virginia Commonwealth University, 2010.

INDEX

Abortion: For Survival, 113
abortion rights: access to abortions, 105; and antiabortion tactics, 122–130; and class, access to, 177; clinics, 124–130; clinics, establishment of, 104–105; coalition of organizations, 115–116; and consent legislation, 107–110, 114–120; "counter picketing," 124–129; demonstrations, 121–123; education campaigns, 116; and ERA, 224n30; compared to ERA, 98; as a feminist issue, 97; funding for, 105–106, 108, 118–119, 130–131; geographical support, 121–122; and Human Life Amendment, 106–107; "I'm Not Sorry," 131; and membership to feminist organizations, 112; organizations in support of, 102–103; "Pledge-a-Picket" campaign, 130; and post-*Roe* activism, lack of, 176–177; as privacy issue, 102–103, 111–112; "pro-choice" as narrow in focus, 98–101; providers, 131, 132, 177, 231n137; and rape victims, 137; restrictive legislation, 106–110, 120, 131–133, 229n114; restrictive legislation, pre-*Roe*, 98; scholarship on, 221n1; and transvaginal ultrasound bill, 132; TRAP laws, 177; in twenty-first century, 176–177; and women of color, 99–101
Adams, Dawn, 192
AFL-CIO, 76–77
Alleghany Foundation, 154
Allen, George, 119, 130
Allen, George, Jr., 147
Allured, Janet, 3, 232n1
Almand, James, 14

American Association of University Women (AAUW): and abortion rights, 115; and ERA, 65–68, 79, 93; and Virginia Pro-Choice Alliance, 110
American Association of University Women (AAUW), Virginia chapters: and domestic-violence shelters, 153; on marital rape, 168–169; and Rape Prevention Resolution, 145
American Civil Liberties Union (ACLU), 125; on abortion consent legislation, 107–108; and ERA, 68, 85; on Fowler and Clarke arrests, 82; Southern Women's Rights Project (SWRP), 37–38, 40–41, 105, 125; and Virginia Pro-Choice Alliance, 110; and women of color, 68
American Law Institute, 98
Ames, Jessie Daniel, 232n1
Annual Women's Musical Extravaganza, 157
Anti-Lynching Society, 232n1
anti-violence efforts, 134, 135–136. *See also* domestic violence; sexual assault
antiwar movement, 27–28
Archer v. Johnson (1973), 55
Atkinson, Frank, 189
Atwood, Bonnie: on anti-violence movement, 179; on divorce policies, 182; on General Assembly, 184; on harassment by legislators, 15; on motherhood, 182; on opportunities increased, 186; and radicalism, 44–45, 47; reasons for activism, 20, 27, 28, 32; on successes of movement, 186; on women's behavior, 181

259

Avalon Center, 140, 143, 164
Avery, Nina Horton, 54, 57
Axelle, Bill, 139

Babe's, 39
Baker, Emily, 164
Baker, Karlyn, 12
Barber, James, 14–15
Barr, Janet, 46
Barry, Warren, 14
Battan, Jesse, 232n1
Bauer, Pat, 12
Beall, Mary Ann, 88, 92, 156
Beckman, Lisa, 21–22, 31, 32, 182–183, 190
Bergeron, Mary Ann: on abortion rights in twenty-first century, 177; on anti-violence movement, 179; and antiwar movement, 28; on change, slow pace of, 189; and domestic-violence shelters, 150–151, 155; on ERA failure, 94; on General Assembly, 184; on generational assumptions, 188; on governors, 184–185; on laws, changing of, 186; on media climate, 181; on motherhood, 182; on opportunities increased, 186; on political climate against movement, 183; on privilege of activists, 155; on rape law codes, 145; reasons for activism, 17, 28, 29–30; on sexual-assault awareness, 136; on successes of movement, 186; on Virginia and feminism, 189; on women of color, exclusion of, 33, 40; on workplace environment, 29–30
Best Products Foundation, 153
Bevacqua, Maria, 234n6
Beyer, Don, 113–114, 117
Biden, Joseph, 165
birth control, 99
Black, Dick, 171
Blackman, Julie, 234n6
Blackwell, Pat, 37
Black Women's Alliance, 202n24
Bladen, Philip, 37
Blair, Susan, 64
Block, Sharon, 232n1
Blue Lantern, 150
Bluford, Robert, 104–105

Bobbitt, Lorena, 170
Boucher, Fred, 147
Boyd, Cynthia, 86
Boyle, Martha, 64, 67
Bradford, Lynn: on abortion rights in twenty-first century, 177; on change, slow pace of, 189; on General Assembly harassment, 15; on generational assumptions, 188; on gerrymandering, 184; on household labor, 182; on opportunities increased, 186; reasons for activism, 29
Bradner, Alison, 43, 46–47
Brandt, Sandra: on ERA, 94; on ERA in twenty-first century, 176; on post-*Roe* activism, lack of, 177; reasons for activism, 20–21, 22; on women in politics, 185; to young feminists, 190–191
Brat, Dave, 192
Brehl, Pat, 75
Bridge, Junior, 65–66, 92
Brinson, Betsy: on abortion rights, 105, 125; ERA, failure of in Virginia and response to, 94; and ERA, militant tactics, 85; on Fowler and Clarke arrests, 81–84; on lesbians, tension with, 42–43, 71, 72–73; and March for Women's Lives, 121; on opportunities increased, 186; reasons for activism, 26; on successes of movement, 186; on women of color, exclusion of, 40–41; to young feminists, 190–191
Brock, Nancy, 169
Brooks, Gene, 149
Brooks, Kathryn, 66, 84
Brzonkala, Christy, 164–165
Buckley, Jill, 63
Buck v. Bell (1927), 101
Burke, Tarana, 174, 180
Burns, Christy, 43
Bush, George H. W., 144
Byrd, Harry, 4, 11, 107
Byrd, Harry, Jr., 52
Byrne, Leslie, 114

Callister Marion, 87
Campus SaVe Act, 178

Canada, A. Joseph, 70, 78
Cantor, Eric, 192
Capone, Audrey, 51
Carlton, Holt, 45, 47
Carlton, Mary Holt, 51–52
Carreras, Cecilia, 172
Carter, Mary Dean: on change, slow pace of, 189; college experiences of, 31–32; on employment discrimination, 30; on lesbians, tension with, 42; reasons for activism, 19, 27; on social forces against movement, 183; on successes of movement, 186, 187, 188
Castleman, Judy, 115
Catholics for Free Choice, 101, 115
Center for Reproductive Law and Policy, 131
Charity, Ruth Harvey, 33, 93
Charlottesville Rape Crisis Center, 138, 139
Chase, Carol, 102
Chichester, John, 89
child care, 175
Chisholm, Shirley, 68
Choices, Inc., 158, 162
Christian Broadcasting Network, 5
Christian Coalition, 5, 108
Church of the Brethren, 79
Church Women United, 53
"Circus Saints and Sinners" club, 14–15
civil rights movement, 10–11, 16; as gateway to feminist activism, 22–27
Clark, Adele, 52, 54
Clark, Patricia Harding, 104
Clark, Paul, 149
Clarke, Jean Marshall Crawford: arrested, 82–84; on CPCs, 124; and ERA, 74, 76, 81–84; in General Assembly harassment, 13; on secret memo, 81; on Thomson, 78
Clery Act, 178
Clinton, Hillary, 190, 191–192
Clute, Sylvia, 56, 159, 160
Cohen, Bernard, 114, 147
Coleman, J. Marshall, 78, 113–114
college campuses: and activism, 23, 25–26, 27–28, 31–32; and assaults, 171–173, 178, 179; and sexual violence, 164–165
Collins, Patricia Hill, 41

Combahee River Collection, 202n24, 205n34
Common Cause, 75, 77, 78
Commonwealth Women's Clinic, 128
Congress of Women's Organizations, 53, 59, 145, 146
consciousness-raising movement, 203n24
Contact Peninsula, 141
Cooper, Natalie, 54
Corbin, Lizzie, 76
Corry, Carolyn, 118
Coulling, Mary, 19–22, 175, 191
Covington Business and Professional Women, 156
Crandall, Richard, 13
Crater, Flora, 29, 49–50, 54, 60, 61, 68
Crawford, Jean Marshall. See Clarke, Jean Marshall Crawford
Crisis Center, 140
Crisis Pregnancy Clinics (CPCs), 123–124, 131
Crooks, Viola, 76
Cuccinelli, Ken, 124, 131
Culpeper shelter, 162
Currie, Kathleen, 78

Dalton, Eddy, 106, 114
Dans, Suzanne, 161
Dart, Melissa, 172
date rape, 31–32, 141–144
Davis, Angela, 222n16
Davis, Eileen, 176
DeBolt, Margaret, 103–104
DeCrow, Karen, 66
Denyes, Mary. See Wazlak, Mary (Denyes)
Department of Community Services (COSAR), 139, 168
DeVos, Betsy, 178
divorce law, 55–56
Dobbins, Del, 34, 35–36
domestic violence: and class, 155; and college campuses, 159; feminist response to, 166–167; and Freedom of Information (FOIA) act, 161; funding for, 158, 161–162, 163; and gun reform, 179; hotline, 163; law codes, 149, 159–160, 165; law codes, response to, 160–163; and mandatory arrests, 162–163;

domestic violence (*continued*)
and police, 163; and public education campaigns, 158–159; reporting of, 149, 166; scholarship on, 232n1; compared to sexual violence, 167; shelters, establishment of, 151–154, 155; shelters, funding for, 135–136, 157; shelters, need for, 149, 150, 156, 158, 159–160, 166, 179; and stalking, 166; statistics, 166; and survivor services, 160; and victim impact statements, 161; and women of color, 166, 173–174

Domestic Violence Awareness Month, 159

Domestic Violence Project, 152

Dorr, Lisa Lindquist, 232n1

dress codes, 32

DuVal, Clive, 13, 68, 89

Echols, Alice, 2

Ecker, Fran, 157

economic factors, 182

Eller, Regina Pack, 140

Ellis, Garrison, 57

Emerge Virginia, 6, 185, 192

employment discrimination, 29, 56, 76, 186

Episcopal Women's United Thank You Offering, 152

Equal Employment Opportunity Commission, 56

Equal Rights Amendment (ERA): and abortion rights, 71–72, 224n30; and activism, entry into, 50; boycott of non-ERA states, 79; and civil disobedience, 86–88; and coalition for support, 49, 53, 59, 61–62, 69–70, 79, 84, 86, 89–90, 91 (*see also individual organizations*); and coalition for support, splintering of, 70–73; congressional extension of, 79; effect of in Virginia, 59–60; and election of 1977, 77–78; and election of 1981, 88; as entry issue into activism, 78–79, 88, 92–94, 94–95; ERA week, 69–70; expiration of, 91; expiration of, extension, 85; failure to ratify, 43, 50, 90–91, 175–176; failure to ratify, reasons for, 91–92, 93–94; fund-raising efforts, 84; and House Privileges and Elections Committee, 52, 60, 64, 67–68, 81–84, 88, 89, 91, 94, 176; and image, concern with, 71–73; and labor support, 76–77, 85–86; legacy of, 94; and media stereotypes of proponents, 56–59; national ratification, 69; opposition to, 50, 53; and radicalization, 80–81, 85–88; rallies for support, 86; "secret memo," 60–61, 81; Senate vote, 70; in South, 74, 84; stalled, 84; and state legislatures, 50–51; support, arguments for, 54–56; supported by Virginians, 78; testimony for, 81; in twenty-first century, 1, 91, 94, 176; and women of color, 69, 93

ERA Central, 58

ERA Legal Defense Fund, 82

ERAmerica, 73, 78, 89–90

ERA Supporter's Handbook (1974), 62

ERA Task Force Report, 59–60

Ervin, Sam, 211n16

eugenics, 99–101

Evans, Sara, 2

Exum, Rosalind, 33, 83, 93

Ezekid, Judith, 232n1

Facebook, 172, 174, 180

failures of movement, 181–184

Fairfax Commission on Women, 145

Fairfax County Hospital, 126

Fairfax County Women's Commission, 147, 157

Fairfax County Women's Shelter, 152

Fairfax Donor's Center, 126

Falwell, Jerry, 5, 85, 86, 108, 224n30

family leave policies, 175

Family Resource Center, 162

"Farm Team," 185

Farris, Holly: on feminist networks, 186; on motherhood, 182; reasons for activism, 18, 20, 28, 42; to young feminists, 191

Federation of Business and Professional Women's Clubs (BPW): and domestic-violence shelters, 155, 156; and ERA, 65–68, 77, 88; on rape law codes, 146

Feimster, Crystal, 232n1

feminist scholarship, 2–3

Fisher, Delvia, 155–156
"flexible solidarity," 41, 43
Fowler, Marianne: arrest of, 82–84; and ERA, 64, 74, 88, 90; on marital-rape law, 169
Frazier, Demeter, 38–39
Freedman, Estelle, 232n1
Freedom Caravan, 113
Freedom of Choice Coalition, 125, 221n1
Freedom of Choice Tidewater Coalition, 101
Freedom of Information (FOIA) act, 161
free-love advocates, scholarship on, 232n1
Fried, Marlene, 99
Friedan, Betty, 41
Fullenkamp, Anne, 143
Fuller, Georgia: on abortion rights, 111–112, 113–114, 126; on abortion rights in twenty-first century, 177; biographical information, 17, 21; and ERA, 92, 93, 94; on generational assumptions, 188; on patriarchy, 189; on radicalism, 47, 87–88; reasons for activism, 26–27; on social forces against movement, 183; on successes of movement, 187
Funds for a Feminist Majority, 113

Galvin, Paul, 122
Gandy, Kim, 130
Garcia, Cathy, 155
Gavey, Nichola, 234n6
gerrymandering, 184, 189
Giesen, Arthur, 60–61
Giesler, Jerry, 89
Gilmore, James, 130
Glasscock, Samuel, 147
Goldberg, Judy, 15
Goode, Virgil, 89
Goodman, Patricia. *See* Winton, Patricia
Good Shepherd Catholics for the ERA, 79
Gordon, Jerry, 85
Gordon, Linda, 232n1
Graham, Hannah, 171
Griffee, Ellen, 63
"A Group of Women," 86–88

Hailey, Evelyn, 59, 160–161
Hall, Diane, 151

Hall, Irene, 139
Hall, Jacquelyn Dowd, 232n1
Hall, Susan, 170
Hansard, Sara, 146
Harding-Clark, Patricia, 115
Harrington, Morgan, 171
Harris, Judy, 68–69
Harrison, Edie, 109, 115
Harrison, Ted, 112
Harrison, Vera, 76
Harrison, Yvonne, 112
Hatwood, Mary, 77
Height, Dorothy, 112
Heinz, Elise: election of, 78; and ERA, 53, 58, 62, 66–67, 90; and General Assembly harassment, 12, 13–14; on marital-rape law, 169; on rape law codes, 147; and VWPC support of, 63
Hellmuth, Jean, 70
Henderson, Vera, 54
Heyer, Heather, 184
Hillcrest Clinic, 104, 124–125, 129–130
Hobson, Richard, 82–83
Hodgson v. Minnesota (1990), 116
Home Builders Association, 153
Hopkins, R. Clint, 102
hotlines, for assault: and awareness, 137–138; and public funding, 234n6
Houck, Edd, 119
House of Delegates Committee on Health, Welfare, and Institutions, 159
Housewives for ERA, 89
Housing and Urban Development, 157
Howren, H. H., 14
Hughes, Jennifer, 192
Human Life Amendment (Hatch Amendment), 106–107
Hunt, Lois, 151
Hyde Amendment, 105

"I'm Not Sorry," 131
International Women's Year, 73
intersectionality, 25, 38–39, 167, 173, 180–181. *See also* lesbians; women of color
Iverson, Sheila, 38

Jensen, Pat, 67, 69, 80
Johnson, Sonia, 87, 141
Jordan, Carol E., 232n1
Joyner, Nancy, 55
Junior League, 156

Keller, Suzanne: and antiwar movement, 27–28; on General Assembly, 184; on patriarchy, 22, 190; reasons for activism, 22, 31; and school segregation, 16; on social forces against movement, 183; to young feminists, 190–191
Kelly, Suzanne, 86
Kenley, Betty, 97
Kennedy, Florynce, 222n16
Kincaid, Anne, 119
King, Deborah K., 35
Koestner, Katie, 142–143

Labor for Equal Rights Now (LERN), 77, 79–80, 86, 93
Largen, Mary Ann, 135
Laster, Max, 149
"Lavender Menace," 41
Lawrence, Eleanor, 136
Leach, Caroline, 160
League of Women Voters (LWV): and domestic-violence study, 158; domestic-violence task force, 163; and ERA, 52, 64, 65–68, 74–75, 85; on ERA opponents, 53; as nonpartisan, 64; on reproductive rights, 102; and women of color, exclusion of, 40
League of Women Voters (LWV), Virginia, 58; and abortion consent bills, 108; and abortion rights, 103, 109; and ERA, 54, 56, 74–75; and *ERA Supporter's Handbook,* 62; and Virginia Pro-Choice Alliance, 110
League of Women Voters (LWV), Virginia chapters: and abortion rights, 102–103; Conference on Legislative Actions Affecting Women, 147; and domestic-violence shelters, 156, 157; and ERA, 67, 72; and rape hotlines, 138; and VERARC, 69

Lee, Denise: on abortion rights, 116, 117, 119, 130, 176; on abortion rights in twenty-first century, 177; on diversity in movement, 33, 34, 182–183; early activism of, 24–25; as NOW Virginia president, 100; on social forces against movement, 183; to young feminists, 190–191
Legal Momentum, 163, 164–165
lesbians: and anti-violence movement, 43–44; and ERA, 72–73; exclusion of, 41–44; and LGBT issues, 57–59, 182–183, 201n17; and the military, employment discrimination, 30; in politics, 192; and racism, 39; tension with, 42–43, 71, 72–73
Lesbian Womyn of Color, 39
Lett, Ardelle, 79
Linnell, Charlene, 149
Love, Yeardley, 171
Loving v. Virginia (1967), 16
Lucas, Louise, 117
Lucy, William, 80
Lunde, Anne, 63
lynching, 232n1

Maher v. Roe (1977), 96
March for Women's Lives, 121
marital rape, 144, 145, 146, 168–171; scholarship on, 232n1
Marschak, Beth: on ERA support, 71–73; on General Assembly, 185; on inclusivity, 40, 42, 43, 70–71; reasons for activism, 18–19, 25–26, 27, 30, 32; on successes of movement, 186, 187; on violence against women, 179
Marshall, Mary, 13, 147, 148
Marshall, Robert, 171, 192–193
Mason, Vivian Carter, 62
massive resistance, 4, 16
Mathews, Nancy, 234n6
McAuliffe, Terry, 120, 188
McCoach, Pamela, 146
McCord, Kate: on abortion rights in twenty-first century, 177; and anti-violence movement, 164, 173, 179; on coalitions, 173, 180–181; on intersectionality, 180–181; on

marital-rape law, 170–171; on rape culture, 178; reasons for activism, 20, 31; on sexual assault, 172

McCoy, Emily: and abortion rights, 109, 116, 123, 176; on CPCs, 131; on divorce policies, 182; and ERA, 80, 88, 90, 94; on generational assumptions, 188; on laws, changing of, 186; on marital rape, 168; on media climate, 181; on parental notification, 117; reasons for activism, 21; on successes of movement, 186

McCoy, Fred, 88

McDiarmid, Dorothy, 53, 60, 64, 68, 80–82, 89

McDonnell, Bob, 132, 188

McEachin, Don, 176

McGlothlin, Don, 12, 14

McGuire, Danielle, 232n1

McKewan, Megan, 112

McKinnon, Kathleen, 144–145

McMurtrie, Andrew, 103

McPherson, David, 123

media images: and ERA, 71–73; image, concern for, 80–81; negative stereotypes, 44–47

Meese, Lulu: and ERA, and House Privileges and Elections Committee, 81; and ERA, failure to ratify, 83, 90, 91; and ERA, Virginia as target state, 63, 74–75

Melvin, Kenneth, 171

Men's Advisory Council, 153

#metoo, 174, 180

Milano, Alyssa, 180

Miller, Andrew, 60–61, 81

Miller, Clinton, 11–12

Miller, Emilie, 112

Miller, Nathan, 90–91

Millner, Joseph, 121

Miss America pageant, 44

missionaries, 19–22

Moral Majority, 5, 85, 108

Moran, Jim, 115, 116

Mormons, 53, 58

Mormons for the ERA, 79, 87, 141

Morrison, Antonio, 164–165

Morrison, Theodore, 147

Moss, Thomas, 12, 14, 169

motherhood, 182

Motley, Donna, 137

Mount Vernon Mental Health Center, 151

Mount Vernon Mental Health Institute, 138

Ms. magazine, 21, 31

Munford, Joan, 89, 110

Murdoch-Kitt, Norma, 74

National Abortion Rights Action League (NARAL), 113, 120, 124, 131

National Association for the Repeal of Abortion Laws, 221n1

National Association of Black Women Attorneys, 38–39

National Association of Social Workers, 79

National Black Feminist Organization (NBFO), 36–37, 69, 202n24

National Clothesline Project, 159

National Council for Negro Women, 112

National Council of Jewish Women, 53, 115, 153

National Council of Negro Women, 115

National Domestic Violence Awareness Week, 159

National Institute of Law Enforcement and Criminal Justice, 149

National Organization of Women (NOW): and abortion rights, 98; NOW-PAC, 88, 112–114, 115; NOW Reproductive Task Force, 104; and Virginia Pro-Choice Alliance, 110

National Organization of Women (NOW), Virginia: and abortion rights, 113–114, 123; and abortion rights and consent/notification bills, 109, 117; and abortion rights and CPCs, 131; and abortion rights and membership numbers, 114; on antiabortionist harassment, 126; and domestic-violence law codes, 161–162; and ERA, grassroots support, 68–69; and ERA, protests, 68; and ERA and elections, 74; and ERA and membership numbers, 92; and ERA caravan, 74; and ERA organization, 53–54; and *ERA Supporter's Handbook*, 62; on marital rape, 168, 169; and Virginia ERA network, 176

National Organization of Women (NOW), Virginia chapters, 103; and abortion rights, 107, 113; and abortion rights, demonstrations, 121; and abortion rights and consent/notification bills, 108, 116; and abortion rights and CPCs, 124; and abortion rights and lobbying, 115–116; and abortion rights and membership numbers, 112; anti-rape task force, 135; on Bobbitt case, 170; and counter picketing, 128; and domestic violence, 151, 154, 155, 156–157, 164; and domestic violence task force, 149, 159; and ERA, 54; and ERA, fund-raising for, 84; and ERA, protests, 68; and ERA and new chapters, 92–93; and ERA and respectability, 57; and ERA fund-raising for, 63; and ERA lobbying, 67, 90; and ERA rally, 65; geographic reach, 3; and lesbians, tension with, 42, 43; on marital rape, 170; on *Planned Parenthood v. Casey*, 122; and radical feminists, exclusion of, 47; on rape, prevalence of, 136; and rape awareness campaigns, 139, 141; and rape law codes, 145, 146; and traditional gender norms, 45–47; and TRIS, 137; on VAWA, 164; and woman of color, exclusion of, 32–36, 37, 40

National Walkathon for Equal Rights, 75
National Women's Conference, 73, 75–76
National Women's Party, 89
National Women's Political Caucus-Virginia (NWPC-VA). *See* Virginia Women's Political Caucus (VWPC)
Neustadt (Mrs.), 58
New Right movement, 102, 107
Nolan, Kathleen, 80
Nordlinger, Zelda, 34, 46, 59, 71, 145–146
Norment, Tommy, 176
Northern Virginia Rape Crisis Hotline, 138
Northern Virginia Women's Medical Center, 128
Northern Virginia Women's Medical Clinic, 125–126
Nottingham, Mary, 128
NOW-PAC, 88, 112–114, 115
NOW Reproductive Task Force, 104

Off Our Backs, 31
Ohio v. Akron Center for Reproductive Health (1990), 116
Older Women's League (OWL), 157
O'Neal, Alice Page, 161
O'Neill, Alyse, 53
Operation Rescue, 124, 126, 128–129
oppressions, interlocking, 35–36, 38–39. *See also* intersectionality
oral history, use of, 6–8
Our Bodies, Ourselves, 181

Painter, Nell Irvin, 232n1
Parsiani, Mary, 62
Parsons, Jane, 149
Patey, Marian, 34
Paul, Alice, 75
Paulk, Beverly, 137
Payne, Sarah: on domestic-violence shelters, 154; and ERA, 91; reasons for activism, 20, 29; on successes of movement, 186; and women of color, exclusion of, 32
Payne-White, Melanie: on domestic violence and police, 162–163; and domestic-violence shelters, 154; on political climate against movement, 183; reasons for activism, 22, 27; on violence against women, 179
Peaslee, Kay, 75
Pendleton, Terrie: biographical information, 17, 20, 25, 30; on diversity in movement, 182–183; as lesbian, 30, 39; on successes of movement, 187; and women of color, exclusion of, 33, 39
Peninsula Medical Center, 104
Peninsula Rape Crisis, 140
Peoples, Napoleon, 36–37
Perkins, Lee: on abortion rights in twenty-first century, 177; biographical information, 17; and ERA, 87; on ERA, need for, 175; on generational assumptions, 187–188; reasons for activism, 30; on reproductive rights, 175; on successes of movement, 187
Petchesky, Rosalind, 99, 111
Philpott, A. L., 14–15, 81, 91
Physicians for Choice, 110

Pilley, Jane, 115
Planned Parenthood: and abortions, begins providing, 105; ad campaign, 122; better baby movement, 99; on consent/notification legislation, 107–108, 114–115, 117, 119–120; as conservative organization, 98; on lobbying efforts, 112; and *Roe* anniversary, 117; on TRAP laws, 97; Virginia League of Planned Parenthood, 117, 131; and Virginia Pro-Choice Alliance, 110
Planned Parenthood v. Casey (1992), 118–119, 122
Pleck, Elizabeth, 232n1
police: and domestic violence, 149, 162–163, 164; and domestic violence charges, 159–161; and mandatory arrests, 165; and rape awareness, 138; and sexual assault, 140–141
Pomerleau, Clark, 234n6
Popinko, Cynthia, 57
"Positive Action Pro-Choice Campaign," 115
Powell, Kathy, 138
Pratt, Barbara, 12
Pratt, Larry, 88
President's Commission on the Status of Women, 147
Pro-Choice Alliance, 115–116, 124, 126
Pro-Choice Coalition Lobby Day, 115
"Project Stand Up for Women," 128
Pro-Life Virginia, 130
property laws, 55
Pudliner-Sweeney, Carol, 74

Quixote Religious Center, 127

racial slurs, 25
radicalism, 47, 80–81, 173–174
Ralston, Whitney, 172
rape. *See* sexual assault
rape crisis center, 140
rape shield law, 145–148
Rape Victim Campaign Program, 137
Raschke, Karen: and abortion rights, 114–115, 117, 131; on abortion rights in twenty-first century, 177; on antiabortionist violence, 129; biographical information, 17; on feminist networks, 187; on General Assembly and harassment, 15; reasons for activism, 30; on successes of movement, 187
Ray, Freddy, 36
Reagan, Ronald, 85, 87
Reagon, Bernice Johnson, 166–167
Reinelt, Claire, 234n6
Religious Coalition for Abortion Rights (RCAR), 102, 110, 115, 117
Reno, Kim, 130
reproductive rights: at National Women's Conference, 76; and women of color, 112. *See also* abortion rights
Reproductive Rights Task Force, 103–104
Republican National Committee, 87
Republicans for Choice, 113
respectability, 45–47, 57; and *ERA Supporter's Handbook*, 62; and women of color, exclusion of, 207n58. *See also* media images
Reuss, Candy, 147
Richmond ERA Ratification Council, 70, 73
Richmond Lesbian-Feminist Organization, 42, 43, 72–73
Richmond Medical Center for Women, 104–105, 107, 129
Richmond Organized Against Rape (ROAR), 136–141
Richmond Women's Clinic, 128
Right to Choose, 123
Robb, Chuck: on abortion rights, 106, 119; and domestic-violence reform, 159, 161; election of, 78, 88, 90
Robb, Lynda, 91, 147
Roberts, Gretchen, 109
Robertson, Pat, 5, 85, 108, 130
Roem, Danica, 192–193
Roe v. Wade (1973), 96
Rogers, Edythe, 38–39
Rogers, Kathryn, 165
Rosen, Ruth, 2
Ross, Loretta, 99
Rothstein, Joe, 63
Rouse, Ruth, 109–110
"Ruler campaign," 113

St. Joseph's Villas, 152
Salvi, John, 129–130
Sanders, Juanita, 12, 88
Saslaw, Dick, 117
Schlafly, Phyllis, 50, 52, 54, 56, 60; and *ERA Supporter's Handbook*, 62
Scott, Buffie, 53
Scott, Eva, 53
Second Presbyterian Church, 141
Service Families for Reproductive Freedom, 101
700 Club, 85
sexual assault: and abortion rights, 137; awareness campaigns, 138; criminal code, 144–148; and date rape, 31–32, 141–144; diversity of activists, 148; compared to domestic violence, 167; feminist response to, 166–167; and marital rape, 144, 145, 146, 168–171; and #metoo movement, 174, 180; and police response to, 138, 139; and pregnancy, 31–32; prevalence of, 136; racialized, 232n1, 234n6; and rape kits, 146; and rape shield laws, 139, 163; reporting of, 142–143, 144, 146, 179–180; scholarship on, 134–136, 232n1, 234n6; and victims' advocates, 138
Sexual Assault Project, 140
Sexual Assault Victims Bill of Rights, 144
Shackelford, Carroll Kem, 59
SHARE (Shelter and Housing to Alleviate and Resolve Emergencies), 157
shelters. *See under* domestic violence
Silent No More, 122
Silent Scream, 113
Singer, Toba, 7–8
Sisisky, Norman, 15
Smeal, Eleanor, 80, 82
Smith, Andrea, 99
Smith, Barbara, 141
Smith, (Muriel) Elizabeth: and domestic-violence shelters, 153; and ERA, 52, 69, 73, 81, 85, 93; on personal potential, 181–182; reasons for activism, 19, 22, 26; on successes of movement, 186, 187; and women of color, exclusion of, 40; to young feminists, 191

Sobrio, Kathy, 45–46
Socialist Workers' Party, 70–71
social media, 131–132, 190; Facebook, 172, 174, 180; Twitter, 174, 176, 180
Sommerville, Diane, 232n1
Southern Christian Leadership Conference, 25–26
Southern Women's Rights Project of the ACLU (SWRP), 37–38, 40–41, 105, 125
Sparks, Grace, 117, 131
Spevacek, Hoann, 13
Spiders Against Sexual Assault and Violence, 172
Spinks, Dorothy, 83
Spitz, Donald, 130
Spitz, Lela, 54, 60–61, 62
Stapleton, Jean, 74
State Board of Health, 105
state seal of Virginia, 80
sterilization, 99–101
Stevens, Phyllis, 86
Stoner, Gayle, 92
STOP-ERA, 50, 88
STOP-ERA, Virginia, 53
Storey, Frances, 116
Students for a Democratic Society, 203n24
Subcommittee to Study Battered Spouses, 159–160
Suhler, Cornelia, 159
Supreme Court, U.S., 16

Taft, Shirley, 109
Take Back the Night (TBTN), 135, 141, 143, 144, 164
Tanner, Waverly, 149
Tashjian, Pat, 139
Task Force for Battered Wives, 160
Taylor, Joan, 116
Terry, Mary Sue, 13, 113–114, 158, 185
Terry, Randall, 124, 128
Thames, James, 149
Third World Women's Alliance, 202n24
Third World Women's Network, 203n24
Thomas, Clarence, 119
Thomas Jefferson Women's Club, 153

Thomas Road Baptist Church, 5, 85, 86
Thomson, Jim, 52, 60–61, 67, 77–78
Ticer, Patsy, 120
Tidewater Coalition for the ERA, 54
Tidewater Rape Information Services (TRIS), 137–141, 168–169
Tighe, Carol, 156
Title IX, 165, 172, 173, 178, 186
Title XX, 150, 160
Tomlin, Lily, 77
transgender, 192
Transvaginal Ultrasound Bill, 229n114
TRAP laws (Targeted Regulations Against Abortion Providers), 96–97, 120, 177
Trump, Donald, 183, 193
Turner, Ted, 113
Turning Point, Inc., 158
Twitter, 174, 176, 180
Tyree, Stephanie: on abortion rights, 222n9; on domestic-violence shelters, 153–154; and ERA, 91, 175; on General Assembly, 184; reasons for activism, 29; on social forces against movement, 183; on successes of movement, 186; and women of color, exclusion of, 32, 33
Tyson, Helen, 76

United Methodist Church, 79
United Way, 152
University of Virginia: and women, exclusion of, 18–19

Valos, Lynn, 146–147
Van Audenhove, Kristi: and anti-violence movement, 21, 149, 173–174, 179; biographical information, 17; on coalition, 166–167; on domestic-violence legislation, 180; on feminism, 193; on marital rape, 168; on sexual assault, 178–179; on successes of movement, 186; on women in politics, 185
VanValkenburg, Schuyler, 192
VERA-PAC, 73–75, 77
VERARC (Virginia ERA Ratification Council): after ERA fails in Virginia, 91; coalition divisions, 73; and direct action, 65–68; and election of 1975, 63–64; establishment of, 61–62; on Fowler and Clarke arrests, 82; on lack of rights, 55–56; member organizations, 61–62, 79; and Thomson, 77
Vickry, Raymond, 83
Violence Against Women Act (VAWA), 158, 163–165, 234n6
Virginia Association of Counties (VAC), 145
Virginia Citizens Coalition, 58
Virginia Committee on Sexual Assault Reform (COSAR): founding of, 139; on marital rape, 168
Virginia Education Association, 73
Virginia ERA Central, 54, 57–58, 59, 60, 66
Virginia ERA network, 176
Virginia Federation of Women's Clubs (VFWC), 52
Virginia Military Institute, 22
Virginians Against Domestic Violence (VADV): and domestic violence law codes, 161–162; and domestic violence statistics, 166; establishment of, 155; hotline, 158; and lesbian activists, 43; Lesbian caucus, 158; and shelters, 158; Women of Color caucus, 158
Virginians Allied Against Sexual Assault (VAASA): and date rape, 141–144; establishment of, 139–140; geographical reach, 140; on marital rape, 168, 169; public funding for survivor services, 148
Virginians Organized for Community Expression (VOICE), 102, 106–107, 109, 110, 115
Virginians Sexual and Domestic Violence Action Alliance (VSDVAA), 43, 164, 173, 180–181
Virginia Nurses' Association, 115
Virginia Organization to Keep Abortion Legal (VOKAL): on abortion consent bill, 107–108; abortion rights, educational campaigns, 123–124; and counter-picketing, 125; and ERA, 71–72; founded, 101–102; on funding for abortions, 105; on lobbying efforts, 112; and Virginia Pro-Choice Alliance, 110; and Wazlak, 71–72, 127
Virginia Peninsula Council on Battered Women, 156

Virginia Pro-Choice Alliance, 110, 112
Virginia Sexual and Domestic Violence Action Alliance, 149, 166–167
Virginia State Crime Commission, 141
Virginia Wives and Mothers for the ERA, 55, 57
Virginia Women Attorneys Association, 89
Virginia Women's Political Caucus (VWPC), 51, 61, 72, 144–145, 150; on abortion and sterilization, 100; and abortion consent bills, 108; abortion rights and membership numbers, 112; election of 1981, campaigning for, 89; and ERA direct action, 65–68; and ERA fundraising, 63–64; on ERA in twenty-first century, 176; and ERA lobbyists, 67; and lesbians, tension with, 42–43; on marital-rape law, 169; on restrictive abortion laws, 97–98; and Virginia Pro-Choice Alliance, 110; and VWPC-PAC, 88
Volunteers of America, 153
VWPC-PAC, 88

Washington Area Clinic Defense Force, 129
Watt, Pat, 72
Watt, Vivian, 74–75
Wattleton, Faye, 100
Watts, Vivian, 14, 120
Wazlak, Mary (Denyes): on abortion clinics, 125; on abortion consent bill, 107–108; on abortions, funding for, 105; on antiabortionist tactics, 123; on date rape, 31–32; on diversity in movement, 182–183; on ERA and abortion rights, 71–72; on media climate, 181; on motherhood, 182; reasons for activism, 20, 31–32; on reproductive rights, 101, 104; on threats received, 127–128; to young feminists, 190–191. *See also* Virginia Organization to Keep Abortion Legal (VOKAL)
Webster v. Reproductive Health Services (1989), 33, 110–116
Weiss, Connie, 86
Wells-Schooley, Jane, 107
West End Lutheran Church, 69

Weybright, Becky, 143–144
Weyrich, Paul, 85
White, Bessida: on anger, 47; and ERA support, 69, 93; on intersectionality, 38–39; on lesbians, tension with, 42–43; reasons for activism, 23; on successes of movement, 186; and women of color, exclusion of, 32–33, 36–37
White, Deborah Gray, 232n1
White, Juanita, 71
white supremacists, 183–184
Whole Woman's Health v. Hellerstedt (2016), 96, 120
Wilder, Douglas, 113–114, 116, 117–118, 119
Williams, Carrington, 61
Williams, Meg, 144–145, 150
Williams, Stephanie, 170
Williamsburg Women's Center, 141
Wilson, Wendy, 144–145
Wilson, William, 91
Winston, Jameis, 165
Winton, Patricia: on ERA, legacy, 92; on ERA and Miller, 90; on ERA and "secret memo," 81; on ERA boycott, 79; and ERA caravan, 74; and ERA fundraising, 88; on Fowler and Clarke arrests, 82
Wittner, Judith, 234n6
Wodell, Irene, 161
Woman Space, 151
Women for Political Action, 61–62, 100
Women in Crisis Center and Response, 137–141, 168–169
women in politics, 12–14, 191–193
Women Matter, 176
women of color: and anti-violence movement, 135; and black feminism, 37–38; and domestic violence, 166, 173–174; enslaved women, scholarship on, 232n1; and ERA, 69, 93; exclusion of, 33, 40–41, 135, 173, 182–183; and reproductive rights, 99–101, 112
"Women of the Tidewater," 141
Women's Alliance of the First Unitarian Church, 97
Women's Center, 42

270 INDEX

Women's Commission, 138
Women's International Terrorist Conspiracy from Hell (WITCH), 44
Woodward, Deborah, 84
Woodyard, Maude "Boots," 18, 88, 181
Woody Guthrie Community Center, 25
Wren, Harold, 54
Wright, Louise, 67, 70, 73
Wyatt, Addie, 77

Yard, Molly, 113
Young Women Committed to Action, 137, 151–152

YWCA: and abortion rights, 121; as domestic violence shelters, 151–153; and rape, 136, 139; and ROAR, 138; Victim Advocacy Program, 152–153
YWCA, Virginia chapters: on abortion rights, 112; and date rape, 141, 143–144; and domestic-violence shelters, 156, 157, 158; and ERA support, 79; and lesbians, tension with, 42; and VAASA, 140; and Virginia Pro-Choice Alliance, 110

"zap actions," 44–45
Zero Population Growth, 221n1